PASSING

LIPIKA PELHAM

Passing

An Alternative History of Identity

HURST & COMPANY, LONDON

First published in the United Kingdom in 2021 by
C. Hurst & Co. (Publishers) Ltd.,
41 Great Russell Street, London, WC1B 3PL
Copyright © Lipika Pelham, 2021
All rights reserved.
Printed in the United Kingdom by Bell & Bain Ltd, Glasgow

The right of Lipika Pelham to be identified as the author of this publication is asserted by her in accordance with the Copyright, Designs and Patents Act, 1988.

A Cataloguing-in-Publication data record for this book is available from the British Library.

ISBN: 9781787383814

This book is printed using paper from registered sustainable and managed sources.

www.hurstpublishers.com

For Rishi, Sara Radha and Arun:
"Not mixed, not half this and half that; you embody equally two heritages."

CONTENTS

List of Illustrations   ix
Acknowledgements   xiii

Introduction   1

PART ONE
STRADDLING THE COLOUR LINES

1. Anansi's Web: Rebirth in Chains and the Dawn of Passing   23
2. The Castle of Your Skin: Rewriting the Past in Jim Crow America   41
3. The Chameleon Dance: Hierarchies of Complexion   65
4. Mistaken Identity: Living in Racial No Man's Land   83

PART TWO
BENDING THE BINARIES

5. Male Like Her: Impersonating the "Opposite" Sex   99
6. The Wild Side: Slipping Between Genders   113
7. Nobody's Business But Ours: Passing In and Out of the Closet   139

CONTENTS

PART THREE

BEYOND HERITAGE

8. Born Again: Shifting Religion and Caste 163
9. Hidden Nations: Collective Passing 185
10. Mindsets of Belonging: Socio-Cultural Passing 209

PART FOUR

TRESPASSING

11. Heart of Whiteness: The Quintessential Reverse-Passing of Richard Burton 239
12. Something of His Selves: The Passing, Appropriating and Identifying of Rudyard Kipling 251
13. Who's Passing for Who? The Curious Curse of Cultural Appropriation 267
14. Represent: Passing and Appropriation in the Performing Arts 291

Epilogue: A Prequel to Passing 311

Notes 321
Further Reading 339
Index 345

LIST OF ILLUSTRATIONS

1. Escaped slave Ellen Craft in disguise. From Wilbur Henry Siebert, *The Underground Railroad from Slavery to Freedom* (Macmillan, 1898, Albert Bushnell Hart second edition), p. 162.
2. Ellen and William Craft. From *The Liberator* newspaper (1831–65).
3. Nella Larsen, author of *Passing*. Photograph by James Allen, 1928. Library of Congress, Harmon Foundation Records, Manuscript Division (7–14).
4. Josephine Baker in banana skirt. Photograph by Walery (Stanisław Julian Ignacy Ostoróg), 1927.
5. The author and her siblings. Family photo, mid-1980s.
6. The black *Goddess Kali dancing on Shiva*. Gouache on ivory with pencil, c. 19th century. From Mildred and W.G. Archer, *Indian painting for the British* (London, 1955), pp. 66–8. Wellcome Library no. 582091i.
7. Neymar da Silva Santos Júnior. Photograph by Antoine Dellebach, 2017. Creative Commons BY-SA-2.0.
8. Population Registration Act, 7 July 1950, p. 3. Parliament of South Africa, *Statues of the Union of South Africa*, 1950.
9. Barack Obama with his grandfather, mother, and half-sister, early 1970s. From U.S. Embassy, Jakarta.
10. Meghan Markle with her mother. PA Images / Alamy Stock Photo.
11. Pope Joan discovered. Woodcut illustration printed by Johannes Zainer at Ulm c. 1474, in Giovanni Boccaccio, *De mulieribus claris*, trans. Heinrich Steinhöwel. Penn Libraries Inc B-720.

LIST OF ILLUSTRATIONS

12. Hannah Snell, British soldier. Engraving by John Faber Jr., c. 1750.
13. *Viola in Shakespeare's Twelfth Night*, dressed as a boy. Stipple engraving by W.H. Mote, 1836. Wellcome Library no. 673000i.
14. *Discovery of Achilles on Skyros*, oil on canvas, by Nicolas Poussin, c. 1650. Juliana Cheney Edwards Collection 46.463, Museum of Fine Arts Boston.
15. Hilary Swank as Brandon Teena in *Boys Don't Cry*, 1999. United Archives GmbH / Alamy Stock Photo.
16. Artist Lili Elbe, 1926. From N. Hoyer (ed.), *Man into Woman. An Authentic Record of a Change of Sex. The true story of the miraculous transformation of the Danish painter Einar Wegener (Andreas Sparre)*, (London: Jarrolds, 1933), opp. p. 40.
17. Gender-fluid couple Sophie & Jess. Photograph by Sophie Green.
18. Hijra Ananya with fellow friends of the third gender. Photograph by Kabir Akon.
19. Chris Gunness with his husband Ari. From Chris Gunness's photo album.
20. The author's father. Family photo, c. 1982
21. *The four classes of society in Japan during the Edo period*, by Ozawa Nankoku, 1883.
22. An *auto da fe* of the Spanish Inquisition: *Torture of the Condemned*, engraving by Bernard Picart, 1722. Reproduced with kind permission of the Jewish Historical Museum Collection, Amsterdam, JHM M003973-B.
23. Landowning womaniser Anne Lister, painting by Joshua Horner, c. 1830. Free online exhibition, Shibden Hall.
24. 'Male genius' Gertrude Stein. Photograph by Carl Van Vechten, 12 June 1934. Prints and Photographs Division, Van Vechten Collection, Library of Congress.
25. V.S. Naipaul: internalised whiteness. PA Images / Alamy Stock Photo.
26. Reverse-passer Richard Francis Burton in Persian disguise as "Mirza Abdullah the Bushri", 1848. From Lady Isabel Burton &

LIST OF ILLUSTRATIONS

W.H. Wilkins, *The Romance of Isabel* (New York: Dodd, Mead, 1904), p. 51.

27. Kim 'transcends identity'. Illustration by John Lockwood Kipling, from Rudyard Kipling, Kim (Garden City, NY: Doubleday), 1901, p. 352.
28. Justin Trudeau playing dress-up at Amritsar. REUTERS / Adnan Abidi / Alamy Stock Photo.
29. Justin Trudeau in blackface, January 2001. Photograph shared by CBC. Creative Commons BY-SA 4.0.
30. Thomas D. Rice as a Jump Jim Crow minstrel. Lithograph by Edward Williams Clay, cover to an early edition of Jump Jim Crow sheet music (New York, NY: E. Riley), c. 1932.
31. Blackfisher Martina Big. Photograph by Michaelbig, 1 October 2017. Creative Commons BY-SA 4.0.
32. Rachel Dolezal at a black rights rally. Photograph by Aaron Robert Kathman, 2 October 2015. Creative Commons BY-SA 4.0.
33. Actor Fredi Washington in the trailer for *Imitation of Life*, 1934.
34. Mickey Rooney as Mr. Yunioshi in the trailer for *Breakfast at Tiffany's*, 1961.
35. Helena Bonham Carter filming *The King's Speech*. Photograph by Lancashire County Council, 18 December 2009. Creative Commons BY 2.0.
36. Bollywood actors Nargis and Dilip Kumar playing Hindus in *Andaz*, 1949.
37. The author's grandmother. Photograph by the author's father, c. 1982.
38. The author's father's self-portrait, among the gods. Photograph by Sakshi Chouhan, 2020.

ACKNOWLEDGEMENTS

When I first started thinking about writing a book on the history of identity performance, I had no idea what a colossal challenge it would soon become. During the first stage of my research I became immersed in racial and socio-cultural examples, voraciously reading stories of black-to-white, lower-class to upper-class "passing" in the mid-nineteenth-to early-twentieth-century literature and public records. I studied Hollywood films of the interwar period, when the industry thought it was going through a progressive period of social realism, and "optically white" black people passing featured as a mainstream theme. Unsurprisingly, in the first draft, race and class dominated.

As I went back further into the past, the history of performing identity revealed the Victorian-era "reverse-passing", when the act of identity assumption was usurped by the likes of Richard Burton and Rudyard Kipling: the former a diehard faker and manipulator, the latter somewhat caught between colonial duty and human confusion.

And it was human confusion, or rather blurred lines, around identity that got me talking to Michael Dwyer of Hurst Publishers about writing a book on "passing", in the context of the Indian subcontinent's religion, class and caste communities. I told Michael about an unpublished novel loosely based on my late father's quest for identity, *Seven Seas Thirteen Rivers*. He asked if I would be willing to extract the actuality from the text and zoom out to a much broader history of the self. That was in 2018. I am grateful to Hurst for giving me the opportunity to delve into two years of intellectual lockdown—which then extended into that of the coronavirus pandemic—to complete this book.

More and more types of passing that I hadn't covered in my initial reading kept popping up, throwing me into a dizzying world where

ACKNOWLEDGEMENTS

it seems that we're all performing identity, in one form or another. But no areas posed a greater challenge than those of gender and sexuality. At one point I even wanted to leave these chapters out, because of the complex sensitivities around them, both historically and in our time. My wonderful editor, Lara, and my daughter Sara—who's now 18—came forward to help me out. I shall get back to Lara, but let me first say that, without my daughter's help, I would not have been able to navigate today's gender and sexuality debates among the very young: she unfolded before me the intricacies of pronouns, gender-neutral spaces, and many incredible soundtracks, from Sampa the Great to the other "final forms" born of our current age's chosen identities and pride in "melanin". Also, how would I have finished the final draft, Sara, had you not taken over home-schooling your little brother during the first two months of the UK's Covid lockdown?

As I describe in the last chapter of this book, in the world of performing arts, black people and other people of colour were once openly caricatured; and the usurpation and erosion of their identities and experiences have since continued, much more subtly, in the toxic trends of whitewashing and "pass-casting": on today's stages and screens, most roles are still played by white, cis and straight actors, even when the character was originally from a minority. I would like to thank my eldest son, Rishi the film-maker, for his valuable insight into the film industry, where race-passing is still permitted in the name of art, and for sharing his experience and that of his colleagues who are racially ambiguous.

Another small person who has been unbelievably interested in my chapter on passing in the performing arts is my youngest, *Doctor Who*-obsessed son, Arun, who came up to me one day saying, "Did you know the new Doctor is a woman, who didn't know after regenerating that he had become a she?"

"Different sex. Same person." The famous Woolfian phrase fluttered about me as trans artist Sophie and her trans partner Jess took me around the Liverpool quayside. Thank you both.

I am grateful to West Yorkshire Archives and Zohrah Zancudi, Director for Public Services at Calderdale Council, Halifax, for letting me into the library outside opening hours and showing me Anne Lister's diaries. Also, I'd like to thank the kind caretaker who

ACKNOWLEDGEMENTS

allowed me into Shibden Hall when it was closed to the public due to renovations.

Thank you, Tirtsah Levie Bernfeld, for once again helping me evoke the tragic identity performances of those wandering, shape-shifting Sephardi Jews in Iberia and Europe during World War II. I am very grateful to Heide Warncke, curator of the Ets Haim Library in Amsterdam, for connecting me to images that could illustrate the death awaiting Jews whose collective passing in Spain and Portugal had failed to spare them the Inquisition. In that connection, thank you to Anton Kras of the Jewish Historical Museum, Amsterdam.

My gratitude to Rabbi Shulamit Ambalu is indescribable: for welcoming me into the community when I came back to London from Jerusalem in 2013, and for her most insightful observations about my children—the dedication quote is hers.

I would like to thank the wonderful Dr Alix Agret, for "introducing" me to Josephine Baker, and enlightening me with her expertise on 1920s Paris and its dalliance with darker-skinned models and performing artists. Thank you, Rahul Sarnaik, for dropping "Mezz Mezzrow" during a nightly debate on white artists identifying as black. Sam Mills, for being there in the initial brainstorming session for a subtitle—"An Alternative History of Identity" fit so well. Hugh Fraser, for relentlessly telling me multifarious passing tales: from Tiresias to the preposterous Dutch age-passer, Emile Ratelband.

Rafiq Husseini, thank you for taking the time while you were in Amman to reply to my frantic queries about the Palestinians' fractured identity since the Israeli–Palestinian conflict began in the 1920s. Fida, as always, I am proud of you. You continue to weave a better yarn for your people, even though you now live in North America, proving how geographical shift is sometimes vital for preserving the remains of our shattered selves. No doubt Trudeau's Canada will be much enriched by your presence.

Beatrix (Payne), thank you for sharing over lunches your South African childhood, and the absurd racial categorisations you witnessed in the 1980s and '90s, and also for the book tips. Lois Thomas lent me several by her colleague, psychoanalyst M. Fakhry Davids's books—these, as well as Lois's own explanations, were invaluable in unpacking the complex terrain of internalised racism.

I am immensely grateful to Professor Tim Hubbard, Head of Genome Analysis at Genomics England, who explained to me the

ACKNOWLEDGEMENTS

secret of genetics in relation to skin colour: that it is only skin-deep. Race science couldn't be made more redundant than by the fact that just eight gene variants colour our skin, all of which have been widely shared since before our species evolved in Africa 300,000 years ago. Are we *all* passing as a race we're not supposed to be?

Charlie (Haviland), thank you for letting me stay in your house and use the kitchen corner during the reading of the first proofs, when my London house was being renovated. Thank you, Annick and Lorenzo, Judith and Emmanuel, for your support and encouragement. Fuchsia, you made me follow the same strict 9–4 offline regime as we worked together—you on your book and I on mine. Thank you, we both did it again.

Daisy Leitch, production director at Hurst, thank you for your hard work and professionalism to bring the book to completion; Alison Alexanian and Rhianna Louise, many thanks for your enthusiastic publicity campaign, and for getting the book accepted by Jewish Book Week 2021 before I'd even handed back the first proofs! And I cannot thank enough Alice Clarke, Hurst's new editorial assistant, for meticulously fact-checking the entire text, finding missing images for the plate sections and pointing out misquotes, among other crucial contributions.

Finally, I return to Lara Weisweiller-Wu, my editor. A linear narrative as it comes to the author's mind may not necessarily reflect how the reader would be best served in a literary journey. This is where the editor comes in. Lara taught me to be more focused on specific, structured themes, and less reliant on what could be described as a stream of consciousness. During the editing process, Lara's favourite phrase has been "clearing the trees so we can now see the wood". Every time I felt tempted to introduce yet another tangent, this phrase would pull me back. She did make me work hard, and at one point I thought I was doing three post-grad degrees simultaneously. Throughout our collaboration, I trusted your judgement, Lara, from the broadening of the book's scope to reordering themes of identity transformation. We've pulled together something more than a checklist of passing stories: an all-round *and* alternative history of the self. I hope the readers will think so too.

London, October 2020

INTRODUCTION

In the early 1990s, I moved into a commune in Brixton, south London, with four others. I was the youngest—not only in age, but also as a Londoner, having just arrived in the UK with an eyeful of dream, like any typical émigré from Britain's former colonies. I had come from what was once the British Empire's Jewel in the Crown, to the place that had been the centre of the Raj chronicles for 200 years. I would now be able to put together the pieces of that jigsaw puzzle, the England of my imagination. There was always the "first time" of things: the first time I would see daffodils to make sense of Wordsworth, or Stonehenge to earn my love of Thomas Hardy. The first years were full of these moments. Sooner than I imagined, the heat and the hyacinth of my past years fell away as I strove to fully belong in my adopted city.

My first impression of London was that the metropolis was familiar to me; with all the red brick Victorian buildings, it resembled a polished Kolkata, the old epicentre of British India, built after a similar architecture in the 1700s. London had the same over-populated feel to it too, if not the grunge. I found the city no less intriguing than an *Ajaib Gher*, Wonder House, as Rudyard Kipling's Kim called his beloved Lahore Museum in 1880s India. Just as Kim's formative years were spent in British India, with him passing as a "native" Indian—an act he performed seriously, passionately and sometimes playfully—over 100 years later, I was trying to live in London as pukka a Briton as possible. I had to face that typical fate of the ex-colonised: suddenly finding myself amidst the actual experience of the former Empire, and the challenge to prove my worthiness, to assimilate perfectly.

This was what separated me from Kipling's characters. As we'll explore in Chapter 12 of this book, they were passing "down", using their privilege as the coloniser, while I was passing as more privileged than I was, which is what the concept generally refers to: a process of crossing over, often secretly, from one lower-status culture, community or identity to another, higher-status one, for safety or opportunity. Passing is the act of living or imitating a life belonging to an identity other than the one you have been assigned by society, and the "passer" is someone who actively emulates this new identity's traits, hiding or omitting their own.

In so doing they adopt those traits as their own, internalise them and inhabit them, sometimes for a whole lifetime; the successful passer excels so well in their act that, at least outwardly, there may not be any discernible difference between the passer's assigned identity and the one they have now assumed. Often, this blurring of the lines also takes place within the passer themselves. While some passing is purely driven by necessity, with no emotions attached, passing can become inseparable from identifying. Abandonment of the role or identity chosen for us by our society or family background can lead to confusion of the self, especially in the long term. In many cases, passing doesn't start as a deliberate choice to begin a deception: appearance is key to how we assign other people an identity, and often those who are wrongly perceived as a member of a dominant or privileged group—a queer person assumed to be straight, a light-skinned biracial person assumed to be white—will go along with this mislabelling, to gain a social freedom that would otherwise be beyond reach.

The passer does not always anticipate the ultimate emotional weight of this decision; they are simply trying to overcome the barriers placed in their way by society's labels. While our public identity will always impact on those in our private lives, some types of identity make passing primarily a personal act that will have profound internal consequences for the individual, but a transformation that won't outlive them. This is particularly true of those who challenge, either by their nature or by their disguises, binaries of gender and sexuality; we will meet many such people in Part Two of the book. On the other hand, some kinds of identity are inherently rooted in family and community, past, present and future; in these cases, which we'll pay particular attention to in Part Three, the decision to transform into a new self requires leaving behind, or reimagining, one's social and cultural inheritance.

INTRODUCTION

As we will explore in Part Four, inherent to the idea of passing is the idea of legitimate and illegitimate identities—of moving to a category you are not "supposed" to be in. You may identify yourself with a certain religion, class or gender in a way that some will call passing, because they don't believe it is possible for you to "really" belong to that category if you were not placed in it at birth; you are perceived to be faking. Or you may be the one who feels that you don't belong in the category you're claiming for yourself: you may be going through the pain of forced passing, living as a normative sexuality or gender in a society that won't accept an alternative, even if it is the truth of your identity. Or you may be racially passing as white, knowing that you can't ever really be the persona you're inhabiting—not because you believe "race" has an inherent truth, but because you are acknowledging the hard reality that your experience, and a white person's, will have been shaped very differently by society's belief in race.

So the nature of passing is as variable as the nature of identity and belonging itself. For those who are reverse-passing—posing as a member of a less privileged group, like Kipling's characters—the passing can often stop at any moment they choose. For some forced passers, the identity performance can end by choosing to emerge into the light, to stop hiding one's true self—by coming out, as queer or as a religious convert, for instance. For others, the passing can only be ended with discovery of the "deception", followed by a return to the original assigned identity; this happens when the boundaries and hierarchies of that type of identity are so strictly drawn that no passing is considered legitimate—as was the case with gender roles in the past, and as is still the case today with race.

Part One of this book begins our journey with an exploration of racial passing and fluid racial identity. This is because the term "passing" was first used in nineteenth-century America, to refer to light-skinned slaves who escaped to freedom by claiming a white identity. It was then popularised in the early twentieth century by the writing of African American authors, primarily mixed-race, who sought the meaning of identity: what it meant to belong, or not, to the nation they were part of thanks to the displacement of their forebears. As the sociologist Nicole Rousseau put it:

PASSING

The historical connotation of the term ... is intimately connected with black America, and "passing," "crossing over," or "going over to the other side" typically refers to a black person whose appearance is such that they can *pass* for white. The vivid language of the term itself evokes many images: passing one's self off as white; choosing to pass over into white society; the passing away of a person's black identity, reborn as white.[1]

But passing is as old as human history. As the idea of "variable identity" becomes more and more widespread today, we have stretched the word "passing" back to various past cultures to explore identity performance in those societies. Many interpretations and perceptions have enriched and complicated the terminology in the twenty-first century; and more and more types of "passing" are being redefined as "identifying", as we expand the range of commonly accepted identities.

This has resulted from the age's predominant trends: global migration, conflict and refugee transfer, changes in social class, growing mixed-race generations, fluid gender and sexuality. Historically, the going in and out of multiple identities was conditioned sometimes by choice, but more often than not by the randomness of fate: being born in the wrong place at the wrong time in the wrong group. But in modern society, it would not be untrue to say that we pass all the time.

My Brixton housemates in the '90s all possessed unusual identities that they had not specifically been allocated at birth.[2] To my newly-arrived *mofussil* eye—the Indian subcontinent's version of an ignorant country bumpkin[3]—all four of these housemates belonged to the Wonder House that was my London. Here's how each one of them defined themselves:

JENNY was bi-racial—half-European and half-South Asian, white in appearance, but belonging to various Black groups, and, to my naïve bewilderment, calling herself "black".

ALAN was gay, but definitely defined himself as "Gay-Asian". The Asian-ness was as important as his sexual orientation.

AMY was newly-arrived like me, but from an English-speaking country on the other side of the world. She said to me on our first meeting, "I am lesbian, but waiting to 'come out'." I, a truly mofussil girl, didn't know at the time what "coming out" meant.

INTRODUCTION

KATIE was brown, but also identified as black. This baffled me; it was the first time I'd come across blackness breaching the barrier of complexion to include other minorities—and to exclude some too. Katie was a feminist by activism, too. "There're too many children in the world," she said, "so I decided to forgo motherhood." She challenged her doctor, who refused to sterilise her. Katie won the right to have her tubes tied.

I managed to upset each one of my flatmates within the first week of my arrival. This is how I did it:

I said to Jenny, who called herself black, "But you're white! You *look* white."

I asked Alan, my gay housemate, why he always had to add Asian to his identity. Why so many labels?

I said to Amy, "You're far away from home, why don't you just 'come out' anyway?" I guess she had explained to me by then the meaning of the phrase.

I showed pure horror at Katie's decision: "Can't you just take precaution during sex rather than go for such a drastic action?" She looked at me in disbelief. To her, I was infringing her human rights—her ownership of her body.

Jenny and Alan did not think much of my unforgivable, imbecilic audacity, and cut me off from further talk on identity.

Katie, however, would give me an answer to my question many years later, when we met again in India. "I didn't at the time even *accidentally* want to become a mother. Only, now I do, and I can't." Katie's parents had come to Britain in the late 1960s as economic migrants from southern India. She was born in the UK, but in her mid-twenties had found herself searching for her roots in Kerala. Dangling our feet in the cool greenness of the Keralan backwaters where I had gone to see her and the man of her life, a native South Indian, I remember wondering about the essence of identity. How we feel about belonging is not necessarily set in stone. Identity is fluid, and this fluidity in itself can be a mark of one's selfhood—for more people today than ever.

I am aware as I am writing this that the narrative of this book will probably upset some, in the same way as my early remarks about my housemates' choices of self-definition had left them unsettled and annoyed. But this book is also about why we need to define ourselves to others, why we deliberately or inadvertently fall into a particular group. Identity here assumes an independent power dynamic; its appeal and appearance to a particular individual or group become a force that must be reckoned with.

All those years ago, I was coming to terms with the pressing need of each of my housemates—all immigrants of the first or second generation—to define themselves in particular ways. Amy, a fellow Commonwealth citizen, was the only one at the time who did not react to the idiocy of my comments. She calmly replied to my questioning of her hesitation to come out in the openness of London. "Oh, I can be lesbian when I want to be, and appear straight when it's needed," she explained, as she headed for the Fridge, a gay nightclub on Brixton Road where she would dance all night with a gay woman followed by a straight woman. Perhaps she was bisexual? I wanted to ask, but Amy liked to leave it vague. Today she would be defined by some as sexually fluid.

Amy's grandmother had emigrated to New Zealand. Not being UK-born herself, Amy was more understanding of my outsider's curiosity at the discoveries of identity and belonging in London of the '90s. She was in the UK on a special visa for young Commonwealth citizens. We were conjoined by one searing reality: Britain's vast Empire which, in the past half-century, had lost its integrity. Both my and Amy's ancestors had been tossed about, and we had come to Britain to reclaim our self-worth. She had lost hers in an experiment of invasion and settlement by her own cultural ancestors, while mine had been disturbed by invasion and colonisation over two centuries—leaving us both with a burning quest for "true" identity.

We arrived in the enchanting British Isles to claim a life away from the parochial, the *mofussil*; a life of travel, adventure, sexual freedom, gender rights. We both came to our Mother Nations—she to a "natural" mother, I to a stepmother, but a mother all the same. We felt we had to prove our prowess as skilled young women selected from among many who had failed the process set by our former colonial masters. Amy and I stood in the same separate queue at the airport when we came back into the UK. It did not feel at all odd, we were even grateful to be there; we had visas for the country that had once ruled our own, and we had got here by put-

INTRODUCTION

ting on our best performances of integration. We thrived in the anonymity that was available to us in London even as new immigrants, and that felt welcoming.

But what we did not address at the time was the massive dose of secrecy still needed to bypass identity questions written there on the main pages of life, and suddenly exposed when we came into contact with the system, the authorities. Because of the extraneous effort to pass as "normal" in Britain, we overlooked the adverse circumstances that were there: borders, visas, racial, sexual and gender profiling, acculturation. Instead we focused on how well we had mastered the culture—and in my case language—of the former ruler, constructed from the pages of English literature and "History of England" in the post-colonial curriculum. As children of the colonies, we had achieved what Derek Walcott called "cunning assimilation", and it paid off.

Yet this kind of socio-cultural passing, which we'll explore in Chapter 10, came with the trepidation that is always an inherent quality of passing: the fear of being caught in the act of "deception", of being exposed as not belonging. A dash of apprehension was there, fear of rejection stole my sleep, and I knew I must not reveal the sense of insecurity that from time to time overwhelmed the process of belonging in London, of performing Britishness. In what we had thought would be a post-racial world following the fall of Empire, the legacy of a still-European educational system back home was still playing a crucial role—including in the lives of those from the "colonies" now reconstructing their selfhood in the West.

* * *

Amy's and my shared story points to a naked reality: that the history of invasion and colonisation—why is it always the Huns and Ottomans who "invaded", while the Western Europeans "explored", "discovered" or "colonised"?—has left a lasting legacy, a strange metamorphosis and a bereavement of identity. In other words, we may think of globalisation as a recent phenomenon dating to the end of the Cold War, but in fact the transformations and ambiguities of identity that come with global connection and movement date back centuries. In my early days in London, I found myself searching for serenity and an anchor, for a permanent sense of belonging—refusing to admit that an idea such as this, a permanence in being, does not exist in a post-colonial, post-slavery, post-digital world. It continues to be an elusive mirage that generations have been running after ever since the Europeans first sailed out to other lands, and brought ideas and identities together.

The role of upheaval in how we understand ourselves has been a theme throughout my life, and it is touchingly summarised in a single stanza by one of the greatest poets born and working during the exploration of the "New Worlds", when Europeans became the masters of the ocean. Here, from Shakespeare's *The Tempest*, is the song of Ariel, the colonised spirit-servant of Prospero, who has settled on Ariel's island.

> Full fathom five thy father lies;
> Of his bones are coral made;
> Those are pearls that were his eyes;
> Nothing of him that doth fade,
> But doth suffer a sea-change
> Into something rich and strange.[4]

The burial at sea of "a father" is also the burial of the past, the loss of heritage for those who leave behind their original community—either by compulsion, as with slaves and refugees, or out of choice, as with passers. The passer perpetuates childhood, going on inventing and changing where they came from, never moving to an adult position of owning a true past that can be passed down to their children in turn. At its extreme, this constant state of flux leaves the passer with a kind of loneliness, a perpetual beginning without an end; a permanent sense of dissociation.

But leaving behind your heritage is not always the death of identity. Instead there can be new realities of life, a metamorphosis into something rich. We'll see throughout this book that a journey away from the old life, triggering the birth of another self, is a recurring theme through every kind of passing. Even runaway slaves in the New World, who were the first to be described as "passing", survived their loss of past, of continuity. For those forcibly dragged in chains through this rupture of self, new identities were still built—from bits of reverie, from secondary sources,

INTRODUCTION

from reconstituted memories salvaged from oceanic fragments. Among the most transcendental of these enduring fragments are the tales of the god-man-spider Anansi—his transformation and survival will be the theme of Chapter 1, about the birth of "passing" amid the horrors of slavery.

So one is never without history, in the same way one could not really be without a childhood. Passers are simply the inventors of new history, reinventors of self. From its original use to describe slaves and slave descendants hiding their blackness, passing has not passed out, but has expanded, taking into its conceptual fold other modern identity transformations—both individual and group. Not only "white-looking" people of colour, but also gay and trans individuals, the low-born, the religiously marginalised and even entire communities have turned a story of displacement into a history of regeneration. In the chapters to come we shall look into characters both real and fictional who sang the song of Ariel and spun the tale of Anansi, adapting to their personal and collective histories of exile and transmutation.

Strategic negotiation of identity has inspired entire communities of Jews passing as Gentiles for their own safety; low-caste families passing as high-status to escape stigma and poverty; Syrians claiming to be Yazidi for fast-track asylum in Europe; queer office workers letting colleagues believe they're straight for the sake of keeping things simple; light-skinned African Americans crossing the colour line for love; tanned Caucasian actors playing Mexican or mixed-race characters in Hollywood movies; trans people moving from a life of hiding their gender dysphoria to a life of hiding their birth-assigned sex; colonials passing as "natives" to satisfy their own curiosity. The list of old and modern passing is long and complex.

Passing usually begins under pressure, but it is also a self-imposed state of being. Most passers pass in a daze, with no time to sift through possible consequences. They want to succeed, they stand by their decision and the circumstances that led them to arrive at such a crossing over. Self-indulgence, though steeped in private pain and a secret sense of loss, is second nature to many passers, who thrive at times on keeping up the act—the impersonation, the erasure of the former self, the guarding of an identity they were not allotted at birth. Passing is a process untamed, unpredictable from the moment of its inception; even if undertaken in fear, it can sometimes be an adventure, a head-rush, a delirious dare. It is also easier for some than for others. Amy and I, we did not deny that we were both class-privileged; our performances in the act of mingling, belonging, fitting in, came easily. In our life in Brixton there were elements of adventure and curiosity, as well as the romanticising of loneliness that often permeates the lives of outsiders in England.

But this rebirthing process is never easy: it is also a process of deracination, and there is an immense sense of discord. As passing is a state of going in and out of communities or social categories, it inevitably leads not only to personal disorder, but also to social disorder. The most scrupulous and extreme of these secretive performing acts will often remove the last contact with the memory of one's past, even one's family. There are moments of reckoning, but the passer is not able to address these, for fear of losing all in an accidental revelation of the life before. Being caught in the act of performing identity—having one's past catch up with you—could mean all sorts of things. In societies that refuse to recognise or protect the identity that's been exposed, it can mean imprisonment, disinheritance and, in extreme cases, death. Many successful passers have taken their secrets to the grave. In the liberal West today, the fear is just as great; but it is a fear of public shaming, alienation, loss of job, tabloid exposure and, worst of all, social media lynching.

* * *

As I endeavour to take a look at this new era of identity, and at the history of passing both temporary and permanent, I am fully aware that my research and my understanding of the concept are not going to produce a straightforward narrative. Allyson Hobbs, a historian of African America, writes in *A Chosen Exile*, that any study of passing is immensely difficult due to the act's clandestine nature: "Conventional wisdom is that few sources exist because those who passed carefully covered their tracks and left no record of their transgression, and that writing about passing is an undertaking fit for novelists, poets, playwrights, and literary critics, but not historians."[5] My challenge has been to combine the perspectives of all of the above.

INTRODUCTION

We will explore tales of passing old and modern, fictional and historical, to see what has or has not changed in our understanding of belonging, particularly in the West—including attitudes about who has the right to present themselves as what. The universal quest for identity will be explored against apartheid, colonialism, slavery, religious persecution, class mobility, sexual freedom and gender dysphoria. I shall take the reader on a journey to show that this has never been as topical a venture as it is now. The truth and reality of fluid identity are stranger than fiction, as my own life has shown. And indeed how do I do this—judge others on their assumption of identities they were not "meant" to have—without bringing in my own demons, which have been living with me, taunting me, laughing at me since early childhood?

A dear friend once told me that if you were to eat meat, you must be prepared to kill the animal—wring the neck of the chicken that you want to see on your plate roasted, glazed and tantalising. I cannot dissect other stories of passing and of personal or political confusion without addressing why I am writing this book. Alongside all the historical and artistic details, I must review my own lifelong struggles in defining an identity that I could believe in. I cannot be ploughing through other people's lives and intimate stories, their dilemmas and subterfuge, without sharing a little of my own search, my own acts of, yes, passing. I cannot talk about the pain of passing without coming to terms with my own confusion over the many lives I have lived.

Long before I ever pondered the meaning of identity, I was already faking, pretending, or at least believing in my being someone I had not been assigned to be. These words, as they force their way onto this page by my tapping the keys of my laptop, have left me perplexed. This must be why those who commit passing of much greater magnitude keep their stories of transition all to themselves. Because by the end of their lives, "the truth" of their identity as others would perceive it becomes somehow irrelevant. When, all those years ago, I had inadvertently hurt the feelings of my Brixton housemates by questioning their need to identify a certain way, I had also been living my own multiple creations of selfhood. Of who I was then, who I had been before and who I would be. As I hoodwinked society—letting myself be known at different points in time with different national and ethnic identities—I was left wondering who the other "original" self was—what my *origins* were, as people kept asking me.

My "passing" had been germinating long before I was born. It had been passed on to me by the realities of division and the ruptured identities that my ancestors had suffered. I was not a midnight's child of the Indian subcontinent, but my birth coincided with the tumultuous years around its final split. The partition of India at the end of British rule in 1947 created independent India and Pakistan as majority-Hindu and -Muslim states respectively; but it failed to create two clear-cut nations: a third force was brewing, and it was not content with this division along religious lines. East Pakistan, formerly East Bengal, refused to pass as Muslim, and so a conflict broke out—the war to create Bangladesh, in 1971.

I was the grandchild of a remarkable oral historian, a thin dark woman with very long hair of a ripened jute colour, who was caught between three countries, two religions, and much more. She was pregnant with my father when her husband died of a "heart attack"—so says the family legend. There are no records of my grandfather's life apart from conflicting word-of-mouth accounts. Snippets of what I have collected, and embellished with imagination in my later years, present a man with a massive rupture in his self-perception. Perhaps the pressure of the new identity born of partition, separating East Bengalis from centuries of Hindu ancestry, was just too much to bear. One account says he went travelling and never came back. Luckily he died before politics did away with his homeland once more.

It was my grandmother who had to witness the split of her India twice, while her own life remained stationary in a self-imposed spiritual and political enclave. She remained stuck in the no-man's-land created out of the haphazard splits and multiple definitions of what was once Hindustan, the Land of the Indus. Was it a land for the Hindus, or was it for everyone? Why had one half of Hindustan—the name given India by the first Muslim travellers and colonial invaders—been split and renamed as Pakistan? When had Hinduism and India become one? Why were Hindu nationalists seeking to pass India off as Hindu? What does it say about Pakistan that the people of Bangladesh hadn't wanted to be passed off as

INTRODUCTION

Muslim before all else? These questions are being asked today, too, in full view of world news and social media. India's political reality since the start of the Modi government in 2014 has been led by a cohort of leaders engaged in even more identity politics: who is the most Hindu of them all?

As I remember my grandmother in her last days, despite all the geo-political turmoil, she was always sure of who she was, of where she lived. The British Raj had once ruled her Hindustan, and in its memory there was a sort of continuity. She was not happy with the unrest, the wars, the religious divisions, the multiple changes to her national flag. So she held onto the royal family. As her body was embalmed for her funeral, the pictures of the British royals went on smiling. Right to the end, they provided an anchor, a sense of stability.

The place where the old woman had found herself living at the end of her life, Bangladesh, is one where belonging is so fluid that you literally just have to swim across a muddy river to go to the other side of identity, to a different country: the Indian state of West Bengal. If only it were so easy to cross over from one selfhood to another; if only identity were as simple as two sides of a muddy river.

My grandmother's world had seen an almighty, shattering split of society and geography. As her country had broken into three, this discontinuity would be echoed in the split religious identity of her family: herself, her son and her grandchildren. Her own progeny became the confused third entity, the Bangladesh of (un)belonging. This remarkable woman did not live to see me, her virulently godless eldest grandchild, go to England, study the "old Indian" ways of Hinduism and Buddhism, and—after all that studying and re-exploring—decide she was going to have a Jewish family. I wish I could tell her about my many rebirths in the former headquarters of her beloved Raj.

In Chapter 10 we will meet the Trinidadian Sam Selvon, a writer of the Windrush generation who described the wasteland of 1950s London, strewn with lost souls, in his novel *The Lonely Londoners*. Amy and I often talked about this book as we sat on the steps of our Victorian terrace, watching our predominantly West Indian neighbours go by. Here in Brixton, everyone and no one was an alien. It was a true post-colonial exile, where the inhabitants were perpetually being reborn. Late one night, I caught my housemate Katie speaking in a fast-paced south Indian dialect—presumably to her mother—but as soon as she saw me, she broke into English. She was London-born, bona-fide English, she could not be asked where she came from.

I too was always mindful of being caught off guard as I dealt with day-to-day life in London. During the 1992 general election that confirmed John Major in power, Amy and I would join in conversations and marches, shout slogans, express our views on poll tax, even hold placards saying "Troops Out Now" at demonstrations commemorating Bloody Sunday. What did they mean, these struggles with which we had no historical affiliation? And what did we feel about joining them as part of "Southall Black Sisters", when we were South Asian, white or mixed-race with European-Indian ancestry?

I did not want to get it wrong. I was trying to understand the strands of blackness. Despite having the second darkest complexion in our house, I felt guilty representing a "black" group. But that was decades before I learnt about cultural appropriation, and "black experience". In the black Caribbean hub of 1990s Brixton, our little commune lived in its own make-belief blackness. The identity of the exiled could be renegotiated, reconfigured as suited the time and place. The post-racial euphoria of "multi-culti" London constituted the raw material we, the new arrivals, had to work with, to make our British life.

Amy and I wanted to be part of the trendy, subversive London. If it wasn't realistic to belong to the mainstream, which was both white and English—Amy was white, but not British; the others were British by birth, but not white; I was neither—surely then the parallel city, the fringe London of marginalia would hide us, our insecurity and self-doubt. It was a classic case of fluid identity—so full of ironies, so steeped in contradictions. There were those who felt black but did not look it, and those who looked black or brown, but did not feel so. The choices of identity expression were purely personal, without the coercion or hardship that drives people to pass. As we entered London adulthood in the final decade of the last century, we could turn the flow of social mobility to our benefit.

INTRODUCTION

Passing had passed onto something strange and new, as its new cousin, identifying, was born.

* * *

Increasingly in modern times, passing is what social historians call "a chosen exile", where "Identity is a series of networks and a set of connections."[6] After all, who in today's world has not "passed themselves off" as something at some point in their life? But two things haven't changed: unless and until you begin to pass or identify, identity is a label put on you by somebody else; and how others perceive our identity, and therefore whether or not we can pass, still comes down to our looks. The way we dress, speak and move has a huge effect on people's assumptions of our sexuality, our class, our nationality. Our complexion still tells people our race, or so they think. In Chapter 5 we will meet various characters and real-life figures living outside a gender binary reliant on visual cues, as well as Eddie Izzard, someone wrongly gender-identified because of his appearance.

But there has been one truly seismic change in the twenty-first century, with identity transformation growing again to encompass areas that are not just visible, but also virtual. Passing itself has entered a different realm: social media, a revolution steeped in the art of self-making. Our pervasive online presence means anyone can assume any identity, pass as who they like; they can promote their ideas or product, interact and form relationships without the visual signals and assumptions that come with face-to-face encounters. Identity in our time—black, white, woman, man, older, younger—can often be just that strike of the return key. This is not only the digital age but the global age: our economies are now borderless and this brings people together through technology. A call centre in India may introduce its agents as William and Mary; when they leave the office, they go home as Bhaskar and Lalita.

These new realities, this empowerment of people looking for temporary disguises or new definitions of selfhood, are simultaneously available to rich and poor, privileged and marginalised. For others, the Web has provided a new freedom *from* passing, a place where one can identify honestly instead. It has created online spaces for ethnic-minority gay people from orthodox religious backgrounds, who have to hide their sexuality from their community and their religion from the white cultural majority.

Amid the transfers and connections of people and power, amid migration, settlement, nostalgia, exoticism and revision of race and identity, the generations born of these reshuffles—such as my Brixton housemates and I—have continually been trying to fit in like the passers of old; but to fit in where we choose. The identity groups of yesterday are not universally defined and fixed characteristics; they are elective factors in an individual's life, and variable. Strong expressions of personal identity in the twenty-first century have gone hand in hand with rejections of all labels.

In our time, "passing" and "identifying" often get mixed up; they overlap, creating confusion, but also buying time for the undecided to find their place in the realm of identity politics. One Dutch court case from 2018 reveals how identity performance can be taken to extraordinary lengths: a Dutch man went to court to lower his age by several decades, because he felt emotionally of that age, and did not want to miss out on his chances to date younger people. He did not just want to pass as someone he was not officially meant to be; he wanted to make his "younger" identity legal—to have it recognised, and his birth certificate declared wrong. Emile Ratelband told the judge that he saw no difference between his desire for freedom in this respect, and that of a trans person wishing to have their gender identity legally changed: "We live in a time when you can change your name and change your gender. Why can't I decide my own age?"[7]

The legitimacy of claiming a particular identity has never been so fiercely debated as it is today, as we will see in Part Four. Passing has expanded to ironic levels, even seeing a total reversal of the term's popular concept. We all know this from the infamous exposures of Rachel Dolezal, who rose to a high position in African American society by posing as a black activist, and Jessica Krug, the African history professor who was "outed" as white Jewish and publicly apologised in September 2020 for her "immoral" "gaslighting".[8] White-to-black passing—reverse-passing not for adventure as in Kipling, but as a sincere expression of a chosen identity—who would have thought that would be possible? In these two cases and

INTRODUCTION

others like them, the passer exposed and condemned as an impostor is a member of the dominant privileged identity, presenting herself as a member of a community or identity with less power than her own.

This also brings us to today's most talked-about social heresy: cultural appropriation, which is intrinsically related to the act of passing. What was once seen as endearing—an English woman appearing at an Indian wedding in a sari—is now seen as insensitive. These enthusiastic acts of misguided socio-cultural passing by the privileged are no longer acceptable, viewed as the historically powerful having a fun day out trying on exotic native cultures, because they can—because they are able to go home afterwards and be who they are. In Part Four we will question when passing becomes trespassing, endeavour to understand why "passing" or "posing" continue to dominate the identity politics of our time, and see that we cannot achieve a post-identity world without first addressing the stereotypes and intersecting power hierarchies of race, gender, sexuality, class and so on.

The aim of this book, therefore, is not only to look at histories of passing, but also to explore how we view this history today, and how passing occurs in the contemporary world, where there is more freedom of identity than ever before. What are we left with, in terms of passing's own social, political and ideological transition to the new millennium? What are we to make of white Americans claiming to have Native American DNA, or Ali G's "multicultural" street vernacular? When did British racism and tribalism move beyond skin colour to reject Eastern Europeans? And what about all those who fall between the gaps of these shifting gates—the growing number of people with mixed identity, or multiple identities? In Chapter 4 we will look at the difficult choices (and sometimes revelations) facing such people today, from the memoirist Bliss Broyard, who didn't know her father was African American until he died, to London theatre director Anthony Ekundayo Lennon, brought up in a white family but doubly stigmatised: first by whites for his "African features", and later by people of colour for identifying as black.

If you find today's range of identities a ridiculous self-indulgence of snowflakes obsessed with ever-expanding labels, you should take

17

a look at our history. How humanity has categorised itself into groupings of self has never been fixed across the world—as we'll see in Chapter 6 with the Indian subcontinent's transgender hijra community, traditionally held to be culturally important and auspicious, not seen as an aberration from what is really a Western binary. Nor have Western categories for belonging been fixed over time.

We once called religion our identity—that was probably humanity's first effort to categorise fellow humans, as we moved into an organised society. This definition of self was in fact selfless, because its allegiance was to a group identity; belonging was ethno-religious. Later, in the early modern period, the old structures started to fracture across the globe, and the scope for individual identity became a pressing question. For the first time people were able to ask, independently of their inheritance: "Who am I? What am I?" In the case of the West, the first new question was, "Am I a Protestant or am I a Catholic?" In the colonies, it was the brutal European slavery and rule that reshaped previously divided allegiances, quarrelling clans and ethno-religious hierarchies among indigenous populations, both creating new and unified "national" identities in the rejection of a foreign yoke, but also fracturing societies, thanks to official European policies of divide and rule.

Empire also perpetuated the categorisation of identity, and so colonialism changed the fabric of traditional societies in another way, too: insisting that people were either one thing or another, and that these rigid classifications were fundamental to how people should be treated. Today the Victorian laws still have a cultural legacy in post-colonial societies, from caste hierarchies to sexual intolerance. In Western society itself, the law no longer organises people and their status by their identity, and it may seem that we are more open to people choosing or refusing their own labels—but we still categorise people, institutionally indexing them through census data and equality laws.

And so, the world over, the struggle for new self-definition continues as it always has. When identity is suddenly no longer compartmentalised the way it was before, as has happened many times throughout history, there are endless possibilities and parallel realities for those who combine many belongings, or who express a chosen identity that hasn't been socially allocated. Nothing is fixed and

INTRODUCTION

all is uncertain. The same goes for this book's attempt to understand what makes us who we are. The following chapters are a dialectic in which all of the above and more will collaborate in a search for equilibrium: the quest for identity that is passing will teach us that there are no absolute markers to measure our being or belonging.

PART ONE

STRADDLING THE COLOUR LINES

1

ANANSI'S WEB

REBIRTH IN CHAINS AND THE DAWN OF PASSING

In West African, African American and Afro-Caribbean folklore, Anansi is a trickster, a cunning shape-shifter, and a divine passer. He is the son of the sky god Nyame, and therefore a god himself; but one who lives on Earth. One day he goes to his father—who is the keeper of stories—and asks if he can take some to tell his people, the Akan of West Africa. Why will you tell them stories, Nyame asks; what good will that do? Story is knowledge, Anansi replies. Knowledge shall make them gods.

Nyame is not amused by his son's insolence, but instead of rejecting his request outright, he sets him a condition, hoping he will fail: Anansi must complete a series of difficult tasks. They include bringing back four highly dangerous species, one each from the reptile, animal, insect and spirit worlds. This is deemed impossible for anyone to accomplish, for the python is the most poisonous and shrewd; the leopard the greediest and hungriest; the hornets the deadliest and vilest; and the irascible fairy highly elusive, because she is invisible. Yet Anansi tricks them all, traps them and brings them to his father.

Nyame, being a god, cannot break his promise—he has no choice but to dispense the elixir of stories to his son. The victorious Anansi carries them to his people for human consumption. Humanity until this point has consisted of a bunch of dry-witted, miserable workmen, and women without a pastime. Now, Anansi endows them with a treasure chest of ready-made tales, and teaches them how to make new ones to pass on to other peoples of the universe.

Henceforth, Anansi remains above all a dispenser of stories. He appears before his audience in various forms—sometimes as a spider, sometimes a creature with a human head and spider limbs, sometimes other shapes. He is the story of many stories that adorned the lives of people from West Africa, and his stories crossed the ocean on the sad voyage of the slaves.

When the world around them appeared to be doomed and the loss of their African life seemed irrevocable, men, women and children in chains kept alive their hopes of survival with the tales of Anansi. These people shipped from the West African coast as captive property managed to keep with them at least one possession of their own, a divine one for that matter: their oral history. Anansi, the original teller of stories, the godly shape-shifter whose identity is variable. In Africa, everyone had gathered around in the village yard to hear these stories, which had given them strength and a common cause. Anansi epitomised the spirit of the community. As masters tried to beat the homeland out of their slaves, Anansi clung on, with his tales of taming the powerful through mesmerising tricks of transformation. Even in slavery, Anansi stories were a life force, a source of merriment, of social bonds and wisdom. For his enslaved people, Anansi would weave the web of continuity for the next 400 years.

By the time massive, commercial-scale transatlantic slave shipments began, Anansi had already spread his web in the West Indies. His stories were there for the later mass arrivals and their children to cling to, as they endured not just the initial transfer to the Americas, but also subsequent sales from owner to owner that would often break up families and couples—a perpetual continuity of absence, and absence of continuity. For the lone slave, separated from land, family and friends, Anansi stories were the meaning of home in dark nights on the plantation. Millions of Africans were robbed of their collective memory as a people, but the trickster Anansi had managed to slip across the Atlantic unnoticed. The man-spider-god was a master in the art of living, always managing to escape terrible situations and survive in some new form. He was a liminal character straddling two or more worlds, and providing the enslaved in the Americas with the secret of identity survival: folklore.

Anansi stories were and are an integral part of the narrative culture of the Creole inhabitants of the Caribbean and the surrounding mainland. Over centuries of significant black migration into Europe, from both Africa and the Americas, Anansi gradually transformed into a world citizen.[1] Through the oral history of plantation songs, sung from the depths of an increasingly blurred African consciousness, Anansi hopped from West Africa to the New World and beyond to poke his people with his wit and his hopeful stories. For "the tribe in bondage", as Derek Walcott puts it, "What seemed to be surrender was redemption. What seemed the loss of tradition was its renewal. What seemed the death of faith, was its rebirth".[2]

In 2008, a Dutch professional teller of Anansi stories, Hilli Arduin, said in an interview:

> The people were taken and scattered over the Caribbean area and the south of North America. And then Anansi got another function, right. I thought it was a very important function he then got. All these people could take with them were their thoughts. 'Cause nobody can take those from you. And in those thoughts they went back to their mother-lands, of course, and turned Anansi into some kind of hero.[3]

In *Slaves to Racism: An Unbroken Chain from America to Liberia*, the writers Benjamin and Anita Dennis tell a story of confronting an "uncle" in 1943, asking why he, an African American, always talked about the good old times in Virginia before the family's emigration "back" to Africa. The uncle replied, "Well, our history is dead if we don't keep tellin' it."[4] What Uncle Dennis meant was that whatever scraps of history his people could salvage, they must—even if that history began under slavery, in a cold, cold land where they had to work hard to survive; even if that history was African American, not African.

The variability of Anansi's nature—not just his quick-witted shape-shifting, but also his sudden turn from dismay at humans who did not tell or know stories to be god-like to optimism when facing his father's dire tests—inspired some slaves wrenched from their homeland to struggle to live. With tremendous resilience and amidst horrific suffering, the deracinated people brought across the Atlantic built new identities, new stories, and ultimately new nations; and indeed their descendants have sought to pass on their wisdom and enlighten fellow nations, as Anansi taught them.

Today, the #BlackLivesMatter hashtag has been used more times than there are descendants of African slaves. From its first appearance on Twitter in July 2013—following the acquittal of George Zimmerman in the lethal shooting of Trayvon Martin—through to 2018, the hashtag was used nearly 30 million times on Twitter, an average of 17,002 times per day.[5] Its use has become a virtual people's court, where race crimes will not go unheeded. In 2020, this court broke out into the real world in a louder, more widespread way than ever before: following the police killing of George Floyd in May, the history of transatlantic slavery and empire was once again put on trial, by black descendants of the enslaved and many allies. This is Anansi's true legacy, carried forth by all those who have built new lives and new selves in the West.

As Anansi's people adapted, evolved, altered and invented new selves, a new word came into existence: passing. Throughout the history of human selfhood, nothing has pinned us to a social identification more often than our appearance, and this is truer for racial identity than any other label. Race is not an ethnic identity; it is not religious or cultural. When it was invented in the age of transatlantic slavery, its creators tried to pass as scientists, but in fact race was determined purely by subjective impressions of how a person looked. And so, though the activity of passing has existed for as long as there have been public identities and people wishing to escape or subvert them, it was in relation to race that passing first became conceptualised and vocalised. With the mass enslavement of black people in the Americas, identity became more brutally and forensically policed on the basis of appearance than ever before. This forced slaves seeking freedom to put on a new identity, to disguise themselves—and so the term passing was born.

* * *

A racialised slave trade did not start as soon as the early modern Europeans arrived on West Africa's shores. The first Europeans—sailor-merchants and other fortune-seekers from Iberia—treated coastal kingdoms or cities like Benin as general trading posts, bought many things besides labour, and negotiated deals with African chiefs to their mutual economic, military or political benefit. They also made marriage alliances known as *cassare*, from the Portuguese *casar*, to marry, and "there is no question that the *cassare* marriages, in ritual as well as practice, were more African than European".[6] These strategic partnerships were no different from those between different European powers, strengthening trade and diplomatic ties. And, even after large-scale commercial slavery started, the powerful West Africans' daughters who had married Europeans under *cassare* inherited their husbands' property after their deaths—including their enslaved fellow West Africans.[7]

As we know, over time, the balance of power changed, with mutual trust and amicable relations replaced by gunboat diplomacy; merchants and navigators by a whole cultural and economic takeover operation. The increasing—and increasingly large-scale—transfers of Africans to European-owned slave plantations in the New World became part of the Christian "civilising mission": "[t]he sailor who killed a heathen savage remained untroubled in his conscience, reflecting that he had just rid the world of one more false and accursed soul."[8] An othering process had begun, both feeding and fed by the commercialisation of bulk-trading Africans as human chattel.

West African kingdoms had long been practising slavery—but not mass-market slavery, not a pan-African trade or an export trade out of the continent. Rather, slavery had been internal, with what we would today call prisoners of war being captured and used as life-long unpaid workers. European merchants frequently came across these warriors-turned-slaves in their dealings with African monarchs, and some of the early Portuguese navigators were gifted them. That said, there was also some long-term and even large-scale slavery in Africa before the age of European colonialism. The fifteenth-century Europeans were not history's first international slavers. People as property are in the stories of the Bible: a good Jew, and a good Christian, is told how to treat their slaves well—a fact later used as a justification for transatlantic slavery—and of course the Book of Exodus features the enslaved Jews building the Pyramids for the Egyptians. More concretely, the Arab Caliphates of Late Antiquity used East Africans as slave-soldiers. From the fifteenth to the early nineteenth centuries, the Barbary states of North Africa oversaw so-called chattel slavery of Europeans, including children.

Chattel slavery was also a predominant feature of Viking life, with those captured in raids on European towns and villages sold to wealthy clients from Russia to Baghdad.[9] Other examples of internal European slavery include Ancient Rome, many of whose gladiators were slaves or former slaves (the most famous being the rebel leader Spartacus); and early colonial North America, where more than half of European immigrants to the British colonies were white indentured workers labouring without pay, as a commodity to be bought and sold.[10]

So what was different about the transatlantic slave trade? Well, as the above examples show, complexion and slavery were not always intertwined. Until the invention of race, white was not necessarily the colour of privilege. And this status quo prevailed in West Africa at first. Reprobate sailors did convince African chiefs to sell them their slaves of war, but Christian missionaries were there long before the arrival of professional slave-traders; to them, even if heathen and African were synonymous, slave and African—let alone black and African—were not. Even once mass-scale slave exportation was introduced to meet the urgent demand for more robust labour in the New World—the enslaved natives there having been killed off by European diseases—the triangular trade was still not initially framed as being about race. But this would soon change.

It was still local rulers and middlemen bringing their fellow Africans to the shore for European purchase and export—for instance, the former Ashanti capital of Kumasi, in present-day Ghana, prospered from this newly expanded slave trade.[11] But race and identity became two sides of the same coin in the mid-eighteenth to nineteenth century, when race science was invented in Europe. At this juncture, as supposedly Christian powers sought an explanation to excuse their wholesale enslavement of fellow human beings, racial identity became rigid—and black people were dehumanised. On the wings of transatlantic slavery—the gravest crime against humanity for hundreds of years, the most shameful chapter in our global history—race was constructed to categorise people on the basis of their skin colour, hair texture, head measurements and other absurd visual assessments, justified by a political, anthropological and religious system run by white colonials.

As we'll see, laws about blood and family were technically what was supposed to determine Americans' racial categorisation; in reality, however, by the mid-nineteenth century one's destiny and the way one lived depended purely on what one looked like. Sometimes, this led to wrong assumptions about a person's identity. This opened an opportunity, and individual plantation slaves learnt to flout the system: if they looked sufficiently white, they could take cover under a more privileged identity, and try to win their freedom.

Wanted: Will Pass For White Where Not Known

Throughout the antebellum period in the nineteenth century, slaves in America changing their identity became a much-publicised phenomenon, in local newspaper adverts and in handbills posted around inns and bars across the country. All over, slave men and women, even teenagers and children, were passing as free whites to escape the hardship, brutality and tortuous indignity of plantation life. But even if they had a few of Anansi's tricks up their sleeves, this was not a playful endeavour: these light-skinned slaves were setting off on an unimaginably risky journey to freedom.

Here's a typical example: according to legend, in Virginia there lived a planter who had two sons. One was illegitimate, born to a slave woman. He appeared to be very fair-skinned, but was classed as black and born into slavery, and therefore his father's property. The other son was "legal", though he very closely resembled his "black" half-brother. One day, the legal son left for New Orleans to sell his brother at a slave auction. The two half-brothers were handcuffed together for the long boat trip, to stop the slave brother from running away. Shortly before the end of their voyage, there was a storm. The boat lost its course, there was commotion on board, and the boat sank. During the scramble to reach dry land, the slave wrestled the key from his "white" brother, uncuffed himself, and handcuffed his free brother instead.

After they swam ashore, the slave brother proceeded to place his now handcuffed brother on the auction block. The free man protested furiously, saying there had been a mistake and that the man claiming to be a slaver was actually his own slave, but his pleas were met with jeers by the bidders, who were used to such claims from "white Negros"—as optically white slaves came to be known—trying to pass for free men as they went under the hammer. The story goes that the planter's son told the bidders his "slave" tended to hallucinate—thinking he was the master. With the proceeds from the sale of his legally white half-brother, he hurried to the North to start a new life as a free man.

The white rulers of this society were very aware of the possibility that slaves could escape by passing, and this must have provoked inner doubts about the meaning or value of whiteness. This was often betrayed in the dark and convoluted language of the handbills calling for a "passable" slave's recapture, excessively detailing their physical appearance (the supposed foundation of their racial difference): "Stop Mabin!! … about twenty years old, chunkily built, a bright mulatto, with grey eyes—hair straight and sandy—a great deal on his head and rather bushy. He will pass for a white man where he is not known."[12]

One of the most famous real-life examples of white-passing slaves is the story of Ellen Craft, documented in her husband William's 1860 autobiography *Running a Thousand Miles for Freedom*. In 1848, the Crafts ran from Southern slavery to a Northern free state. They were later forced to flee again by the Fugitive Slave Act of 1850, which licensed bounty-hunters to roam not only the South but even into the free states to capture escaped slaves. To get away from these bounty-hunters, the Crafts ultimately crossed the ocean from Boston to Liverpool. But it is the first part of their journey that has most fascinated historians.

The Crafts' story has frequently been mentioned in studies of passing and identity performance, because their escape from slavery is a tale of multiple identity transformations. Ellen and William's passing to freedom encompassed race, gender, class and disability impersonations. Ellen was the daughter of a wealthy slaver and a mixed-race slave woman. She looked a lot like her father's legitimate white children. In order to put an end to the gossip around her husband's infidelity, the planter's wife had sent Ellen away as a wedding present for her daughter, to Macon, Georgia. There, Ellen had met William Craft, a slave who was trained as a carpenter. Soon after their marriage, the couple decided they did not want to have and raise their children in slavery. William came up with an ingenious plan, which he puts forward at the outset of his memoir: "[I]t occurred to me that, as my wife was nearly white, I might get her to disguise herself as an invalid gentleman, and assume to be my master, while I could attend as his slave, and that in this manner we might effect our escape."[13]

And so the quadruple-passing plan was hatched. Ellen would flee with her husband by posing as a wealthy white slaver, with a slave—William—in tow. This meant she would not only have to race-pass and class-pass, but also to gender-pass, as a woman could not own property, including slaves. And she must pass as disabled, too, with her right arm in a sling, to avoid having to sign or write anything; as a slave, she was illiterate.

> For the Crafts, the crossing of the boundary from South to North becomes contingent on the crossing of other boundaries, of the limits whereby identity is conventionally fixed: gender, race, class—Ellen traverses the dividing lines of each, becoming in the course of the narrative black and white, slave and owner, woman and man, wife and master. Drawing the lines of these categories in order to (double-)cross them, Ellen sets in motion questions about authentic, essential identity.[14]

By passing, this scholar says, *Ellen sets in motion questions about authentic, essential identity*—but does she? What is or was her "real" identity? She never "truly" felt white, or identified with any of these characters she was playing—this was only pragmatic, short-term passing. We could perhaps more comfortably say that it's not Ellen's passing that challenges the idea of an authentic or essential identity, but the fact that she was able to pass. Just by being who she was, she challenged the idea of rigid and fixed social categories based on supposedly inherent biological differences. Her white appearance and her black slave status made American race law seem ludicrous, and she went on mocking it to her freedom.

In the moment, though, there was some confusion of self—as there always is with passing. At least for the duration of their long journey north, the optical illusion was more real than what reality had once been. Note William Craft's interesting, almost Woolfian language in the quote above. Throughout his autobiography, Craft alternates the pronouns and titles used to describe his wife, Ellen, versus her disguised male persona. He meticulously maintains her various articulated identities and addresses her accordingly, even in private moments when she returns to him as his wife. Craft even speaks admiringly and proudly of Ellen's presentation as a "most respectable looking gentleman".

This emotional investment in Ellen's alternative persona is unsurprising when you think of the stakes. We shall see throughout this book that passing is only passing when it is successful, realistic. The slightest detection of "Mr Johnson" being anything other than what he seemed would have been highly dangerous for both Ellen and William, and there were several near misses where they were almost caught. But Craft the narrator never slips up, always using "him" and "my master". It's as if Craft doesn't even dare to remind the reader of Mr Johnson's true identity. When the officer of Baltimore—the last slave port before freedom—demands that Mr Johnson show papers for William (as his slave), or else face imprisonment,

> My master looked at me, and I at him, but neither of us dared to speak a word, for fear of making some blunder that would tend to our detection. We knew that the officers had power to throw us into prison, and if they had done so we must have been detected and driven back, like the vilest felons, to a life of slavery, which we dreaded far more than sudden death.[15]

William's narrative has totally suspended disbelief about the Crafts' identity, and they were not the only ones attempting this. As he charts the loopholes through which he and his wife passed, from one side to another and back again, Craft writes about both whites and blacks bending the law, using the cracks in it to secure profit and privilege, and by doing so categorically contesting the capricious workings of race. Right at the start of his memoir, Craft confronts the absurd reality that, ultimately, slavery in America was not confined to persons of any particular colour:

> there are a very large number of slaves as white as any one; but as the evidence of a slave is not admitted in court against a free white person, it is almost impossible for a white child, after having been

kidnapped and sold into or reduced to slavery … ever to recover its freedom.[16]

Craft's narrative becomes more discursive as we hear about a German teenager, Salomé Muller, who was orphaned during her voyage to America and, on arrival, kidnapped and sold into slavery. By his careful use of such examples, Craft strikes a raw nerve for white American readers: watch out, your child might be next. He warns that, if action is not taken to abolish slavery, America's race politics may turn on its head. Race was so arbitrary in antebellum America that it frequently breached the colour-coded legal boundaries. And racial profiling was so ubiquitous that, even when a slave was granted freedom, his complexion forever bound him to the enslaved identity.

As dramatised in the acclaimed 2013 film, the memoir *Twelve Years A Slave* (1853) documents the experience of Solomon Northup, a New York State-born free man, who was kidnapped by two men and sold back into slavery. This demonstrates the point Craft makes, which is that racial categorisation is not in fact based on "realities" of blood, but on common consensus—and such a consensus can be overturned. The injustice of Northup's tale rests on the fact that he has been enslaved even though he is "supposed" to be free. But the real injustice is that it is heinous to enslave any black person. To Northup, and to the audience complicit in this artificial ranking of who has the right to life, his free status is more important than his colour; but to his captors and enslavers, of course, it is the reverse. He *looks* like a slave, and so he belongs among slaves. Ellen Craft uses the same consensus to gain freedom, nonchalantly fooling one Southerner after another. She looked white, and so she was allowed to travel openly out of her slave life.

William Craft's account is a modern read. His and his wife's story could not emphasise more that categorisation of identity is futile, because the "real" and the "assumed" selves are mirror images of each other. There is no "true" beginning or "false" ending. Craft narrates this identity fluidity sardonically, adding a light touch to the terrifying flight from "the jaws of the wicked". He seems to take great pleasure in playfully narrating the elaborate deception, whether Ellen is successfully engaging with fellow steamer passengers on the old subject—"the niggers talk"—or being wished good health in the clean air of Philadelphia, or "hobbling" off the boat as the frail Mr Johnson, assisted by a white hotelier: "The proprietor made me [William] stand on one side, while he paid my master the attention and homage he thought a gentleman of his high position merited."[17] Two young women in a train compartment swoon over Mr Johnson, the perfect gentleman, and one tells her father, "I never felt so much for a gentleman in my life!" Craft chuckles, "'they fell in love with the wrong chap!'"[18]

Running a Thousand Miles for Freedom was written in William's voice, but we have evidence that Ellen, too, enjoyed this cunning victory over an illogical racist society. Her disguise is described at great length in the book, and an engraving was made to illustrate the story's first publication in the *London Illustrated News*, on 19 April 1851. We see here a fine-featured young white gentleman in a top hat and cravat, with tassels on his coat—the costume of a wealthy Southern slaver. He has curly, cropped hair that comes up to his ears, fine lips, a small cleft chin and intelligent eyes behind semi-opaque glasses. On that thin mouth we can detect a faint smirk, as if "Mr Johnson" is having a roaring laugh at her ability to fool white men, from Georgia to Boston.

* * *

Like the tale of those two Virginia brothers, the Crafts' escapades were well publicised all over North America—first in the handbills advertising for their recapture, and then of course in the memoir. It is hardly surprising, then, that contemporary fiction started to reflect these extraordinary stories. The best-known nineteenth-century novel on slavery was *Uncle Tom's Cabin* by Harriet Beecher Stowe (1852). By this time, thanks to bounty-hunters' and slavers' handbills, the word "passing" had already entered American parlance, and Stowe likewise explores this new hot topic of the day.

In the first part of the book, the plot revolves around the character Eliza Harris, and her family's flight to Canada in disguise. This spectacular escape to liberty is achieved through an ingenious cover: altering every possible prediction of subterfuge made by their white masters. This episode in Stowe's novel is seen to be breaking a series of taboos in America's gender, class and racial hierarchies. The family's passing is multi-fold, as they devise a new class, a new identity and a new nationality, on the road to Canada. Eliza assumes a white, male persona, cutting her hair and dressing in "white" clothing. Stowe herself enters the book as a character, the little boy called Harry, who is dressed up by Eliza as a girl and renamed Harriet. In this way, the author "places herself within the narrative as the wide-eyed, 'peeping', and disbelieving child of the primal scene ... of American cultural intercourse, the imagined and unimaginable coupling of race and gender."[19]

In escaping to Canada, Eliza and Harry/Harriet are following in the footsteps of Eliza's husband George. He too defies the arbiters of colour and, like Ellen Craft, has flipped it on its head to win his freedom, using white America's blind faith in racial binaries against it. When he escaped from his slaveholder, Mr Harris, the master circulated a handbill advertisement:

> Ran away from the subscriber, my mulatto boy, George. Said George six feet in height, a very light mulatto, brown curly hair; is very intelligent, speaks handsomely, can read and write; will probably try to pass for a white man; is deeply scarred on his back and shoulders; has been branded in his right hand with the letter H.[20]

George knew his master's mind well, anticipating that he would imagine his mulatto slave passing as white in his flight to freedom. But of course George, the "very intelligent" slave, is hugely underestimated by his master. He has not tried to pass for a white man. Instead he chooses to escape by doing the opposite: slightly darkening his skin, rather than accentuating his very light complexion. Despite looking white, he rejects the obvious path in favour of passing as an olive-skinned Spaniard called Henry Butler. Toward the end of the novel, we find him lamenting, "if I wished anything, I would wish myself two shades darker, rather than one lighter."[21]

Stowe's account of George's chosen "third way" was a reflection of real history. Some mixed-race slaves who were not light enough to pass as white did manage to escape through an alternative identity, such as the black-haired, "well-set Fellow" called Jem who found freedom as early as 1763 by passing as a Native American tradesman. The handbill for his recapture read:

it is supposed, he will change both his Name and Dress, as he has been seen with his Hair comb'd out straight, and an Indian Match coat on: I am informed he intends to make his Escape in that Disguise, pass for an Indian, and profess himself as a Shoemaker.[22]

But the character of George Harris seems to be a special case; for reasons of wit and perhaps defiance, he *chooses* not to pass as white even though he has the complexion to do so.

Here we come back to an important insight into the "master" class highlighted by William Craft: the slave will eventually revolt, because they have worked out the ruling elite's deep insecurity; once slaves realise this, and the power of the majority, there will be a slave rebellion. Any revolution or successful mass defiance in human history has happened when the mighty become too complacent. The history of passing—though not a universal form of protest at oppression—is underwritten by underprivileged people who have diligently observed their dominators' great weakness: their preconceived ideas about identity and their enforcement. George Harris's successful performance stems from an assessment that his master is aware his own position is untenable in the face of a smart, mixed-race slave, and anxious about it. As the literature professor Julia Stern puts it:

> Why does he mention the fact of George's mulatto heritage not once but twice? Why, in his second use of the word, does he modify the term with the phrase, "very light"? Why is the "boy" of color in the first line of the ad imagined to be feigning the role of a white "man"? How do high intelligence, eloquence ("speaks handsomely"—connoting a mastery of language that borders on the aesthetic), and, most significant, literacy ("can read and write") work to transform the abject and infantilized slave ("boy") into a bonafide adult ("will try to pass for a white man"), entitled to citizenship and human dignity?[23]

Having claimed this dignity for himself, without having to conform to his master's ideas of a dual racial hierarchy, George Harris confidently walks into a Kentucky inn. His Spanish masquerade is complete and successful, and fast turning into a risky adventure. Mr Harris's handbill about George is pasted on the wall. But white onlookers in the tavern admire this tall, handsome Spaniard, tanned and dark-haired—"a well-dressed, gentlemanly man", who arrives in a one-horse buggy, "with a colored servant driving". He walks to the bar, where everyone is transfixed by "the admirable contour of his finely-formed limbs", his "expressive black eyes" and his glossy black curls.[24] The men in the bar watch him and think there is something uncommon about him, but theirs is the fascination with a fine-looking stranger from exotic southern Europe, not the suspicion of a possible fugitive. He politely tells the landlord that he would like a private apartment, as he has to get on with some writing "immediately".

George Harris has just thrown his best card: his literacy, which is of the highest order. Not only can he "read and write" as the handbill proclaims, he is posing as an author. Stowe has not only created an educated slave at a time when slaves were not generally allowed to be literate, but she has compelled her readership to feel very confused about what to make of a runaway slave who speaks and acts so "handsomely". A huge number of her readers in the 1850s must have been slaveholders, or deeply prejudiced about black people.

Stowe herself was defying identity conventions of her time, writing as a social and gender reformer and as a woman author, daring to challenge the world of male slaveholders and landowners. She was perceived to be trespassing into a man's world. During her later campaign for women's property rights, when she was editor of the women's magazine *Hearth and Home*, Stowe argued the married woman was in many respects "precisely similar to that of the negro slave".[25] Whatever she earned or inherited became her husband's property at the moment of marriage. Like a slave, a married woman passes out of legal existence.

And yet, here she is, unmasking the prejudices of those who control others—herself armed with the power of the pen, Stowe, a small woman, stood up to America's obsessive attachment to binary social roles based on fictions of gender and race. Stowe's portrayal of "nice slaves" such as the title character, Tom, uses the patronising racialised language of the time, and is sometimes credited with cementing or popularising racial stereotypes—she would be lambasted for it by anti-slavery activists. But *Uncle Tom's Cabin* was the biggest-selling book of the nineteenth century after the Bible. This novel about powerful men behaving abominably, and black heroes who outdid them, remains one of the most effective campaigns against the corrosive institution of slavery. Abraham Lincoln, upon meeting Harriet Beecher Stowe after the start of the American Civil War in 1862, apparently said: "So you're the little woman who wrote the book that started this great war."[26]

Atlantic Amnesia: Parcel'd Out to All the World

As the appearance of a person can be changeable, or deceiving, so can their identification with any other form of being or belonging. Identity is not inherited; it is to be found, determined or defined by the individual, without necessarily corresponding to perceived norms of "biology" or society. Nowhere is this more evident than in these early stories of slaves' racial passing. Escapees were able to manipulate the weakness of the identity society had assigned them, their success exposing race as a constructed fiction.

William and Ellen Craft, playing out their parts of master and slave, inhabited temporary identities for a thousand-mile journey—fooling not only those who would hunt them down or turn them in, but even, at times, themselves—just in order to find a place safe from identity, where they could be anonymous, and therefore free. Only on arrival in Pennsylvania, as they head for a boarding house run by abolitionists, does William Craft's narration acknowledge Mr Johnson's true identity:

> On leaving the station, my master—or rather my wife, as I may now say—who had from the commencement of the journey borne up in a manner that much surprised us both, grasped me by the hand, and said, "Thank God, William, we are safe!" and then burst into tears, leant upon me, and wept like a child.[27]

The Crafts' personal battle against slavery is won.

But for as long as humans have categorised themselves and each other, there have been safe and unsafe identities. Runaway slaves were not the only or the last black people in the West who had to fight just to be, and the victory of the individual performing a fluid identity couldn't bring down the system itself. At one point on their journey, the Crafts meet a fellow slave, Pompey, who advises William that once he reaches the free state of Pennsylvania, he must not only run away and be a free man. He must also pray for his fellow people to pass into freedom. In a Biblical allusion, Pompey pleads with William, "God bless you, broder, and may de Lord be wid you. When you gets de freedom, and sitin under your own wine and fig-tree, don't forget to pray for poor Pompey."[28]

Passing is a contingency against a blockade: the constrained seek to master the act of outpacing their assigned selves, as an insurance policy; to make space for the brutalised selfhood to be negotiated and reclaimed. This has long been, and still is being, pursued by many persecuted communities and floating peoples, at every blockade against freedom of movement. Experiences of departure—both forced and voluntary, both physical and spiritual—bear the same hallmark of loss, exile and the search for an adopted "home"— whether geographical, social, cultural or emotional.

In having their roots torn from them, and in shifting their identity once the return to their origins was made impossible, we can argue that the children of empire, starting with the transatlantic slaves, were the first modern beings. Through their search for identity, and their rejection of the labels placed on them by a society that wouldn't recognise their humanity, they gave us the gift of diversity—the courage to break free of cultural exclusivism and rigid categorisation, in favour of new concepts of convergence. As the Martinican writer Édouard Glissant said in his essay "Caribbean Discourse", these were identities "neither uniform nor predictable but extending 'in all directions.' The image of slaves' drowned bodies—individual bodies that are freefloating and yet immersed in a greater whole—challenges a notion of selfhood characterized by boundaries".[29]

Running a Thousand Miles for Freedom and other tales of white-passing runaways represent the story of people who went out roaming a treacherous world, in search of a place where they could claim safety and plant the seeds of a new life. Black slaves, violently separated from both their original communities in Africa and the privileged white majority in the Americas, had to carve out their own culture and identity. The St Lucian poet and essayist Derek Walcott talks about "Atlantic amnesia", the erasure of the slaves' memory and origins that triggered this process, ultimately birthing new selfhoods. There couldn't have been one without the other: were it not for the original uprooting, no new identity would have taken root; but the new self will still eternally search for those lost roots. For though the body may have complied with the key requirement for passing, the soul carries on with its quiet rebellion.

Nobody knew this sense of disconnect better than the slaves taken to the New World. In his magnificent poem *Doomsday*, the seventeenth-century English poet and priest George Herbert prays for a reunion of the dislocated body with its soul: Herbert says it is the origin of the segmented man.

> Come away,
> Help our decay.
> Man is out of order hurl'd.
> Parcel'd out to all the world.[30]

The disintegration of body from soul was a terrifying part of the Middle Passage: between 1 and 2 million Africans died crossing the Atlantic from West Africa, and their bodies were routinely thrown into the sea, even though devout Christians believed in burial as a crucial pillar of the faith, being paramount for resurrection. If the souls of the enslaved had not been saved, says Herbert, why would their history have been?

For descendants of the enslaved, this trauma of separation from the familial and the familiar, and the necessity of rebirth, have continued to shape life long past the end of slavery. In the next few chapters, we will see how ideas of racial passing, and the formation and un-formation of racial identities, have played out in the wake of slavery and empire, right up to the present day.

2

THE CASTLE OF YOUR SKIN

REWRITING THE PAST IN JIM CROW AMERICA

The Muse of History

As we have seen, historically racial passing from black to white resulted from the social and cultural and legal oppression of white rule. In the pages to come, we shall see that "free" African Americans still often felt forced to pass if they could, decades after the abolition of slavery. They were still living under a codified and constitutionally sanctioned system of white supremacy and racial segregation that continued to define their lives, run on the same assumptions about identity as the slavery era. Today we call this system Jim Crow America.

For almost a century, from the late nineteenth century to the end of the Jim Crow laws in the mid-1960s, a colour line divided white from black in the Southern United States, attempting to keep the "races" separate from one another, and African Americans locked into their designated place. There was no room for the concept of "mixed-race"—you were white, or you were black, and your identity papers and social security documents set this in stone. Throughout this era, and beyond it, those on the wrong side of this colour line felt their unfreedom just as the slaves had felt theirs—some longed to cross over. The other side was white; the other side was mainstream; the other side was free; the other side was higher-class.

Some lucky passers did manage to cross into privilege: as Anansi knew, there was always a way for the cunning and brave to "bend the rules, finesse the system."[1] But there was a cost. In this period of

American history, white-passing evolved from the temporary identity shift put on by escaping slaves to become a permanent double life. The Crafts and Harrises stopped passing as soon as they had reached safety—but light-skinned African Americans passing as white in the century after slavery never truly found security or freedom. The other side of their successful transgression was a dark tale of loss and disconnect.

First of all, the passers had to cross over to anonymity, relocating away from their birthplace so that no one could recognise them. Only then could they transform—if they had the right complexion, the right skills, the right education and the right courage—into someone different, freed from the prison of their black life. By doing so, they would lose all connection to their old world, as they searched instead for new ground—a new belonging, a new identity that was less deadly and more liveable.

> Passing works as a prism: it refracts different aspects of what we commonly think of as racial identity and reveals what is left once the veil of an ascribed status is stripped away. Behind that veil what we know as "race" is simply the lived experience of a people, expressed perhaps as an ache for family and interconnections or sometimes as a longing for music, humor, and food. Thus passing unmasks race as conventionally understood.[2]

Those able to leave their "putative racial identity" could enjoy a better quality of social and economic life, in the shelter of their pale complexion. But they were often alone here. Many light-skinned and mixed-race African Americans had darker-skinned family members who could not pass and so must be left behind. Even when the entire family could pass as white, they would then have to sever ties with their community, their neighbourhood, their friends. The result was relentless isolation, and a burden of secrecy. Passers struggled to overcome the legacy of loss: of music, food, humour, the feeling of embeddedness in a community in dark times. They also risked the judgement and moral superiority of the "left behind", who either couldn't or wouldn't pass. In a racially segregated society, whiteness is a long-term quarantine.

Amidst these auguries of loneliness and abandonment, many of those who could pass did. The irony of Jim Crow America was that

African Americans' only way to live an authentic life—one that fulfilled them, and reflected their aspirations, values and talents—was to claim it illegally. Black Americans passed to become actors, singers, lawyers; poets burdened with words that would otherwise never have been published. Whiteness became the journey's end for dejected individuals weary of prejudice and injustice. Why should you be dominated by the laws of segregation, if you could circumvent them? In what way was it "right" to accept perpetual disenfranchisement not only for yourself, but also for your children and children's children, all for the sake of loyalty to the community? Did it really matter, wrenching oneself from one's origins, if the law was already keeping lovers apart, friendships from forming?

No one has put it more sorrowfully than Derek Walcott in one of his early poems, written in 1949 when he was only nineteen. The black speaker, a poet, laments the impossibility of reaching out to his white lover, described as a delicate, china-white figurine of a shepherdess, because of the distance in their "complexion": "You in the castle of your skin/I the swineherd."[3] In the end, the identity of the white-complexioned beloved in her castle of superiority does not really interest the reader. Instead we are transfixed by the haunting language of the poem, which Walcott weaves with the anguish of the dejected lover. By mastering one important tool of the dominant race, the English language, the poet has outmanoeuvred the otherwise impenetrable fortress of whiteness, and the castle of his own black skin.

* * *

But not everyone can turn longing and frustration into a love poem. Others were not skilful or educated enough to fight racial division with the pen. Those of African ancestry who did have another kind of "privilege"—a light complexion—sought fast-track entry into the castle of opportunities. But this was not really a choice of the privileged. This was a chance opportunity grabbed by the disoriented individual, "divided to the vein" as Walcott put it,[4] when there was no other way to overcome racial segregation and hierarchy.

The irony of ironies in America was that race laws had made racial mixing much more pervasive. The Great Migration, also known as the Black Migration (1916–70), saw African Americans move northward out of the rural South, where segregation ruled and opportunity was slim. Among them were tens of thousands of light-skinned migrants, mostly descendants of women slaves and their white rapists, who passed in the booming urban centres of the North and married "pure whites". It is estimated that more than 150,000 legal "blacks" crossed the colour line in the 1940s alone;[5] and that, by 1950, a little more than 20 per cent (28 million) of America's 135 million whites had black ancestry within the past four generations.[6]

In the novel *Pudd'nhead Wilson* (1894), Mark Twain uses the phrase "a fiction of law and custom"[7] to describe the arbitrariness of how white and black were defined by a regime caught in its own trap. The blanket principle called the One Drop rule, which was devised during the days of slavery and which openly ruled American society until the civil rights movement of the 1960s, classified anyone with one drop of "black blood" as black. A child born to a black African and a white European becomes a mixed-race or "mulatto" person—like Ellen Craft's mother. When that "mulatto" has a child with a black person, that child is a "griffe"; when with a white person, a "quadroon", like Ellen herself. The "octoroon" is one-eighth African American; the "'steenth" one-sixteenth—very likely white-skinned, but still categorised as black.

Thomas Jefferson (1743–1826), third president of the United States, explained these darkly comic equations of American law in a letter written after his time in office: "By the third cross, of the result of 'q, (quarteroon) being ¼ negro blood crossed with C [Caucasian]—q/2+C/2=a/8+B/4+C/2' was an *e* (eighth), and having only 1/8 of negro blood, was no longer a mulatto."[8] [These absurd conceptions and the obsession with "cross-breeds" lasted into the twentieth century, when the Jim Crow laws were in place.] The eugenicist Madison Grant wrote in *The Passing of the Great Race: Or the Racial Basis of European History* (1916):

> The cross between a white man and an Indian is an Indian; the cross between a white man and a Negro is a Negro; the cross between a white man and a Hindu is a Hindu; and the cross between any of the three European races and a Jew is a Jew.[9]

But in fact, as Mark Twain hinted, this principle was a lie. First of all, given the very possibility of passing, we know that race—as a social status and a life experience—was determined not by biology, but by appearance. In job interviews, or before being conscripted, for example, if the official wrote "W" next to the name of a light-skinned slave descendant, they would be selected to live a completely different life from other members of the same family. Secondly, the One Drop system was created not to preserve the separation of races, but in response to their already having mixed. What the racist system wanted to ensure was that no "white Negros" could be considered white—an acknowledgement in itself that such a possibility existed. But the reverse was already happening too, making a mockery of the system: after many centuries of systemic sexual abuse, genes were sufficiently diluted for black families sometimes to produce "white" or "mulatto" children. The stigma and fear of this blood reality was deeply ingrained in white society. As Malcolm X put it, "the guilt of American whites included their knowledge that in hating Negroes, they were hating, they were rejecting, they were denying, their own blood."[10]

So if the choice is between a world full of brown people, or a world without people—which would you go for? This primal fear of seeing their nation tainted by black blood may have been after the horse had bolted, but it persuaded even the abolitionists of the mid-nineteenth century to advocate for a mass export operation of African Americans: a national homeland for former slaves, as we will see in Chapter 9. This reminds me of the argument that it was fear of a Jewish takeover of Europe after the Holocaust that prompted a guilt-ridden Europe to support the creation of Israel.

The fear of a brown world has not dissipated in today's America. The white Christian self being synonymous with America, race has not left the arena of identity politics as had been hoped after the civil rights movement, and then again with the "Obama moment". In an intrinsically racist society, identity's main vehicle is usually race. In her 2016 essay "Making America White Again", Toni Morrison wrote that, 150 years after the end of slavery, "for many people, the definition of 'Americanness' is [still] color".[11] Today the fear of a black takeover is focused on black nationalism, the idea that African Americans would take over through a democratic process and run America officially: "Another black President? A predominantly black Senate? Three black Supreme Court Justices? The threat [to the collective identity] is frightening."[12]

White nationalists still join mass gatherings, their appearance emblemised by distinct identification badges and logos—no longer the cone-shaped hats, but hats all the same, vowing to make America great again. These campaigners do not say how America became less great, but the implication is clear. Until a few years ago, "cultural protectionists" and white intellectuals who express alarm at the high birth rate of Muslims, Asians and other minorities as a kind of Western apocalypse would have been considered shameful reactionaries. Today white protectionism has become mainstream in Europe too, as we'll see in Chapter 10.

But the "apocalypse" has already happened, and it has been allowing white-passing for centuries. Thanks to sexual relations and abuse in plantation society, the dreaded "pollution" of white America by much more than one drop of black blood is as old as the history of slavery. The historian Allyson Hobbs states in her book, *A Chosen Exile*, that passing revealed "the bankruptcy of the race idea".[13] The multi-racial (if I may use this description) American philosopher and conceptual artist, Adrian Piper, was born in 1948. When she traced her ancestry, this is what she found:

> To date, what I *think* I know is that our first European-American ancestor landed in Ipswich, Massachusetts, in 1620 from Sussex; another in Jamestown, Virginia, in 1675 from London; and another in Philadelphia, Pennsylvania, in 1751, from Hamburg. … My great-great-grandmother from Madagascar, by way of Louisiana, is the known African ancestor on my father's side, as my great-great-grandfather from the Ibo of Nigeria is the known African ancestor on my mother's, whose family has resided in Jamaica for three centuries.[14]

In fact, despite the One Drop illusion, miscegenation had happened early even in America's highest political milieu. Take the civil rights activist Walter Francis White (1893–1955), who had blond hair and blue eyes. This NAACP figure was the great-grandson of America's ninth president, William Henry Harrison, who had six "illegitimate" children by Dilsia, an African American woman he owned. Harrison was the son of Benjamin Harrison V (1726–91), a planter and governor of Virginia—a founding father who signed the Declaration of Independence. Walter White wrote of his own experience of passing while travelling in the South in an all-white train carriage: a white passenger grabbed his hand and placed it next to his, boasting that he could tell a pure white man from anyone with a drop of Negro blood by examining his knuckles and the halfmoons of his fingernails. White sat through the journey nervously, placing his halfmoon-free fingers on the table.

* * *

The One Drop rule drove many either to work actively on creating a new white identity or simply not to correct assumptions when they were taken for white. Racial categorisation often depended on administrative whims—a white interviewing officer might well not bother to carry out a "proper" investigation of a job applicant's race—assessing the kink of their hair, thickness of lips, sloping shoulders and so on—if the person simply appeared white. In the next chapter we'll explore a novel set in apartheid South Africa, *Playing in the Light*, in which a character, John, chooses to look the other way when a lucky error is made on his identity papers: "Why fuss over a spelling that made not the slightest difference? Or if it did, if that was all it took to turn him into someone new, a man of the city with prospects, who was he to complain? The name could easily be corrected…"[15]

But John did not correct it. He moved to a faraway city where no one knew him, where he found wealth and recognition.

Whiteness—even accidental whiteness—was a status card, an entry ticket to a free zone. It was an escape from the smoking car packed back to back not only with all the blacks on the train, but also the white misfits, drunks and criminals; from often poor, overcrowded, squalid neighbourhoods; from lack of access to proper jobs, to adventure, travel, simple pleasures of life like dining out with friends in downtown restaurants or drinking from a "white-only" water fountain. The biracial author James Weldon Johnson (1871–1938) describes his white-passing narrator's experience of degradation and dehumanisation in *The Autobiography of an Ex-Colored Man*, first published anonymously in 1912:

> All the while, I understood that it was not discouragement, or fear, or search for a larger field of action and opportunity, that was driving me out of the Negro race. I knew that it was shame, unbearable shame. Shame at being identified with a people that could with impunity be treated worse than animals.[16]

In the Jim Crow era, being black could feel like a windowless room full of family members who had no way out. Sometimes amidst this, on a sleepless night, a resentful light-skinned face would look into their future, and decide they did not want to be identified with a roomful of blackness.

From the nineteenth to the mid-twentieth century, white-passing was a powerful social disturbance that could devastate African American families. Being optically white wasn't enough to pass. At a time when race laws searched for "Negro" blood even in the eighth generation, Atlantic amnesia wasn't good enough—and inventing a seamless white backstory was not an easy job. Passers had to change places, cities, countries, states, in order to invent stories that would be convincing to the white vigilantes of lineage. In an echo of the challenge facing the transatlantic slaves, the abandonment of roots left the leavers of black life with a reckless streak, a feeling that they had nothing to lose. The voluntarily disinherited went out into an unfamiliar wide world to find new knowledge, new family, new opportunities; to remould their fate in the freedom of whiteness.

It was incredibly dangerous, and had irreversible personal consequences. Of those who successfully passed, most could never go back to their black families, not even when their parents died in some segregated towns. Nor, if they passed for long enough to start their own family, could they always confide in their white spouse and children that they had transitioned from one race to another. In other words, the passer did not enter free white society so much as a parallel, alternative society, where the newly "liberated" still live in the prison of their chosen identity. The social historian Hobbs says that "the core issue of passing is not becoming what you pass for, but losing what you pass away from."[17] In the end, African Americans taking on a white identity found themselves standing before a set of closed doors—and the door they had just shut behind them, back into their black life, also stayed closed.

Fig. 1: Mixed-race slave Ellen Craft disguised as a disabled, white, slave-owning man.

Fig. 2: Ellen the 'master' and husband William the 'slave', during their flight to freedom in 1848.

Fig. 3: Harlem Renaissance author Nella Larsen, whose novella *Passing* (1929) popularised the term as we understand it today.

Fig. 4: Josephine Baker, whose *Danse Sauvage* played to interwar Parisian audiences' prejudices about black women.

Fig. 5: The author (far right) and her siblings, characterised by four different "complexion descriptors".

Fig. 6: Kali, Hinduism's black goddess, dancing victorious over her husband, Shiva.

Fig. 7: Biracial Brazilian footballer Neymar da Silva Santos Júnior: "It's not like I'm black."

(b) (i) all persons who are not South African citizens and are within the Union on the fixed date and were prior to the fixed date born in any part of South Africa included in the Union or admitted to the Union for permanent residence therein; and

(ii) all persons who are not South African citizens and are after the fixed date born in the Union or admitted to the Union for permanent residence therein; and

(c) (i) all persons who are not South African citizens and are within the Union on the fixed date for a temporary purpose; and

(ii) all persons who are not South African citizens and are admitted to the Union for a temporary purpose after the fixed date.

Act No. 30 of 1950.

5. (1) Every person whose name is included in the register shall be classified by the Director as a white person, a coloured person or a native, as the case may be, and every coloured person and every native whose name is so included shall be classified by the Director according to the ethnic or other group to which he belongs.

Classification of persons whose names are included in the register.

(2) The Governor-General may by proclamation in the *Gazette* prescribe and define the ethnic or other groups into which coloured persons and natives shall be classified in terms of sub-section (1), and may in like manner amend or withdraw any such proclamation.

(3) If at any time it appears to the Director that the classification of a person in terms of sub-section (1) is incorrect, he may, subject to the provisions of sub-section (7) of section *eleven* and after giving notice to that person and, if he is a minor, also to his guardian, specifying in which respect the classification is incorrect, and affording such person and such guardian (if any) an opportunity of being heard, alter the classification of that person in the register.

6. The Director shall assign an identity number to every person whose name is included in the register.

Identity number to be assigned to every person whose name is included in the register.

7. (1) There shall, in respect of every person whose name is included in the register, other than a native, be included in the register the following particulars and no other particulars whatsoever namely—

(a) his full name, sex and ordinary place of residence;
(b) his classification in terms of section *five*;
(c) the date and place of his birth;
(d) his citizenship or nationality, and in the case of an alien, an indication of the fact that he is an alien;
(e) his marital status;

The particulars to be included in respect of every person whose name is included in the register.

Fig. 8: Apartheid South Africa's Population Registration Act, which classified everyone by "race".

Fig. 9: Barack Obama, the first black president of the United States, with his grandfather, mother and sister, early 1970s.

Fig. 10: Meghan Markle, who has chosen not to pass, with her mother.

Those who passed over and, outwardly, found their place in white society often secretly longed for things and people they had left behind; but they usually never looked back. When dark-skinned relatives came across them in public places, they might pretend not to know each other. The newly re-racinated were already on the other side of the chasm called segregation.

Divided to the Vein

We know all this because, by the early twentieth century, passing had started to feature prominently in African American—particularly mixed-race African American—writing. Marriage was not legal between whites and blacks, and those of mixed heritage were doubly stigmatised: seen as black by the white side, and white by the black side. White-passing characters appear frequently in the literature born of this community—for example, in the works of bi-racial Harlem Renaissance novelist Nella Larsen. Her characters cross the porous boundary of race in New York City into the white world, and back again into the black. In the city's crowded, individualistic and fluid landscape, it was possible to reinvent one's personal identity. Larsen's 1929 novel *Passing* introduced the term to the urban lexicon, popularising it.

The subject was close to Larsen's own experience. Daughter of a Danish mother and a mixed-race father, she lost her father young. Her mother remarried a fellow Danish immigrant and the family moved to a white-majority neighbourhood. Nella did not fit in and was sent abroad to live with relations. She eventually came back to the United States and, despite the recognition and prestige her writing brought her, remained on the periphery of race, belonging to neither side. Like many passers, she passed away unceremoniously—dying alone, in virtual anonymity.

Passing opens with a quote from "Heritage", a poem by Larsen's fellow Harlem Renaissance writer Countée Cullen:

> One three centuries removed
> From the scenes his fathers loved,
> Spicy grove, cinnamon tree,
> What is Africa to me?[18]

PASSING

Passing reflects two African American women's struggle to find their place in the present, amid a loss of connection with their roots. Both of them are "passing", one by chance, and one by design. Irene Redfield, the heroine, finds herself passing on occasion: due to her "white" appearance, she is accepted into white-only spaces. For the other woman, her childhood friend Clare Kendry, it is a chosen, permanent exile.

This is a source of tension between the two characters: many African Americans saw white-passing as disloyalty to fellow blacks, denial of one's origins, racial self-hatred. Even if nobody from the old life blamed you for your choice, a sense of shame may still have been there, and always an awareness that you had sacrificed "the history, wisdom, connectedness, and moral solidarity [of] family and community".[19] Irene disapproves of Clare's disowning of her people, and throughout the book more broadly the "black" characters who look white are shown to be suspicious of each other. In cafes and jazz bars, they watch each other, speculating as to who is truly black and who is passing. Here we see how fragmentation of the mind and fragmentation of society are intertwined in questions of identity. The novel is full of terrorised figures who walk around like shadows, their presences subdued, the cloak of their altered identity held closely and carefully.

At one moment Irene—continuously straddling the black and white worlds—breaks down in despair under her many burdens, including the most confusing one: race. Irene has remained in her black neighbourhood with her physician husband and their black family, but ventures out from time to time to taste and tease the white world. It is during one of these resentful social research trips to a white-only cafe that Irene meets her long-lost friend, Clare. They are cautiously thrilled to have found each other again, but soon Irene is horrified to learn about Clare's double life. Clare has left her home in Harlem to marry a racist white man, moved with him to a white area and had a white child.

Of course, her new family has no idea that she is in fact African American. In James Weldon Johnson's *Autobiography of an Ex-Colored Man*, the white-passing narrator explains this fear of being exposed to the white love object:

> The dread that I might lose her took possession of me each time I sought to speak, and rendered it impossible for me to do so. That

moral courage requires more than physical courage is no mere poetic fancy. I am sure I would have found it easier to take the place of a gladiator, no matter how fierce the Numidian lion, than to tell that slender girl that I had Negro blood in my veins.[20]

When Irene visits Clare at home, Clare's husband makes vile comments about blacks, without any knowledge of his wife's own background. Larsen describes Irene's deep, despondent rage:

> Sitting alone in the quiet living-room in the pleasant fire light, Irene Redfield wished, for the first time in her life, that she had not been born a Negro. For the first time she suffered and rebelled because she was unable to disregard the burden of race. It was, she cried silently, enough to suffer as a woman, an individual, on one's own account, without having to suffer for the race as well. It was a brutality, and undeserved.[21]

Allyson Hobbs calls what Irene and Clare are going through "painful familial ruptures."[22] Irene is upset because Clare's rejection of race is much more than just passing from one identity to another; it has left in its wake a permanent separation from the old emotion of what it means to belong to a community. Clare tells her friend that she has even decided to forgo trying for another child, lest it turn out to be dark-skinned. Passing is not about lying, though it may require this; it is about perpetually transitioning into different beings. Irene may feel Clare is living a lie, but for Clare herself, she is just living what is right for her. Her new reality has quickly become her own, and while it doesn't disqualify the past, it erases it. The past is overwritten with the present.

All, however, goes horribly wrong for Clare in her white life, as the weight of the daily pretence becomes too much to bear. The rupture gets too messy. When her husband finds out she has been passing, the fiction of her white life comes to an abrupt end. Her edifice of self-denial falls to dust, and Clare herself falls to her death—whether pushed by her husband or Irene, or whether jumping voluntarily. For Larsen, who had struggled to live with her white mother, white stepfather and white half-sister, passing asks too much of someone in requiring them to abandon their history. When Clare's enraged husband exposes her deception in front of company, she realises she has run out of room for manoeuvre. With her black best friend and her white husband both feeling betrayed by her passing, she is no longer able to choose between two identities. The book's powerful last line hints that there is no way out, except for a deadly one: "Let's go up and have another look at that window."

How does a passer deal with the memories of the past, or those deliberately erased in order to implant new ones? This is what frustrates Irene, that she has been carrying not only the burden of suffering as a woman and an individual, but also her stigmatised black identity, assigned to her by social construction. The danger of an inferiority complex among the colonised and racialised is still one of the most visceral drawbacks in the process of integration for millions of outsiders in the West, even when they can get by perfectly as members of the privileged class (see Chapter 10). It is the memory of inferior status, converted into an impostor syndrome, that continues to gnaw at the passer, threatening their ability to shake off the past. Eventually, as with Clare Kendry, it will catch up with them.

Larsen's novel established passing's meaning as the choice to transition away from one's assigned identity. But she was documenting a widespread real-life phenomenon among African Americans of the Jim Crow era: here are the real stories of some remarkable people who memorialised the complex, sometimes liberating and sometimes painful essence of performing a racial identity.

La Danse Sauvage

In a New York Jazz club, Larsen's heroine Irene is told by her friend Hugh that he knows "lots of people 'pass' all the time." She replies, "It's easy for a Negro to 'pass' for white. But I don't think it would be so simple for a white person to 'pass' for coloured."[23] They are talking about jazz-lovers among the white community who pretend to be black in order to grab a twist with the best black dancer in the club.

The 1920s were the heyday of jazz, which offered for the first time a powerful, popular alternative to the traditionally white world of classical music. Many whites fascinated by this new music were drawn to explore, develop or invent romantic associations with "Negro blood". As we know, the border between black and white society had long been porous, as far back as the beginning of the nineteenth century. Now, in the age of jazz, whites of a Mediterranean hue occasionally literally reverse-passed, joining the black music scene by artificially darkening their skin. The Russian-Jewish jazz musician Mezz Mezzrow (1899–1972) wanted to be a "Negro musician" and self-identified as "a voluntary Negro".[24]

Other white performing artists didn't go quite so far, but still catered to this emerging white urban craving for jazz and soul in hip Western cities on both sides of the Atlantic. This wasn't mockery, as in minstrel shows, but a serious—if often exaggerated—imitation of perceived "black traits". This kind of identity performance was for the performance's sake, and was not a permanent reconfiguration of the artists' sense of self—today we would call this cultural appropriation. But black musicians performed this way too, playing on and living up to the West's romanticised stereotypes of what black should be and how black people behaved. The jazz and soul revolution offered "Negro musicians" an opportunity not just to make a living, but to thrive and prosper—especially away from Jim Crow America. For African American performing artists, emigration to Europe was the chance of a lifetime.

The extraordinary Josephine Baker sailed to Paris in 1925 and established herself there as a supremely successful performer. Baker spoke frequently over the decades of the dire racism she had faced during the early years of her career in New York City; she had run 3,000 nautical miles to find self-respect in Paris, to enjoy simple human liberties that most people take for granted—going out to eat, using public toilets and, yes, drinking water from a public fountain. Baker's enthusiasm for the relative freedom she enjoyed in France would seem undimmed decades later in this famous line from her speech at Martin Luther King's March on Washington: "I must tell you, ladies and gentlemen, in that country I never feared. It was like a fairyland place."[25]

In her new fairyland, Josephine Baker found the jazz-infused euphoria of the interwar period. Society was changing, and Europe's musical establishment was being challenged. Young trendy Parisians were fixated on African American culture, dancing the Charleston and expressing interest in African art. The urban French were so obsessed with jazz that Baker even started a unique, unforeseen craze: white desire for black skin. Fashion magazines offered tips on how to emulate Baker, including rubbing walnut oil into the skin. And, long before the tanning frenzy took over the white world—long before the ethnic-minority influencer revolt against the white-centric beauty industry—Baker launched her own "dark is beautiful" brand, offering beauty products including the Bakerskin darkening lotion.[26] People went mad for it.

Further feeding the white Parisians' curiosity, Baker immortalised *La Danse Sauvage*, the Wild Dance, wearing nothing but her famous "banana skirt"—a string of plastic bananas around her narrow waist. The name of the dance was deliberately ambiguous, speaking directly to white preconceptions of black "savagery". Instead of trying to fit into traditional Parisian culture and offer a performance passing as white, Baker played to—and with—her audience's fantasies of black sexuality as exotic and uninhibited. Famously, she would roll her eyes on stage and pretend to swoon in ecstasy, to the rapturous delight of the white audience, who believed they were in love with black culture.

According to Morgan Jerkins, writing in a special issue of *Vogue* published for what would have been Baker's 110th birthday in 2016, the *Danse Sauvage* was an extraordinary artist's attempt to change how the world thought about race.

> Aside from … surface-level interests [in black popular culture], there was a much deeper and disturbing fascination with the widely accepted belief in black people's inherent primitiveness. When she swung onstage in that fiercely swinging banana skirt in 1926, Baker brilliantly manipulated the white male imagination. Crossing her eyes, waving her arms, swaying her hips, poking out her backside, she clowned and seduced and subverted stereotypes.[27]

Baker reclaimed dignity for herself and for black people by entering the white imagination. She didn't sell herself or her identity, merely deigning to pass as a black stereotype. Her public persona was a glorified form of the otherwise inglorious act of transgression. This was how she could fit in and live a life in the mainstream, and she did so in the most spectacular of fashions, earning $1,000 a month in the late 1920s. This made her one of the highest-earning entertainers in Europe at the time.

We may say that, in the end, Josephine Baker achieved her life's goal—to be raceless. Baker had no biological children, but adopted a dozen from all over the world, creating an international family that she called her "rainbow tribe" and raising them in a castle she bought. During ticketed tours of the Château des Milandes, visitors could watch the children play. Sure enough, Baker was criticised by some for using them to communicate her views on race politics, but in the thriving, international intellectual circles of Paris at this time, she was lauded for her vision of what humanity must look like, which she spread to the world through her life, work and activism. Picasso painted her, and Hemingway spent many hours in bars speaking to this extraordinary woman.

In 1963, at the age of 57, Baker flew back to America, to appear before perhaps the largest audience in her life. Wearing her uniform from the French Resistance, in which she had been a spy against the Nazi occupation during World War II, Baker addressed the 250,000 gathered at the March on Washington, where Martin Luther King would deliver his famous "I Have a Dream" speech. Baker shared with the huge audience her own dream, and how she felt she had achieved it: overcoming race.

> Ladies and gentlemen, my friends and family, I have just been handed a little note, as you probably say. It is an invitation to visit the President of the United States in his home, the White House.
>
> I am greatly honored. But I must tell you that a colored woman—or, as you say it here in America, a black woman—is not going there. It is a woman. It is Josephine Baker.[28]

As Jerkins put it in her *Vogue* tribute, Baker "radically redefined notions of race and gender through style and performance in a way that continues to echo throughout fashion and music today, from Prada to Beyoncé",[29] who is among those of today's musical legends who have recreated the Danse Sauvage. Rihanna has worn dresses inspired by Baker. And her rainbow family model was the inspiration behind Angelina Jolie's multi-racial brood.

Josephine Baker's failure to fit into her own segregated society propelled her into the international arena. Her war against the separation, categorisation and caricaturing of people on the basis of race, class and gender took a revolutionary turn. By blurring the lines in the early twentieth century, she made history.

Black Like Him

The Jim Crow laws were enforced in the South until 1965, but they began to be dismantled following the famous *Brown v. Board of Education* case, a 1954 ruling that desegregated schools. However, even when social restrictions were removed, black Americans did not suddenly become free people, and many white-passers chose not to shake off their cloak of secrecy and claim their birth identity. The racism was still there, with or without visible segregation. In the 1950s and 1960s, "whites only" signboards were slowly being removed from public areas and bars, but those places didn't become accessible to blacks overnight. In late 1959, one white man decided to try and shake his country awake, in a desperate attempt to expose its dark history and make the nation take responsibility for the everyday brutality African Americans still faced.

One day that autumn, a white American journalist walked into a doctor's surgery and made an unprecedented request. He asked for melanin injections to darken his skin—not as a fashion statement or an adventure, but as a disguise in which he could investigate the odious crimes committed against black people by his fellow white Americans. His mission was to write a scathing report on how American racism dehumanised the descendants of former slaves. But this unlikely experience also turned out to be an incredible feat of self-inflicted trauma. John Howard Griffin knew that passing as "coloured" would be a passport to shame and servitude—that was the point—but he didn't anticipate how deeply it would affect him to put on someone else's selfhood.

At the outset of Griffin's book about his experience, *Black Like Me* (1961), he describes the most terrifying part of the passing act—it is not just the total memory loss, but the fact that, once your roots are lost, you are left with a haunting sense of rejection by both the old society and the new: "I felt the beginning loneliness, the terrible dread of what I had decided to do."[30]

As he travelled for weeks as a black man in New Orleans, Mississippi, Georgia and South Carolina, Griffin quickly found that his reverse-passing was disorienting him. He was struck with an amnesia about his abandoned life similar to that of the white-passing African American. His children and wife, still living in their affluent suburb in the safety of white privilege and economic sufficiency, seemed like a dream. His past suddenly became a blur, as if he had never been a white man. His life, he felt, had surely always been the same as it was now, as he stood in a windowless bedsit in a poor black neighbourhood, looking into the mirror at a wild-eyed, bald black man. This amnesiac attack happened just weeks after his chosen exile into black life. He could not make sense of his present state: "The strangeness of my situation struck me anew—I was a man born old at midnight into a new life. How does such a man act? Where does he go to find food, water, a bed?"[31]

Griffin's writing is full of references to this new self—to being born again, to being a child again. His account is a despondent one of shocking transformation—not just outwardly, as he'd expected, but inwardly too. Griffin had thought that being medically altered to a black man was just a job, but he was fast losing his former self. He described his experience as being imprisoned in the flesh of a total stranger, "an unsympathetic one with whom I felt no kinship. All traces of the John Griffin I had been were wiped from existence." Now, his life was defined by "the fruitless struggles against the mark of blackness."[32]

Those passing in the traditional sense—passing for their own sake, in search of safety or opportunity—may feel joy and exaltation as well as apprehension; but inhabiting a new identity is also baffling and frightening. When Griffin needed somewhere to spend the night, and was unsure about the black neighbourhood of Hattiesburg he had just stumbled into, he called up an old (white) friend. The man came to pick him up, but while they were driving Griffin found himself speaking in a "strangely stilted manner". He realised that it was because he had become so used to the contempt a white person would show a black man. His nervousness kept growing: he felt he was trespassing by riding in the front seat with a white man, and he feared for the safety for his friend's family, lest the KKK see them.

The danger and strangeness of the situation wasn't only apparent to Griffin. When they arrived at the house, his friend's wife addressed him, "Well, hello, Uncle Tom." "Once again," Griffin writes, "the terrible truth struck me. Here in America, in this day, the simple act of whites receiving a Negro had to be a night thing and its aura of uneasiness had to be countered with gallows humor."[33]

Griffin's terror—both his "own" white fear as an impostor and his internalised fear as a black man—was so great that he almost freaked out as he started writing a letter to his wife. On the blank page, in his own handwriting, he saw the words *My Darling*—a term of endearment that no "Negro" could address a white woman with. His wife was in the castle of her skin, where he was only a black swineherd. Griffin was frightened at what he had just written, thinking to himself that a black man like him could not be married to a white woman: "Never look at a white woman—look down or the other way. What do you mean, calling a white woman 'darling' like that, boy?"[34]

The chills running down Griffin's spine at this racial "transgression" were well-founded. The fear of rape of the white woman by the hyper-sexed black man has long been a preoccupation of racist white consciousness, and in the mid-twentieth century even more so—it was all but impossible for many Americans to imagine that a mixed-race couple could in fact be consensual lovers. As Griffin hitchhiked through the South, he found that within minutes his conversation with white drivers would turn to whether or not black men such as himself really did possess humongous phalli, and whether or not Griffin had ever had sex with a white woman. In *Black Like Me*, Griffin suggests that this white fixation is the white man's subliminal admission of guilt—a collective fear of the historically oppressed black man striking back, taking revenge for the centuries of institutional rape of black women by their slave masters.

The journalist in Griffin can analyse the situation, but it's clear that he is nowhere near as distant from the experience of blackness as he might have liked, even writing it up a year later. As a member of the ruling white race, once he had finished his research on racism in America, he could return to privilege again. But he began to fear that this was never going to be possible. He had been taking melanin pills every day, and to transition he would have to come off them; the blackness would only disappear gradually. For a frightening few weeks, though his skin was lightening, Griffin remained black. In this life with unending despair, he cries aloud, "The black man is wholly a Negro, regardless of what he once may have been. I was a newly created Negro who must go out that door and live in a world unfamiliar to me."[35]

Even after passing back into white society in Montgomery, he remained apprehensive. He knew from the friendly treatment he received from whites in restaurants and white areas that his return had been successful, but still he did not leave his hotel room until late at night. Seated next to a white diner, he was surprised that "no one said, 'What're you doing in here, nigger?'"[36] When the racial passer crosses into whiteness, and survives, it seems like a miracle. Griffin's internalisation of blackness after so many weeks on the road was such that he was experiencing this same insecurity. Here, we return to the epic loneliness of the shifter of identity, imprisoned in secrecy, all versions of their self, and no version at the same time. As Nella Larsen's heroine Irene shows, you don't have to pass for life to find yourself adrift and burdened.

At the same time, the real insight into identity experience that emerges from *Black Like Me* is the story of Griffin's mistake and realisation: the well-meaning journalist had seen blackness as a short-term costume he could put on and take off, suggesting that he, like his society, thought of race in visual terms. Griffin had never before had to think about his whiteness (and so his identity), because whiteness was the default against which African Americans' appearances were demarcated. His skin colour didn't constantly threaten to disrupt, limit and define his life, and so it didn't occur to him that changing it might also change this. What Griffin learnt from his stint as a black man was that blackness is not, or not just, a visual, but a state of being—in America, a permanent state of siege. In this way, the moral of his book is one that would become the zeitgeist in our own twenty-first century, as we'll see in later chapters: that you cannot understand race unless you live with it.

John Howard Griffin was successful in his mission. He passed as black and gained the insight he needed, and then he successfully returned to his old white self, his old community, and his old life as a journalist, writing about his experience. His book was well received, and did enlighten white audiences as he'd hoped. At the same time, Griffin was left deeply scarred by his weeks as a black man for the rest of his life—but, like all reverse-passers, he had chosen that trauma, even if he hadn't known it. His dark memories of confusion and fear were not the same as the experience of a white-passer, who faces living the remainder of their life isolated, floating in lost memory and unable ever to be fully themselves.

One Drop of Black Blood

Bliss Broyard is an American author and the daughter of a *New York Times* columnist, Anatole Broyard (1920–90). Just two months before her father's death, Bliss, then in her early 20s, became aware of a curious piece of news that involved her ancestry. Her father's family was officially black, going back to the mid-eighteenth century. And so, under America's One Drop rule, Anatole Broyard was born black—but had spent his life passing as white. After Anatole died, Bliss's mother said that his secret had caused him more pain than the cancer that had killed him.

This discovery of her black heritage would set Bliss on an intriguing trail of family secrets, and a long journey to a sense of her own belonging—but we'll come back to that in Chapter 4. For now let's go back to the moment during World War II when Anatole Broyard realised he could bend the law. Of course, America's armed forces at the time were segregated; there were no black officers. But Broyard, from a mixed-race family that had left the South when he was a child, was taken to be white at his enlistment. By securing on his ID paper that magic letter "W", he was able to train as an officer, and after the war he never looked back.

There was some uncertainty—Bliss would later find in the archives that on her father's social security form, he tried every tick-box in the section on race, scribbling and crossing out various categories before settling for "white". These deliberations and equivocations are typical of the passer's personality, even if their public choice is absolute—and, in Broyard's case, final. There were two pressing reasons why Broyard might have wanted to claim a white identity. The first was his ability to write those winning letters next to "Father" on his daughter's birth certificate: "WHITE".

The other reason was more personal and immediate. Broyard wanted to be a writer, but he did not want to be stigmatised as a "black writer" or "Negro author". He didn't want to write about black longing for the unreachable white beloved, about black suffering or black aspiration. In a dilemma still familiar to authors of colour today, as quotas have become tokens, Broyard knew that he was in a culture where black literature is measured against the underprivilege and desolation from which authors have worked their way up—with a little patronisation from the white system. He wanted more than this, he wanted to be an *author*—colourless, uncategorised.

He succeeded, and would die a prominent essayist and literary critic. But—as always with passing—there was a price. He severed his connection to another important identity, distancing himself permanently from his Puerto Rican first wife and child, and his family in the black part of Brooklyn. His light-skinned parents had been passing in their workplaces too, but they had always come home black. This was partly due to Anatole's sister Shirley, who was born dark-skinned and could not have passed. But Broyard didn't want to stay together anymore. He moved away, and did not see his family. When someone commented on the light kink in his very dark hair, he would refer vaguely to a "distant black ancestor". Writing in *The New Yorker* six years after Broyard's death, Henry Louis Gates Jr added, with subtle irony, that if anything, Broyard had some distant white ancestor.[37] It was this article that made his secret life public knowledge.

It was to New York's Greenwich Village that Broyard had relocated when starting his new white life—a trendy hub full of artists and writers. Even in this liberal neighbourhood, Anatole could not be who he had been brought up to be; but it was somewhere he felt he could call home, because everybody there was self-made, or re-made. Anyone experiencing fractures of continuity could belong in the Village. Broyard explained this powerfully in a 1979 *New York Times* column, though of course he didn't reference his black heritage:

> I ran away to Greenwich Village, where no one had been born of a mother and father, where the people I met had sprung from their own brows, or from the pages of a bad novel ... Orphans of the avant-garde, we outdistanced our history and our humanity.[38]

This language suggests that Broyard was not ashamed of his transition to a new self, that he had found a way to romanticise it as part of an open-minded, intellectual, transcendental way of life. But by passing, Anatole had not only tampered with the narrative of his own life, but also his children's. He was pleased that his son and daughter—whose mother is of Nordic origin—showed no visible sign of their black ancestry. As we saw with Larsen's character Clare, who only dared have one child for fear of chance genes giving away the secret, this is another common anxiety that weighs on race-passers: that blood will out. What an absolute sense of loss Anatole Broyard must have felt as his daughter and son were growing up, without getting to know their father's family or their rich Louisiana Creole ancestry. For as long as their father lived, Bliss and her brother did not visit their grandmother, never saw their darker-skinned aunt Shirley.[39] Like Clare Kendry, the passer jumps into the unknown of a world to come, and then must live with the consequences.

If potentially catastrophic for the individual and the family, white-passing African Americans have long been intriguing too, and it is not surprising that novelists have been obsessed with them. Some have said that Coleman Silk, the "Jewish" professor protagonist of Philip Roth's *The Human Stain*, was partly based on Anatole Broyard, whom Roth knew well. One thing that Roth's novel explores is how quickly passers often adapted to the language of white society, even its racism. Bliss Broyard's memoir recalls an incident, poignant in hindsight, of her father guarding his "white" identity. While waiting for prospective house-buyers to arrive, Broyard saw black children playing outside in the street. He expressed exasperation that white buyers might not go for the property if they saw this.

Some who learn to suppress the reflexes of the past make up for the emotional vacuum this leaves by emulating the cruelty of the world into which they have now catapulted themselves. You could call this—or passing in general—hypocrisy, or over-compensation, but you can also see it as irony, a device writers have often used when tackling a subject as intricate and baffling as race-passing. In *The Human Stain*, Silk finds his secret identity on the verge of being exposed when his college wrongly accuses him of racism against two black students.

* * *

Anatole Broyard invented his own version of transatlantic amnesia, and grafted it with utmost solemnity onto his black past. By redefining himself through the quick wit of Anansi—intellectualising his transformation into part of his artistic identity—Broyard re-emerged as a master storyteller himself, acclaimed by the white mainstream for his way with words. We will return to the English language as a form of identity redemption against historic trauma in Chapter 10—for the descendants of the enslaved, colonised and racialised, it is both a gift and an inheritance, however bitter. What survived the wrongs of slavery's and Jim Crow's assigned binaries has transformed into creativity, with African Americans today producing some of the country's most jaw-dropping art, music and literature.

It is said that Broyard was writing a memoir or autobiographical novel during the last decade of his life, but he never published it—he didn't because he couldn't, because he was still living his life of secrecy. Was his love of jazz that of any twentieth-century intellectual, or was it the one remaining connection he allowed himself to his "coloured" family from New Orleans, his source of consolation amid ties forever severed? We can never fully know what Anatole Broyard's experience of passing was. But there are many other "racially ambiguous" people who have documented the passer's pangs of disconnect. Some have felt exalted by a sense of victory, however pyrrhic—a muted elation at having found success by duping a racist society. Others have felt remorse or shame. Most have found their past catching them by surprise, encroaching on their adopted identity. All who survived that uneasy tussle between origins and rebirth had to take on the mammoth task of maintaining their new biography, perpetually tweaking it, finding or making a history in defiance of their racial destiny. Some things about passing as white are universal.

3

THE CHAMELEON DANCE

HIERARCHIES OF COMPLEXION

We have seen how some African Americans were forced to pass as white in a legal system destabilised by the very thing it was designed to prevent: miscegenation. This chapter will reflect further on racial passing and identity in societies where racial mixing is acknowledged and incorporated into the structures of racist categorisation. As we shall see, the result is to create social hierarchies based not on a rigid racial binary, as under Jim Crow/One Drop, but a racial spectrum, a plethora of complexions—a pigmentocracy. This system—where skin tone gradation and social stratification are interchangeable—is a timeless part of culture in India, while in Brazil it is official and legal. But nowhere have hierarchies of colourism been so deeply ingrained in both law and culture as in apartheid South Africa.

Under the white-supremacist and segregationist regime that ruled South Africa from 1948 to the 1990s, the "right" complexion could be a variety of different shades, but the "wrong" complexion was certainly black. The system was somehow both utterly ruthless and bizarrely arbitrary. Different members of the same family could be allocated different races, while one person in the course of their lifetime could be born black, classified coloured, reclassified white, and then rejected in court by a white judge, who could reinstate their previous status.

As we know, arguments for preservation of racial purity were nullified as far back as the mid-1800s in America: nothing made clearer that it was "too late" than the full-scale racial passing taking place everywhere in the world under white Christian dominion. In a story echoing that of the transatlantic slave trade, at first in South Africa there was a cooperative relationship and conditional harmony between European farmer-settlers and natives, based on mutual dependence and familiarity; and there was considerable mixing of communities. According to the scholar Sarah Yates, for example, "Afrikaans was necessarily created not by those who identify themselves as white Afrikaners today, but dialectically through contact between the Dutch and those they found in South Africa."[1]

As elsewhere, society was divided into European colonials racialised as white, and indigenous inhabitants ethnicised into different tribes. But

> there were many instances of intermarriage between the two groups, as well as between the Xhosa and the Khoesan. White nationalism in South Africa was therefore accompanied by a profound sense of doubt about national and racial identity which necessitated the creation of an Other in opposition to which the Afrikaner nation could define itself.[2]

In other words, just like America's, South Africa's race laws were based on insecurity around the truth, not on truth itself. The reason barriers had to be built between rigid identities was because there was no such thing.

The policy of *apartheid*—Dutch for "apartness"—was introduced by the white Afrikaner rulers, who adopted the old European colonial policy of divide and rule. It was codified by two laws passed in 1950—the Population Registration Act, which classified South Africans by race, and the Group Areas Act, which restricted non-whites to specific segregated areas. But apartheid categorised race not on the basis of history or ancestry, but—in practice—on the basis of complexion.

Apartheid organised, divided and ranked society not only into black and white, but also by inventing an entirely new racial class: "coloured". This category—which the Ugandan academic Mahmood Mamdani has called that of the "subject races"—covered anyone not white, but also not an indigenous inhabitant, as defined by the colonial regime: Indians whose families had been brought as labourers from the subcontinent by the British; descendants of slaves and other mixed populations, with an array of titles—coloureds, mestizo, creoles.[3] By instituting this grey zone between blacks and whites, the two could be kept further apart—and the conditions of the supposedly fundamental difference between black and white could remain only vaguely defined. Constant tweaking and redefinition of race laws and categorisations stopped people from belonging to any one large group, minimising the threat of a mass uprising by the racially persecuted.

In this demented hierarchy, coloureds—the visibly in-between—were given some limited freedoms and privileges denied to the black tribes, but kept well below the white Europeans. Unsurprisingly, they were unable to assimilate into white society, yet distrusted by the black communities of the ghettoised shanty towns. Defined by what they were not, rather than by anything they certainly were, those classified as coloured were in a state of perpetual transition and alienation, caught in a no man's land. "The result was to produce a double contempt: they were held in contempt by those who ruled over them and held in contempt by those over whom [blacks] they held petty authority."[4] More broadly, this gradation of "race" meant that South Africans began judging their own worth in society, in their community and in the world according to their complexion.

The apartheid regime, failing to come up with a consistent, simple narrative as to what separates whites from non-whites, reflected in its legal system these inherent doubts and confusions. The bizarre spectacles this produced in the courts must have resembled a post-apocalyptic world of surrealism, with a depraved humanity at the centre. Any South African who liked their chances could petition a judge to have their race reclassified, offering up their hair texture, the shape of their lips and, of course, their skin tone as evidence. The fact that the magistrates could not definitively judge identity on the strength of a quick physical examination was shown in the nebulous language of their rulings, which regularly used circular phrasing or amended past definitions to describe whiteness or "colouredness".

Depending on the judge's mood on a particular day, an individual's life could either be forever doomed to the black zone, or rewritten as coloured—or, if they were very lucky, white. It was a risk many felt worth taking: the courts could hardly cope with the number of individuals rejecting their racial status and fighting for a new legal identity. In *Long Walk to Freedom*, Nelson Mandela shares his own experiences of such "race trials". He represents before the Classification Board a man "who was colored, but had been mistakenly classified as African,"[5] the social historian Allyson Hobbs recounts. It turned out that one specific trait could exonerate Mandela's client from blackness:

> I had formidable documentary evidence to establish my client's case ... But the magistrate seemed uninterested ... He stared at my client and gruffly asked him to turn round so that his back faced the bench. After scrutinizing my client's shoulders, which sloped down sharply, he nodded to the other officials and upheld [our] appeal. In the view of the white authorities in those days, sloping shoulders were one stereotype of the Coloured physique [and not the black African's]. And so it came about that the course of this man's life was decided purely on a magistrate's opinion about the structure of his shoulders.[6]

A second amendment of the 1950 Population Registration Act, passed in 1962, made racial categorisation even more contingent, and more open to random misrecognition. It left the already confused population even more unsettled. The apartheid laws were such that they more or less encouraged non-white South Africans to pass, even though passing was illegal. This created an environment of chaos as people strove to improve their circumstances, with those too "African-looking" to pass for white at least seeking to be mistakenly categorised as coloured. The hope was that perhaps your children would turn out to be more white than brown, and then they might one day make it into that world of ultimate opportunity. It was a racial stampede in which you pushed your way along the colour spectrum through to the spotlight of whiteness, where the Selection Committee awaited you.

Those who got themselves misrecognised as white by the system were known as "play-whites". The survival of this "floating" group— the long-term success of being able to pass whiteness down to the next generation—depended on continual passing: as with the African American passers of Chapter 2, it was not enough to con-

THE CHAMELEON DANCE

vince people that you yourself were white—for racial security, you also had to hide your non-white origins, including from those same children who have unwittingly inherited a bureaucratic mistake. In Zoë Wicomb's 2006 novel *Playing in the Light*, the protagonist is Marion Campbell, a woman of Afrikaner background, who grew up white in the last decades of apartheid; but—like the real-life Bliss Broyard—she discovers a family secret. She is the child of a "play-white" couple. Marion's coloured father had gone for a traffic officer's job, missing the clause that said the opening was for whites only, and got it. When the interviewer did not question his racial credentials, he suddenly bagged that miraculous lottery win—membership of the ruling race.

Marion is baffled at the meaning of whiteness as stated by the racist system, and wonders if she will ever be able to find words to describe her own, newly complex identity, armed with nothing but the indefinite definitions of the Population Registration Act:

> A 'white person' is a person who (a) in appearance obviously is a white person and who is not generally accepted as a coloured person; or (b) is generally accepted as a white person and is not in appearance obviously not a white person, but does not include any person who for the purposes of classification under this Act, freely and voluntarily admits that he is by descent a native or coloured person unless it is proved that the admission is not based on fact.[7]

The absurdity and impenetrability of this language rivals the "mathematical" formula of Thomas Jefferson's letter explaining the One Drop Rule. In the ironically titled *Concrete Poem*, the South African poet Michael Chapman powerfully portrays the farcical division of the races, using the bullet points of officialdom:

> *The Chameleon Dance*
>
> *The Minister of Home Affairs, Mr Stoffel Botha, disclosed that during 1985:*
>
> * 702 coloured people turned white;
> * 19 whites became coloured;
> * One Indian became white;
> * three Chinese became white;

* 50 Indians became coloured;
* 43 coloureds turned into Indians;

...

* 249 blacks became coloured;
* 20 coloureds became black;
* two blacks became 'other Asians';

...

No blacks became white, and no whites became black.[8]

As we can see, except for the "confirmed" blacks and whites, all other South African racial identities were very fluid. In this sense, stories like Marion's in *Playing in the Light* show that apartheid South Africa—typically thought of as an extremely racially rigid society—in fact pushed the boundaries of whiteness, unleashing an avalanche of identity inventions. As Marion tries to piece together her past, she recalls her father's comment, that "Whiteness is without restrictions. It has the fluidity of milk; its glow is far-reaching."[9] In order to bask in its glow—which meant being listed as white and eligible for better housing and opportunities—her mother plasters her body with heavy makeup, so her deep bronze skin would look white. This image is evocative of the escaped slave handbill advertisements of antebellum America: "Run Away … Mulatto, or Quadroon Girl, about 14 years of age, named Seth, but calls herself Sall, sometimes says she is white and often paints her face to cover that deception."[10]

Thanks to her parents' efforts to "cover the deception" of their colouredness, Marion herself will not have to "play" white—she just *is* white, classified as such from birth. The only risk of racial insecurity after that first generation of passers would have been a biological "throwback"—a child randomly inheriting the complexion or features of more visibly coloured ancestors. The latter would be stripped of their family's whiteness, and thrown among the other groups. This led to great anxiety before the birth of each child, but a markedly different terror from that of African American passers like Clare Kendry, which was a fear of discovery: since the Jim Crow/One Drop system couldn't recognise mixed marriage or heritage, the entire edifice of a family's assumed status would be brought down by a single "throwback" child. In countries like South Africa where individual relatives could officially be classified as being of a different race, the fear was of separation. The new baby's survival with dignity was hitched to the amount of melanin under their skin.

That said, from eighteenth-century Maryland to twentieth-century South Africa, the story of ambiguous appearances challenging a racist authority has varied little. Time and time again, however hard the system tries to pretend there's nothing to talk about on the clear-cut subject of race, the fiction of racial laws and customs is eventually forced into the mainstream and, before long, exposed—and then race politics emerges from the underground. Both sides—the racial supremacists and the racially persecuted—are then caught in a cycle of historic embarrassment or shame and reprisal. The hope is that a middle ground will eventually be found, with both sides making cautious steps—if not to forgive and forget—then toward a dialogue about the past.

In South Africa, the post-apartheid restorative justice process of the Truth and Reconciliation Commission tried to achieve just that. This is how Marion's personal history is unravelled in *Playing in the Light*, after the Commission throws up information about her family's identity. In a neighbourhood and home where blacks and coloureds can only enter as servants, Marion's playwhite parents have brought her up in a carefully guarded environment where she would not have to bear the burden of her country's racialism—until she learns about it and does exactly that. Whenever Marion has asked her parents about their background—there is no extended family around—she has been told what passers usually say, to others and each other: "Ask no questions and you'll hear no lies."[11]

But Marion, faced with a dilemma over her rightful place, does the opposite: she searches for the true meaning of her past, and recognises the importance of historical memory. She has inadvertently been playing an imposter, living in an exclusive neighbourhood for the rich in Cape Town, with "a glorious outlook on the sea, with the classic view of Table Mountain on the left and Robben Island on the right".[12] Now that she feels she has been a passer from birth, it is time to search for her identity. At a crucial juncture in the novel, Marion confronts her father John. He confesses that, as a young man, he stopped seeing his family—or rather, his family stopped seeing him, in order to give him, the "white" one, a chance to make a better life.

But part of this passing over to privilege has been an acceptance or adoption of racism, and its language of mistrust. When Marion suggests earlier in the novel that John get a gardener, this former coloured man, now frail and bedridden, uses the white language of fear of the "other", of obsession with savage black criminality:

> he'll have none of it. They kill you in your own garden, hack your head off with your own blunt spade. Haven't you seen in the papers? ... he says, [referring to the city's rising crime levels,] these kaffirs of the New South Africa kill you just like that, just for the fun of it.[13]

But when John's cover is blown, he has a different moment with his daughter. When transgression is no longer necessary for survival, when the secret will no longer hurt in the new "rainbow nation", he lays bare his vulnerability. Marion's father breaks down in tears, saying that the anxiety and trepidation of a terrible life in the coloured zones made him sever his history and deprived Marion of hers. This self-imposed amnesia had enabled him to pass as white in South Africa's bizarre and depraved system of apartheid: one that enforced, in Marion's words, "an era of unremitting crossings".

Phorsha, Kalo, Tostado, Quase-Negra

In apartheid South Africa the riddle of complexion perforated every layer of the social comfort zones where an individual could have taken shelter. I would also like to reflect on two other places where complexion-based identity has been a national obsession: Brazil and India. The number of official racial categories in Brazil is similar to the apartheid system, but in Brazilian society, the way variations in skin shade are detailed off the record beats all other openly practised cultural racisms in the world—except perhaps that in the Indian sub-continent. Though colour was never formally codified in India, it intrudes into every sphere of life to discriminate against the darker-skinned, particularly women.

When I was growing up, the immediate description for a person would be determined by their skin colour, followed by their height, then their body mass index. We might also have added the clothing they were wearing and, lastly, the beauty or ugliness of their eyes, teeth and so on. If we said a certain girl—it was mostly girls who had to be scrutinised for attractiveness—was beautiful, *sundar* (or *shundor* in Bengali), it definitely meant she had fair skin. And if we wanted to describe someone almost as beautiful as a fair-skinned person, we would say, well, she is dark, but she's really tall, she has doe-like eyes and long black glossy hair. A number of secondary attributes would make up for her complexion.

My parents had names for their own skin tones, and for those of their four children. My father was *phorsha* (light-skinned) and my mother was *shyamla* (medium-brown). Their children were:

1. a *ghono shyam*, a dark brown daughter (that's me),
2. a dark son, almost *kalo*—black,
3. a *khub phorsha*, a very light-skinned daughter, and
4. a *halka shyam borner*, their light-brown youngest daughter.

We, the three girls and one boy, each had a different complexion—*varna* in Sanskrit, or *borno* in Bengali. We routinely heard people around us talking about which of us was the most marriageable; whether my father's *phorsha*—light-skinnedness—could make up for the fact that I, the *ghono shyam*, was dark brown, and win me a light-skinned husband; or whether my complexion could be overlooked because I, like my father, was strikingly tall for a Bengali—not usually a positive attribute in girls, but one that people endearingly associated with my tendency to be top of the class at school. Historically, and still today, education, wealth and family name have often worked as a "whitening" effect on the Indian subcontinent. In addition to social position, other qualities that help to blur the colour lines include fine features and height, particularly in men. The matchmakers managed to find my very tall, light-skinned father for my mother despite her "medium brown" complexion. His impoverished background was balanced by his being self-taught and about to receive his BA, making him the first person in the village with a college degree; but it also made it easier to match him with my dark-skinned mother.

Even today, skin colour is stipulated and detailed in the "Brides and Grooms Wanted" sections of Indian newspapers. Poets as great as Tagore have tried to alleviate the social stigma around darker complexion with words of beauty:

> *Kalo*, black? However black she is,
> I have seen her black doe eyes.[14]

Most of us know the word "avatar" or incarnation—the Indian gods use their avatars to pass themselves off in whichever form they fancy. Some of the more popular incarnations—particularly among lower-caste Hindus—include the blue gods Krishna and Shiva, and the black goddess Kali. Indian gods, ironically, are less discriminatory than their human worshippers when it comes to the complexion or class of their love interests. The blue god Krishna transmogrifies into a brown cowherd's son to woo an older woman, the milkmaid Radha who would become his eternal consort—this is a culture where marrying off young girls to older men had been and still is the norm. The gods often pass as humans to taste the mortal things, and they frequently class-pass for love. A god impersonating a herdsman to go for a milkmaid is a big deal in a tradition where women are treated as second-grade, even worthless; it makes Krishna a much endearing, "human" deity.

Numerous poems, songs and rhymes—mostly folkloric—eulogise Kali's *kalo* blackness. She is neither "medium brown", "deep brown", nor any other euphemised dark skin; she is pure black, as black as can be, a powerful incarnation of the goddess Durga—who is otherwise light-skinned, like all the Aryan gods of the Hindu pantheon. But Kali, in her ferocious battle to rid the world of dark forces, is not seen as a white goddess temporarily passing as black in order to win her war on the demons. Her blackness has been made permanent by her devotees. She is the victim of colourism and racism incarnate, her ethereal white power metamorphosed to earthy black humanity. In colonial times, one infamous cult of Kali equated the dark forces she fights with white British officers. The Thuggees grouped together in disused temples and jungle hideouts to strike against imperial power, and to worship the black and the powerful. But beyond Kali worship, back in daily life, colourism still rules attitudes on the Indian subcontinent.

* * *

Another country that would probably exceed India's colour hierarchies is Brazil, where attempts to codify the idea of "mixed-race" have reached absurd levels. On paper, self-identification is considered a valid basis for collecting ethnic or "racial" data, and must legally be respected when it comes to Indigenous Brazilians; in practice, however, "states often violate the right to self-identification by imposing particular census questions and ethnoracial categories and forcing people to identify with—or reject—them."[15] The Demographic Census of the Brazilian Institute of Geography and Statistics does just this, offering a set of tick-boxes like censuses all over the world. Officially, then, Brazil's colourism has five main categories: white, brown, black, yellow and Indigenous—these are the terms used, along with a skin colour continuum that ranges from 1 (light) to 10 (dark).

A 1976 survey by the Institute showed that Brazilians do not recognise these limited and over-generalising criteria as an accurate description of their identity. However, those polled didn't exactly reject the idea of an identity based on complexion. Asked to describe their skin colour, they came up with 136 variations.[16] Responses from the relatively fair included: *alva* (snowy white), *alva-rosado* (pinkish white), *trigo* (wheat), *melada* (honey-coloured), *canela* (cinnamon), *ruiva* (redhead), *trigueira* (brunette), *sarará* ("yellow-haired negro"), *tostada* (toasted) and *puxa-para-branca* (somewhat toward white). For the darker-toned, the labels offered included plain old *preta* (black), but also *turva* (murky), *sapecada* (singed), *pouco-clara* (not very light), *pouco-morena* (not very dark), *quase-negra* ("almost Negro") and so on.

As this list shows, Brazilians—like many Latin Americans—generally prefer to describe themselves in terms of colour rather than race. It is no coincidence that the term "pigmentocracy" was coined by the Chilean anthropologist Alejandro Lipschutz. Brazil has the largest black population of any country outside Africa, having enslaved eleven times as many Africans as colonial North America. Today about half the country is mixed-race, which has elevated its unique status in the world as a *democracia racial*. For a century, sociologists and visitors have been intrigued by Brazil's racially fluid society, where intermarriage has always been allowed. Many black or mixed-race people, particularly the moneyed classes, marry into white families. But an all-pervading colourism and its divisive effects on the so-called racial democracy meant that complexion is still, ultimately, synonymous with race—and it still determines a Brazilian's life chances.

For this reason, attempts to cross over into the status of whiteness are just as common as they were in apartheid South Africa. For the period 1950–90, when there was a particularly high level of inter-racial marriage, sociologists have also recorded an increasing number of black Brazilians reassigned as brown.[17] The natural expectation of this pattern is of course a new generation of white, or at least "honey-coloured", children. The forward who captained Brazil's Olympic Gold-winning football team in 2016, Neymar da Silva Santos Júnior, has a white mother and a black father. In a 2010 interview, he shocked a world used to the binaries of American race with his reply to an interviewer who had asked him whether or not he faced racism. "Never," he said. "It's not like I'm black, you know?"[18]

Throughout the twentieth century, football mania has dominated much of Brazil's popular culture, and it was sport that first brought Brazil's colour spectrum to international attention. During those 2016 Rio Olympics, people across the planet saw a kaleidoscope on their television screens. As had been the case in South Africa during the 2010 World Cup, the first to be hosted by an African nation, there was a sense that Brazil's many shades were a hopeful message for building a world of one common humanity. A colour-blind, post-race world. In 2012 the evolutionary biologist Stephen Stearns celebrated the fact that, over time, humanity will become more and more diverse—in a few centuries, he said, we'll all look like Brazilians.[19]

In the slums of Rio de Janeiro, Manila and Bombay, in the leafy avenues of New York's Greenwich Village, in the dusty suburbs of Cairo, along the muddy banks of the Ganges, children played football in the yellow shirt of iconic player Edson Arantes do Nascimento, known worldwide as Pelé. In reality, though, Pelé—who, like Neymar, avoided discussing racism in public—had another nickname at home: *gasolina*, Portuguese for "crude oil". When spectators from more ethnically homogeneous countries see Brazil playing, it's important to resist any urge to romanticise the country as some living illustration of racial harmony. What they're seeing is simply a country where colourism has taken different forms; a country with distinct racial quagmires of its own.[20]

Following Brazil's abolition of slavery in 1888—making it the last country in the Western hemisphere to outlaw the practice—some millions of white Europeans were brought into the country with the promise of free land and other perks. The idea was to balance out the descendants of the 4 million slaves who had been trafficked in, to completely dilute Brazil's then black majority. Mixed marriages were encouraged. The history of the Brazilian kaleidoscope is therefore intimately tied to a hierarchy of desirable and undesirable complexions—just like in Jim Crow America. Countries like Brazil, South Africa and India may have inherited racism from the European colonisers who invented it, but they have implemented its legacy just as viciously.

The stamping out of the black majority worked: today, Brazil's social engineering is going in the opposite direction, to try and compensate. Discrimination based on hierarchies of complexion is rife, and has provoked Brazilian universities and government institutions to implement affirmative action policies, quota-based recruitment for black and brown candidates. But the problem is that race is still assigned to you by the state, in an explicitly colour-based system; this means that just looking white is good enough for Brazilians to be considered as such. Those who come forward to benefit from positive discrimination are often accused of "passing"—that is, reverse-passing. Based on their appearance, they are judged to be taking illegitimate advantage of these opportunities. There have been cases where those looking "too white" have been taken off the list of those eligible for quota-based places.

In 2015, Maíra Mutti Araújo, a law graduate, applied for a local prosecutor's job in her hometown, the north-eastern coastal city of Salvador known for its large African-heritage population. At this time, affirmative action was relatively new in Brazil. Despite feeling apprehensive about being seen as a "diversity hire", Araújo specified her race on the application form: *pardo*—brown, or mixed-race. Not in Araújo's wildest dreams could she have imagined that she would end up disqualified as a candidate, be vilified by black activists in her community, and possibly face criminal charges for fraud.

PASSING

All quota candidates had to submit verification of their race: a photo of themselves and a short form to fill out (some of the questions on these forms have been highly controversial). The selection panel assessing Araújo's case refused to recognise her, along with eight others, as black or brown; she assumed this was based on her photo: although she was clearly brown-skinned, it showed that she had straightened hair and "mixed features". In language straight out of the apartheid courts, she was told that she could not be a candidate for the *pardo* quota, as she did not have the required "Afro-descendant phenotype". Only after an appeal was the decision overturned, as reported in *Foreign Policy*: "'After careful consideration of the photograph at hand,' wrote one panellist [on the review board], 'I am of the opinion that the candidate is *negro* (*preto* or *pardo*).'"[21]

Brazil's ruling elite is still white. Those running affirmative action can't understand why those who could pass for white—who are white, as far as the officials looking at them are concerned—could possibly want to claim a non-white identity, unless it was to latch onto the "privilege" of quotas. Many among those of black ancestry are fighting not to let the world forget Brazil's state-sponsored and state-funded history of brutal racism, that today's diverse society was not the natural endpoint of humanity, but the result of deliberate policies to whiten Brazil's blackness. The irony of all ironies is that many of those coming forward to claim their black origins are now accused of freeloading. Otherwise, the establishment reasons, who in their right mind would want to call themselves brown or black, when they could identify as olive, toasted, or somewhat toward white?

You Can Always Tell

Talking about the colour spectrum in various cultures reminds me of makeup store displays. Browsing a cosmetics store in central London, I was amused to see rows and rows of labels on face powders, foundation and other products of different hues, using the exact same uncomfortable distinctions—light, deep, medium deep, dark, medium dark and so on. British readers might think that their society is less obsessed with labelling people by their colour than these foreign countries, but here we are.

THE CHAMELEON DANCE

Britain abolished slavery thirty years before America, in 1833, and the population of these small islands was largely protected from its horrors by the Atlantic: pre-abolition, the Empire ran slaves in satellite plantations of the Americas, and even after 1833 Britain continued to benefit indirectly from the profits of slavery that was raging across America, at a distance. After World War II, however, Britain came face to face with its own imperialism—and that face was black and brown. Today, these migrants into Britain—many of them from the West Indies—are commonly known as the Windrush generation.

The late 1940s and the 1950s saw significant transfers of non-white labour from former and present British colonies to the home isles, brought on ships like the *Empire Windrush* (1948) to fill the acute post-war shortage of labour and help lift the country back on its feet. As a result, mid-century race politics in Britain was almost as fraught as in Jim Crow America—but less openly. Even if racial stratification wasn't as insidious as in the United States, the new levels of diversity in Britain—as in South Africa, India and Brazil—produced a colour spectrum, and a hierarchy based on it. British society was not officially organised along racist lines, but the lines were very much there—and so was passing.

It is true that Britain has had a non-white population for centuries; and, particularly in the ages of oceanic diplomacy and Empire, dignitaries of colour were frequent visitors. North African ambassadors and Indian Rajas regularly came to Britain and were revered, immortalised by court painters. But the mid-twentieth century was different. No longer exoticised Orientals making an appearance in the great halls of state, these were ordinary men and women who had come to participate in society; they were next-door neighbours on a council estate. And instead of the international trade networks, bejewelled turbans and diamante robes of the Lord Mayor's seventeenth-century guests, these newcomers brought simple clothes, salt fish and curry powder.

No sooner had they arrived than they found themselves caught up in the liminality, insecurity, isolation and shame of the racialised. Their natural expectations of welcome were very quickly dashed, with hateful stares from the white working class, harassment by the police, and discrimination on the part of individuals and institutions alike, including governmental authorities. This baffling betrayal made a mockery of the place known in British and former British colonies as Mother England. These emergency labourers from warmer shores huddled in the frozen, rainy, grey heart of London, driving buses and cleaning toilets. In ill-fitting suits, skirts and plain saris, they flitted across the Midlands and the North, seeking lowly employment and crowded accommodation in dingy backstreet rentals.

The numbers of those passing for white grew as the Windrush generation became more settled in Britain's urban centres. The process bore the same hallmarks of racial passing as in the United States: self-invention, rebirth and opportunity, but also loneliness, alienation, uncertainty and terror. This was reflected in 1950s popular culture. The 1959 film *Sapphire* was made shortly after the 1958 Notting Hill riots, and exposed in graphic detail the prevailing British prejudice against black people, especially white-passers among them.

Set in a grim, cold, drab London, the film follows a Metropolitan Police investigation into the violent murder of a young biracial dancer from the West Indies, who, the officers discover, had been passing as white. In the opening shot, we are already shown the consequence of this transgression: Sapphire's lifeless body on a misty Hampstead Heath. As *Time Out* puts it, "the film's 'impartiality' leads it perilously close to condoning what it sets out to condemn."[22] Its white director and white writer appear to succumb to prejudice in telling the story of Sapphire's passing, for instance by hinting at the victim's dubious morals with the discovery of sexy petticoats in her room—these are received by the investigators as evidence of "the black under the white". According to Ann Ogidi, writing for the British Film Institute, "The film is littered with casual, unchallenged racism."[23]

As the narrative unfolds, we learn more about Sapphire's life. She was being pulled in both directions, her roots and identity against her future prospects in London's white-dominated cultural scene and her love for a self-made working-class Englishman. She wanted to be seen as a white college student like her boyfriend, to go to white bars—Britain didn't need Jim Crow segregation for society to divide itself—and to live in an ordinary rental house with hot water and a kitchen. One of Sapphire's landladies tells the Metropolitan Police chief investigating her death: "She wanted so much to be counted in, to belong!"

Another landlady says to the police, "So you knew she was coloured then? You can always tell, eager to please, laugh too much, noise with the gramophone, but I don't mind as long as they don't look it." This prejudice was far from unusual, as Sapphire learnt from the reaction of her boyfriend's family after they found out she was black. But, as ever, passing is no easy way out. With the blessing of her brother—her only relative in England and optically black—Sapphire had embarked on a separate double life, but she sometimes experienced self-loathing, and her act was constantly on the verge of being exposed. She couldn't help laughing louder than white English culture would allow; she loved music too much. The fear of being apprehended left her in a constant state of jitteriness.

We don't discover Sapphire's story from her own point of view, but this sense of threat and uncertainty that the police discover in her life story echoes Nella Larsen's *Passing*. In tone, atmosphere and language, *Sapphire* is no celebration of the Windrush experience, as commemorations of the NHS and the broader phenomenon often are today. The film shows us dingy neighbourhoods where black workers dwell, the despair that leads some to drunkenness, the racism that motivates Sapphire's murder, and the indifference of the police once they find out that the dead girl is not "really" white. As if America's "One Drop" rule was the law in 1950s Britain, this biracial individual is automatically assigned the lower-status race, with less social power. Even in death, Sapphire bears the stigma of her black blood, the human stain.

Her lonely, brutal death on the frozen hill of a quintessentially English park has a tragic irony to it: even when she is no longer able to perform whiteness, already having died, Sapphire succeeds in convincing the authorities that she is white, on the strength of her appearance alone. She is finally given that status when her identity is assumed to be white English—until her clearly black brother comes to the police station. In *Sapphire*, we see a fractured consciousness mimicking a fractured body and a fractured life. The Caribbean woman's passing has ultimately been a sacrifice of all three.

PASSING

Any changer of identity—and any migrant—has to balance their severed emotional connections to their roots, key to their survival in the new persona, with their need to connect with a new self, without which they will fragment. This dissociation is shown again and again in literary and cinematic depictions of British race-passing in the early to mid-twentieth century, and the end result always seems to be the same: passing is a doomed strategy, a desperate mode of escape which ultimately fails to provide salvation to the passer. In a society of stringently policed racial divides, whether officially binary as in Jim Crow America, officially plural as in Brazil and South Africa, or unofficially so as in Britain and its former colony India, racial passing is undertaken as a leap to freedom—but often only amounts to transgression from one prison to another.

4

MISTAKEN IDENTITY

LIVING IN RACIAL NO MAN'S LAND

I often think the term mixed-race is problematic. It sounds like the product of a haphazard biological experiment, a creature whose wholeness as a person is hit or miss. I will always remember the words of a visionary rabbi on a day very close to my heart, my daughter's bat mitzva at a North London synagogue. In her sermon, Rabbi Shulamit Ambalu said that she was celebrating the rite of passage of a special person; that my daughter embodied both of her two heritages; that she was a complete being with a unique identity—not mixed, not half this and half that. For those of multiple heritages more than anyone, identity is not simply something one is given at birth. Sense of self for the "mixed-race" has to be made, discovered, negotiated through one's life—and sometimes defended.

Britain may no longer be as hostile a place for people like the tragic Sapphire as it once was, but authorities still think about things in terms of race. We're assured that information on the matter is requested only for monitoring purposes, to try and ensure a fair distribution of opportunity. When you apply for schools, universities or jobs, you're likely to come across a series of tick-boxes—a limited set of options for describing yourself, based on where your parents come from and (implicitly) what colour your skin is. Although my own racial identity is clear-cut, I always leave that box empty. It does not feel right, participating in a system that can't recognise children like mine. If they choose to go for one identity, regardless of how they look, they will not be telling the whole truth. Unless they want to inhabit that partial lie, there is no box for them to tick except "Other"; and then they are expected to offer—in one line—an explanation. For why and how they don't fit into the racial categorisation on offer from the authorities; for why they exist.

Being of dual or multiple heritage is never simple enough to define or express in a single line. In this chapter we will look at the dilemmas of identity facing mixed-race individuals, even when they do not choose to pass; they still have much in common with passers of all kinds, caught between others' perceptions and their own experience, between one sense of self and another. This is how Marion put it in Zoë Wicomb's apartheid novel *Playing in the Light*:

> My parents were the play-whites; *they* crossed over ... but if those places are no longer the same, have lost their meaning, there can be no question of returning to a place where my parents once were. Perhaps I can now keep crossing to and fro, to different places, perhaps that is what the new is all about—an era of unremitting crossings.[1]

According to Wicomb, of mixed heritage herself, a biracial person's acceptance of non-white identity is an act of "denial of shame".[2] But when there has been passing, it is more complicated than ever to embrace or even discover that identity. At first Marion tries to find her "colouredness", but the family connections—a lost aunt called Elsie, uncles, cousins—have been severed. Ultimately she decides on a compromise: to keep moving forward, to keep crossing to new places and personas. She will draw on what she has gained from the discovery of her family's past, rather than mourn what she has lost. But Marion has realised the sad reality of many mixed-race people in a world obsessed with racial labels: a perpetual search for the "true" self.

In Chapter 2 we met Anatole Broyard, an African American writer who passed as white all his life, and his daughter Bliss, who discovered the truth after his death and set about writing a personal narrative of her "coming out" in order to find answers: "Overnight my father's secret turned my normal young adult existential musing of *Who am I?* into a concrete question, *What am I?*"[3] This project would come to challenge Bliss's own sense of identity, and the very question of what identity means in a "mixed" world.

MISTAKEN IDENTITY

Her 2007 memoir, *One Drop*, charts her determination to declare and understand her "African" or mixed-race ancestry. Broyard writes that, once she learnt of her father's origins, she found herself wanting to tick "black" on her graduate application form. Technically speaking, under America's official definitions of blackness at the time of her birth in 1966, Broyard's father was black, and therefore so was she. Had Anatole not been passing, her birth certificate would have given his race as "Negro", the word used for those who were black up to the known "octoroon" level, and sometimes beyond.

But her case, like that of all the passers we have met so far, shows us that official definitions of race—based on false science—have nothing to do with practical definitions. There are social complications to identifying as black while "looking white"—as we know from my own reaction to my housemate Jenny's "chosen" black identity. Broyard confesses in her memoir that, the few times she experimented with describing herself as black, it did not go well. Her high school sweetheart's response, when he heard she was "black", was: "How can you be black? That doesn't make any sense."[4]

Broyard was feeling a sense of imposter syndrome: she felt that, for as long as her father's race was listed "white" on her birth certificate—the physical symbol of how she had been stamped as white from the moment she entered the world—she couldn't convince herself that she was not lying or deceiving anyone by calling herself black. She decided to go for "biracial". But that is rarely the end of a search for identity. Broyard may have felt uncomfortable identifying as black while she looked white, but she felt equally uncomfortable denying her heritage by omission, being forced by society's limited understanding to continue "passing". Broyard's description of her dilemma will sing powerfully with anyone of more than one background:

> when it came to identifying themselves, the de facto method of racial identification required that you choose only one label. And if you chose white over black, then—no matter what you looked like or how you were raised—you were passing or ashamed of the stigma of being black or denying your true self.[5]

In the end, though, caught in a quandary, Broyard felt it was the lesser betrayal to decline a black identity. She reflected after learning of her heritage that she knew people who were part-Caucasian, but did not generally identify as anything other than black. So why was it not the same for her in reverse? Why did she feel such hesitation calling herself black?

Like Wicomb's Marion, Bliss Broyard grew up sealed off from her black ancestry, with her white-passing father and Norwegian mother. She was so much a part of white society, so completely inhabiting a white mentality, that she even exoticised black people—as she confesses in her book, describing a night club encounter with a black dancer who kisses her. She mentally crossed "kissed a black man" off her list of romantic experiences to collect. Further on in the narrative, once Broyard is fully immersed in unearthing her family's black history, she writes that she still cannot say aloud that she is technically black. She feels it would make her the appropriator of an identity she did not grow up with.

Broyard knows that being black is not only about skin tone; in actual fact, it may not be about skin colour at all. Bliss and her brother both took ancestry DNA tests, and the results were yet another shock for the family. It turned out that while Bliss was just 17 per cent African genetically, her blond, Nordic-looking brother Todd had much more African DNA, closer to that of their aunt Shirley—the sister Anatole had left behind with their parents when he started his new life, because she was too dark to pass.

This just shows, once again, how fictional race is. So what does make you black? Many black British and African American people today will tell you that black is also a cultural identity, and a social or political experience. I may be darker than many people with some African heritage, but I cannot and would not ever call myself black. Race is only skin-deep, but it is still skin-deep: we will always have a racial identity put on us by others, based on our appearance, primarily our colour. And that label is central to our life experience. If anybody knows that, it's the man we're about to meet next.

32% West African

The London theatre director Anthony Ekundayo Lennon has a complex and interesting story to tell. His parents and grandparents are white Irish, but he and his brothers, especially Anthony and his brother Vincent, were born with "African" facial features, dark skin and curly hair. When they were growing up on their West London estate, people always thought they were mixed-race. Lennon often uses as his Twitter profile photo a childhood snap of the three of them, and you can see it. Anthony even wore a natural Afro as a boy and young man. Now he is shaven-headed, but that has made his striking features more prominent. If you accept that race is an appearance, then looking at Lennon you would think you are seeing a biracial man of European and African descent.

As far back as the Lennons can stretch on their family tree, all known ancestors are white. So how did this happen? Did the mother have an affair? It would have to have been a longstanding one, since all three of her boys were born looking this way. These were the questions and speculations Anthony Lennon grew up with, from immediate family, friends and mere acquaintances. His parents only separated when he was 12, his father didn't suspect infidelity, and the family has always maintained that there was no affair—but that didn't make their lives any easier. In the open racism of 1960s Britain, Anthony endured vicious taunting and racial slurs, including from neighbourhood children, who called him "dirty nigger". What more proof do we need that race is a social construct? But does it necessarily follow that someone of this history can call themselves black?

Lennon participated in a 1990 BBC documentary called *Chilling Out*, which followed black British actors to shed light on their experience. It is fascinating viewing. He confesses to his mates on camera that his family are white, but when they ask him what he sees when he looks in the mirror, he confides in them that he feels black: "When I'm alone in my bedroom looking in the mirror, thinking about the stuff I've written down, thinking about my past, relationship-wise, pictures on the wall, I think I'm a black man. I've not said that to anyone. And I won't say it outside."

This brings to mind James Weldon Johnson's fictionalised memoir, *Autobiography of an Ex-Colored Man*. The novel's protagonist, like Anthony Lennon, finds his sense of self put under a difficult test, and both men experience a moment of internal specification and simplification of their race; but the Johnson story is the reverse of Lennon's. This is a mixed-race man raised black in a black family, experimenting with and committing to his "white side", as the novel's title suggests. Johnson describes a childhood episode where he is singled out in class as coloured. He rushes home and stands before the mirror. He searches for signs of colouredness in his reflection, but gazing back at him is a white boy:

> I noticed the ivory whiteness of my skin, the beauty of my mouth, the size and liquid darkness of my eyes, and how the long, black lashes that fringed and shaded them produced an effect that was strangely fascinating even to me. I noticed the softness and glossiness of my dark hair that fell in waves over my temples, making my forehead appear whiter than it really was.[6]

Johnson (or his fictional alter ego) is in love with what he sees, but for him it is reassurance—that he can pass if he needs to. What the young Anthony Lennon concluded was that he couldn't. From the expression on his face during his hesitant retelling of his own "mirror moment" in the BBC film, it seems clear to me that Lennon had come out of his bedroom that day fully determined that he had no option but to live a black life. Not to pass as black, because those who pass have a choice—to accept that he *was* black. A hard recognition, terrifying even. But one that others have told him—as the mixed-heritage Brazilian law grad Maíra Mutti Araújo was told—is only "stealing" an identity for personal gain.

When I first came across Lennon, in a *Sunday Times* exposé accusing him of misappropriating black identity and opportunities, I admit that I was confused for a moment. But as I delved more into Lennon's life, I realised that he had been living a non-white life long before he joined Talawa, a Black British theatre company. Not only had he stated his parentage publicly in the BBC documentary early in his career, but his "black" life had been germinating since childhood: he was given an Afro comb by a black neighbour because his mother could not manage his curls, and when he first started expressing interest in acting, his friends teasingly called him Sidders, after the black actor Sidney Poitier. James Weldon Johnson writes in his novel about his character's preparations for joining the life ahead, life as a coloured man. He started teaching music to a class for coloured people, and secured membership of a black church. "This was really my entrance into the race. It was my initiation into what

I have termed the freemasonry of the race. I had formulated a theory of what it was to be colored, now I was getting the practice."[7] Lennon's account of his own entry point into his chosen race, of claiming ownership of the culture that came with it, is strikingly similar: "When rap and hip-hop hit the UK I got really intoxicated by it, and began to develop a sense of ownership of who I was through music and other aspects of black cultural expression."[8]

Lennon came to widespread public attention in 2018, after he received a share of a £406,500 Arts Council grant for four recipients of non-white backgrounds. A journalist "outed" him for passing as black, and the case was taken up by several national newspapers, calling him a conman and accusing him of hiding his white parentage. Apart from a few close friends and his fellow members of Talawa, the black theatre company where he still works, Lennon came under fire from reputable black British actors, directors and other leading figures, who took up the attack on a man seen to have hijacked an award meant for a person of colour, to have been "self-identifying as something else".[9]

But Lennon had always felt like "something else" in Britain's pigmentocracy—and even if he hadn't looked in that mirror and been convinced he was mixed-race, he had been *made* to feel that way. He just had to go out of his house, walk down the road and everyone would see a mixed-race person. As in Brazil, his right to self-identification had been erased in favour of an imposed skin-tone category. Like Anatole Broyard, a fellow artist, Lennon's identity was determined by society but modified by its bearers, because of the only objective reality—how one looked. But Broyard used his colour to bypass his "Negroness" and become a mainstream author; in Lennon's case, opting for white would have been difficult. He is some shades darker than Broyard, and has also been judged by his other "black" physical features.

Thanks to the process of casting, the world of performing arts is often a racially segregated one, as we'll see in Chapter 14: actors of colour audition for specific complexion-based, often stereotypical roles, mostly catering to a white audience; or they don't get an audition at all. There are barely any mixed-race parts. Some of Lennon's critics said that he was a failed actor (to explain why he had "fraudulently" gone after this funding), but it was in fact the racist attitudes of the industry that had failed him. Lennon's best chance of breaking into the mainstream was to go for black roles, in the black theatre scene. With the company Talawa, he has toured the country teaching young black people acting and leadership skills.

Lennon's loyal supporters included some influential black British actors such as Michaela Coel, and the artistic director of Talawa, Michael Buffong, who has stood by him and his "complicated ancestry". I did, however, find myself wondering: would Lennon have gone for black identity if he had still believed himself to be mixed-race, but had physically resembled his parents' white Irishness? If he had been able to get the roles that were there for white actors, would he still have joined the theatre world as a black artist?

It's clear that opportunity—the classic motive of the passer—was not the only or even the most important thing driving Lennon to embrace a black identity. He told *The Guardian* that, more than anything else, it was the prejudice he had experienced as a child and young adult that made him identify as black. The reporter Simon Hattenstone describes Lennon as saying that his grandmother and his father, who was a Sunday School teacher, "may have thought his appearance was something to be ashamed of, but he didn't. If their attitudes were representative of being white, he was happy to renounce his whiteness."[10]

Lennon's mother has accepted her "black" son, but his father, who died in 1999, did not. He apparently told Anthony on his deathbed that he was white, that he was just having an identity crisis and looking for a way to be different. The identity crisis part is probably not entirely untrue, given that Lennon went through five different name changes—a combination of Yoruba, English and South African variations—before settling on Anthony Ekundayo Lennon. The middle name is Yoruba. Though he says that he was driven to identify as black because society treated him as black based on his appearance, he also became sure of his African ancestry, and it was important to him to prove it. Like Bliss Broyard, he took a DNA test. His genetic make-up came back as follows:

46% Irish and Scottish.
22% English, Welsh and north-west European.
32% West African.

Lennon says he had always known. He had chosen his West African middle name long before this ancestry testing—which is not set in stone, but which, even returning 32 per cent approximate African genetic information, vindicates his gut feeling and his right to call himself black. His "identity crisis" may have been provoked initially by other people's superficial identification of his race, but ultimately he felt compelled to prove his blackness by relying on science; today we might turn to DNA tests rather than the eugenics and phrenology of race science, but strangers' judgement of Lennon's blackness based on his physical characteristics seem to have landed him back in the same place anyway, defending himself with reference not to his experience of racism, but to his African ancestry.[11] His story shows us how our need for labels can be more powerful than our understanding of them, reminding me of those problematic tick-boxes.

Lennon's DNA discovery also reminds me of the historian David Olusoga's work on the "hidden" descendants of the black Georgians. Prominent among them were the famous grocer, composer and Lettrist Ignatius Sancho, who lived in Westminster; the coal merchant and property-owner Cesar Picton, in Kingston upon Thames; and, of course, the former slave and writer-campaigner Olaudah Equiano. These "extravagant strangers", as Shakespeare described Othello, lived, had families and died in eighteenth- and early-nineteenth-century Britain. They were clearly visually black or mixed-race, a population that numbered in the thousands, but later "disappeared" from view, as their "black" features were diluted through generations of intermarriage. Their descendants today bear no trace of that "one drop".

Olusoga interviewed one of these descendants, Cedric Barber—optically white, but with a freed slave ancestor on his father's side. In almost folkloric language, he outlined for Olusoga the lineage from his forebear Francis Barber, who became servant, secretary, "adopted son", friend and heir to Dr Samuel Johnson, of the famous *English Dictionary* (1755): "Francis had a son called Isaac; Isaac had a son called Enoch; Enoch had a son called Edward; Edward had a son called Norman; and Norman has a son called Cedric; and that's me."[12]

Barber talked about his feeling of going around "in disguise, in camouflage", a curious kind of "passing": he is walking about the place and "many people don't know" that he has black ancestry. In the mid-eighteenth century it was estimated there were 10–15,000 black people living in Britain. If they all had average numbers of children, it is thought that there could be up to 3 million white people with a black ancestor from that time, all camouflaged like Cedric.[13]

Except, every now and then, there is the odd "throwback"—and we suddenly find three boys in the same white family looking as "African" as they do "European", challenging everything we think we know about race.

The President and the Princess: Unwilling Icons of the In-Between

For Anthony Ekundayo Lennon, the race question has finally quietened down after a stormy childhood and a stormier youth, when he grappled with the stigmatisation of being a presumed bastard, racist street abuse and threats of violence. He was not what the racist attackers said he was, but his identity reflects both the skin he felt comfortable in, and what others have hoisted on him since childhood. One thing is certain, he never "passed" as black. It was society that passed a black identity to him; he just became fed up of protesting and embraced it. In a twisted world where social labels are based on your looks, those whose appearances tell a complicated story have to manoeuvre their way through life, find a way to adapt to being "something else" and belong—especially if that person is a public figure.

The artistic director of Talawa, Michael Buffong, issued a statement expressing the company's unending support for Lennon's mixed-race identity. Buffong said that this case, having drawn much attention to contemporary identity politics, is ultimately a positive thing. Lennon's story shows that, in debates on identity, "there are nuances and grey areas."[14] Amid the media finger-pointing and accusations of "passing as black", it is important to see that moving between racial identities is not about abandoning a "true" self in favour of another one that is "false". In the words of Professor Samira Kawash, author of *Dislocating the Color Line*, it "is about the *failure* of blackness or whiteness to provide the grounds for a stable, coherent identity. Blackness and whiteness as they emerge in the passing narrative belie the possibility of identity or authenticity that would allow one to be unequivocally black or white."[15]

Take, for example, Barack Obama. Two years after Zoë Wicomb published her tale of a mixed-race heroine struggling with her identity in post-apartheid South Africa, history was made following Obama's election as America's first non-white, and first black, president. If we applied Rabbi Shulamit's description of my daughter to Obama—one whole, equally belonging to both heritages—then he was a white president as much he was a black president. Certainly his "white side" helped him to get elected, defusing his "otherness" for white voters and making him a more acceptable, less threatening "first black" president. This was not only about his light skin and white family, but also about his socio-cultural roots. Only really forming connections with his Kenyan father's family in adulthood, he was brought up by a white mother and white grandparents, and a brown Indonesian stepfather. Bliss Broyard didn't feel she could identify as black because her background and upbringing were white; yet the same principle clearly doesn't apply to Obama.

The difference is society's view, and once again it's a view based on colour: Broyard can pass as white, but Obama can only be black, because he is not light-skinned enough to be considered otherwise. This is still the same American race binary that goes back to the Jim Crow era. The world has identified Obama as "black", and so that is the way he has lived in this world, with the disadvantage that creates—regardless of his white family. Just as Broyard must accept the universal lifelong judgement that she is white, and forgo a black identity, it wouldn't make sense for Obama to feel any other way than black.

As for Meghan Markle, Duchess of Sussex, her race and what it means has been just as hotly debated as in Obama's case; but she has been able to offer her own answer to the question. Her mother Doria Ragland is visibly black, but she herself is not. Markle has made clear right from the start of her public life—first as an actress, then as a duchess—that she is mixed-race. What makes her different from Bliss Broyard, Anthony E. Lennon and Barack Obama is her ability to choose. On paper, Obama and Broyard are neither white nor black, but society tells one he is black and one she is white. On paper Lennon was fully white, but society told him he wasn't; then society told him he was not black; and now at last he has a new "on paper" identity, the DNA test showing his diverse ancestry. Meghan Markle's appearance has entitled her to have a say herself in what she has become.

Markle could have passed for white due to her light skin, and people would have thought she had some "exotic" heritage—southern European or Middle Eastern, probably not African. Instead, she identified openly as mixed-race—and, paradoxically, the fact that she had a "passable" complexion opened up opportunity for her as a mixed-race actor. She was cast in the legal drama *Suits*, and then reoriented her role to make her character explicitly of mixed parentage, with an African American father. No such chance for Anthony E. Lennon, whom no audience could have mistaken for "pure white": he said he was told by his agent that there were hardly any mixed-race roles in theatre. This was what pushed him to identify as black—rather than spending his life telling incredulous casting directors that his parents were white.

Markle's proximity to whiteness has taken her to the very top of British society. Just as they did after Barack Obama's election victory in 2008, the dreamers of a post-race world were basking in optimism on 19 May 2018, as Meghan married Prince Harry in the 500-year-old Windsor Castle chapel, in the presence of her mother Doria Ragland and many other black guests. Writing in *The New Yorker*, Doreen St. Félix made this powerful observation:

> A millennium of world-shifting encounters—of violence and of romance and of acts in between—produced this scene: the sixty-one-year-old Ragland, an American who teaches yoga and does social work in Culver City, California, sitting in the opposite and equivalent seat to Queen Elizabeth II. They'd agreed on green, the color of beginnings—Ragland in churchy, pastel Oscar de la Renta, the Queen in electric-lime Stewart Parvin. One is a descendant of the enslaved, a child of the Great Migration and Jim Crow and seventies New Age spirituality; the other, the heir to and keeper of empire. Blood had long ago decided what life would be like for both.[16]

Yet here Ragland was, in pride of place at a royal wedding— without needing to be able to pass for white. Billions of people watched live around the world as she sat in graceful silence in "one of the oldest halls of whiteness",[17] in a chapel no doubt renovated many times over with the wealth generated by slavery. Her daughter entered the chapel on the arm of Britain's next monarch, Prince Charles, whose ancestor King George III (r. 1760–1820) had been against the abolition of slavery in the American colonies, because it was still one of the Empire's most profitable trades. Ragland's profoundly symbolic presence "represented the fraught lineage of a nation".[18] To some, her face in that chapel was the face of faith in humanity, of hope after fear; for a few, the graceful presence of this slave-descendant was a source of anxiety about things to come.

Race and hereditary monarchy have a lot in common—partial, illogical, the most irrational of institutions that we still keep aloft. You have to be firstborn to be king, and in the racial hierarchy you have to *look* white to truly claim a slice of the white kingdom. Meghan Markle is not the first black member of the British royal family, but she's by far the most important and prominent. Would she have still entered the royal family if she had been born a shade or two darker, like Obama? If she hadn't had a choice in declaring herself biracial, if she had clearly been African American, would she still have been anointed a "black duchess"? One look at the *Daily Mail*'s talkback comments below any article on Meghan will tell you how much racist vitriol she has had to endure, even being as close to whiteness as she is.

Markle is about as close to approximating visible and socio-cultural whiteness as a biracial person can be—so why is she still treated like such an outrage and such a threat? I've often wondered if the British tabloid onslaught against the Duchess might be because of the old fear raging through popular white consciousness that she is a black woman class-passing. Meghan came to the royal family as a self-made millionaire with a thriving acting career built on hard work against the odds in a racist industry. This was not just another royal spouse like the others, who met their modern knights either through belonging by birth to the aristocracy or through acquiring it via new wealth and members' clubs. That makes her a dangerous example of what an African American woman can achieve; and, for those who believe that "black" and "aristocratic" are incompatible, and that "white" and "aristocratic" are synonymous, her royal status amounts to passing. She may not be pretending she is from a fully white family, but she can still never truly belong. She can only ever play at being an English duchess.

Others, on the progressive side of the Meghan Markle battlefield, also agree that she can never belong in the royal family—but not because black or mixed-race people aren't good enough for royalty. This camp argues that her infiltration of the British establishment is nothing to celebrate for ordinary black people, because the establishment itself is racist. Neither side seems very interested in asking Meghan where she feels she belongs herself. No wonder she and her husband have had enough, deciding in 2020 to leave behind their royal duties, and the United Kingdom altogether.

In our time, race remains a primary tool for defining personal identity, our own and other people's. The result is that imposterism is projected onto people of multiple heritages. Anthony Lennon didn't suffer from "an identity problem", as his father put it; the internalisation of the need for arbitrary racial identity is the problem. His brother, Vincent, apparently responded to his imposed black identity by becoming a skinhead and a petty criminal, but he was killed in a tragic incident involving a train door. It has not been ruled out that Vincent may have taken his own life. When he died, he was described by a witness to the accident as a "half-caste". So there we are, the truth of race—a series of labels dependent on appearance, no more than skin-deep, but following us even into death.

PART TWO

BENDING THE BINARIES

5

MALE LIKE HER

IMPERSONATING THE "OPPOSITE" SEX

There is another kind of socially and legally conditioned identity. Like race, its enforcers depend on a binary against which everything else is measured; and, as with race, this socially constructed identity also depends on "biology" as a supposedly clear-cut, "objective" marker. What's more, racial passing was not around before the invention of race in the late eighteenth to nineteenth centuries; whereas gender identity, and therefore gender passing, is ages-old. Throughout history, there have been many who found themselves in between society's understanding of male or female identity, whether by choice or by nature, momentarily or fundamentally.

Literature, art and religion are full of gender-bending and gender-crossing stories. Myths in all cultures involve quite random sex changes according to the divine will and whim. We started this book with Anansi, the transformative god of the Ashanti and other West African peoples, and in Chapter 3 we saw how Indian mythology is inundated with cross-gender incarnations of gods (as well as humans). Ancient Greco-Roman literature is similarly full of such transformations, both of godly creatures themselves and imposed by them on hapless men and women—the mockers and the mocked in the divine and earthly orbits.

One of the best known works of classical literature—a mock epic for that matter—is Ovid's *Metamorphoses*, a vast work consisting of fifteen books, under the common theme of mythological transformation. We see gods and humans turned not just from mortal to divine and vice versa, but to animal, tree, stone—and, frequently, between man and woman, in a complex navigation of rape and escape, bondage and freedom, transgression and punishment, consciousness and oblivion. Jump ahead 1,500 years, and the English language's own legends—Shakespeare's plays—are filled with characters who are not victims of a capricious pantheon, but transform their gender by their own choice, dressing as men to dupe a male system and establish their authority before a misogynistic audience. The Bard's cross-dressing female characters exude agency and intellect. Rosalind of *As You Like It*, Viola of *Twelfth Night*, Portia in *The Merchant of Venice*—all are seen in early feminist criticism "as role models for modern (and postmodern) women."[1]

Then and now, cis men and women have passed as one another, when a sought opportunity would have been beyond reach in their assigned selves. This has mostly applied to women because, across human history, just as whiteness has been privileged to shut out people of colour, so has maleness been privileged to the exclusion of women. Women have often not been allowed to pursue certain professions or lifestyles in a patriarchal system, and the intrepid among them chose the means of passing as the only way—or the only safe way—to access wealth, wisdom, love, self-knowledge or meaningful work. These gender-passers may not be identifying as men or trans, or feeling themselves to be "in between" like mixed-race white-passers, but they are still resorting to passing as the only way they can be themselves.

As with the passers we've already seen, some would take their secrets to the grave; others would be exposed with tragic consequences, sometimes death. In this chapter we will uncover the stories of some incredible women who performed gender identities in pursuit of a social status largely unattainable for their sex. One in particular rose all the way to the very top of her society.

Top Girls

The legend of Pope Joan has been a source of embarrassment for the Roman Catholic Church since its emergence, and was originally batted away as anti-Catholic propaganda by early Protestants. But the shameful story of a female Pope in the ninth century—even worse, a pregnant Pope—has never gone away. She has become an enduring presence in the history and consciousness of European Christianity—a deeply unsettling tale of transgression for the Church, and an inspirational and empowering figure for some others, breaking down the highest and most sacred gender barrier of all.

Supporters of the "She-Pope" myth point to a piece of evidence in the Vatican's collection: a curious *sella stercoraria*, a chair with a large keyhole cut out of the seat used during papal election ceremonies. Legend has it that, with the would-be pontiff sat on this chair and submitted to an examination, a deacon would kneel down and look under it, to make sure through the hole that the occupant was male. Was the Church really so paranoid that it would pre-empt the possibility of a Pope Joan with such an awkward, elaborate procedure? Then there is the suggestion in some accounts that, since the thirteenth century, papal processions have avoided passing the spot where Pope Joan was supposed to have been unmasked and to have met her gruesome death—the stretch between the Basilica of St John Lateran and St Peter's in Rome. But the Vatican and most historians are against the idea that Pope Joan truly existed.

Pope Joan, whether a historical woman or a powerful legend, was born in medieval Europe. In this culture, female intellect was not only seen as a threat to the exclusively male religious elite and near-exclusively male political establishment; a woman of intelligence was an evil occurrence. Her tale is one of a woman in a male disguise, partaking in the forbidden elixirs of education and Christian theological teaching. The chronicles of the thirteenth century onwards that recount the histories of other pontiffs tell us that Joan was the daughter of English missionaries in Germany. She was 12 when she was told to step aside from conventional education, then reserved for boys. Joan ran away, apparently with one of her teachers, in a long monk's robe, passing herself off as a young student of theology.

She settled in Athens, where she excelled in her learning of classical Greek literature and philosophy. She then travelled to Rome, in the same male disguise, and soon became the right-hand "man" of the then pontiff, Leo IV. After his death, Joan was nominated as Pope John in 855 CE. She would hold the Holy See for two years. Once she had gone that far, there was no turning back—not without endangering her life. This was a transgression of the gravest kind, a woman's sinful "trespass" into a man's territory—an unforgiveable apostasy by papal decree. In the end, according to some sources, it was a visible reality of Pope Joan's womanhood that blew her cover. She went into labour during a papal procession, prompting the public to uncover her gender and the elaborate subterfuge she had gone through to gain the highest of all ecclesiastical positions. Depending on which version you read, she was either stoned to death or literally torn apart by an angry lynch mob.

One question that has puzzled social historians and writers since the inception of the legend is this: was Joan transgender, or simply a woman forcing her way through doors locked to her, by any means necessary?

Pope Joan has coloured the imagination of writers, sculptors and lay worshippers for centuries. As well as the medieval chronicles written by papal chamberlains, bishops and archbishops, many modern plays, novels and films have been written about Pope Joan. In all these texts, both medieval and more recent, the interpretation of her papal passing has generally pointed to the act of a cis woman hoodwinking an institution guarded exclusively for and by men of a certain pedigree. Donna Woolfolk Cross's bestselling historical novel, *Pope Joan* (1996), was made into a feature film in 2009. An earlier 1972 film had Liv Ullmann in the title role. All three works identify the constraints on girls and women as the motivation for Joan's decision to pass, whether to escape an arranged teen marriage or to continue her education—her gender identity never comes into question.

The most famous artistic depiction of Pope Joan—Caryl Churchill's 1982 play *Top Girls*—has the same focus, bringing together historically important women from different periods to show that the struggles they faced are still relevant to the central character, modern-day career woman Marlene, who invites her iconic guests to discuss how women have traditionally been constrained and how their achievements are viewed now, drawing uncanny parallels between the past and the present. Pope Joan, of course, arrives in the restaurant in male disguise. If Joan were clearly a real historical figure, then we could argue that she might have been a gender-dysphoric individual in a society with a narrow and moralistic understanding of identity, and thus her true motivations and feelings have been hidden from the record by its male ecclesiastical gatekeepers; but the legend is clearly written from the outset as a tale of a woman's transgression in patriarchy.

This brings us to a second question. If the Vatican's vehement denials of Pope Joan's existence are accurate, how and why did this popular legend come into being? How has it made its way not only into modern culture, but into the medieval monks' chronicles? The only logical conclusion is to remind ourselves once again that gender-passing and gender ambiguity are as old as our history, regardless of whether this specific individual ever lived. Her very presence in records of the past—the very idea of her—exposes as delusional a certain twenty-first-century intolerance based on normative nostalgia for a supposedly perfect past. In that narrative, gender was always clearly and permanently defined, until liberal thinking in our age destabilised it, leading to social chaos, break-up of the family and a whole host of catastrophic events. Pope Joan stands in defiance of this fiction.

Passing is a performance that follows the simple rule of the survival of the fittest. And the best-equipped in the social hierarchy—historically and now, as *Top Girls* demonstrates so memorably—are men. The extremity of the stakes for Pope Joan simply reflects just how far she sought to rise beyond the position society had given her, how very low that position was. But beneath the level of the papacy, and long after the disempowerment of the Middle Ages, there has been a whole world of women passing as men in less dramatic, more anonymous ways, just stepping in from the margins.

* * *

Throughout history, women have passed as men out of a desire to be liberated, to enjoy the freedom of choice and the power of knowledge in a man's world. For some, this was a lifelong career move, whereas for others, it was a limited pursuit, a taste of the vast and inaccessible world historically barred to women. Curiosity about the exclusive power of male spaces has drawn some women into them, undercover. To give one obvious, physical example, until recently, the Western world's "gentlemen's clubs" did not allow women membership or even entry—the ridiculously termed "cigar room" amounts to a fortified place for cliquish, elite male bonding. At the other end of the spectrum, working-class masculine culture is just as strong. The journalist Norah Vincent wrote a fascinating account of working-class male bonding in her 2006 book *Self-Made Man*, for which she passed as a member of a men's bowling club. Only by disguising herself as man was she able to gain insight into the social culture of visiting a strip club after a few drinks with the lads.

That was a limited act of research, but women have also passed as men for a life of adventure, particularly in the armed forces and the world of exploration—both traditionally male-dominated or exclusively male professions. Often, as with the racial passers who found themselves unexpectedly miscategorised on a piece of paper, the passing was almost thrust upon these women by circumstance, only for them to see a future in it. One of Western history's better-known women sailor-soldiers is Mary Anne Talbot, who fought in the French Revolutionary Wars in the 1790s. One of many illegitimate children of a wealthy English lord, Talbot had faced a series of unfortunate events since her birth, eventually ending up the mistress of a sea captain, Essex Bowen. On a voyage to the Caribbean, Mary Anne joined him as his footboy, "John Taylor". Later, Captain Bowen's regiment was enlisted to serve in the Flanders campaign against the French. At the battle for Valenciennes, Bowen was killed, and "John Taylor" slashed in the leg. Talbot tended to her wound herself for fear of her gender being revealed, picked herself up, and—despite the original reason for her passing now lying in a grave—went on working as a male sailor.

Another British woman who passed as a man for personal reasons, but ended up making a career of it, was Hannah Snell (1723–92). After her husband, a Dutch seaman, left her when she was pregnant, Snell borrowed her brother-in-law's clothes and assumed his name, James Gray, in order to go around looking for the missing Dutchman. As it turned out, he had been executed for murder. After the birth of her daughter, Snell put her male disguise back on and enlisted as a soldier in the British Army. She later joined the Royal Marines, which saw her unit transferred to capture the French colony of Pondicherry in southern India.

Snell was seriously injured on several occasions, and suffered injury to parts of her body, including her groin. Like Mary Anne Talbot, Snell braved it out without medical help, looking after her wounds herself so that she could guard her secret and resume her swashbuckling male life after recovering. The armed forces were and probably still are among the most apt places for an exploration of machismo—where better for a woman passing to taste the full-blown power and freedom of masculinity?

Male-passing was not always about gaining access to a social world or a dangerous lifestyle; it could also be about gaining professional opportunities. We saw in Chapter 2 that Anatole Broyard passed as white out of a longing to be regarded as a writer, not a "Negro writer". Mary Ann Evans wrote under the pseudonym George Eliot for a similar reason: in order to be treated as a mainstream author, rather than a "woman writer". She is just one of many women in the history of literature who have sought to overcome their marginalised identity by adopting a male persona, thus avoiding their societies' preconceptions that women's writing is light-hearted, easy reading, and limited to certain topics only of interest to other women. Ellis Bell is celebrated today as the author of a gritty novel on class, gender, hate, self-hate, adulterous love, perverse sexuality, coarseness of being, sadomasochistic relationships, madness, and a total negation of heteronormative happiness. Ellis Bell is Emily Brontë.

The "Plaguey Things" of Sexual Norms

As in real life, so too in fiction—one of the most famous gender-passing stories of all time is Shakespeare's *Twelfth Night* (c. 1601–2). As in several other Shakespeare plays, shipwreck and storm are used as a juncture of identity change, a rebirth into something "rich and strange" (*The Tempest*). At the start of the play, Viola and her twin brother Sebastian are separated following their shipwreck. In the land of Illyria, Viola decides to pass as a man to gain access to the court of Duke Orsino. Viola transforms into Cesario, who is sent by the Duke to woo on his behalf a reluctant love interest, Olivia. Viola's dressing as a man is the source of the play's comedy, creating as it does both subterfuge and confusion. The riotous main plot twist sees Olivia falling in love not with the Duke as planned, but with "Cesario", thinking that he is a man; it is Cesario—really Viola—who falls in love with the Duke.

This "mistaken identity" plot may seem to revolve around heteronormative relationships, and this "natural order of things" is where the play ultimately ends up; but gender theorists have also seen *Twelfth Night* as an exploration of homoeroticism. The Duke is full of worldly admiration for "Cesario" when the effeminate man turns up at his court. His eligibility for the job of convincing Olivia of the Duke's love seems to be his "womanly" characteristics, as Duke Orsino praises Cesario's feminine looks and voice:

> For they shall yet belie thy happy years
> That say thou art a man. Diana's lip
> Is not more smooth and rubious. Thy small pipe
> Is as the maiden's organ, shrill and sound,
> And all is semblative a woman's part.
> I know thy constellation is right apt
> For this affair.[2]

The play frequently refers to Cesario's womanly beauty in this way, and the device of "all but identical" twins, one man and one woman, further suggests that gender and sexuality can be no more than a role-play, open to nuance, influence, interpretation. When Sebastian, Viola's twin brother, shows up, Olivia marries him, thinking that he is "Cesario". *Twelfth Night* is named after the eve of the feast of Epiphany—held on the twelfth night after Christmas, when traditionally servants dressed up as masters, men as women, and women as men, to indulge for a day in misrule and revelry. Shakespeare applies this symbolism of ambiguous identity to the themes of fluid sexuality and gender.

* * *

This brings us to another reason why women have passed as men: intolerance of their sexuality. Today the concept that we know as "queer"—which denotes a whole range of sexual and gender affiliations—has not long existed in the lexicon of identity markers. In societies where straight was considered the only comprehensible, legitimate or morally acceptable sexual identity, this has often led those who are not heterosexual to gender-pass.

The much-overlooked 2011 film *Albert Nobbs*, based on George Moore's 1927 novella, stars Glenn Close as a woman born into poverty and abuse in nineteenth-century Ireland, who escapes the misery and misfortune that is her birthright by posing as Albert Nobbs, a butler in a classy hotel. "Albert" meets a painter-decorator working in the hotel called Hubert Page (Janet McTeer), and each discovers that the other is a woman. "Hubert" is passing as a man not only to improve her prospects like "Albert", but also because she is in love with a woman—her wife. The intersectionality of gender, sexual and class-passing is skilfully portrayed through the film's minutely observed characters, and the contrast between their experiences of living as a man. *AfterEllen*, the pop culture website for lesbian and bisexual women, put it this way:

> For Albert, passing as male is a necessity that has protected her—but also enchained her—for decades. In contrast, the painter "Hubert Page" views passing as male as a form of freedom. Whether Hubert is lesbian, genderqueer, or transgender is irrelevant for this era. Passing as male gives her the freedom to marry her wife, a relationship that is clearly romantic and probably sexual, and to live beyond the constraints normally imposed on women at that time.[3]

The sexual interests of the protagonist, Albert, are far from clearcut as the story unfolds; but this is clearly not the point. Scene after scene, this fantastically shot film transmits the oppressive class divides of the time through the segregation of hotel locations: the banqueting room full of rich diners; the kitchen full of maids and butlers; the guestrooms full of lust, lechery and sexual exploitation of the hotel workers by the rich; the creaky, run-down top-floor bedroom where Albert meticulously dresses as a man every day, binding her breasts like Brandon Teena, and putting on all the paraphernalia of the era's male attire, as befitting a butler. For Albert, this costume is a passport not to gay freedom, but to social mobility.

Albert takes inspiration from the happily married Hubert, and sets about wooing a hotel maid; but this is not about sexual desire. Instead, Albert is looking for marriage to serve her aspirations of socioeconomic independence and status. She dreams of one day buying and running her own tobacconist shop with living quarters above—impossible without the male disguise, at a time when women could not own property—and decides that a pretty wife might complete the picture of social success.

For Albert, passing is a lifelong project of banishing poverty to memory; by the time we meet her in the film, in her butler role, she has been living as a man for thirty years. Only once do we see her dressed as a woman, in a scene where she goes to visit Hubert after the latter's wife has died. They put on the dead woman's dresses and go out for a walk on the beach, but both are uncomfortable in this sole episode of public womanhood. Just as John Howard Griffin became convinced that he was a black man while undercover and later struggled to readjust to his white life, the audience here gets the sense that it is now being a woman that feels to Albert and Hubert like "dressing up" in an ill-fitting persona. Albert realises—remembers—how cumbersome women's clothing is, how greatly limiting and awkward.

This brings to mind a great passage from *Orlando*, which uses the same metaphor to convey women's unfreedom in pre-twentieth-century British society. After the hero has become the heroine in Constantinople, she sails home to England in the eighteenth century. Orlando buys herself an expensive dress fit for a woman of rank and sets in motion a new gender construction, boarding the aptly named *Enamoured Lady*. There is nothing romantic about the experience of restrictive womanhood for Orlando, though: feeling the "coil of skirts around her legs", she thinks to herself, "giving her legs a kick, 'these skirts are plaguey things to have about one's heels.'"[4]

"Funny Women"

In all these tales of women passing in a man's world, we've seen the importance of cross-dressing in gender-passing, just as skin tone is central to the ability to race-pass. Again defying the arbitrary hierarchy that sets one socially constructed identity above another, women have only had to put on the costumes and mannerisms of men to be accepted into the world of privilege, education and freedom traditionally reserved for men. But what about the other way around? When and why, in a historically gender-unequal world, do cis men pose as women?

Sometimes, the very fact of women's restricted status can be helpful to men: temporary disguises may enable them to enter areas reserved for women, for voyeuristic or romantic purposes; or to escape as an unthreatening woman when they would have been in danger as a man. Here we get into a phenomenon that we will look at more closely in Part Four in relation to race: reverse-passing, or passing "down". This is not passing out of the deep desperation or bold defiance of the underprivileged and marginalised—people of colour, trans and gay people, disempowered women, persecuted religious minorities, those of low caste or class. Instead these are transformations undertaken casually and temporarily to serve a particular interest.

In Greek mythology, Achilles is a celebrated war hero, immortalised by Homer in the *Iliad*. But there is one episode in his life that is not so well known, being more recent than Homer's version of the tale: somewhat unheroically, Achilles disguises himself as a girl and hides among King Lycomedes' daughters to avoid becoming a soldier. This is at the instigation of his mother, Thetis, who was told by an oracle that her son would die in the Trojan War. When the war breaks out, Odysseus and his Greek commanders, sent to track down Achilles and enlist him, decide to trick him into revealing himself. They visit Lycomedes with jewellery, clothes and other finery for the women of the household, cunningly placing a sword and shield among the gifts. Achilles, the natural born warrior, instinctively reaches for the weapons, thus revealing his true identity. All's well that ends well, as Achilles goes to meet his masculine destiny.

There can be nobler causes for which men pass as women. Henk Jonker (1912–2002) was a member of the Dutch Resistance and a photographer. Just a few years before John Howard Griffin set out to record and expose racism in the South, Jonker disguised himself as a female nurse to document the German occupation of the Netherlands during World War II. His aim was peaceful, and in protest at military force, but one real-life story of a man gender-passing that beats any fiction involves the Israeli general and prime minister (1999–2001) Ehud Barak. Before entering politics, in the 1970s

Barak led a number of bold and inventive undercover missions. In 1973, his squad travelled to Beirut by rubber dinghy with Barak disguised as a woman. They sought out their targets—the three Palestinians accused of masterminding the murder of eleven Israeli athletes at the 1972 Munich Olympics—and killed them.[5]

The common theme running through all these stories is a consistent underestimation of women and their agency, which daring men have turned to their advantage in the rare tricky situations where their own room for manoeuvre as a man—normally significant—has been curtailed. This comes back to the assumed inferiority and marginalisation of women in many societies through human history. In European cultural history, for example in Elizabethan plays, women were not allowed to act. The actors playing Viola and Olivia at the first performance of *Twelfth Night* in 1602 would have been men. The same was true in public performances throughout the world—such as Japanese Kabuki theatre—until fairly recently, and even once women were permitted on stage, acting was seen as an "unladylike" profession for low-class women of loose morals. In the case of the stage, men's gender-passing has actually been used specifically to further the exclusion of women.

It is no coincidence that cross-dressing in the entertainment world most often involves men appearing as women, rather than the other way around. The West has created a whole theatrical world of caricatured male to female personalities, where drag queens—sometimes transgender, sometimes not; sometimes hetero men, sometimes not—are commonplace. Cross-dressing entertainment is an important part of the queer space, and one that we'll explore further in the next chapter. But despite drag culture's defiance of the norms of strictly policed gender boundaries, it still upholds gender *norms*: it defends the right of men to cross into the "women's realm", and revolves around the exaggeration of stereotyped "female" traits, just as "Negro musicians" and Josephine Baker played to tropes of blackness for the delectation of a white audience.

Drag culture takes the performance and the performers seriously; but male cross-dressing is also a source of comedy in popular culture. What does that say about gender inequality? Why is a man pretending to be a woman a hilarious thing? Is it because womanhood is something lowly, something no man would ever seriously aspire to? Somehow unworthy of the mainstream and therefore to be made fun of, the way comedies also make fun of "lower-class" accents?

In films like *Mrs Doubtfire* and the *Big Momma's House* series, male actors wear prosthetics masks, fake breasts and latex "fat suits" to portray caricatures of femininity—a motherly housekeeper and a "big black woman" respectively—apparently to tickle the audience. Somehow this use of gender-passing as a source of comedy feels different from Shakespeare's. The fact that three films have been made revolving around a man wearing a Fat Black Lady body suit, frolicking around the place, playing Twister and making a fool of himself, suggests that the (male) film-makers are in cahoots with a target audience that really does find such denigrating portrayals of women funny. None of this is passing as we understand the term in this book. As the gender theorist and literature expert Valerie Rohy says: "passing is not simply performance or theatricality, the pervasive tropes of recent work on sex and gender identity, nor is it parody or pastiche, for it seeks to erase, rather than expose, its own dissimulation."[6]

However, sometimes cross-dressing in entertainment is part of a genuine gender identity expression. Eddie Izzard is a well-known British stand-up comedian and actor. He sometimes likes to arrive on stage wearing stilettos while still in "men's" clothes. Izzard has said publicly that "transvestite" would be the wrong term to describe his identity, since he is only wearing a dress as a way to express himself—the implication being that his clothes are separate from his sense of himself as a man or otherwise. Even if he did identify as trans, Izzard has explained, his transvestism would still have nothing to do with his gender identity; as he famously put it, "Women wear what they want and so do I." But over the years he has introduced himself as something of an in-betweener, describing his gender identity as a bit "boyish" and a bit "girlish".[7] He has said that he doesn't care what pronouns people use to address him.

The best conclusion we can draw from this collection of statements might be that Izzard uses cross-dressing to express his identity, but the identity being expressed is one that rejects gender binaries and labels. Transvestism is as old as other human identity transgressions, but in our time, social scientists have argued that cross-dressing as art challenges age-old thinking. Marjorie Garber sees cultural figures like Grayson Perry as questioning "the categories of 'female' and 'male', whether they are considered essential or constructed, biological or cultural."[8] Izzard is ready to challenge those in his audiences who—accustomed to thinking in binary terms—feel he has compromised his gender performance or identity by wearing makeup, high heels or dresses.

Maybe, in a world where we stopped policing other people's gender identity for them and placing them in a power hierarchy accordingly—where, instead, we learnt to understand them through what they say about themselves—maybe there would be no more need for, or even possibility of, gender-passing. The freedom to be gained from such a world, and the harm done in its absence, is shown most clearly in the experience of trans people in a transphobic world—this is the world we will turn to next.

6

THE WILD SIDE

SLIPPING BETWEEN GENDERS

So far, we've seen examples of what is traditionally or most commonly meant by "gender-passing": cisgender individuals, real and fictional, passing for the "opposite" sex. But now we will explore just how brutally the gender binary is upheld and policed by looking at the struggle of trans individuals to have their gender identity accepted and recognised, by looking at those who have been compelled to pass as cis. We will start with a famous tale of such a man, forced by our obsession with DNA to declare a biological sex he had not in fact been assigned at birth, as the only way society would let him claim his true, free gender identity.

Long before his life was dramatised in the film *Boys Don't Cry*, Brandon Teena was born as Teena Brandon in Lincoln, Nebraska. Over the years, Brandon became quite accustomed to living as a man, but with a great deal of anxiety around the preparation and paraphernalia involved in pretending to have been assigned male at birth: the usual breast-binding, stealing tampons from shops and hiding periods, stuffing a pair of socks into his pants, carrying a plastic dildo for when he made love to his girlfriends, so that they wouldn't find out his sex. In the early 1990s, he moved to the little town of Falls City, where he believed no one would know that he was biologically a she. There, he carried on confidently with this daily routine of deception—until he found love.

Everything started to go wrong when Brandon fell in love with a local girl, Lana Tisdel. In a brutal, hateful act of betrayal, his new male "friends" in Falls City tried to expose his female anatomy to

Lana (who was not in fact interested to know) on Christmas Eve 1993, to prove that he was "passing" as a man. Brandon was locked in the bathroom and disrobed, his genitalia exposed. A week later, on New Year's Eve, the same so-called friends brutally killed him. Brandon was 21. The story shocked America and the rest of the world. Discussion of transgender identity, and trans visibility, have increased significantly since the murder, partly thanks to the media outcry around the case, which continued throughout the 1990s. A book was written, then adapted into Kimberly Peirce's Oscar-winning 1999 film *Boys Don't Cry*, starring Hilary Swank.

Brandon Teena's murderers, John Lotter and Marvin "Tom" Nissen, tried to justify the killing on the basis that Brandon had duped an "innocent" local girl by hiding his biology; that such fakery was against natural law. They found Brandon's subterfuge, what they saw as his illegitimate intrusion into masculinity, a more offensive crime than their killing of him. The scholar Elaine K. Ginsberg explains their intolerance:

> the law and social custom insist on the relationship between an individual's gender identity and his or her physical being, and when that relationship is subverted, the cultural logic of gender categories—and privileges—is threatened ... Thus it seems that Brandon's murder was a tragic consequence of a female's transgression and usurpation of male gender and sexual roles.[1]

But it was not a failure of Brandon's "male makeover" that had led him to be exposed—his attackers, like his girlfriends, had had no problem believing Brandon was a cis man based on his appearance. It was during an ID check that Brandon was arrested and sent to prison, where he was kept in the female cell. The news of his arrest was posted in the local paper under his birth name, Teena. As with the fiction of race, we see here an attempt to prioritise "inherent" "biology" that is in fact based on visual judgements, in turn driven by our obsession with determining other people's identity.

Societies throughout history have demonstrated an almost existential need to police people's labels, and this same need to enforce a gender binary prompts transphobic tendencies among ordinary people. Our very first identity, assigned at birth, is defined by what our nether-regions look like—the earliest marker of us as individuals in society, male or female. But in the case of trans or intersex people, nature takes over nurture: assigned sex no longer reflects gender identity. The difficulty of society's intolerance for this gap often leads trans people to opt for surgical correction, which can make it easier for them to belong. But many individuals, as we shall see in the pages to come, cannot immediately afford or do not have a legal avenue to change their sex to match their gender. Some, like Brandon Teena, will find themselves "going undercover", claiming a cis identity when a trans one is too dangerous or alienating.

This attitude was evident in the gruelling questioning that Brandon faced after reporting the Christmas Eve incident to the authorities. Chronicling the subsequent interrogation of Brandon in *The Brandon Teena Story* (1998), the documentary-makers Susan Muska and Gréta Ólafsdottir unearthed the following exchange between the victim and the Richardson County sheriff, Charles Laux, whose failure to address Brandon's plea and protect him led to his tragic murder days later by the same tormentors. This police interview was so aggressive and intrusive that it has been termed a "third rape" by *Boys Don't Cry* director Peirce.[2]

The exchange is also depicted in *Boys Don't Cry*. The scene is powerful and painful to watch. The audience is left feeling humiliated along with Brandon, as he endures the Sheriff's questioning:

Sheriff Laux: ... after he pulled your pants down and seen you was a girl, what did he do? Did he fondle you any?

Brandon: No.

[...]

Laux: Why do you run around with girls instead of, ah, guys being you are a girl yourself?

Brandon: Why do I what?

L: Why do you run around with girls instead of guys being you're a girl yourself?

B: I haven't the slightest idea.

L: You haven't the slightest idea? You go around kissing other girls? ... the girls that don't know about you, thinks [sic] you are a guy. Do you kiss them?

[...]

B: …I have a sexual identity crisis.

L: A what?

B: I have a sexual identity crisis.

L: You want to explain that?

B: I don't know if I can even talk about it.

Talking about a difference in gender between how one has been labelled and how one feels has been a taboo subject in most cultures. In intolerant societies, transgender and transsexual "identity crises" top the chart of "unnatural" behaviours, deviant and freakish. This leads many trans and intersex people to pursue a kind of double life.

One of the best-known early recipients of sexual reassignment surgery was the Danish landscape artist Lili Elbe. Until surgical confirmation of her gender, she had lived publicly as a prominent male artist, Einar Wegener, all the while concealing her increasingly emergent female self, Lili, celebrated privately with her wife Gerda and some close friends.

Like Brandon Teena, Elbe had to pass as cisgender—but, in her case, by *continuing* to live as her assigned sex. She cross-dressed only in the evenings, at intimate parties among a trusted circle, emulating "female" body language. Maintaining the Einar persona in wider society, one half of a regular heterosexual married couple, drove Elbe to suicidal depression—a common side effect of the loneliness and dehumanisation experienced by those hiding their gender identity. A society uncomprehending of the trans experience will strip trans people of the dignity of personhood. In *Boys Don't Cry*, when Lana's mother learns of Brandon's biological sex, she asks for "it" to be out of her daughter's life. How could Brandon "even talk about it" with a Sheriff, when he is regarded as against "order", let alone law?

Gender transitioning is distinctly different from passing. Passers—including the cis individuals we met in the previous chapter—do not generally have an extensive emotional affinity with the public persona they have taken on; they are acting out an identity, not truly claiming or expressing it. For a trans or intersex individual, the life that is a lie is the life *before* they transition.

THE WILD SIDE

When Teena from Lincoln became Brandon in Falls City, he became who he really was; the deception on his part was the claim that he had always been a biological man. As we've seen in Part One, passing is often not only done for the sake of opportunity, but for survival; trans people passing as cis are no different from race-passers in this respect. It is a life of pain, mostly; and, as Brandon Teena's case shows, it can be extremely dangerous. On that fateful New Year's Eve, Brandon joined Clare Kendry, the suburban American housewife, and Sapphire, the British Caribbean dancer, on the long list of those who have died for their passing; as we meet sexual, religious and class-passers in later chapters, other names will be added to his.

For some trans people, it is a lifelong journey to reach the phase where they do not have to prevaricate or pass, when their self-expression will no longer be inhibited by anxiety around their gender presentation—what to wear, how to behave in a restaurant, in a pub, at a family gathering, which toilet to use, when or whether to tell your parents, siblings, close friends. Until they are able to come out as trans, they hide in the shelter of their more easily acceptable, assigned identity.

Transgender identity is often misunderstood even by sympathetic cisgender people as a crisis in sexual orientation, somehow "gay" in nature. *Boys Don't Cry* shows Brandon's cousin Lonny worrying about his safety as he goes out to drinking joints to seduce local girls. Lonny tries to help Brandon, suggesting, "Do you wanna admit you're a dyke?" Brandon simply replies, "I am not a dyke." In *The Danish Girl*, during one of Lili's first public outings, a gay guest at the same house party detects her biological sex—this is before she has had surgery. He takes this as a cover for the artist's sexual orientation, assuming that he is dealing with a fellow homosexual man, and makes inappropriate advances accordingly.

* * *

This need to frame gender dysphoria and trans identity in a way that "makes sense" to society's established norms is really about affirming gender itself as a norm—as something fixed. Pulling down a so-called gender-passer's underwear, as in the first assault on Brandon

Teena on Christmas Eve, is a recurring offence committed by people with only one intention in mind—to shame gender non-conformists. This ordeal has featured in much fictional writing about the trans experience. In Jeffrey Eugenides' epic novel *Middlesex* (2002), the narrator Cal—an intersex teenage boy passing as a cisgender male—is attacked in San Francisco's Golden Gate Park. As well as robbing, beating and finally urinating on him, the mob pulls down his pants, and shouts at him, "Crawl back into the hole you came out of, freak."[3]

Middlesex is an ingenious title for this brilliant study of identity; it not only refers to the neighbourhood where its narrator grew up, but also reflects his search for self-definition, caught between the two recognised sexes. The theme of hermaphroditism in Greek mythology was an inspiration for Eugenides in writing the book, and Cal likens his own state to that of Tiresias, the blind prophet(ess) transformed for seven years into a woman—"first one thing and then the other".[4] Cal is born an XY male in 1960, but appears to have female genitalia due to a syndrome called 5-alpha-reductase deficiency. She is brought up as a girl—Calliope, or Callie. But Callie has always known there is something different about her that sets her apart from other "girls".

In the mid-70s, the teenage Callie's parents take her to a sexologist in New York, who plans to operate on her to permanently "correct" her sex to female. When she learns the truth about "her" birth sex, Callie runs away and becomes Cal, travelling to San Francisco to live as a he. At the end of the novel, Cal's mother asks if it would not have been easier just to "stay" the way he was—as a girl. But, Cal explains, this is the way he always was. Not to live as a man would have been denying his very self.

Along each stage of the way, Callie sheds a layer of the socially visible markers of gender identity. The transformation begins as she swaps her girly suitcase with flowers for her father's, buys androgynous—what we would probably call today "gender-neutral"—clothing at a Salvation Army charity shop, and walks into a barber shop to cut her very long hair. Here comes the archetypal mirror scene that we've already seen in race-passing narratives both real and fictional—that moment when an individual caught between identities is self-scrutinised by their reflection. Cal bids farewell to Calliope, named after the Greek mythical muse: "And there she was, for the last time, in the silvered glass: Calliope. She still wasn't gone yet. She was like a captive spirit, peeking out."[5]

In short hair, and more or less passable as male, Cal arrives in New Jersey by bus, from where he starts hitchhiking across the States, eventually finding himself in San Francisco. Callie's metamorphosis is as painful as birth, the labour pains a journey away from the familiar self, as his lonely soul faces "the fraught, giddy, emotional abandon brought on by assuming identities not your own."[6] The necessity of the transformation doesn't get rid of the fear of loss, of the step away from "normality". "If normality were normal," Cal knows, "everybody could leave it alone. They could sit back and let normality manifest itself."[7] But the ongoing journey of rebirth is mired in denial, shame, loneliness and the tell-tale dread of stigma. And so, even once "Cal" is born, he cannot bring himself to live openly as trans or intersex; he hides the past, and lies by omission in the present.

Under cover of the dark Californian underworld he now belongs to, Cal's journey to his assumed personhood has only just begun. He doesn't go as far as Brandon Teena in hiding his sex characteristics, but he goes along with society's assumption that he is a boy and always has been, and he plays up to it in his behaviour and appearance. There is the socially prescribed "manly" gait, "a swagger", a "Clint Eastwood squint"; there is a consideration of whether it is more masculine to handle loose change out of his pocket rather than his palm.[8] But this is not enough. As we know, identity performance is first and foremost an act to be believed by the performers themselves. To convince himself that he is Cal, he must unlearn his memories of Callie.

The Blank Slate of Personhood

The passer seeking to cast off the identity they were assigned at birth must improvise a credible past and a convincing present, and carefully navigate between the two. The problem for the gender-passer or sex-passer is that they must conceal not simply an official legal arbitration, as with white-passers; they must conceal an entire lifetime's experience. Hiding that he is intersex requires Cal to literally erase the past, wiping out childhood film footage that shows Calliope's mother handing her a baby doll.

When Cal is exposed in the Golden Gate Park, it's not because he couldn't get away with passing. As with Brandon Teena, and as with the race-passers we met in Part One, the very act of successfully passing has overcome the idea that an imposed identity is in fact inherent. Cal was betrayed not by an unconvincing male appearance, but by a piece of paper: searching him, his tormentors found his school ID card from when he had been living as a girl, his assigned sex at birth.

We've seen the importance to the white-passer of paperwork to help rewrite history, either forged or unwittingly gifted through some official misapprehension. The latter mistake is unlikely to happen with trans individuals. Thus, even more so than for racial passers, an important part of radically reworking one's gender history—rewriting one's self, both practically and psychologically—is geographic displacement. Only by physically leaving the past behind can you avoid bumping into known faces who would expose your assumed identity, shame you, imprison you, even. A successful identity defection is often also a bodily one, marked simultaneously by guilt and exhilaration in a mutiny against both the learned self and society. In *Middlesex*, the anonymity of travel and the "shifting feeling" of San Francisco itself offer Cal the time and space for his own personal shift. After the rite of passage travelling along Route 80, his new adulthood as a man looms out of the unknown.

The unknowability of the road ahead helps create what Eugenides calls the "blank slate of personhood".[9] It helps the new person-to-be to defamiliarise themselves with the past. One of the best-known depictions of transsexuality in popular culture is the Lou Reed song "Walk on the Wild Side" from his 1972 album *Transformer*, following the journey of a trans woman across the United States as she steps into "the wild side" across the drawn gender binary.

Sophie Green is a trans artist with a studio in Liverpool. She went through various cities in the Midlands and the north of England—Leicester, Leeds, Derby—before finally settling there to be what she calls comfortably "female-identified". When we meet, she explains to me the early days of her soul-searching in the 1990s, around the same time that Brandon Teena's murder brought the gender question to the forefront of public consciousness on both sides of the Atlantic. As with Brandon's cousin—"Do you wanna admit you're a dyke?"—Sophie, who was assigned male at birth, was often taken for gay at the time. There was no recognition of her, or anyone's, trans identity.

> When I was about 18, I contacted one of Leicester's LGBT groups, I tried to explain how I felt. But there wasn't anything trans-specific then. They said, come along to our meeting—the LGBT meeting, the Q wasn't really around then. I went to the meeting, it was essentially a gay bar, lots of gay men in a pub really. And there was me, trying to talk to people how I feel, how I like dressing up as a woman ... how I perceive myself, where I think I might wanna go, and because they were gay men, they didn't get it, you know. They went, like, oh, everyone likes to dress up a bit, don't worry, it'll go away. I was like, you know, you're not listening. I never went back there, there was nobody like me. Even remotely like me.[10]

There was no question, then, of living as a trans woman; of making any kind of change from the socially imposed default of "cis man". This forced passing was just as unbearable for Sophie as it had been for Teena/Brandon in real life, and for Callie/Cal in *Middlesex*. The constant anxiety and sense of inner dishonesty remind us of the tortured white-passers we met in Part One, ever trapped in a made-up version of themselves:

> This bounced around my head every day. Especially in my 20s, it was on the mind all the time: "This is not right, this is not how I'm supposed to be living." The way people perceive me, the way people react to me ... not being able to be open, not being open to my family, [able to] talk to my family, work, and everything else. The weight of maleness was put on me, I felt this could not go on, really.

The only way Sophie could get away with not fully conforming to male identity was by adopting an "androgynous look". "I was a bit like an indie kid at school. I started growing my hair when I was sixteen, dying it red; I've been dying it red for a long time." Sophie laughs as she tells me this, coiling and uncoiling an orange-red lock around her index finger. This adolescent look helped cover up her anguish, and lighten that "weight of maleness" throughout Sophie's university life. But navigating society's expectations still caused her discomfort and anxiety. After graduating, she cut her hair and got a job in "a very macho male establishment" as a graphic designer. She began to dress as a "proper male", and moved into a flat with a girlfriend. "I was wearing black trousers and black tops, I thought I was getting away with it. But my ears were pierced, my hair was in a bob, I was still, like, male at work. Looking back now, it seems ridiculous!" This haunting double life, reminiscent of Lili Elbe's many decades earlier, was not just in the workplace. Even once she had started socialising as a woman, Sophie was still "male" with her loved ones.

> I lived away from my family—they were all in Leicester, I was in Derby, so I didn't really need to tell them, till quite late on. I spoke to my sister, told her that I was trans, then I showed her photos [of me in make-up and women's clothes] and told her, look, that's me, that's how I see myself and how other people see me.

Sophie is speaking to me standing at Liverpool's historic harbour. The city's World Museum has an impressive queer collection, celebrating among other things gay life at sea and the city's most famous trans woman: the model April Ashley, one of the first British people to undergo sex reassignment surgery. The slavery museum on the other side of the harbour bears testimony to how European prosperity came about, particularly in port cities like this one: through the triangular slave trade and the spoils of empire. Just as the British exported white-supremacist race science and ethnic categorisation around the world, they also spread and codified into law rigid Western Christian ideas about gender and sexuality that still wreck lives in former colonies today, as we will see later on.

Standing on the edge of the waters, I feel dizzy with the weight of history. My reverie is broken when Sophie says that she has come a long way since her childhood trauma; from the burden of society's attempts to nurture her as a boy "to here!" Pointing to the top viewing gallery of the World Museum, she proudly states, "There, in Liverpool Museum—just across from the museum of slavery, they had my wedding dress on display for a long time, in their LGBTQ exhibition."

Who did she get married to? What she tells me is not something I expected to hear. Three years ago she married Thom, a computer programmer, also from the north, in a typical wedding—Sophie in a fabulous backless white wedding dress, Thom in a smart suit. (Sophie would later tell me the suit cost more than the dress!) Back then, says Sophie, Thom occasionally liked to cross dress, but identified as male; now that has changed. Where is Thom, then? I ask her. You'll meet them, she says. And later I will indeed meet Jess, Sophie's trans spouse.

As Sophie and I stand on the historic pier—which has witnessed the departure of the first transatlantic slave ship and, 300 years later, has displayed a trans woman's wedding dress—we muse that our species are a variable lot. Even the darkest chapters in our history often evolve into something rich and strange. As Sophie points out, she is lucky to be part of that history; I can't help thinking that her and her partner's story is remarkable. Unlike Brandon Teena, and many fictional trans or intersex characters like Eugenides' Cal, Sophie and Jess have been able to give up the life of passing for cis. They have found a wonderful freedom and fluidity, on this very spot from which the British Empire once exported race science and Christian gender morals to an unassuming world.

Sophie and I walk toward the centre of town. We meet Jess on the way, and the three of us head into a wonky Victorian pub. Jess is like a classical painting: delicate-limbed, very tall, with yellow hair in ringlets down to her shoulders. She towers over me, and even Sophie, who is around 6 foot. Dressed androgynously, Jess appears to be more gender-fluid than Sophie in her short denim dress. The first thing I ask, as we get a table in the noisy pub, is which pronouns I must use. "She, or they; but I won't be offended if you can't be consistent!" Jess tells me. That puts me at ease.

Close to the Liverpool estuary, The Globe—now famous for the sloping floor—was established in 1888. Sophie, Jess and I talk about the Victorian constraints that came before the early-twentieth-century genesis of the gender revolution. Liverpool played a huge part in evolving and maturing the way we think of gender and sexuality today. After all, this is the city of April Ashley, the 1960s trans icon who underwent reassignment surgery and did pioneering work to eradicate the social stigma of transgenderism in the popular media. Ashley, born as George Jamieson in 1935, "in a way that was insouciantly subversive ... passed as a woman, and was celebrated as an object of heterosexual male desire",[11] working as a lingerie model until she was outed as a former man by a tabloid newspaper. She then lost her marital wealth and social position.

Inevitably, Sophie and Jess bring up Ashley. They tell me how, because of what she did for the trans cause, they both have a right to the life they need to live. For both Sophie and Jess, now in their 40s, this has included a shift not only in gender identity, but also in sexual orientation. As Jess began transitioning, Sophie's sexuality evolved and adapted to the new reality; they are now regarded by themselves and others as a lesbian couple. Sexually, Sophie says, she is probably now pansexual. Her partner, who started out like Sophie and Lili Elbe—alternating between Thom and Jess in their private life—is now medically transitioning. Sophie is helping them with the process, as they helped her when she was going through hers.

We're squeezed between a group of rowdy Scousers, all sitting with large pints. Our trio can see our reflections in the mirror behind the bar—a trans woman, an Indian woman and a transitioning woman with androgynous appearance. We could not look more different from these white, middle-aged publicans. My companions must have seen their reflections in this mirror many times in the twelve years since they moved to Liverpool and started coming here. The former Sophie and Thom are now looking at Sophie and Jess. Has it made a difference to the way they feel toward each other?

Not at all, they say in chorus—which takes me to yet another famous mirror scene in an identity transformation novel.

Virginia Woolf's 1928 *Orlando: A Biography* heralded a powerful but contained explosion of the previous century's social constraints. It hammered through the age's binary thinking not only around gender, but also around sexuality, transsexuality and, to some extent, race. Orlando travels the continents, living for 400 years, changing class, position, geography and, finally, sex. The character's many transitions make the idea of "gender-passing" or "cis-passing" completely irrelevant, as Orlando becomes what or who they appear to be, repeatedly and with ease, in a natural progression from one state to another.

Woolf marketed this great novel as a biography, as if to say that there is not much difference between the strangeness of fiction and that of truth. Orlando's incredible story of gender transition and love affairs—first as a man with a woman, then as a woman with a man—is not so incredible if we look at Woolf's own life. Orlando's flamboyant character is based on the writer Vita Sackville-West, Woolf's long-term lover (both were married). Sackville-West also cross-dressed from time to time, not out of any gender identity crisis, but for fun; because she could. For her, passing as a man—"Julian"—was a pastime. Sackville-West and Woolf were prominent members of the Bloomsbury Group, known for its "modern" attitudes.

Partway through the novel, Orlando has woken up in his bed after a political riot in Constantinople, where he has been sent as Britain's ambassador. He "stood upright in complete nakedness before us ... looked himself up and down in a long looking-glass, without showing any signs of discomposure, and went, presumably, to his bath." Here the author steps in, as if to guide her readers, toward the greatest quiet gender revolution of Woolf's time and, perhaps more importantly, in the history of the English novel:

> Orlando had become a woman—there is no denying it. But in every other respect, Orlando remained precisely as he had been. The change of sex, though it altered their future, did nothing whatever to alter their identity. Their faces remained, as their portraits prove, practically the same. His memory—but in future we must, for convention's sake, say "her" for "his," and "she" for "he"—her memory then, went back through all the events of her past life without encountering any obstacle. Some slight haziness there may have been, as if a few dark drops had fallen into the clear pool of memory; certain things had become a little dimmed; but that was all. The change seemed to have been accomplished painlessly and completely...[12]

In the film version of *Orlando* by Sally Potter, the full dramatic effect of Orlando's transition is felt when Orlando, after seeing her reflection in the mirror, looks straight to camera and tells the audience: "The same person, no difference at all! Just a different sex."

*   *   *

If we took away the law, and social preconditioning—if we got rid of rigid binaries—we would be left with much healthier, more fluid societies, where identity would not be "this" or "that", or even a "third" gender (see below). In an ideal world, no legal or cultural labelling would be necessary; we could simply be who we feel we are, and be accepted for it. In the old Victorian pub near the Liverpool waterside, Sophie—who has not read *Orlando*—echoes the memorable line as she says contemplatively, "There isn't a great difference between male and female."

The shiftability of gender (and sexual) identity was always on Sophie's mind as she was growing up in a northern working-class family. She and Jess, who have known each other for decades, have been trying to define themselves—Sophie undoubtedly as a woman, and Jess as gender-fluid. But the journey has not been straightforward. They both "passed" as straight and cis at various points in their lives, at work in particular, throwing away that "put-on" identity as soon as they came home to their own space. Thom would elaborately dress up as a woman and Sophie would "glam herself up in high heels et cetera", and the two would go out in the evening, to private parties where they would not be reviled for their gender-switching and complex sexuality.

But even once the transition is fully public and open, that doesn't mean the period of identity anxiety is over. Sophie says that you can never arrive at or fully own one single "true self". This applies to all identity reassignment processes, but gender reorientation in particular is as much emotional as it is physical. The pre- and post-transition stages do not completely merge into a clear-cut state of being, even when physically and socially it may seem like a one-way street. When Orlando transitions from male to female, the memory of the male past readjusts organically. But in real life, this memory is not something that trans people look back on nostalgically. It marks a time when they had no option but to pass as cisgender, because failure to do so would have meant ostracisation, mockery, violence, even death.

In the Liverpool bar, to my shame, I keep referring to Jess as he, primarily due to their appearance, which is still gender-fluid. Sophie comes to my defence, saying this is Jess's fault for not "fixing the pronoun thing" yet. I only hope that Jess is not too mad at me. I ask them both how they bridge the past, transitive and present memories of their respective selves. How does one remember one's childhood after changing gender? How does a transgender person's family react to them, deal with the new pronouns—when a brother is now a sister, or a mother is now a father?

Sophie refuses to reveal her birth name, proclaiming she has always been "Sophie" to herself, ever since she was a child. "My name was going to be Sophie, my mother said, had I been born a girl"—that is, with female genitalia. Just as Anthony Ekundayo Lennon's father denied his son's black identity even on his deathbed, Sophie's father found it hard to see her as a woman. But others, including her older sister and mother, adjusted more easily to her transition. Her big sister, whose clothes Sophie used to try on,

> was great, she was very excited to tell the rest of the family. My family got on board with it quite quickly. My relatives thought, when they saw me, "Oh, that's what it is! That's what the thing was that we couldn't quite work out"—it was like, "Oh I get it now! What a relief!"

It turned out that the main source of confusion was not Sophie's gender identity as a woman, but her having passed for such a long time as cis.

Sophie said when we entered the pub that the men in there didn't really care who we were, so I take another look at the faces sitting around us and at the bar. They seem friendly, but when I follow their eyes, I see them linger on Sophie and Jess, who are holding hands. I feel certain that I can read their thoughts; they are wondering whether Sophie and Jess are just a regular straight couple out for an evening drink, or something else. At a glance, Sophie's appearance is of a cisgender woman with striking red hair, but Jess, in jeans, a shirt and with long hair, has a kind of Orlando-like ambiguous look about her. Their life is certainly happier and freer than Brandon Teena's or Cal's, but it seems we're not yet in the Woolfian utopia where trying to put people in boxes no longer makes sense to us. Sophie says:

> When I was younger, I conformed to be male, and I countered it up by being more androgynous. ... Then when I transitioned ... things started going the other way. Now I need to conform to the stereotype of a woman. It's like now I need to take care of my parents, I need to get my hair done, nails done, all of these little add-ons ... And I guess in the social circle you hang out in, I have many cisgender female friends, and hanging out with them—some of them kind of quite girly—there was a period when going out for cocktails (and everyone had their heels on) was glam, it was fun. But looking back now, I ask, was I just pushed to conforming to a strong female identity?

Sophie, who has undergone reassignment surgery, is no longer passing as biologically female: she just is. But still, at first, she found herself feeling the need to perform a woman's identity, copying hand and eye gestures thought to be feminine. We've seen Brandon Teena and Cal of *Middlesex* do the same, Cal—transitioning the opposite way—overdoing his "maleness" like a new religious convert. Today, Sophie no longer feels that pressure. "When it comes to gender, you're just trying to pass as yourself," she says. "You don't want to go from one box that caused you anguish and upset, to jump into another tight little box—that's not liberation."

That fear of the social and legal accusation of transgression had lingered on from Sophie's gender-dysphoric childhood, when it was always there. "I didn't want anybody to know. It just felt like a very, very bad thing," she replies, when I ask her if she was scared of the awakening inside her when she was so young—7 or 8, when children just about start conforming to their socially allocated identity. The age when boys become boys and can't like pink, when girls become girly and are supposed to. When they stop playing together as children, and start interacting as boys and girls.

I am saying this from my own experience of raising three children, each eight years apart, so encompassing some twenty-five years of three childhoods. As I write this in 2020, my youngest is 9. I am seeing first-hand his gender awareness, which has less to do with how he is being brought up at home than with how society perceives him. The expectations have been similar across several countries where we have lived and the children have gone to school: in London, Rabat, Amman, Jerusalem, La Roque, a little village near

Toulouse, and for a few weeks in Pushkar, western India. My daughter was obsessed with Bob the Builder as a child; she refused to wear pink, or girly clothes, so she was pegged by society as a "tomboy"— as if being interested in building and engineering is an essentially male or boyish trait. When my eldest son didn't show any interest in football, despite growing up as a young boy near the Arsenal stadium, people thought it was odd. The pressure to conform is huge, and even very young children can sense it.

Deep down, most parents want their children to fit in, mainly out of fear of their being cast aside. My daughter, who's now 18, fought for two years in her early teens at a North London school for a gender-neutral toilet—without success. I have never voiced this before doing so here on this page, but I always secretly hoped that she wouldn't end up drawing negative attention in school with her outspokenness about gender and sexuality. I wanted her to feel safe, and not to get herself labelled in any way that would make her stand out, or make her vulnerable to social taunting. Here we're back at those boxes again—why do we constantly put people in them?

This brings us to the intersection of sex and gender. On the one hand, trans people often have to fight to have their gender identity recognised when it does not correspond to their birth-assigned sex. On the other, many—even with the cultural shifts of the new millennium—do not feel fully at peace and at home with themselves until they have made that biological change, through surgery. Empathy in tolerant societies has led us to describe the transgender experience as gender dysphoria, but even now, medical reports are filled with language associating trans identity with illness, describing a gender "disorder" or chromosomal "abnormality".

This way of thinking about gender dysphoria—as a fault to be fixed—extends to the language some trans people use to talk about themselves. For them the aberration in need of correction is not their gender identity, but the "wrong body" they are trapped in. In the 2015 biopic *The Danish Girl*, Lili Elbe explains why she needs the operation: "God made me this way, but the doctor is curing me of the sickness that was my disguise." In *Middlesex*, Calliope has always felt at odds with herself, but the decision to transition to Cal only comes once she reads a medical report and discovers that society has conspired against her knowledge to "fix" her to her assigned gender.

Even those who would otherwise be content in their bodies, provided they could live as the right gender, feel an external pressure to be not just transgender but transsexual. Sophie was selected by the National Health Service for sex reassignment surgery—also known as gender confirmation surgery—in 2013. She didn't want people in women's changing rooms to "freak out", stare or isolate her for having male genitalia. She didn't want to be spotted with a penis in women's toilets and asked to leave; but she also didn't want to attract attention in men's toilets for looking female. Toilets were a test in Sophie's earliest memories—while she was still discovering her gender dysphoria, they left her feeling torn, fearful. The Harvard professor Marjorie Garber explains this in her brilliantly titled book on cross-dressing, *Vested Interests*: "The restroom as site of gender identification accords with a child's earliest training in the use of public accommodations, whether in schools, in airports, or in train or bus stations, and therefore with some of his or her earliest public declarations of gender difference."[13]

Sophie told me, "It was a conundrum." Jan Morris took this word as the title of her autobiography, in which she gives a similar account of the quandaries of trans experience. She describes a situation in Mexico where some hotel maids asked her, post-reassignment, whether she was a man or a woman. She "whipped up" her shirt "to show [them her] bosom", using her sex characteristics as proof of her gender.[14] The celebrity and former athlete Caitlyn Jenner, star of *Keeping Up with the Kardashians*, is a male-to-female transsexual. Following the 2017 surgery that completed her transition, she said:

> It is not something I talk about. Yes, I had gender confirmation and that for me was important. For many trans people it is not important to them ... for me it was. Femininity and womanhood is in your brain and in your soul. That is the issue ... It is not what is between your legs.[15]

But the fact that Jenner felt the need to state this shows that, thanks to society's enforcement of the gender binary, even an openly trans person can still be accused, offensively, of passing. Without the physical evidence of femaleness, there will always be those moments when you risk being "caught out", exposed and stigmatised. It's not enough to transition your self-identification, to come out as trans to the people in your life and to be happy with it; society will constantly try to reverse, deny or invalidate that transition, unless you can conform as far as humanly possible to society's preconceived notions of what a man or woman is. We can see this in today's culture war between trans activists and radical feminists such as Germaine Greer, who says that even a surgical sex change does not make a man a woman, and talks about "fake femaleness", "false sex".[16]

Most feminists would agree that a cis woman and a trans woman's experience of patriarchy will have been different in some ways, but implicit in the Greer worldview is the idea that trans women are impersonating "real" women, in order to take up space and enjoy privileges that rightly belong to cis women. In actual fact, trans women do not have it easy to say the least, as we've seen. Anti-trans feminists forget that most cultures stigmatise men who are considered to look or behave like, let alone identify as, women. They are namby-pamby, effeminate—because women are of lower status than men. Why else is it so easy for cis women to wear trouser suits (often described as "power-dressing"), and so impossible for cis men to wear a skirt? Without gender dysphoria, how can we explain those assigned male at birth forgoing their privilege in favour of terrible mockery, alienation and abuse? But these arguments still enjoy acceptance and airtime, and their hostility has an effect on the psychological and physical security of trans women. After her surgery, Sophie felt she was finally no longer a "fraudster". She was not cross-dressing, she was not gay, she was not passing. She was a woman, now outwardly too.

This insecurity around living as transgender, but not transsexual, is sometimes reflected in (mis)representations of the trans experience in the arts. When Sophie was growing up, she says, any trans people she had encountered in popular culture were always desperately negative. Trans TV characters were either deviants, or victims "trapped in the wrong bodies"; they were utterly miserable. "I was like—I don't want to be one of those people." As Sophie struggled with her trans identity in 1990s Britain, Neil Jordan's film *The Crying Game* reflected the challenges of trans individuals finding recognition and understanding, in a powerful exploration of race and gender against the backdrop of the Northern Irish Troubles.

PASSING

The film depicts the complex relationship between an IRA operative, Fergus, and a trans woman, Dil. Fergus forms an unusual friendship with Jody, a black British soldier held captive by the IRA until his death. Jody shows his minder the picture in his wallet of Dil, his "woman". After Jody dies, Fergus comes to London to find Dil, and the two become involved romantically. To his shock, and initial revulsion, Fergus discovers during a sexual encounter that Dil is a trans woman who has not undergone reassignment surgery. Dil is a hairdresser, and Fergus interrogates her about her colleagues outside her salon:

Fergus: Do they know?

Dil: Know what, honey?

F: Do they know what I know?

D: Know what?

F: Know what I didn't know. Don't call me that.

D: Can't help it, a girl has her feelings.

F: You're not a girl.

D: Details, baby, details…

F: So they do know.

As we can see, Dil is largely unfazed by Fergus' emotional and discombobulated questioning, telling him that gender is a social construct, founded primarily on visible features; and that society's allocations of identity amount to no more than "details". But Fergus remains obsessed with his discovery of her biological sex. In another scene, he goes to a bar frequented by Dil, and tells the barman, who referred to Dil as a she, "She's not a girl." The barman's reaction is uninterested: "Whatever you say," he replies, walking away.

The agony of cis-passing among trans and intersex people is proof that society's labels are not good enough. "Whatever they say" is exactly what should define an individual's identity. Though not without its problems—the film didn't go as far as telling the story from Dil's own perspective, and the ending is far from a happily ever after—*The Crying Game* set down some important ideas and sympathies. Fergus loves Dil, continues their relationship once he has come to accept her trans identity, and ultimately sacrifices himself for her. And all of this is possible for Dil even though she has chosen not to hide her trans identity. As Dil says to Fergus' confused but caring self, "Can't help what I am."

The Third Gender

On the Indian subcontinent, the gender binary has been circumvented since antiquity—in one specific, limited way. The community that we know as hijras represents an official "third gender" category, socially and legally accepted in India, Bangladesh and Pakistan. The three sovereign nations born of the split of British India have long seen transgender people in mainstream culture and even in politics. The hijras are an important part of traditional entertainment, typically cross-dressing men in saris and shalwar kameez, performing with exaggerated "female" gestures—similar to drag queens in the West. But whereas the gender identity of drag queens is not a fundamental requirement of the job—many, for instance, are gay, cis men—the hijras are, and always have been, the only people on the subcontinent recognised as legitimate gender-benders.

The idea of the hijras is not as unusual as it might at first seem. The pressure of a binary status quo around sex often dictates that societies initiate some kind of third term to address those left outside the rigid male/female duality. Intersex, hermaphrodite, androgyne—these are some of the words that have been used in the West, and some Western gender theorists believe that the nineteenth-century European concept of the "invert" (Freud et al.) may not just have been a description of homosexuality, but an early recognition of a third sex. Marjorie Garber again: "The 'third' is that which questions binary thinking and introduces crisis … The 'third' is a mode of articulation, a way of describing a space of possibility."[17] Allowing for another sex or gender concept pushes cultures to make room for empathy for the other, beyond the notion of negative-positive ignition that is said to trigger (pro)creation. In Indian culture, understanding of the hijras and their role descends from that of the eunuchs, and their place in royal politics and culture.

These servants within the emperors' courts and harems literally belonged to a "third sex". It was assumed that, without a fully developed penis, the eunuchs—some intersex from birth, others castrated in early childhood to join the profession—would not be involved in heterosexual activity with the royal women, whether wives or concubines. It was a trusted position that could wield power. The offshoot hijra tradition goes far back, long before the arrival of the British; hijras were deemed to have been endowed with spiritual powers, and were called to bless special occasions such as weddings and house-warmings. The community became a formal institution, led by a "guru" and rules on clothing, public performances and so on. The profession grew quite lucrative at one point, so much so that it grew beyond its original intersex and gender-fluid identity.

Like transitioning in the West, becoming hijra is a long and complex process. The transformation away from maleness follows ancient tradition, today codified in new ways: "First, *hijras* make a pledge to hand over all earnings to the guru, who in exchange supports them inside what is effectively an alternative home as most *hijras* are runaways or evicted by their families."[18] Then comes an elaborate physical transformation. Before the initiates can go out in public as hijras, guru-appointed "pluckers" from the community must get rid of their facial and other unwanted hair in a painful threading process. "Joining this group that traces its roots back to antiquity is not something to be taken lightly."[19]

Today on the Indian subcontinent, the hijras live on the periphery of society. In these societies' cultural consciousness, "hijra" has become an umbrella term for the entire queer community. The hijras' historically auspicious status is rarely recognised, and people no longer call for them to dance and sing at family celebrations. Many resort to begging in busy traffic junctions. Nowadays, rather than the traditionally gender-fluid or intersex people, the majority of the hijras are trans women, gay men, or cis men who like cross-dressing—none of whom could easily live openly in what is still a conservative society. But, as with all passing, adopting a hijra identity is not an escape to complete freedom of selfhood: inherent in the concept of the "third gender" is the idea that one is either male all one's life, or female all one's life, or neither. Biological men who identify as female join the community to live as women, but being hijra does not make the concept of "trans women" acceptable, even for the lucky few who have gone through sexual reassignment surgery.

THE WILD SIDE

In February 2016, I was in the Bangladeshi capital Dhaka to make a BBC documentary when I found myself among a small but confident LGBT community, who took me along to a rally for World Human Rights Day. There was a mood of celebration: the band party—a legacy of the British Raj—came out in their white and red uniform, turbaned with their trumpets, while a decorated elephant bore two huge discs, one on each of its flanks, proclaiming that everyone is equal. I didn't sense any discomfort among the onlookers at many of the participants' nonconventional gender or sexual presentation. There were families with small children who had come to see the rally; street food sellers were noisily trying to entice them with free samples. A trans woman came up to me and put a cap on my head with an embroidered rainbow logo.

Later in the day, I met one of the trans activists who identified as hijra for lunch. Assigned male at birth, the 45-year-old Ananya told me that she had always felt "trapped in the wrong body". Ananya was not born into the hijra community, but joined them in order to live the way she needed to live. She told me that she had no other choice but to identify with the hijras, because she would never be accepted as trans in mainstream society. Ananya was immaculately dressed in a sari. Under the dimmed red lights of too many plastic lanterns in the Chinese restaurant, just to look at her, I would never have known she was trans. Only her voice revealed that she may not have been assigned female at birth.

This made me think that hijras are accepted by society *because* they do not look like "real" women, but instead are seen as their comic impersonators. If we think back to the hate crimes against Brandon Teena and the *Middlesex* protagonist Cal, it seems that what drove their attackers' phobia was the *shock* of discovery: the fear that these individuals in fact made perfectly recognisable men, despite being trans. Does acknowledging the "third gender" create the safety of a buffer zone between a strictly policed male and female, in the same way that the apartheid regime used the category of coloured to keep black and white further apart?

At the time we met, Ananya hadn't had reassignment surgery. Many trans and intersex people's sense of their sex or gender identity is separate from their physical characteristics. What Ananya wanted above all else was to be seen as a woman.

"Beggars can't be choosers", she smiled, and she felt optimistic about the future—she was jubilant over Bangladesh's recent legalisation of the "third gender", showing off her new passport, which bears her female name at last. Ananya believes that this recognition of the hijra community will pave the way for other non-binary people, and queer people more generally: "Bangladesh has a long history of tolerance of individual sexual identity. This is the start of a revolution. The next would be legalisation of the gay and trans communities."

She is not wrong about traditional popular attitudes. Historically, the Indian subcontinent has been more liberal than the West about sexual and gender identity. On a practical level, queer relationships have long been made easier by the fact that there is a kind of tolerance of same-sex proximity: two men or two women hugging or holding hands in public is a common sight, in contrast with the various strict codes of behaviour between heterosexual couples. Meanwhile, the third gender is celebrated in ancient Indian texts like the epic *Mahabharata* and sexual manifesto the *Kama Sutra*. The hijras also appear in medieval Sufi erotic poetry, and in the seventeenth-century Mughal erotic canon.

Lack of understanding and intolerance in fact dates back to the Mother Nation's export of its own sexual morality to British India in the 1860s. Section 377—a legal "transplant" of Britain's 1533 Buggery Act—criminalised non-procreative sexualities; hijras, too, were declared socially deviant. It was then that trans people within the hijra community were forced into either reverting to their birth-assigned sex, or going underground and passing for cis women, with their own secret language and customs. This criminalisation of a gender-fluid community of historical prominence in Indian society led its members to take on gender-restricted appearances, and the subcontinent's mainstream still conforms to this narrow interpretation of sex and gender today.

In Pakistan, where the law to accept the third gender came into effect in 2012, Bindiya Rana was the first trans woman to run for provincial office, and her voice has been loud and clear. She has often said that traditional Pakistani society is more accepting of transgender and transsexual people than the state. Even with the hijra law's acknowledgement that gender is not as simple as a binary, most people living on the subcontinent as hijras—trans women assigned male at birth—are still not supported to live as they wish to. This continues to necessitate a lot of painful subterfuge.

In India, the Supreme Court ruled in 2014 that, in all official papers, transgender, transsexual, eunuch and transvestite communities will once again be recognised as a third gender. There too, however, many of those currently living as hijras are not fully happy with the law. Ananya and her co-activists say it is discriminatory, forcing people who should be known by their chosen gender to perform a prescribed gender category of "other". Campaigners for trans rights say this is another way of controlling and silencing bodily identity—a legacy of colonial-era body-policing.

When law produces identities, identity will inevitably be controlled by law-enforcing authorities. Ananya told me that what she would really like to see one day is more progressive legislation that doesn't label gender by numbers—first, second, third. It would simply recognise the universal human right to difference. "So I can say, without having to add trans or hijra, *I am a woman!*"

7

NOBODY'S BUSINESS BUT OURS

PASSING IN AND OUT OF THE CLOSET

Not No Queer

"'I'm not no queer,' and Jack jumped in with 'Me neither. A one-shot thing. Nobody's business but ours.'"[1]

From Nebraska to Dhaka, we have seen how societies' intolerance of genderqueerness has forced trans people to pass as cis; so it should come as no surprise that homophobia has also pushed non-hetero individuals to pass as straight. Our cultures' distrust of variations in sexuality has only recently transformed from recognition of a single acceptable identity—straight—into a qualified reception of yet another binary: first assigning most people the label "heterosexual" and a small minority "homosexual", then expanding the conceptions and definitions of queerness to include, for instance, "bisexual" or "fluid"—but these "alternative" sexual identities are still defined against the norm of straightness. While growing numbers of people today view sexuality not as a binary, but as a spectrum, the mainstream has not shaken off the idea of "sexual minorities", again establishing a standard, privileged identity from which some people's identity deviates, at a cost to their social status.

Society's preoccupation with who we have sex with—which strangely echoes historical policing of inter-racial relationships, and has its present-day mirror image in transphobic people's obsession with genitals—has made either partial or full-time straight-passing a pre-requisite for countless individuals. Given our reliance on the *absence* of visual cues to label someone as "straight", it might seem that sexuality passing is a lot easier than race-passing or gender-passing; but, as for trans people cis-passing, the fallout can be terrible. The straight-passer is motivated by an internalised shame: the deep fear of being shamed by society and bringing shame on their family, if their true identity is exposed. This is different from the external degradation dreaded and avoided by people of colour race-passing, or women male-passing. But those hiding their sexuality may also feel shame at their denial of self, an emotion felt by many passers.

We have seen again and again in this book that passing is driven by limitations placed on one's life because of one's identity: depending on how severe these limitations are, passing is sometimes about freedom of choice, and sometimes freedom from fear. But often straight-passers are subjected to more severe moral judgement than others who have assumed an identity. In a seriously homophobic society, it is physically safer to simply pretend to be straight; and, as the opening quote above suggests, in less hostile places it is widely accepted that society should have no say or interest in how we live sexually. Yet, much of the time, when we talk about sexual passing—in life and in art—we do so from a starting assumption that, if you are sexually queer, the "right" or best thing for you to do is to "come out" to society as a whole and to live openly—regardless of the consequences, and regardless of the realities of your relationship.

This idea frames the narrative and drives the tension of one of the most famous fictions of straight-passing: the short story "Brokeback Mountain" by the American author Annie Proulx (1997). Here, we meet two Wyoming country boys and high school dropouts, Jack Twist and Ennis del Mar, who are spending the summer of 1963 working on the eponymous fictional mountain grazing sheep. During these isolated, idyllic days, they form a sexual relationship that is to last even after they part ways, get married and have children. Throughout the years, each is haunted by the ferocity of their attraction for each other during that first summer, and over the decades they manage to meet on remote campsites or in anonymous motel rooms, to relive that brief and intense emotional experience.

These clandestine liaisons are described by Proulx in understated, economical prose, interludes organically woven by the two men into their long stretches of straight-passing as husbands, fathers, ranch hands, friends and neighbours in their insular rural communities. The sparse language of the narration reflects a key theme of the story, and of our chapter here: the normality of silence, and the power of speech, in sexual identity. The protagonists of "Brokeback Mountain" do not talk about their sexuality, except in a sentence or two as quoted above. In that exchange, they are questioning whether or not their sexual orientation should be a matter of social or family concern. While they agree that what they do is personal and private, there is also a suggestion that what they do is not who they are.

When Ennis declares, "I'm not no queer," and Jack agrees, "Me neither," they are saying, to themselves, each other and American society as a whole, that they can fully conform to straight identity and perform a social persona as tough American men—herders of sheep in the wilds, good family men. While Jack and Ennis start out on the same page in their separate pursuits of a straight life, their growing difference over whether or not they can live this way drives the story's tension, and the men's relationship to breaking point.

The fear of homophobia runs through the story, with its multiple implicit references to the "tire iron" of the lynch mob; it seems like there is no way for Jack and Ennis to express their homosexuality except up the mountain, away from society. In the "real world", there's no one like them around; so they put away the idea that being gay is "like them". Ennis is even very attached to his wife, Alma, and their two daughters. "Brokeback Mountain" explores what it looks like when sexuality is not permitted to impact someone's sense of themselves—in mid-century rural America, that means their sense of themselves as a man:

> Ennis and Jack don't depart in any substantial way from the boundaries that define socially constructed norms of gender, and indeed … they exemplify many of the characteristics that Americans associate with the dominant ideal of masculinity, but both must confront and struggle with a society in which homosexuality is equated with unacceptable gender behaviour.[2]

These behaviours are not calculated. By passing as "normal" strong American cowboys, they are not putting on a conscious show so much as avoiding accepting an important part of their identities that they have been programmed by their cultures to fear, to be ashamed of. But, towards the end of the story, after repeated disagreements over whether they should take steps towards a greater commitment to the relationship, Jack has formed an intention to express his gay identity, or at least fulfil his sexual desire with other men when Ennis is unable to offer him more than just "a couple a high-altitude fucks once or twice a year".[3] Even now, he is performing normative masculinity, expressing his distress in terms of a man's sexual "needs".

But, in at least some limited way, Jack wants to stop passing as straight. He has pushed for them to start a ranch together, without success, and now suggests eloping to Mexico. Perhaps more significantly, by referring to his desire for other men, he has broken the covenant of Brokeback Mountain: that their sexual encounters are contained to their relationship and have no broader meaning for their identity. Ennis reminds Jack of this, that they have not even dared to declare their sexuality to each other. He tells Jack, "'I got a say this to you one time, Jack, and I ain't foolin. What I don't know,' said Ennis, 'all them things I don't know could get you killed if I should come to know them.'"[4]

Ennis is vocally in denial—he has perfected his straight act, and even during their "once or twice a year" meetings, he tells his lover Jack that what they're doing should not have a name, ever. In the words of American literature professor Eric Patterson,

> For Ennis, loving another man has to be reduced to being a part of his life that can be kept separate and hidden, confined to certain times and certain places by boundaries that prevent it from intruding on the awareness of others—and of Ennis himself—and contradicting his identity and status as a supposedly normal heterosexual man.[5]

Jack threatens Ennis' need to hold onto his social status as "not no queer". Ennis's world collapses as his passing for "normal" is jeopardised by his lover's demands for acknowledgement. He lashes out at Jack, attacking him with "the force of narcissistic homophobia"[6] as the external social violence working upon both men manifests in Ennis' anger at Jack's audacity. He will have none of Jack's tomfoolery, trying to give expression to what had always been "nobody's business" but theirs.

Ennis has internalised his own homophobia such that he sees his sexuality as a problem—but one he has long since resigned himself to: "if you can't fix it you got a stand it."[7] To him, this means keeping it inside, and never sharing it with the world. But Jack can't stand it anymore, and he has a different understanding of how to "fix" the problem—not by getting rid of his homosexuality as Ennis would prefer to do, but by embracing a more open, truthful identity. In the end, Ennis's warnings that public knowledge of Jack's homosexuality may destroy him are borne out, as the fearful imagining of the tire iron makes a final appearance; as with Nella Larsen's character Clare Kendry—another passer backed into a corner, with nobody left to accept her for who she really was—the circumstances of Jack's death are left shrouded in ambiguity.

In the next story, we shall learn about two young people who did make the decision that they could not bear to live a lie, throwing off their passing to be together; "going to Mexico". But we will also see that such a transformation in identification isn't easy, in a hostile world looking to "fix" gay people.

Women in Love

The artist Sophie Green, describing her adolescent gender dysphoria, told me in that Liverpool pub: "it's like I didn't really have the language, I didn't know myself what it was. The thought of saying then that 'I think I am a female' was a step too far. I just wanted to tell people I was different, I [was] working it out, you know." This process of coming to identify as trans went on for fifteen years, until Sophie was in her late twenties. She thought, "Why couldn't I have got here sooner? Why didn't I figure this out earlier?" The answer is simple: there was no visibility.

Sophie was a 13-year-old school student when the UK's queerphobic "Section 28" of the Local Government Act was introduced. The Act prohibited the publication or use in education of any material encouraging "the acceptability of homosexuality as a pretend family relationship". This was the spring of 1988—"exactly the time when I needed people to tell me what was going on in the world, and I didn't get anything," Sophie recalls. "And I never asked because I was scared. I thought this was not a good thing to be."

Just as Sophie was forced to keep her dysphoria to herself without knowing what it was, homophobic social environments have also forced some gay people to pass as straight, regardless of whether they have the language to know that this is what they are doing. Wherever queerness is treated as a dirty secret to be swept under the rug, there will be queer people living in the shadows—even if neither they nor their persecutors could articulate this. I've seen this for myself in south-western Bangladesh.

This is the story of two young women in a traditional society: a Hindu merchant's eldest daughter, Puja, and her Muslim private tutor, Sanjida, who fell in love in January 2013. It is also a story of multiple transformations and transgressions encompassing not only sexuality, but also religion and class or caste. Their secret relationship, which eventually became headline news, challenged a culture that was not prepared to face two village women's sexual revolution.

In the sleepy town of Pirojpur, nothing much happens beyond the mundane sound of rickshaw bells, Muslim calls to prayer and evening chants from the Hindu temple complex. Sanjida, 20, had come to this small town from her village to complete her studies, and rented a room from a Hindu potato merchant who lived with his family near the temple complex. When I was making a film of her story in 2016, she described to me the moment she fell in love with her student. Puja was brushing her hair in the mirror, with her back to Sanjida and the string fastenings of her blouse dangling loosely at her back. The emotions churning inside were not alien to Sanjida, who had had a brief relationship with a married woman a year or so earlier; but she had no means of expressing the ideas of "coming out" or having a sexual orientation. For Sanjida, the first step on her journey to identity, before putting a label on it, had been discovering for herself who she was. At the time, "Neither I nor Puja knew the word 'lesbian'", she told me.

For Puja, the world would never be the same again. She was melting inside, in a tumult of self-discovery. This sexual awakening was shattering, in a conservative society that considered gayness "deviant": not that the two young women knew it, but in 2016 Xulhaz Mannan, senior editor of Bangladesh's first LGBT magazine, was brutally murdered. If she wanted to survive in her community, Puja would now have to join Sanjida in a life of heteronormative performance. This would be straightforward for her in practical terms: Puja was perfectly "feminine", dressing in a traditional sari or shalwar kameez; her long black hair arranged in a plait with a bow at the end, her large eyes kohl-lined, her skin scented with coconut oil. Sanjida, on the other hand, dressed androgynously; her mother referred to them when I spoke to her as "boys' clothes". She was often mistaken for a hijra.

Sanjida was never in the slightest doubt about her gender identity; she was definitely a woman who liked women. But her choice of clothing confused people, partly due to the fact that her society was in denial of lesbianism. The mid-nineteenth-century British colonial law Section 377 had banned homosexuality, specifically "carnal intercourse against the order of nature"; but women were exempt from it, mainly because lesbian sex did not, forensically speaking, fall under the "Buggery Act" that had outlawed gay male sex in the mother country since the time of Henry VIII. In other words, even if people weren't quite sure what to make of Sanjida, it certainly didn't occur to them that she was a gay woman. She too could hide in plain sight.

In a society with no formal, public articulation of homosexuality, Sanjida and Puja also had to wrap their heads around their relationship themselves. Given the way they each dressed, I tried to explain the butch/femme concept to Sanjida. She seemed surprised that this aspect of herself had a name in the West. Puja liked the way she dressed, she explained, and she herself liked the idea of "male role-play" for Puja's enjoyment. I wondered if this was a way for Puja to remain in denial that she was with another woman. Were Puja and Sanjida subconsciously passing as their own socially constructed, deeply ingrained heteronormative conception of a married couple? We will explore this idea—of women performing masculinity to obtain sexual freedom in homophobic societies—in Chapter 10.

In any case, Puja knew that she had found the love of her life—but, while secretly seeing Sanjida, she was forced to keep up a public persona as a young lady preparing for an imminent arranged marriage, to a man selected by her family. Unlike Sanjida, who belonged to the rural peasantry, Puja's husband would have to be a good caste match: she came from the moneyed *kayastho* caste of traders. She was being shown around to various matchmakers, and went along with the process so as not to raise suspicion around her "real" marriage, which society could not acknowledge. In order to make vows to each other, Sanjida had agreed to conform to Puja's idea: to marry in the "Brahmo way", with Hindu rites. One day they set out for the temple for an unofficial marriage ceremony, exchanging garlands of flowers with the gods as their witnesses.

Such a vow would have been valid if made by a heterosexual couple. Puja and Sanjida performed it above all to convince themselves that their union, once confessed before the gods, would be sanctified and sealed by divine blessing, even if socially it was criminalised. Initially they thought they could carry on this way, like in a romantic story of forbidden love. Puja would go into her married life, but the women would continue to see each other secretly whenever they could. Puja even felt a strange kind of pride in the fact that she had received multiple proposals of marriage—a definite ego-booster for a young woman in her society. Puja, I was told, was basking in it, and I kind of believed it. As if in order to join the queue of suitors, Sanjida adopted "male" social behaviours: not only the gender-neutral clothes, but also a "male gait", as Jeffrey Eugenides' Cal adopted in *Middlesex*; an uninhibited, outgoing temperament; a louder laugh.

But the pressure of this double life and the weight of secrecy became increasingly unbearable. They eloped, soon after their secret "marriage". Like the race- and gender-passing figures we've seen, they travelled to enable their identity transition. They moved to a big city and rented a place together, in the hope that here, they could lead a more peaceful life: no one would know them, or raise suspicion at two women sharing a room—a lesbian relationship was not what people would normally think, in a culture where physical proximity between same-sex people is commonplace. This was the perfect cover: two working women, labour migrants from the countryside, sharing a room to save money. Just as the escaped slave Ellen Craft and the trans pioneer Lili Elbe would switch between public personas and a safe private life where they did not have to pass, the couple from Bangladesh shut themselves every night in their one-room lodging house to be their real selves, the women in love.

In conservative rural societies such as Puja's and Sanjida's, homosexuality is typically seen as a "sickness". Sanjida's family had known about her "possession" since she was a teenager, and had tried to get rid of it behind closed doors; but when that failed, she had been allowed to remain in the family home, and later to go out into the world and pursue her education independently. This isn't as unusual in rigid, conservative, buttoned-up cultures as you might think. Naomi Alderman's 2006 novel *Disobedience*, and the film adaptation released in 2017, follow Ronit Krushka, the estranged bisexual daughter of an Orthodox rabbi, as she returns to her family in North London after her father's death. There she meets her former lesbian lover, Esti—their romance, and its uncovering by the community, was what forced Ronit into exile in the first place. But now Esti is passing as straight, as if it never happened: she is married to the rabbi's chosen young successor. Because she has agreed to bury her gay side, she has been allowed to take up a place at the very heart of her community.

For many gay people in rural Bangladesh, so long as they keep their sexual orientation a family secret, or to themselves, they are likely to be left alone. But Puja's family had no idea of her sexuality—how would they, when she hadn't known herself before meeting Sanjida? By eloping, she had outed herself to her family. When I met them, it was clear that they believed Sanjida was a deviant who had drawn Puja into a "brain-polluting" scheme where she had done the inexplicable: leaving the chance of a good marriage, to a man with money and a house, to be with a "crazy person pretending to be a woman." Puja couldn't have made such an aberrant decision independently. When Puja failed to return home one day after her visit to the temple, her father had gone to the local police station and reported his daughter's disappearance as a case of abduction. She and Sanjida found themselves fugitives from law in the big city, like Ellen and William Craft, who were not only running away from their slave-masters, but also from the bounty-hunters out to catch them and bring them back to their former lives.

If they had been men, Sanjida and Puja would have been pursued and tried under Section 377. But the authorities were not sure how to deal with an openly same-sex relationship between two women. So Puja's family came up with an ingenious plan, Sanjida told me.

They tweaked Puja's age to make her under eighteen, a minor in Bangladesh. Sanjida was made to look not just like an abductor, but a child-abductor. Police found the women in their lodging house. A reluctant Puja was reunited with her family and married off to the man her family had chosen for her—a policeman. When I saw Puja's sister, Shipra, she claimed that Puja was far from faking this happy marriage; the fake life had been the one she'd been lured to by Sanjida, a wicked woman pretending to be a man. Sanjida was thrown in jail.

At this stage of her remarkable life, Sanjida, only in her early twenties, faced cruelty reminiscent of the treatment Brandon Teena had received two decades earlier in Falls City, Nebraska, at the hands of the "friends" who had stripped him in a locked bathroom to establish his "real" sex. The worst thing that happened to Sanjida in jail, she said, was not the fact that she was a prisoner, but the humiliation of intrusive physical examinations by her jailers to check if she was a man or a woman. She was subjected to this three times, as female police officers randomly touched her and laughed at her, telling her that her female genitalia proved that she had pretended to be a man to destroy the life of an innocent woman. Other inmates joined in these "inspections" and mocked her vulgarly, repeatedly taunting her that "her face looked so innocent, why was her mind so ugly." This was so shameful to bear, Sanjida told me, that she wanted to die. She contemplated suicide often.

Puja, in a prison of her own—powerless to stop her imminent marriage—gave a brave statement to local journalists, who were fascinated by the women's love story. She said she had asked the police who'd caught them, "If a male can love a female, why couldn't a female love another female?"[8] Why couldn't she and Sanjida be together and live a married life just like others, since they truly believed their union had been sanctified by the vows they took before the gods at Pirojpur's Shiva temple? When their story first came out, it made headlines as "the first lesbian marriage in Bangladesh". But the women themselves refused to label their union with any such terminology. They kept saying that they hadn't known there were specific words to describe their passion for each other, that they just wanted to live their life like other "normal" couples. Nevertheless, Puja's open declaration of same-sex love made history in a conservative country, and was seen as inspirational nationwide.

Sanjida too has been praised by campaigners; I wrote at the time that she was being hailed Bangladesh's "natural born pioneer of gay rights."[9] Women's rights activists secured her bail, allowing her to return to her village in a remote area of Bangladesh. When I went to see her in 2016—three years after her brief marriage to Puja—I was warmly invited into her modest family home, tin-roofed, mud-floored and sparsely furnished. Even now that Sanjida's sexuality was a matter of public record, she was not ostracised from her family; but they still firmly believed that she had a problem: "a man problem" or "hormone issues". Over our cups of sweet, stewed milky tea, one of her uncles even wondered if she was possessed by a wily djinn.

I have heard this before in India and Bangladesh, the invocation of an evil spirit as an explanation of people's nonconforming sexual or gender identities; also of those—mostly women—having extra-marital affairs. As Sanjida's mother said goodbye to me, chewing betel leaf, she went on murmuring under her breath that her daughter had "become sick" when she was much younger, "possessed" at the age of 13 or 14. "We took her to mullahs and healers, but the djinn would not leave her." The religious healers gave her amulets to wear, with prayer parchments inside. Sanjida's religious relatives had also tried to instil in her the fear of God, to distract her from her "deviance". "But nothing cured her," said Sanjida's mother.

That said, this is far from an exclusively Bengali, Indian, Hindu or Muslim way of looking at things. Across the world, intolerant cultures that refuse to recognise or pretend not to believe in homosexuality attempt to "fix" their gay children. From brainwashing camps to Talmudic school to electroshock therapy, tales of attempted "gay conversion" abound in radical Islamic, fundamentalist Christian and Orthodox Jewish communities, for instance. The common theme running through all such stories is an attempt—a belief that it is possible—to "reprogramme" the individual's identity so that they can fit into their society's norms. Of course, it doesn't work.

Having failed to obliterate her homosexuality, Sanjida's family's ultimate solution was to keep that part of her under close guard. When she was younger, Sanjida had accepted and gone along with this. It turns out that she had even agreed to an arranged marriage before she finished school: to straight-pass outside the home, as Puja was now being forced to. But life as a married woman had been "the biggest fakery" she'd ever performed, Sanjida told me. She was forced to fool not only herself, but also her husband and the entire community. She had fled from that life, and she had met Puja. Now she was back home, and so long as she continued to pass in public, her family could accept her. One of her devoutly religious relatives, another uncle who is a *hafez*—someone who has memorised the Quran—said to me that he was not terribly worried. After all, "What can happen between two women in bed?"

Sanjida's fury at his comments was expressed in open outbursts, as if in these moments she became her rage, and felt doubly determined to establish her identity: "I am not a man, nor will I ever be. I am 100% a woman. If my country ever legalises same-sex marriage, I'll be the first one to come forward."[10] As I watched her in all her outspokenness and steadfastness, I couldn't help wondering where she'd got her courage from, being born in a family and a village where no one has ever heard of such a concept as "gay".

The story of Sanjida and Puja shows us that, although labels are powerful, so can be their absence. On the positive side, while putting a name to an identity can help to campaign for rights and recognition, a culture that isn't able to talk about a particular identity can, in practice, lessen social stigma and facilitate acceptance of non-conformist individuals, in limited forms. In the West, the LGBTQ community has long fought for open expression of, and equal opportunity for, the labels behind the acronym. Legally, that battle is increasingly won. But the popular currency and legislating of ideas like "sexuality" and "gay" haven't protected LGBTQ people from alienation. There are many tales of people being disowned by their family after coming out, and unspoken tensions or feelings of betrayal and incomprehension even after reconciliation decades later—your parents knowing what a lesbian is won't stop them throwing you out of the house for being one, if that is how they feel about it.

The very act of disowning a queer family member implies an understanding that nothing can be done about their queerness; normally, it is the end of the relationship. Puja and Sanjida's families allowed them to be persecuted and punished for their sexuality, but in their case that wasn't the end of the story. Both were taken back into the family even after they revealed their relationship in the national media. Instead of lack of acceptance, these young women have faced a lack of comprehension. On a day-to-day basis, the very fact that their true identity is literally unspeakable protects them—so long as they choose to participate in the family's polite fiction by passing.

And this is the disturbing side of a world with no language to describe an identity: refusal to acknowledge gayness can be just as damaging and imprisoning as attempts to curb it. Puja and Sanjida may have been accepted back into the family home, but they have also been stuffed back into the closet—Puja condemned to a heterosexual marriage, and Sanjida (who refuses to countenance such an arrangement) to a lonely life among a family who can't understand her nature. One way or another, their homosexuality has been cancelled. Puja has been bound by a heteronormative institution to a heteronormative life; Sanjida's sexuality only comes up at home in the context of attempts to "cure" her, and otherwise silence must reign. This is conditional tolerance at best: we can accept your self-definition, if you don't shame us by taking it into society.

Possessed by a Dybbuk, or Love?

Puja is far from the only queer person who has agreed to marry—and inevitably straight-pass—to maintain her family's honour and her own position in society. In her culture, it would have been bad enough had she run away with a man; after eloping with a woman, the only way to avoid being outcast was to make reparations by complying with a return to tradition—a return to belonging. The lie of Puja's "perfect" marriage arranged by her parents made me think of another marriage, in another world. Although aeons apart in geographical and cultural terms, the two stories are similar in their interweaving of gender, sexuality, religion and class, and in revealing unions that are not entirely as they seem.

Isaac Bashevis Singer's "Disguised", published in 1986 in *The New Yorker*, is about a young yeshiva student, Pinchosl, who marries a rich, beautiful young woman, Temerl, according to their parents' wishes. However, within a month of their traditional religious wedding, Pinchosl disappears. Temerl, both families and the couple's friends fail to understand why a nice young Hasidic man would do such a thing, particularly as his bride would not be able to remarry under Jewish law until he divorced her—or unless she could prove he was dead. When Temerl turns nineteen, she sets off with a maid from her little hometown to travel around Greater Poland in search of Pinchosl. She stops at many places, until she arrives in a town called Kalisz, where she sees a woman buying eggs in the marketplace.

The woman looks vaguely familiar; she bears a strange resemblance to Temerl's lost husband, Pinchosl. And, when Temerl notices that the woman's face is not smooth—that she has fuzzy facial hair, perhaps a beard—she realises that this is no woman. This is Pinchosl. Temerl chases after him into a run-down muddy alley. The long-lost spouse admits in an emotional voice, "Yes, I am Pinchosl." Temerl, in her bewilderment, asks, "Are you mad? Possessed by a dybbuk?" In Jewish folklore a dybbuk is a wily, wandering spirit, like the djinn held responsible for Sanjida's homosexuality; it takes over the body of a morally weak mortal. Pinchosl explains that she (the pronoun used by Singer) is living in Kalisz with a man. At this, Temerl expresses utter shock and repeats, "With a man?" To which Pinchosl says, "I am not a man anymore, not really, not for you."[11]

They walk together to Pinchosl's house. Sitting there with a glass of soda and homemade pretzel, Temerl learns more about the woman who was once her husband. Now she feels a strange kind of sisterhood welling up inside her as Pinchosl introduces Temerl to Elkonah, a fellow yeshiva scholar and the man Pinchosl now lives with. The two had eloped and found "truth" in the little town of Kalisz, where they lived as man and wife. Temerl stoically hears the person still legally her husband say that she never wanted to marry her; it was always Elkonah that Pinchosl was in love with.

With "deceptive simplicity", Singer depicts Pinchosl's physical and emotional transgression.[12] In Deuteronomy, cross-dressing is a most profane act for a Jew; but, tired of living with lies in a false marriage, Pinchosl has finally decided to come out of his closet. But this isn't a triumphant declaration to the world as we often understand "coming out" today. The philosopher of sex Raja Halwani explains:

[the closet] can have two functions. In the case of an individual trying to determine her life in a homophobic society, the closet can function as a protective shield, especially when important goods are threatened. But in cases in which the only reason for hiding is shame, the closet functions perniciously: it assaults the dignity of the individual, renders her identity invisible, compromises her integrity, and has the net effect of forcing her to lead a morally compromised life.[13]

Pinchosl has effectively come out of one of these closets, but not the other. Married to Temerl while in love with Elkonah, he was deeply anguished by this "morally compromised life". He left to live with his lover in a personal embracing of gayness. But the only way they could share this life was as man and wife. To justify this decision to remain socially "in the closet", Pinchosl, once a devout student of the Jewish rabbinical seminary, refers to the Talmud, explaining to Temerl the double meaning of cross-dressing as a source of both shame and liberation.

> "According to the Talmud, when a man is overcome by the evil spirit and knows of no way out he should wrap himself in black garments and go to a place where he is not known and do what his heart desires.
>
> "This is what we did—Elkonah and I."[14]

Where straight-passing requires some kind of gender-passing, then this can complicate the normally one-way direction of passing, from an underprivileged status to a privileged one. In crossing over to a female persona, Pinchosl has gone from life as a man enriched by his wife's dowry to life as a poor pretzel-seller. And by invoking "her" religious text to defend the secret relationship, Pinchosl defies any simplistic idea of the moral imperative to "come out of the closet" in order to be true to oneself. Everything about this choice of new self raises challenging questions about the nature of "integrity" or a "true self" for the character. As the gender and sexuality studies scholar Daniel Silvermint puts it,

> Intersectional differences help shape the specific balance of benefits and burdens, which affects the morality of pursuing or avoiding them in turn ... the lived realities of some individuals at

the margins have the potential to upend standard arguments about passing.[15]

Singer's short story covers a whole range of identity shifts, and he addresses head-on the ways in which these come together in a morally complicated tale of transformation. As we saw with the pansexual Sophie and the gender-fluid Jess in Chapter 6, these intersections and dilemmas mean that sometimes individuals prefer to remain ambiguous. Pinchosl's comment to Temerl—"I am not a man anymore, not really, not for you"—leaves the reader wondering: is he a gay man, or a trans woman? We know for sure that, by marrying Temerl under social pressure, Pinchosl had been passing as straight; but was he also passing as a cis man?

Singer leaves the answer tantalisingly vague, as if to say: is this character's gender identity really important? Why do you feel you need to know the answer in order to understand them or their story? If Pinchosl feels within herself that her chosen exile is an authentic life, can't we take her word for it? Nobody's business but theirs.

Macaulay's Gay Child

Daniel Silvermint has more to say that complicates our understanding of what "living authentically" means for gay people, with specific relation to passing: "consider the double bind that authenticity presents for groups like queer femmes, who pass as straight precisely by being themselves."[16] In a heteronormative world, anyone who does not have an appearance or mannerisms specifically associated with gayness will be assumed straight unless and until they show up with a same-sex partner on their arm. Women like Puja, for example, whose lack of stereotypically "lesbian" or "butch" clothes and hairstyle mean that she outwardly presents as straight; but others caught in this quandary of misapprehension include bisexuals who happen to be in a straight relationship—and so cannot even be "outed" by their partner's gender—or simply any person on the queer spectrum who presents heteronormatively and keeps their private life to themselves. The rights and wrongs of addressing society's false assumptions in such situations are far from clear-cut.

Chris Gunness, a broadcaster and former United Nations spokesperson in the Middle East, is half-Trinidadian Indian and half-white English, and has always identified as gay. At a glance, he appears white with a lot of freckles—he likes to joke that his so-called Creator didn't shake the DNA jar hard enough to make him fully white or fully brown. However, it was not just racial ambiguity that Chris battled against growing up; his struggle to define his identity was challenged just as much by his sexuality and the choices he seemed to face about how to live with that identity. As he grappled with life in post-colonial Trinidad, and later British boarding school and the University of Oxford, he found himself passing as straight.

"I don't have camp mannerisms," Chris told me, "so it didn't occur to people I could be homosexual." Like Ennis and Jack in "Brokeback Mountain", Chris exhibits the expected amount of stereotypical "masculinity" in his behaviours and appearance, allowing him to pass as heterosexual. But, just like Ennis, Chris always felt that sense of "twoness", that he needed to be one sort of man to his family and friends, and another sort of man to the men he loved. "Being in this situation," Eric Patterson explains in his commentary on Proulx's story, "requires constantly holding back the deepest part of yourself from the people who love you, and who you've committed yourself to love."[17]

Chris's straight-passing in his youth intersected with the fluidity of his race, class and to some extent religious identity. His father's family—his Indian family—had arrived in Trinidad, then a British plantation colony, under Sir John Gladstone's "indentured labourers" scheme in the mid-nineteenth century. Gladstone, father of the British Premier William Gladstone, received the largest sum of any awarded by the Slave Compensation Commission in 1837. Compelled to get rid of more than 2,000 African slaves on his Caribbean estates after abolition in 1833, Gladstone imported indentured servants from India, lured into indebtedness that could be paid off through labour with the promise of schooling, among other opportunities. In reality, the living and working conditions of the British Empire's indentured labourers weren't much better than those of the unpaid slaves who had preceded them.

Some on the Indian side of the family hadn't approved of Chris's father marrying a white girl. In those early days, as

Trinidad approached independence in 1962, there were still distinct socio-racial divides: the whites with their swimming pool parties; blacks with their history of slavery; and the Indian descendants of indentured labourers, a proud and closed community with their own culture and tradition: "As a freckled child going between the white and Indian communities, I was either a little white kid, or was trying *not* to be a little white kid. So I became really an expert on passing."[18]

Given his appearance, what Chris calls passing here others might call code-switching, which we'll explore more in Chapter 10. But he clearly learnt early on how to blend in with different social and cultural groups. This would become rather handy when Chris discovered his sexual orientation, he tells me:

> As soon as I became sexually aware, I knew that I was gay ... Of course I didn't express it. Then I was sent to a private school in England, where although I did gay things with other boys, the question of being openly gay did not arise ... In fact there wasn't ever a particular moment when I declared my sexual identity to the universe.[19]

This tendency not just to move between identities, but to avoid expressing an identity altogether, was closely tied to the aspirations of Chris's family. His parents wanted their son to be Western-educated to internalise "proper" upper-class behaviour, a signal of whiteness and Englishness.

Chris's maternal grandmother was horrified when she found a tape of Chris as Oliver Twist in the school musical—she'd had no idea that he had played the starring role. It turned out that Chris's mother had avoided inviting her to the play, in what Chris diagnosed to me as "a classic case of class-passing on my mother's part": she hadn't wanted her mother, with her strong Hampshire accent, showing up at the public school and giving away the family's working-class origins. Meanwhile, Chris's Indian relatives were looking to overcome the stain of their forebears' untouchability back on the subcontinent, and their hopes were for Chris to be one of "Macaulay's Children"—a term used for Westernised individuals of Indian ancestry who hide or reject their heritage. The family had converted to Christianity after arriving in Trinidad. "I didn't allow my coloured identity to find any expression. I became very good at internal deracination." Chris's first act of passing was therefore about denying both sides of his family, getting his scholarships and using them as a gateway to upper-class whiteness. With an anglicised surname, Gunness—from Indian "Ganesh"—he was comfortable in his new skin.

Building on this foundation of denying or distancing himself from his Indian and class/caste roots, Chris became very good at hiding his sexuality too. Of course, Lord Macaulay's Indian Penal Code of 1862 had been copied and pasted for Trinidad and many other British colonies, including Section 377 and its criminalisation of homosexuality. Chris was facing the same British-instituted homophobia as Puja and Sanjida on the other side of the world. Back at home in the Caribbean, he used to go to concerts regularly, and he won a choral scholarship to Oxford. One of his cousins, who was a pianist, could not play Elton John because the singer was known to be gay. Wealthy people in Trinidad were telling entertainers they could not play Elton John at their parties. "If you discovered Mozart was gay, would you stop listening to his music? That was the kind of world I was born into."

But Chris says that he has witnessed homophobia and racism mainly in the institutions of the Western establishment where he found himself from early adolescence: first the English boarding school, then Oxford, followed by the BBC, all the way to the United Nations, where he became head of communications in the Middle East. "Homophobia and racism exist big-time in elitist organisations. Elitist organisations, and people in them, can often be quite illiberal."

In his days in the 1980s, Chris told me, the World Service newsroom in London was run by people who were openly "sexist, racist and homophobic", both individually and institutionally. One of his bosses used to call him "Kid Chocolate". The World Service, still a bunch of "largely white people ... in charge of largely non-white people" in Chris's day, was specifically set up as a "soft power" propaganda arm of the British Empire. No surprise, then, that it represented and mostly still reflects Britain's former colonial power structures: white upper-class heteronormative men, presiding over a workforce descended from African slaves, Asian indentured labourers and other colonised peoples. "The funny thing is," Chris remarked to me, "the head of the department, always a white man, was ridiculously called a 'controller'—what was he controlling? A building full of black and brown people from the former colonies?"

As for the homophobia, it was strange, Chris told me, because a lot of the newsreaders were gay, yet

> I remember any time a gay story came up, there were titters around the newsroom … I kept quiet. I don't have a camp exterior, it was very easy for me to pass on the sexuality thing, I could just pretend to be straight. I didn't have to lie about anything, I would just sit there and hear the talk of homophobia. I would feel deeply conflicted and wounded, it was a difficult and painful thing.

Here we encounter a new form of "passing"—passing up the opportunity to intervene in people's normative assumptions and declare a "minority" identity. But this wasn't just a passive response on Chris's part; in order to deflect people's attention from his sexuality, he actively projected other characteristics

> that people could latch onto, to like and respect about me; I was the BBC's UN correspondent, I covered revolutions and uprisings that ended the Cold War. It is even painful to say this, but you know, it was like, "In spite of being gay, he is still an amazing journalist", that kind of thing people would say who found out I was gay.[20]

A lot of what Chris was going through, passing as straight or trying to earn people's respect "despite" his gayness, was "self-inflicted, because that's what the repressive colonial administrations do, they teach you to learn how to hate yourself … I am just very good at playing the White Man's game." His family had been playing the same game, with both sides trying to hide their low-born ancestry and perform an idealised English respectability; and we'll learn much more about this game in Chapter 10.

Chris continued to effortlessly pass at work, right up to his career at the UN, almost exclusively posted in the Middle East for a decade and a half as Director of Strategic Communications—until he met his now husband Ari, an Israeli Jew, who had just come out after decades of marriage to a woman with whom he had two children. Chris and Ari married within the year. This upset some in Chris's close professional circle, and the news travelled to Gaza, where Chris was now spending the majority of his time working for UNRWA, the UN agency supporting Palestinian refugees. He had always been careful not to disturb Gaza's deeply conservative society, but the leaked news about his wedding soon found its breeding ground on social media, and a death threat was issued by Islamists. His "offence" in the eyes of that faction was double-edged: first, he had turned out to be gay; second, he had married the enemy, an Israeli.

> The head of the UN in Gaza called me up to say, you can't come here because there are credible threats against [your] life. It was properly investigated by the UN investigations unit at UNRWA: they found out that a person in the education department [had] leaked this about my sexuality.[21]

At this point in our conversation, Chris drops a baffling piece of information: the UN did not take action against this person, trying to contain the talk of homosexuality within the organisation—because the line manager himself was passing as straight, and did not want any further media attention drawn for fear of him personally suffering homophobia. "He was afraid of being outed, which was what happened in the end in any case."

Chris now lives openly with his husband, in the UK. He says: "The great thing about releasing information is that it becomes someone else's responsibility. If they can't deal with the information, then that's their problem." Chris has finally found peace with himself; though he could have continued hiding his many selves from those in his life, he now tells people that he is a member of the BAME community; that his father's family were Untouchables in India; that, although he had a Christian education, he is also half-Hindu.

In many ways, Chris's story is a perfect example of the complexities and dilemmas of a heteronormative world. On the one hand, he ultimately found his forced outing freeing, and has turned it into a positive evolution in his relationship with his identity—a "happy ending" that fits with today's instinctive value-judgements about coming out versus "staying in the closet". Yet Chris's "outing" experience also shows the moral and practical limits of prioritising abstract ideas of integrity or authenticity as the key to happiness. Before that happy ending, his very worst fears did actually come true: his life was endangered when his sexuality became public in his place of work, vindicating his decision to pass for so long.

Once that had happened, Chris couldn't and didn't challenge institutionalised homophobia in a place where his identity was a grave crime against social decency. Nor did he want to draw negative attention to a city ravaged by decades of war by remaining as an international figurehead for besieged sexualities. His only choice, once outed in Gaza, was to move somewhere he could live without fear; his personal happiness didn't result from a determined struggle to live openly no matter the context. Jack and Ennis of "Brokeback Mountain", and many who support gay rights, might feel that it's nobody else's business who we're sexually attracted to—that this is the most deeply individual identity of all. But in practice it is rarely that simple, as all the stories in this chapter have shown. In a world where communities and societies have opinions about individual morals, the personal is also social, and queer people don't live in a vacuum apart from society's demands any more than straight people do.

From straight-passing by choice and straight-passing under coercion, to straight-passing by gender-passing and straight-passing by omission, we've seen throughout this chapter that the pressures leading people to conceal their sexuality, across time and place, are often tied up with religion. Religious identity is about more than personal faith: it is one's culture, one's society, one's heritage and roots. After the often individually determined "inner" selfhoods around gender and sexuality that have informed the transformations explored in Part Two, in the next part of the book we will return to forms of passing that involve moving away not just from a personal identity, but from a community that frames it—starting with a deeper exploration of this link between religion and social status. It can lead those in a religious minority to pass as another god's believer; and even those in the majority faith community are still sometimes compelled to pass, if it means they can escape membership of a religiously sanctioned underclass: low caste.

PART THREE

BEYOND HERITAGE

8

BORN AGAIN

SHIFTING RELIGION AND CASTE

Before I left Dhaka, I wanted to ask Sanjida how she had felt about taking that marriage vow before Puja's gods. But I decided not to. It would have been a tricky question to handle for her; and who was I, after all, but another probing reporter trying to define her identity, as if she hadn't had enough of that already with people scrutinising her gender and her sexuality. Besides, a topic such as religious transgression—even for a short period, and for love—would have been terribly inappropriate to bring up without invitation. In most cultures, renouncing one's birth faith is still considered a sacrilege, and in many societies remains punishable by imprisonment or even death. Religious "fakery"—whether true passing or sincere conversion—is believed in some quarters to lead to social disorder, and can be fraught with fears among the religiously reborn of both social ostracism and divine retribution.

Just as there is bitter transphobic debate over whether a transsexual, let alone a transgender, person can ever "really" be the gender they identify as, there are those who believe that no conversion is legitimate, for it is an act of blasphemy—for them, there is no such thing as a religious convert; only a religious passer. While this is a question of dogma, and perhaps intolerance, around converts, it does relate to a question of serious interest around actual passing: is it really possible to enact a religious identity, which is not simply physical but spiritual, without coming to inhabit it internally? When does religious passing become religious conviction?

This has been an explosive subject since the beginning of culture and the birth of religions. Time and again, religious minorities have been vulnerable to persecution. Individuals, and sometimes entire communities, are either forced to convert to the religion of the oppressor/invader, or pushed underground to practise their faith secretly, while outwardly passing as whatever the majority ruling faith ask of them. The cultural anxiety of the religious passer is as great as the identity crisis of any other passer adopting a persona for their own safety and opportunity—they are faced with the same hidden trauma resulting from the loss of history and family, and the same permanent insecurity in the present. Ultimately, the difference between the religious convert and the religious passer is that the convert leaves behind one sense of communal belonging in favour of another; but the faith-passer, shedding an identity derived from their heritage like the white-passer, is left stranded between communities.

A Hard Nut

As we saw in Chapter 3, like Anansi, the gods in India are no strangers to passing. And, like the gods, my father's many lives would only show in glimpses, through the songs he played on his twin-deck cassette player—the love of his life. Depending on the day and his mood—of which his family had not a clue—he would play songs telling of the god Krishna shedding identities like skins, appearing as a butter-thief in the milkman tribe, an unruly neighbourhood trickster boy, an elusive lover to older women, and back to a benevolent god—this time as friend and advisor to the anguished soldier, Arjun, on the chariot of human dilemma. The dilemma, as all Hindus know, is whether or not Arjun should kill his warring cousins to preserve the order of things. The idea of "one's got to do what one's meant to do" is the primary storyline of the ancient Indian epic, the *Mahabharata*.

To paraphrase Walcott, an epical story of survival is not possible without the splendour of personal metamorphosis. My father's was transmitted to his family in an ingenious way. When Bliss Broyard probed her father for information about his mysterious life and past, just months before his death and "outing" as a white-passing African American, he told her that if his children wanted to know about him, they should read his written work. For my father, it was his cassette tapes—he played them during all his waking hours. The songs carried his soul's screech and whispers. His inner restlessness sometimes found its way in his creative pursuits, which included his role as a stage director and organiser of the travelling village opera—the folk-theatre known as *jatra* was popular in Bengal in the 1970s and 80s. Mostly the songs would be from Hindu tradition, like the ones about the dalliance of the humanoid Hindu god Krishna with his consort, Radha the milkmaid—an older woman, an embodiment of everyday humanity. But sometimes they would be from Indianised or Bengalicised Islamic folklore.

> Come, see who's swaying on Amina's lap,
> The honeyed full moon face is resplendent and bright.[1]

These are the first two lines of a song that I remember hearing on my father's cassette player, growing up. It is about a blessed baby born in Arabia with a face that resembled the full moon. The baby is none other than the future Prophet Mohammed, and Amina is his mother, rocking him as his face glows with the colours of the full moon. These words are by a Bengali poet with a transformative soul. Caught between two religions, Kazi Nazrul Islam (1899–1976), who was a prolific poet and songwriter, drew variously on Hindu myths and folkloric stories around the founder of Islam in sixth-century Arabia.

When the Indian subcontinent was breaking up in the mid-twentieth century, the song of independence took over popular emotion, leading to a two-state frenzy. Nazrul decided to name his son Krishna Muhammad, in a desperate personal attempt to spurn the religious and political turmoil. The division bell had long been ringing, and in the Rorschach of the partition of Bengal, he read the end of India's intercommunal utopia, and the death of his own dual-yet-whole cultural identity—as much Muslim as Hindu. When he was no longer able to straddle the two, he refused to settle for one.

The song invites the listener: come, see who's just born. It never spells out who that is, unless we know the name of the Prophet's mother. The poet is testing his audience's knowledge, or being deliberately ambiguous; he seems mystified by the power Amina's son had over him, as if pronouncing his name would split apart for good the wholeness of his Hindu-Muslim selfhood. Nazrul is teasing his audience, leading or misleading them into thinking their poet might be a secret Hindu, or a secret Muslim—or, like many Indian gods, he is two-in-one.

Like Nazrul, my father lived in an aura of his own making. He would make contradictory statements, mostly to himself about himself, and about the various peoples that came to or from Bengal whose blood flowed through his veins. Sometimes in the early morning, as he would walk around his small courtyard checking the coconut trees for young coconuts, or pruning the overhanging leaves of a lemon tree, he would murmur—just loud enough to be heard by his unassuming wife, sitting before a wood-burning cooker making breakfast, or his children memorising history and physics—that he had some Buddhist heritage; Bengal was once the seat of Theravada Buddhism. The sudden one-liners occasionally went like this: he had come to the city with a kilo of rice to sell, the proceeds of which he used to go to school—the first boy in his village to get a high school education. Who could question the veracity of this founding myth?

Other times, the murmurings hinted that one of his ancestors may have come from Persia. Legends often draw on scattered visible signs of truth: a 6 foot olive-skinned man is not your usual Bengali. Why was he so light-skinned and tall, like an Aryan invader from four millennia ago? His children would look up from their desk at this towering fair man they had always been in awe of, without ever being able to connect to him or to his various moods, as changeable as the incarnations of our household gods.

Through the ages, there have been many wandering men passing through Bengal on their way further east: Central Asian travellers, lost Yemeni Muslims, Dutch Calvinist opportunists, French imperialists, English merchants, roaming Zoroastrians. Some visitors stayed only for a while, some for a long time; some came and went, some settled permanently. If some of my father's ancestors may have come from Persia, what did that mean? A possible union between a lone Persian wanderer and a Bengali maiden—how long ago? What happened to the traveller? Did he stay on like the Mughals, or did he head back to Central Asia, never to return?

My father's "recorded" ancestry barely even goes back to his own father, whom he never knew—he died before he was even born.

BORN AGAIN

The convenient myths of my father's self were his own, his roots an unknown island where he himself was a stranger—and, after his mother died, he was its lone dweller. Unlike those passers and identity-transformers in history who created their own myths after moving to different locations, my father was not self-made, but self-born; he was perennially regenerating within his own shell. His murmurings were like a memory machine that churned out versions of his past so that he didn't forget them; through these vague but repeated variations he wove a continuity into his personal history where there wasn't one. He carried the solitude of rootlessness, the burden of thousands of years of no known ancestors. These murmurs were his way of communicating with the imagined souls that peopled his lonely island.

These people sometimes hinted that, if not Persian blood, then surely there was some high-caste Brahmin DNA in him: look at that Aryan nose, those long slender limbs! But I also kept hearing the opposite, that the available fables of his most recent past suggested a lower-caste connection; that the big void in his familial memory was in fact not without people, but had been a deliberate discounting of nameless bonded farmers, working on land owned by others of a higher caste. The way out was to leave the prison of the lower caste birth for the generations to come. Since you cannot upgrade your social status in a caste-divided religion, the only way to gain access to education or escape destitution is to leave the religion altogether. Islam spread fast among the Bengal peasantry, with its message of equality and humanism, celebrated by Nazrul in that poem of hope and wonder.

When I was a little older, and listened more closely to my father's murmurs regarding his family's possible transition out of a low caste, I found historical evidence in the 1872 census of Bengal, compiled by the colonial officer Henry Beverley. Beverley—rather controversially, and to the chagrin of the landed Muslims—pointed out that the highest percentage of Muslims could be found in the lower Bengal Delta, rather than in the old centres of Mughal rule in northern India. He concluded that "the existence of Muhammadans in Bengal is not due so much to the introduction of Mughul blood into the country as to the conversion of the former inhabitants for whom a rigid system of caste discipline rendered Hinduism intolerable."[2]

Might my father or his forebears have subscribed to this "social liberation theory", as scholars have called the idea of Islam as a less hierarchical alternative to Hindu casteism? Caste relief through conversion has been integral to India's communal history: on the other side of the country, many low-caste Punjabis migrated to the towns of the Sikh gurus, whose new religion was explicitly egalitarian, and converted. And this makes more sense than the story of a liaison between a Persian traveller and his Bengali consort. But then, in a counter-murmur, my father would go back to his unusual features, his physique and skin tone, which could always be explained with the so-called Aryan-blooded superior castes' historical oppression of the darker-skinned lower castes.

Growing up, I liked to believe in the Persian affair theory. It was more romantic, and unencumbered by Hinduism's blighted history of caste segregation. The mysterious aura around my father was partly created by the man himself, and partly by his mother, who lived with us; his children added to the snippets of the stories they heard, and each one of us had a different version of our father's "real" persona. Apart from our grandmother, we never saw anyone from our father's side of the family, which of course added to the mystery. Bliss Broyard and her brother had never met Anatole's relatives, which had made the enigma of his past all the more tantalising.

We never stopped being fascinated by our elusive father, and our equally elusive grandmother. Both were raconteurs who frequently entered their own narratives. Their personal tales were so engrossing that their audience would suspend disbelief and long to hear more, like one of those Bengali *punthi* stories—oral tales passed from storyteller to storyteller, with the characters changing roles each time. At the end of each session, the hair-raising suspense would be left hanging until the next instalment—always "to be continued". In our home, mother and son were the perfect heroes of their own epic, tireless disseminators of stories whose notes of incongruity or anachronism were never challenged by their rapt audience, because reinstating disbelief would mean "the end". We could not imagine life without a "next instalment" in the ever-evolving narrative of our family saga—religion, conversion, self-erasure and reconstruction, new and old cultures, passing, travelling, disappearing.

Apart from the disjointed throwaway comments we picked up, we could not see any coherent thread, and our father's death—another mystery we cannot solve—has left us without closure. At least Bliss Broyard was able to dig out the archival material and trace her father's past. Her ancestors had names. My father is only recorded in the oral history of which he himself was the author-narrator. This self-formed tapestry of identity did not make my father more self-assured. He repeatedly played that Nazrul song about Amina's son whose name is never uttered, just as my father's various rebirths were never truly revealed to his listeners. Was the song, I would later ask myself, his attempt at a self-discovery that he was trying to pass on to his family? Or was it the expression of an ongoing bafflement at his own constant, rootless shape-shifting, appealing to an imaginary audience to tell him how he came to be who he was, and where he found himself?

I cannot end this section without mentioning the last, final mystery of my father, which shook our "to be continued" family chronicle to its core. His children will never reach "the end" of this story. It happened suddenly, and with brutal finality. In Kafka's *Metamorphosis*, Gregor Samsa woke up one day to find he had turned into a cockroach and his parents could not recognise him. My father's last act transformed an elusive self-born man into an unfamiliar dead fugitive.

One July morning in 2012, my father did something which looked like an accident. He injected himself with an overdose of insulin. He had always been reckless, impulsive. He waited and didn't tell anyone, not until the adverse reaction began to show. By then, it was too late. He took with him all the lives he lived or didn't live. His children hadn't been paying enough attention to the songs he had played us, we hadn't understood his life story. None of us were at his bedside to witness his death. There was never a Bliss Broyard moment when we could ask, "Tell us then, Father, your secret. Are you a Muslim, a long-lost Persian throwback, a born-again Hindu? A man of many worlds who did not belong to any of them? What are you?"

A hard nut.

His children did not manage to crack it in his lifetime, nor will they after his death. He took his contradictions and deliberations to the grave. That was it.

For a while, I sometimes believed that perhaps he had tried to leave us some clues, but the map of the labyrinth of his mind was drawn with a shaky hand, never completed. It is hardly surprising that, many years later while researching this book, inspired by Bliss Broyard and Anthony Ekundayo Lennon, I too sent off some DNA swabs to one of the ancestry analysis labs. The result came back with a generous genetic map encompassing 91% South Asian all the way to the edge of Iran, and 7.2% Chinese and Vietnamese. I shouldn't have done it. Now I have this new niggling curiosity—the Far East was not part of my father's murmured myths about his heritage. But this Chinese part is something I would not dare delve into. This lattice work of a non-history is what I would ever get, about my father's and my own unrecorded, ambiguous ancestry. A perfect chronicle of "the unremitting crossings" of those of us who harbour a secret in their family, an internalised history of past oppressions and escapes.

Only two of his children managed to come for the last rites; the rest were far away. Like his mythical wandering ancestors, my father's children had wandered off to far corners of the world.

His files, diaries and transcripts of his text messages travelled to London with me, his eldest child. There I found, amongst a pile of medical papers, an instruction to the team of doctors who had been in charge of looking after him during his last days. He had specifically asked for a Hindu doctor, preferably a Brahmin. His wishes were fulfilled. He recorded in his diaries rough notes of his chats—mostly over the telephone—with this Brahmin physician. His children didn't understand him, he had said to the doctor. Going over the scraps of papers and notebooks and diaries, I could not agree more. But the question is, did he understand himself? When you have multiple personae, either you are resigned to living all of them at once, as part of your unique being, or you are left perpetually hankering after a "true" self. I believe my father's life was the latter, forever searching for an answer to Rudyard Kipling's question in *Kim*: "What am I?"

* * *

"What am I?" is an essential quest that has historically forged the unity of minorities in hostile societies. As they questioned the system, they also formulated their own selfhood—under threat and often on the verge of extinction. Majority groups, who considered themselves superior, pushed the minority to the periphery or the shadows of society. There, the marginalised formed secret alliances and worked out logistics of survival, which included passing as members of the mainstream society. My father's story—or stories—have already revealed the two key identity hierarchies that shape selfhood more than any other on the Indian subcontinent: religion and caste.

The old fluidity and ambiguity that made the mystery of my father possible is fast disappearing in today's India, where the Hindu nationalist government is passing bill after bill to shift the country away from its pluralistic tradition. Anti-Muslim prejudice in India is one of the perilous legacies of the partition of 1947, and the memory of its violence has been rekindled since 2014, as India has become a place where identity must be worn like a badge. The government's agenda has intensified communal mistrust and hostility, as Hindu—or, more specifically, higher-caste Hindu—seems now to determine "normative Indianness".

The introduction of the infamous Citizenship Amendment Bill in December 2019—which allows all immigrants from Afghanistan, Pakistan and Bangladesh a swift route to Indian citizenship, unless they are Muslim—saw an explosion of communal violence. In New Delhi, in the aftermath of the bill becoming law, scores of Muslims were killed as Hindu mobs went out vandalising and looting mosques, Muslim-owned shops and Muslim homes. Indian and international media showed grim footage of Muslims covered in blood from beatings, lying in the street and being forced to prove their patriotism. One reputable British journalist likened the rampage in Delhi to "Kristallnacht—the Night of Broken Glass" in November 1938, when Nazi supporters burned down German synagogues and smashed up Jewish homes, with many Jews escaping by passing as gentiles.[3]

It is no wonder, then, that so many Muslims have passed as Hindu since the partition, or that increasing numbers may be doing so again amidst today's re-energised Islamophobia. In the continuing street violence following the passage of the Citizenship Amendment Act, Hindu nationalist mobs in Delhi killed "At least 37 people, almost all Muslims ... a two-year-old baby was stripped by a gang to see if he was circumcised."⁴ Those who managed to escape, mostly women, did so by pretending to be Hindus. In the longer term, Muslims are passing as Hindus to improve their chances in the job market. One of the most visible platforms for this—as we shall see in Chapter 14—had once been the film industry, with Muslim Bollywood actors frequently taking on Hindu screen names.

In today's India, many of those passing to gain employment are applying for menial types of work such as domestic help, where meticulous background checks are usually not carried out. The agencies that supply such help to wealthy families are often complicit in this passing, advising Muslim applicants to put on Hindu attire and names to get a placement faster. One such case received worldwide attention in 2013, when a Bangladeshi Muslim domestic worker was found dead in the Delhi home of Dhananjay Singh, member of the Lok Sabha, the Indian parliament's lower house. After Mr Singh and his wife were arrested, it turned out that the maid, Rakhi, had been masquerading as a Hindu from West Bengal.

Muslims have passed as Hindus not just for economic reasons; there have been numerous news stories where one half of a couple in love has pretended to change religion, at least for the sake of public ceremonies, in order to marry their partners. This has been turned into an Islamophobic urban legend by Hindu nationalists, a myth called "Love Jihad" according to which Muslim men are passing as Hindu—particularly on social media—to lure Hindu women into marriage, as a calculated prelude to converting them. Partly driven by this myth, Hindu nationalist activists around India have started indiscriminately harassing and cyber-bullying mixed couples.

In more high-profile Muslim-Hindu marriages, neither party has converted or passed—for instance, the Bollywood heartthrob Shah Rukh Khan and his Hindu wife, Gauri Khan. Theirs is in fact an inspiring story of inter-religious love and harmony, epitomised in a 2020 video message from Shah Rukh which celebrated the old, undivided India, and went viral: "My wife is Hindu, I am a Muslim and our children are Hindustan."⁵

BORN AGAIN

Dirty Work

The reality of partition was a codification of religious hierarchy, the legacy of which has never been more insidious in India than now, under Hindu nationalist rule. But even within what is now India's majority religion, Hinduism, there is another hierarchy—a woeful, sweeping internal class system, dictated or justified by religion: caste. The history of class structures is as old and global as human culture, from slavery and feudalism to hereditary wealth and nepotism, eating away at societies behind a façade of legal equality. Caste is one of the most caustic of all.

The most infamous caste system, the one that the word immediately brings to mind, is India's, widely publicised and universally considered a blight on humanity, with its ever-so-intricate, culturally internalised microscopic gradations of social segregation and ostracisation. Indian caste originates from the Vedic story of the *Purusha*, a cosmic being from whose four limbs the four castes were created: from his head came the highest caste, the learned Brahmins; from his arms the warrior Kshatriyas; his legs the commoners, Vaishyas; and from his feet the lowest caste, the Shudras, who are meant to do lowly jobs and live lowly lives—all because they transgressed in their previous incarnations. Then there are the Dalits ("oppressed"), often known as untouchables, who are literally outcaste. Excluded from this four-caste system, Hinduism dictates that they have no hope for salvation. Considered to be polluted and polluting, they have traditionally been confined to "dirty work" like fishing, scavenging, and working with meat or waste.

In a classic case of imperial "divide and rule" tactics, the British endorsed these concepts, using and furthering caste divisions to pamper caste-privileged groups who would uphold British rule and set them against the rest, both lower-born Hindus and Muslims. We can see the ubiquity of caste in the Raj reflected in the prolific writings of Munshi Premchand (1880–1936). His many novels and his oeuvre of short stories, numbering over 300, are a spectacularly vivid portrayal of the transformative powers of his characters, moving between castes, religions and languages. Born as a Hindu of the second-highest caste, a Kshatriya, Premchand's early education was completed in an Islamic seminary, which meant that he started his life as an author writing in Urdu. Later, in both his Urdu and Hindi stories, we meet a Brahmin woman passing down to the third caste; an upper-class Hindu man moving to an untouchable area for loving a Muslim woman; a Muslim Gandhian leader with a mass following of all religions and castes fighting for social justice and end of colonial rule. Premchand's characters are constantly negotiating new definitions of selfhood through their vanishing acts from one identity to another.

While pluralism, and a certain amount of cultural and social fluidity or blending are part of Indian tradition, not everyone stuck with low-caste status in real life can shrug it off as easily as in Premchand's stories. Though caste Hindus and Dalits are no longer confined to their original professions, caste remains everywhere in Indian life. Many of "low birth" will have tried, successfully or not, to pass as higher-caste to escape their inherited stigma. Gandhi once called the Dalits *harijan*, the gods' people, which the Dalit community has since rejected as condescending—the Mahatma, though he chose a life of simplicity and had many low-caste followers, was not himself from a lowly background. Today, in general day-to-day dealings, the Indian caste system works in a similar way to Brazil's colour spectrum: theoretically, these are simply descriptive classifications without inherent positive or negative value; but in practice high-caste Hindus enjoy the status of the upper-class and racially superior. As in Brazil, there has been affirmative action in India since independence, with quotas for Dalits and those of low caste to overcome the historical barriers of their class. But attitudes remain problematic.

Open any popular newspaper and you will find in the classifieds "Brides and grooms wanted"—with clear caste specifications. Along with the right complexion, a proper caste match is what will ensure an auspicious marriage and preserve the order of things; you certainly wouldn't want to marry down. In job interviews, Hindu background and a "minimum caste" are an implicit, sometimes explicit, requirement for successful candidates. So, if the opportunity arrives to blur or hide your historically disadvantaged status, why would you not snatch it? Because life caught on the lower echelon of the caste system would be half a life or no life. Even if I'd like to remain forever fascinated by my father's glorified fantasy of a

Persian wanderer running through his and my veins, ultimately the plausible story here is the one of his low-caste origins, thrown off by moving geographically or converting religiously.

The highs and lows of caste-passing are explored powerfully in Aravind Adiga's 2008 novel *The White Tiger*—the title being a euphemism for something rare, "the creature that comes along only once in a generation",[6] but also evoking a tiger who successfully loses his stripes. The white tiger also symbolises power in some parts of East Asia; the novel is written in the form of a letter to the then Chinese premier, Wen Jiabao. The narrator, Balram Halwai, describes with insouciance his rise up the social ladder through immoral means, including extortion, bribery, lying and, finally, murder—the reader is left to assume that the cycle will repeat once they've finished the book. From a low-caste rickshaw-puller's son to a self-proclaimed "entrepreneur" in India's southern tech city, Bangalore, Balram's path to success is dark and sinister. Frequently referring to himself as a "white tiger", he sheds a series of aliases, personas and statuses. Along the way he carries out and covers up a shocking list of crimes—all so that he can play in the light, never to look back at or be haunted by the "Darkness" in which he was born.

Yet there is darkness in the book: it is with black humour that Balram commits murder and helps cover up the misdemeanours of others of his adopted social elite, all justified in his letter to Wen. Instead of being treated as a parasite, ruled by the system as his people have been throughout history, Balram overturns it, playing by its own pitiless cut-throat laws. For Balram, gone are the days of mass social revolution: even if it did happen, it would take many generations before the people in "Darkness" would reap the benefits. India's new subversives—the children of globalisation and capitalism—are impatient; they want to make an immediate difference to their own place in society. In Balram's case, this desire is insular; passers are often haunted by a spiritual and practical decision that Balram finds easy, and where many passers work to provide opportunity for their progeny, he readily forsakes his family in the hope of personal success.

Balram's literacy and determination to rise above his class were spotted early by a school inspector, who commented that the boy was meant for a "real" school, as opposed to remaining stuck in a place full of thugs and petty criminals. But Balram doesn't want to be a quota-filler. He has much greater plans for his life than pandering to this condescending system devised by the political (and caste) elite, in which he would only pass from the life of a thug to the life of a clerk, driver, or middleman between bribe-givers and bribe-takers. Passing as high-caste to secure a job as a driver of the rich is not good enough; he wants to be the one to be driven around—in fact, he wants to own a whole fleet of cars, which is what eventually prompts him to choose his line of business, running a taxi service in the industrial hub of Bangalore.

Not only does Balram escape the state of darkness where idiots dwell, by caste-passing up and up, in his fast-track journey from slum to triumph he skips over servile mediocrity to become the oppressor par excellence, launching himself into a position of power where he is actually running the corrupt system himself. In this sense, he has simply transferred his identity positioning: he ceases subscribing to one dominant world order—traditional class hierarchy—in favour of another, newer one: global capitalism. Balram's rejection of his birth community—or any community—as the definer of his identity goes hand in hand with capitalism's meritocratic and individualist values. It is hardly surprising that this unrepentant narrator is writing his story to the leader of one of the world's fastest-growing economies. Wen Jiabao would understand the necessary costs of capitalism; China is emerging as a global power, just as India is—so Balram believes.

He envisages a future that is yellow and brown, not white; he sees that "tomorrow" is within reach of the lower-class people who had perpetually been stuck in "today". They can dive into the anonymity of capitalism's big cities, shrug off the stripes of their origins, and be reclassified as "entrepreneurs".

The New Commoners and the "Instantly Inferior"

Caste is not uniquely Indian. The following is the story of Japan's little-known "untouchables", the *burakumin*, who hide within the social mainstream at the usual cost of anxious secrecy and silent trauma, despite their legal emancipation 150 years ago. In the Edo period (also known as the Tokugawa Shogunate, 1603–1868), Japanese society was split into a ruling elite and a common majority.

Fig. 11: The legendary ninth-century Pope Joan gives herself away, going into labour during a procession.

Fig. 12: Hannah Snell (1723–92), who served in India as British soldier James Gray.

Fig. 13: A nineteenth-century Viola disguised as Cesario in *Twelfth Night*, Shakespeare's gender-bending romantic comedy of c. 1601–2.

Fig. 14: Achilles (far right) gives himself away among the ladies with his excitement at a fine sword.

Fig. 15: Hilary Swank as the transphobic murder victim Brandon Teena (1972–93) in *Boys Don't Cry* (1999). Today it would be less acceptable for a cis woman to play this role.

Fig. 16: The Danish artist Lili Elbe (formerly Einar Wegener), 1926. Elbe was among the first recipients of sex reassignment surgery in 1930.

Fig. 17: Gender-fluid/trans couple Sophie (left) and Jess.

Fig. 18: Ananya (centre) and fellow hijras, members of the Indian subcontinent's officially recognised third gender.

Fig. 19: Chris Gunness (left), happily married to Ari and embracing a BAME identity after a lifetime as an "expert on passing".

Fig. 20: The author's father, so tall and fair he could be Persian or Brahmin, in one of his "murmuring" moments in the garden.

Fig. 21: The four castes of feudal Japan (clockwise from top left): peasants, samurai, craftsmen and merchants. Descendants of the outcast *eta* ("abundance of filth") are still marginalised today.

Fig. 22: An *auto da fe* of the Spanish Inquisition, which targeted secret Jews and Muslims still observing their faith after forced conversion to Catholicism.

Fig. 23: "Gentleman Jack": Anne Lister, landlord, industrialist and womaniser (1791–1840), whose coded diaries tell of her sexual conquests.

Fig. 24: Gertrude Stein (1874–1946), who belonged to a set of "male geniuses" and lived openly with her "wife" Alice in Paris.

Fig. 25: V.S. Naipaul (1932–2018): the epitome of Fanon's "internalised whiteness"?

At the top of the pyramid was the divinely blessed emperor, then the court nobility, the military (the shogun) and the feudal lords. Below them, the masses were organised into "Four Occupations", a profession-based structure rooted in Confucian ideas of social order, and remarkably similar to the original Indian caste system.

The four professional classes—the Samurai, peasants, craftsmen and merchants—were also clearly separated from a class outside the caste system: various groups of untouchables, who laboured in graveyards, slaughterhouses and tanneries, or worked as executioners and handlers of faeces. By the end of the Edo period in the mid-nineteenth century, the most important hierarchy was now the distinction between these untouchables, who had come to be known as the *eta* ("abundance of filth"), and the majority. By then, the original "four castes" were being abolished, blended together into a default dominant class known as the *yamato*. This was the term used to refer to the Shinto imperial court in ancient times, and it denoted the idea that this mainstream was set above the rest—both untouchables and ethnic minorities—because the *yamato* class represented the original settlers of mainland Japan.

Until 1871, the *eta* were officially discriminated against, and confined by law to certain areas. The law then changed, and the term *eta* was considered derogatory; since that time, those born into this outcast group—the "new commoners"—have been called *burakumin*, "hamlet people", after the separate villages and ghettos where they still live today. For, despite the abolition of the caste system, social attitudes did not change overnight. Historical class structures can often be found ingrained in our nature. Individuals at both ends of the spectrum have internalised the hierarchy, and will manifest its historical outgrowth in their xenophobic contempt or inferiority complex. The *burakumin* might have had a new name, but—just like the Dalits—were still seen as "unclean", because they had historically been assigned to professions deemed impure. Yet their status had become hereditary regardless of profession, again thanks to Confucian ideas of the family. The only way they could break free of untouchability was by leaving their segregated villages and claiming a new *yamato* identity, usually changing their names.

Officially, there are thought to be 1 million *burakumin* in Japan, but other estimates suggest that the figure could be 2–3 million if you take into account those passing as the mainstream caste. But this remains a challenging process. Marriages have historically been rare between *burakumin* and others, and even highly regarded corporations have regularly engaged in discriminatory hiring, as we'll see below. As in Jim Crow America, even one drop of *eta* blood was seen to be contagious, and future generations would continue to be infected by it. No matter their ethnicity, the mark of *eta* would forever taint their every life prospect. Until recently, just as under Jim Crow and as in India even today, Japan's untouchables were not allowed to eat, drink or socialise with mainstream society.

In a bind that would be familiar to Balram Halwai, the *burakumin* are shamed if they are caught hiding their ancestry, but are also singled out, pitied and patronised if they take advantage of the educational or housing quotas achieved after years of campaigning by social reformers. The only society that *burakumin* can "proudly" join without concealing their identity is Japan's infamous gangster world. A third of *yakuza* recruits have traditionally come from the *buraku* community. This is hardly surprising—the underworld must have been a tantalising prospect if the *yakuza* were willing to accept the *burakumin*, a route to empowerment without having to pass— yet the connection also serves to fortify *yamato* prejudices that the *burakumin* are lowly creatures, tainted by anti-social behaviour.

The plight of the *burakumin* was first brought to light by *The River With No Bridge* (*Hashi no nai kawa*), a seven-volume saga by Sue Sumii that was published in 1961–92, with the first volume translated into English in 1990 under the same title. The novels depict the life of Koji, the orphaned son of a war hero, who—like the author—grows up in a *buraku* ghetto in the early twentieth century, facing mockery and class discrimination until he begins to question the system. Sumii's book sold more than 8 million copies in English translation, and brought to light the doomed life of the outcast *burakumin*—previously unknown both to the outside world and also to many urban Japanese.

Several films have been made based on the bestseller, the most widely released in 1992. That same year, Robert Guest, a journalist based in Tokyo, published an investigative feature in *Far Eastern Economic Review* on the tale of two *buraku* sisters—one, Hiromi, passing as a non-*buraku* Japanese, and the other, Yoshiko, ultimately choosing to hold onto her ancestry. This real-life dichotomy is reminiscent of Nella Larsen's *Passing*; here Hiromi, the sister who's passing, is torn by the same trauma of having to hide her identity as Clare Kendry, powerless to answer back when she hears derogatory comments about her community from her close friends with no knowledge of her *buraku* connection. One says, "I would never marry a *burakumin*."

The only way Hiromi could get a job at one of Tokyo's top computer firms was by meticulously concealing her ancestry. This was no easy task, since she had to pass the screening process many employers carry out to filter any *burakumin* from the list of applicants. Having succeeded in bypassing what would otherwise have smeared her credentials as a candidate for her prestigious job, Hiromi couldn't get away from a constant feeling of insecurity: if her secret came out, she would have to forfeit her social position and "mainstream" friends. "She wants to marry," Guest explained in his piece, "but since the parents of any potential partner are likely to hire a private detective to make sure she's not a *burakumin*, this could be difficult. Her family tree and previous addresses are recorded in her family register, which is kept at the local ward office, easily accessible to a conscientious snoop."[7] Such a list has been in the public domain since the mid-1970s, which led to protests by the Burakumin Liberation League when Google Earth used the list to incorporate into its maps *buraku* villages. Like escaped slaves shying away from the handbills pasted all over town, the *burakumin* live in fear of prospective employers seeing these designations: Japanese corporations can now literally Google job candidates' caste background.

The prejudices are similar to those I have seen in India against Dalits. Japanese society perceived the *burakumin* to be illiterate, second-grade, subhuman, literally—one of the derogatory terms for them is *ningai*, or "other than human". Worse, *yotsu* (four-legged) is also used. And yet passing is extremely common among the *burakumin* because there is no ethnic or visible difference between them and the dominant *yamato*. This is why documentation and Google Earth snoops are necessary to "out" them. Hiromi's younger sister Yoshiko, growing up on the island of Shikoku, had been assumed by others to be of a higher caste; at the time Guest interviewed the sisters, she had just been voted head girl of her school. As she stood up in the assembly hall to accept the title, she decided to announce that she was a *burakumin* and proud of it, to a shocked audience. For the rest of her life, she knew, she would have to work hard to disprove the prejudices in her society.

* * *

As we know, the term *yamato* came into modern use in the nineteenth century after Japan's opening up, as a way to distinguish ethnic Japanese who consider themselves indigenous to the mainland from ethnic minorities and foreign immigrants. In the period when Western race science became obsessed with genetics, Japanese scientists were also pursuing the concept of *yamato minzoku* (Yamato ethnicity), a pure-blooded race. However, in the early twentieth century, new hereditary class distinctions were also created by out-migration: *yamato* who left Japan, and their descendants, became classed separately from, and looked down on by, the *yamato* on the mainland. For example, the term *dekasegi* ("workers away from home") is used, particularly in Brazil itself, to describe the Brazilian Japanese, who first arrived in South America in the early twentieth century to fill the labour shortages on coffee plantations around the city of São Paolo—a shortage connected to the very late abolition of the slave trade in Brazil, in 1850.

Initially the vacancies were filled by Italian workers, whose arrival was partly encouraged by the racist "whitening" policy we encountered in Chapter 3—until Italy stopped subsidising emigration to Brazil. This was when the Japanese started pouring in—like migrant labourers everywhere, they hoped to work hard for a few years, make their money and then return home to Japan. This migration of ethnic Japanese to Latin America grew enormously after the US passed its Immigration Act of 1924, including the Asian Exclusion Act. Brazil today is home to the largest Japanese population outside of Japan: 1.5 million.

The flow of immigration decreased drastically after a return migration movement in the 1980s, which saw many leave Brazil for their ancestral homeland. It was time to go back to their roots. But this has only exposed yet another underclass: the children of the *dekasegi* are known in host societies of the Americas as the *nisei* (literally "second generation"), and they are not highly regarded in Japan. Many of the *nisei* from Brazil, for instance, only speak Portuguese, and in their ancestral homeland they "instantly feel inferior", as Yae Nakayama Wallis, a *nisei* from São Paolo, put it. She spoke to me about the trauma of being "a *nisei* in Brazil and a *dekasegi* upon arrival in Tokyo." The first time she "returned" to Japan,

> They couldn't quite work it out, initially they thought that I was Japanese, but as soon as I started speaking, they could hear that I had an accent. The manner of my speech was totally outdated, and that was when they started asking, are you Korean, or are you Chinese? To offend me deliberately.[8]

Which was more offensive, I asked? "Of course being called Chinese," she mused. "Korean was slightly better, as they're deemed more beautiful!" Yae had just arrived in Tokyo with her English husband, and they were sitting in a sushi place. The fellow diners and waiters were eager to please her husband, giving him saki and trying to make a conversation "in their bad English", while Yae was totally ignored, somewhat "aggressively, deliberately". "I'll never belong in Japan," Yae told me with profound sadness, adding, "even in my biological Japanese mother's world."

Yae's mother was visiting São Paolo in the mid-1970s when she met Yae's father, who was a wealthy and successful man, much older and already married. He secretly committed bigamy when Yae's mother "disgracefully" fell pregnant with her; they wed in the Japanese consulate, without revealing his existing marriage to the authorities. This was too much for Yae's biological mother, who decided to return home when Yae was 9 months old. Just as Chris Gunness's mother kept his working-class grandmother out of his boarding school, Yae's mother left her infant daughter behind in Brazil; it would have been terribly stigmatising for a legally unmarried mother to return to Japan with a child.

Besides, she boasted about having Samurai blood—the family even had a whole Samurai outfit passed down from some ancestor. All the more reason not to display an illegitimate daughter, revealing a pollution of the elite warrior bloodline. The Samurais had been the highest caste in the old Edo system, but—unlike India's Kshatriya warrior caste—they were not born into this privilege. It was in later life, once they had actually become warriors, that the Samurai—less than 10 per cent of the population—"elevated themselves in society, were given land and other benefits".⁹ Yae's mother did not want to bring shame to her ancestors' hard-won position.

For sixteen years, Yae didn't know her biological mother existed.

> When she met me [again], I was 16 years old, and my Japanese mother didn't understand why I wasn't Japanese the way she wanted me to be. I wasn't sweet, I wasn't very quiet, I was loud, my Japanese wasn't good enough. I think she found it really, really difficult that I was more Brazilian than Japanese. From that point on I knew that I wouldn't be accepted in Japan, because if your own mother cannot quite accept the fact that you're so Brazilian... Her perception of how a Japanese girl should behave and be seen was the opposite of what I was.

In the Japanese language, as in any other, there are levels of tone and register, said Yae; and women speak and are spoken to differently. She felt doubly inferior when men in bars and restaurants would address her English husband politely, yet show disrespect or indifference when speaking to Yae. The situation would sometimes change if people learnt that she was now a British Japanese, "which was much better, as was American Japanese, than Brazilian Japanese."

But growing up in Brazil in the 1980s, "you were never a Brazilian" either. And who can blame the native Brazilians, laughed Yae. "All my cultural references were VHS tapes full of Japanese children's programmes, I didn't have any experience of Brazilian cartoons for example." The Japanese colony was too culturally strong, too inward-looking. So was Yae's "all-white" French secondary school, where the only black boy, funnily enough, was called Pelé. Yae's own name, had "another problem", however: *yae*, or *hiai*, means pain in Japanese. The whole school would make fun of her.

Yae grew up thinking that she was a cause of grief, haunted by the breakdown of her parents' fake marriage and her mother's abandonment after she was born. So all her life she tried to fit in, passing culturally and emotionally, and failing on both counts. She would later learn from her biological mother that her Samurai ancestors carried a curse: that her mother was a cursed child, which was why the first child born to her had been a girl, and why she herself would not bring any happiness. Is that why this young woman had named her daughter Pain?

Yae's search for belonging, like other stories in this book, has been multi-layered. What began as socio-cultural passing, in Brazil and later in her married life in the UK, brought caste-passing into its fold as she grew up and began visiting Japan. In a modern-day version of the old association between the *eta* and "dirty", bodily or menial work, the *dekasegi*—Brazilian Japanese—are seen by the majority *yamato* as people doing lowly jobs common to migrant workers such as cleaning.

I was curious to find out whose status was lower, the *dekasegi* and their offspring, or the *burakumin*. Yae said it was still the Japanese-born *burakumin* who were seen to be at the very bottom of Japan's social hierarchy. Did that make her feel any better? She laughed, and said she didn't want to go for either, because both would have prejudiced the views of those trying to put her in an identity box; she usually won't say anything—not even the time when she and her husband unknowingly ended up in a hotel in Tokyo's red light district and people thought she was a prostitute. When Yae jokingly recounted this story, it occurred to me to wonder—though I didn't ask—whether being a Japanese-born prostitute was a better status than being a *dekasegi*, a lowly outsider seen as trying to pass for a "true-bred" Japanese.

"Nowhere else in the world makes me feel instantly inferior as does Japan," Yae told me. These days she doesn't even try to speak Japanese when in Japan. People think she is a moneyed American Japanese *nisei*. "I don't belong to the class that would earn their respect, so it's better for me to pretend that I'm something else." These days, when Yae goes back to Japan, as soon as she gets a chance she throws in the fact that she lives in England. Her settling there came with an interesting twist: she was given a management job at the London office of Mitsubishi, the Japanese car-maker—"because of my Japanese background!"

There has been a shift, at least publicly, in recent decades. The *burakumin* of Japan—and the Dalits of India—still tend to leave their birth towns and villages, change names and reinvent themselves in order to rid themselves of the shackles of their "origins", but more and more mixed marriages are taking place, and these unions between the "unclean" and the self-proclaimed divine have not led to an apocalypse, as the protectors of caste division in both cultures claimed they would. Though the specific professions to which Indian castes and sub-castes are tied can still be passed down through the generations, gone are the days when only caste Hindus or *yamato* had access to education and high positions. With the spread of compulsory universal education for all, regardless of caste or class, the democratisation of travel, and the availability of online portals to teach yourself—not to mention the ease with which outcasts can pass—the rigid hierarchy of caste privilege is becoming a thing of the past.

What this means is that modern passing tales in historically caste-divided societies are now about individual choices to cast off one's family, hometown and even ethnic background—an individual self-determination taken to its extremes as a personal philosophy in *The White Tiger*. The religious passing we have explored in this chapter has likewise been a case of lone people forging a new life for themselves, given the necessities of leaving behind the community in order to shed an inherited identity of disadvantage. In the next chapter, however, we shall see what happens when an entire persecuted community takes on a new identity for its collective self-preservation: mass passing.

9

HIDDEN NATIONS

COLLECTIVE PASSING

A whole people decides to pass for the same reason as an individual: for survival, or to claim dignity and self-determination. And this kind of mass or collective passing has the same consequences we've already seen with individual passers: a chasm or rupture in selfhood, which can only be solved by reinventing and taking ownership of a new history or identity. Because of the way communities have been organised through most of human history, mass passing has principally been in response to religious persecution. Collective religious passing continues in many of today's theocratic and foundationally faith-based societies—we hear frequently about Bahais in Iran passing as Shias, Ahmadis in Pakistan passing as Sunnis. In both countries, public manifestation of these faiths is often met with violent measures. But the past in particular is inundated with stories of "secret nations" that existed in parallel with, and hiding within, the ethno-religious majority. Many of these were born of forced conversion, all of circumstantial necessity.

After the genocide of 1915–16, the remaining Armenians in eastern Anatolia were forcibly converted to Islam by the ruling Ottoman Empire, and most have lived as Muslims amongst both Turkish and Kurdish communities ever since. These Islamised Armenians, today numbering 2 million, created a secret world out of imagined history and made-up reality, to which their oral histories are a testament. At the same time, many genocide survivors kept their birth identity secret in the precarious life of "afterward", their ethnicity and ancestral religion as unknown to their children and grandchildren as

Anatole Broyard's "blackness" was to his. The secret Armenians in Turkey lived with the subliminal knowledge of an inherent connecting tissue which bound the Armenians in Turkey and worldwide.

Many who had been converted became devout Muslims in their daily lives, but others held onto what remained of the Armenian Church, now but a memory to them. These clandestine Christians are still to be found in the mountain villages of eastern Turkey, in Sason, Dersim and so on. The Armenian-Argentinian journalist Avedis Hadjian records a detailed portrayal of the post-genocide Anatolian Armenians in his 2018 book *Secret Nation*. His account informs or complicates our definitions of passing, as we read of entire "hidden" communities of Armenians refusing to be referred to as such—seeing themselves as fully Turkish—yet some of these groups are still clandestinely Christian. These outwardly assimilated Armenians are keen to be "mistaken" for ethnic Turks, their Armenian-ness still an invisible stigma among the majority-Turkish and -Kurdish societies in which they live. The human rights lawyer Kenji Yoshino explains how time changes the way communities are marginalised:

> In the old generation, discrimination targeted entire groups—no racial minorities, no women, no gays, no religious minorities, no people with disabilities allowed. In the new generation, discrimination directs itself not against the entire group, but against the subset of the group that fails to assimilate to mainstream norms. This new form of discrimination targets minority cultures rather than minority persons. Outsiders are included, but only if we behave like insiders—that is, only if we cover.[1]

For the ethnic Armenians in modern Turkey, oppression has evolved from active violent persecution to erasure: the genocide almost wiped them out, the immediate aftermath of forced conversion finished the job, and today everyone is expected to identify as Turkish in the national republic. The ancestors of today's Turkish Armenians will have heard, or maybe even have sung to save themselves, the Young Turk chant "Turkey for the Turks"—a social exclusion movement against non-Muslim minorities within the Ottoman Empire like Armenians and Greeks. After the breakup of the Empire at the end of World War I, this ideology was remodelled as a popular revolution by the leader of Turkish nationalism, Kemal Atatürk. In the new Turkish state, an Anatolian melting-pot forced into a single unifying identity, those who did not belong and refused to assimilate were again massacred, kicked out or sent underground.

For the true converts among the Armenian-origin community, inhabiting Turkishness is a straightforward expression of their identity; this means that, so long as the rest—the secret adherents to the old faith—"cover" their Christian observance, the Armenian community as a whole can successfully present itself as Turkish, because (Yoshino again) "passing pertains to the *visibility* of a particular trait, while covering pertains to its *obtrusiveness*."[2] The default assumed identity in Turkey is ethnically Turk and religiously Muslim: the Armenians don't have to go out of their way to perform this identity, they just have to avoid presenting another one.

Whether Christian or Muslim, these people have, in all practical terms, joined the Turkish mainstream—so can they really still be said to have a secret identity? In Part One we explored the importance of both folk memory and personal upbringing for one's sense of racial identity; if you have lived for a century without an ethnic identity, if some of your progeny don't even know that "they are Armenian", are you still a secret nation? Is your community still passing? The advent of social media has started to suggest one answer: a tiny portion of younger Turkish Armenians have been coming forward over social media to renew their connection with the Armenian diaspora. Something of the old belonging still flickers in the air around those who know of it. If nothing else, we can safely agree with Avedis Hadjian that, since "identity is not an immutable quality, it could be thought of as a state that can be defined along an imaginary spectrum."[3]

Curating Memory

For those ethnic Armenians who have been raised as Turkish first, or Turkish only—especially those who have uncovered a family history that was hidden from them—their Armenian identity comes from an imagined history similar to that of African American slave descendants. Their imagined nation of Armenia is not tied to the modern nation-state of that name so much as to a broader community of genocide survivors that defies national borders: a "connecting tissue between present and past, trauma and acceptance."[4] Memory—in the Armenians' case, the memory of the genocide and its impact—is what generates the life-force of a nation, and a history is constantly being processed from it—most people who have changed country, religion or culture are familiar with this. Passing, after all, is always an act of searching for belonging—whether a positively affirmed identity, as with today's re-emerging Turkish Armenians, or a passive blending into the background, as with their persecuted forebears.

No group has endured this perennial cycle of loss and recovery of history and belonging like the Jews, ever since their dispersion following the Roman destruction of the Temple in Jerusalem in 70 CE, reaching a calamitous apex in the mid-twentieth century in Nazi Germany. Just as Jerusalem's early converts to Christianity passed as Jews to avoid persecution, in the 1930s and 1940s hundreds of thousands of Jews faked gentile identity papers all over Europe to escape the Holocaust. Tragically, some even took this passing as far as internalising the Nazis' false race science codifying "Aryans", "Jews" and so on—"a fiction of law and custom", as Mark Twain described America's One Drop rule. In a desperate bid to avoid capture and banishment to concentration camps, some Sephardi Jews of Western Europe employed German anthropologists to measure their heads, to prove that their "Jewish" blood had actually long since been diluted into southern European or Mediterranean stock.[5]

The story of the Sephardim is a complex one. In the wandering centuries following Roman persecution, the Jews adopted the survival mechanism of versatility, including various stages of assimilation into Christian and Islamic societies to get by unnoticed in their day-to-day life. Under Muslim rule, for instance in the Ottoman Empire, conversion was not forced, and minority communities were governed by separate law. Jews could even rise to high governmental office. Nevertheless, they were wary of unscrupulously flaunting their faith or its symbols, of becoming too comfortable with the limited freedom they were given; Jews were always careful not to overstep the norms set by Islamic law for the minorities, and they often espoused Islamic culture and language.

This was also the case in Muslim Spain (711–1492), where Sephardi thinkers like the Cordovan theologian Moses Maimonides wrote in Arabic. But after the Catholic takeover of al-Andalus in the late fifteenth century, things took a dire turn for the Iberian Jews. They were ordered to convert or leave. Most were forcibly converted, sometimes in mass baptism ceremonies in public squares adjacent to churches that had recently been mosques. These ignominious parades of non-Catholics (Muslims as well as Jews) went on for centuries, until violence and property repossession by the Church had made sure the last flicker of open religious resistance was snuffed out. So deep was the mistrust toward these convert communities that Ferdinand and Isabella, the fifteenth-century Catholic Monarchs who had reconquered the last of Muslim Spain, formed an all-powerful religious authority of vigilantism. They named it the Spanish Inquisition.

The generations of those forcibly baptised after 1492 were known as New Christians. They tried their best to fit in, to avoid raising the suspicion of the Inquisition police by adhering strictly to Catholicism, and to be accepted by the "old" Christians—but persecution and prejudice continued. Meanwhile, a whole new clandestine community grew and survived as "crypto-Jews". A popular story goes that, after the arrival of a new baby, these secret Jews would, like regular Catholics, head for the church in their Sunday best to baptise the newborn; but, once the ceremony was over, the parents would return home, quickly undress the baby, and wash off the baptismal water. These were the Sephardim who refused to give in; to be moulded by the harassment, torture and death of the Inquisition.

Passing as Catholic while remaining Jewish was a highly dangerous performance of group identity. Those suspected of faking Christianity while secretly practising Judaism were disparagingly referred to by the Inquisition as *marranos*, or pigs. If any member of this hidden community were caught, their families would be shamed and rejected as social outcasts, and they themselves would meet their death at the stake. Before that, they were made to wear the yellow robe of shame, the infamous *san benito*, and paraded through streets lined with a jeering mob, to the open squares where they would be publicly burnt alive in the odious *auto da fe*. The *san benito* would then be displayed on the church wall forever, as a cautionary reminder against community transgression.

So there was no freedom, and certainly no safety, in passing as Christians under the Spanish Inquisition, any more than there was in passing as white for Clare in Nella Larsen's novella, or passing as cis for Brandon Teena. As with all kinds of passing, true freedom could only come through self-definition. But, as generations passed, the crypto-Jewish community had no physical relics of their past in which they could covertly search for roots. They had been stripped of their culture and, more importantly, the Torah scrolls. The books had long since been destroyed, the rituals nearly forgotten. In sixteenth- and seventeenth-century Spain, Christian religious festivals marking Old Testament events were celebrated with more vigour and enthusiasm by the crypto-Jews than by the Catholics, as the only remaining trace of their religious heritage. Tales of persecution from the past and present helped accentuate the sense of loss, and fed the psychological process of curating the fragments of memory. For a community that is not just dispossessed but passing, this is done under a shroud of secrecy—if caught, the curator risks losing everything. The secret Sephardim were greedy for memory, stories, legends—the fabric of their identity as Jews. There was just a flicker of a connection to a distant cultural history that kept replaying scenes from lost ceremonies.

The crypto-Jewish community of Iberia produced a vast body of literature, continuing the tradition of Jewish memoir-writing that went back as far as the twelfth century—one of the most celebrated such texts being the log book of Maimonides. Memoirists' takes on life under siege can offer what journalism and historical writing cannot: a subjective picture of the impact of a conflict on people's personal space, and the personal conflict of double or multiple lives. The journalist John Howard Griffin chose not to write a piece of reportage on the plight of African Americans in the South, but to pass through it himself in clinical blackface while keeping a journal that he published after his return. *Black Like Me* has powerfully immortalised his personal anguish, recording the troubled times his country was going through by expressing the meaning of human freedom and human bondage from personal experience.

In *Memoirs of My People*, the American Jewish writer Leo W. Schwarz (1906–67), who edited several anthologies of Jewish personal writings, invites us to

> ponder for a moment the motives that impelled these men and women to record their experiences. With some it is vanity, imita-

tion, profit, discipline, with others the urge for immortality, but with the majority it is the overwhelming need to express themselves. A shattering event has broken their lives, inner pain tortures their spirits, an historic upheaval has cast them from their moorings—they must willy-nilly write down their reactions.[6]

Diaries and autobiographies of Jewish passers from pre-modern times to the present day, Schwarz believed, "afford a glimpse into the curious psychological nature of a mind that was a battleground for the opposing elements of rationalism and occultism."[7] The community of Sephardim passing for Christian made the rational calculation of the secret heretic: to move on and to survive. But after their compelled exodus from Iberia, former groups of secret Jews re-emerged as Jewish communities in other parts of the world, Western Europe and North Africa. As they settled in their Jerusalems in exile—Salonica, Venice, Amsterdam—they enjoyed a renaissance both in their economic and public fortunes and in their Jewish faith.

In some ways, this renewal made the curation of memory more important than ever, particularly as families who had been living as true Christian converts for generations came "back" into the fold, now that Jewishness was back out in the open.

The "New Jews" who had left Iberia and found themselves again called themselves a "nation". Their inspiration and ultimate recovery of their identity—not just surviving, but flourishing—came from the entire Jewish community's faith in circumstantial miracle, one of the most cherished modes of escape for the unfree. For those on the Middle Passage and the grim plantations of the Americas, Anansi was miracle both deified and humanised—he represented the reality of and the hope for survival through rebirth; a return to roots, yet one that transcends the history of rupture and oppression.

Curating memory can be an obsession with the passer, and when it is an entire community hidden in another identity or ripped from its roots, this moves from curating memory to curating collective memory—curating nationhood. Everyone is born with a history, even though for some it is a matter of rediscovery. History is not only built on "achievement and creation"[8] (Naipaul); it is also informed by the collective losses or annihilation of a people as a result of catastrophe—invasion and domination by mightier powers, with their more sophisticated killing machines; dispossession through natural disaster or war.

For those displaced physically and culturally by historical events, self-reinvention can become necessary for a sense of inner peace, or even to be left in peace by others: when the rupture of selfhood has come from the West and its boasts of superior civilisation, a strong foundation to the non-Westerner's sense of identity can allow them to affirm an identity as equals. In Chapter 10 we will meet writers who forged a British Caribbean identity and a black history, defying both the loss of the past among those brought to the New World and the claims that Africa had no history before the Europeans arrived. The lack of physical ruins in much of sub-Saharan Africa has been pointed to by Western cultural chauvinists as proof that Western or Mediterranean civilisation is superior. But ruins often denote the culture of the oppressor, who enslaved people or colonised people's land to build monuments to empire—including the Pyramids in ancient Egypt, the legendary building of which by Jewish slaves is a foundational part of many Jews' sense of their history.

Writers can articulate a more powerful response than anyone to the argument of a community having no memory. Just as there have been reminders of great civilisations before the rise of the West, from India and China to ancient Arabian kingdoms like the Nabataeans and of course the millennia of pharaonic triumph in ancient Egypt, the global community of Jews, one of the world's oldest and largest diasporas, has found ways to fight back against attempts to erase their identity. Pre- and early modern Jewish history is also without ruins. The oppressed and the exiled in Iberia preserved or remade enough memory of their ancestral culture to claim a new Jewish identity after the collective passing was over.

The dilemma of identity-making has featured extensively in the life and work of the wandering Jew. The imagined memory of the very first Jewish roots—the ghost of return to Jerusalem—goes on haunting them millennia after their loss. The story of the Exodus from Egypt, the freed Israelites' crossing of the Red Sea, is recited every year at the Passover seder by Jews all over the world, a tradition marked by the now almost metaphorical longing for return to the spiritual homeland. "Next Year in Jerusalem" both recounts the history of persecution and wandering, and renews the vision for the future—when they will stop "passing" as gentiles. Such oral recital of the memories of displacement has established a Jewish identity in exile; but those memories have also defined the Jews' Anansi-like adaptability and survival as a community—in the case of the once-passing Sephardim, as an indispensable part of European history.

Ghosts of the Displaced

Even today, there are communities passing in order to belong to a world where, as a group, they did not feel safe. Caught in an endless conflict, made refugees or exiles in their own homeland with little but a remembered past, the Palestinians have been building collective resilience and reshaping identity out of their people's sudden loss after the colonial powers divided and quit in 1948. But while most Palestinians, both in what's left of historic Palestine and in the diaspora, have a strong sense of history, identity performance is also just another reality of life within the community under occupation.

Before the Second Intifada (2000–5) and the resultant closures, before the building of the wall and the checkpoints, Bethlehem was very much part of Jerusalem—it was like an extension of the Holy City, providing cheap labour and marketplaces to which Jerusalemites would flock on weekends, as the produce there was fresher, more exotic, less expensive. The windy alleyways of the ancient city also provided a rare escape for the members of the "peace camp", who believed that here, in one of the world's hottest conflict spots, the possibility of co-existence could not be ruled out. Tourism to Bethlehem used to be the city's main source of income.

But since 2002, a massive "security wall" towers over permanent long queues at the checkpoint. To enter the city that houses the Church of the Nativity today, everyone must show their papers; buses from Jerusalem cannot drive through, but must undergo vigorous security checks. Palestinian passengers are required to get off the bus and walk through a caged pathway holding their ID cards, while their bags are put on X-ray belts. Bethlehem's old city squares and lanes, once heaving with foreign tourists and shoppers from Jerusalem, are now deserted. The day visitors trickle in.

The residents are more or less imprisoned inside the city, as the solid 8-meter-high wall surrounds them. It is an ugly, randomly erected monstrosity, a slap on the face of the visitor. There is a subsidiary wall within the main perimeter boundary—a wall within a wall. Once you've passed the huge gates and turnstiles of the outer barrier, you will be hit by another tall concrete barricade that encircles the Jewish holy site of Rachel's tomb, often splashed with colourful graffiti by Banksy and others denouncing the state of Israel. One inscription used to read, "From Warsaw to Israeli ghetto"; another, accompanying a picture of a lost little girl facing the wall, "Could I have my ball back please?"

The area between the main wall and the inner wall is straight out of a bleak futuristic movie where the remaining population of a post-nuclear apocalyptic world is living behind multiple high-security fences. The in-between zone is littered with debris—plastic bottles and bags, soiled nappies, disused barbed wire, empty cigarette packets and used syringes. Here, sprayed on a stretch of the wall in red, visitors may come across the famous lines by Roger Waters: "Tear down the wall" and "We don't need no thought control".

It takes me just ten minutes by car to get from West Jerusalem to the checkpoint. After I show them my British passport, the young soldiers wave me through the high-security wall. As I drive in, I look at the long queue of Palestinians waiting on foot to get through the multi-cubicled, turnstiled hurdles to the other side. I keep going, and in another two minutes I arrive at Jacir Palace, the magnificent but now deserted hotel, converted from an Ottoman-era building, where my Palestinian friend Fida is waiting for me. I have come to meet some of Bethlehem's remaining Christians. Most people with multiple identities find themselves caught between different selves, but Christian Palestinians have to contend with mistrust from all sides, because their identity is politicised.

As a group, they are marginalised for both their national and their religious status, and the community's allegiance is challenged both by other ethnic Palestinians who are Muslims, and by the State of Israel beyond the security wall. A Christian Palestinian's national loyalty may be questioned by Muslim groups, and any observant faith community in Palestine may be viewed with suspicion by the secular Palestinian Authority; on the other hand, those Palestinians who don't practise Islam, whether secular Muslims or Christians, may be seen by the more religious as insufficiently patriotic—too

Westernised to serve the Palestinian interest fully. And, of course, all Palestinians can be seen as outright enemies by Jewish Israelis.

The first of my stop-offs is a kebab joint very close to the security wall, run by two extravagantly moustachioed brothers, who claim to have descended from an original Bethlehem Christian family. They are known as the Abu Shanab brothers—literally the Father of Moustache brothers. Hands covered in minced meat and chopped parsley, Abu Shanab One greets me at the entrance. "We don't use machines here, we mince our meat by hand." I soon meet Abu Shanab Two, behind a huge clay oven where rows of kebabs are being chargrilled on skewers. There are pictures of the Greek Orthodox Patriarch and the Jerusalem Patriarchate on the wall, with other Christian paraphernalia arranged on a table below, including a miniature Nativity scene carved from olive tree roots—traditional Bethlehem handicraft.

Abu Shanab One comes to sit with us. To my surprise, he starts speaking Hebrew to me. He continues even after I tell him that I am not Israeli. Fida whispers to me that the man wants to prove he has intimate contacts with the Jewish State, that he is actually very open-minded. Whatever Abu Shanab is trying to do, he would very easily have convinced me that the brothers are Israeli, had I met them on the other side of the wall in West Jerusalem. His Hebrew has no more of a "give-away" lilt than that of Arab Mizrahi Jews, who speak the language with an aspirated "h" instead of an Ashkenazi "kh", for example.

As we eat, Abu Shanab One talks about his family's long ancestry in the city, adding that he is sad most of the young Christians have left their hometown—or their homeland altogether—to be away from the conflict. Before the Second Intifada began in 2000, Bethlehemites flocked to Jerusalem for better opportunities, but access to Israel has since been restricted by the wall. Now, only a limited number of "Jerusalem passes" are issued by the Israeli government every year, and so young people are desperate for a passage to Europe or the US. Christian Palestinians have a better chance than Muslim compatriots when they apply for American and European visas, as they carry a lesser load of Western prejudices around terrorism. As a result, this once Christian city is losing its Christian residents. But how would I know who is a Christian and who is not?

PASSING

"If I met you in Jerusalem, I would have thought you were an Iraqi or Syrian Jew." When I say this, the brothers start laughing, saying they can pass as Muslims too, and often do so when they cross into Jerusalem with their special temporary passes to attend Christian events. Like many Palestinians, they do not correct people—particularly Israelis—who make wrong assumptions at checkpoints. Often, because they are Arab, the brothers are thought to be Muslims, even by Muslims themselves.

This can be an advantage: being a Christian Bethlehemite has its drawbacks. Many Jews, and some Muslims too, look at the brothers suspiciously when they find out their faith, wondering if they are collaborators of one side or the other. As Palestinians shared their stories with me, I could not help thinking that for many centuries this was how the wandering Jews must have felt in majority-Muslim or -Christian countries. While Iberia's true converts to Catholicism were never accepted by the Christian state, seen as a crypto-Jewish community of passers, they were regarded as morally inferior by the actual crypto-Jews and the Jews outside the Iberian Peninsula, who thought they had failed to protect their ancestral faith.

The Abu Shanab brothers tell me that, even when they go to America, they are accused of passing, as their Christian identity is questioned by incredulous representatives of Homeland Security: "They think I am an Arab pretending to be Christian! To them, 'You're an Arab' means you're ethnically profiled as a terrorist suspect!" He says that this conflation, and the racist assumption accompanying it, has forced his community to wear a crucifix while travelling—but to Abu Shanab it didn't feel right, like he was self-justifying in response to other people's prejudices. Nowadays the brothers no longer correct interrogators who assume they are Muslim; they keep their silence.

"Everyone seems to have a monopoly to decide who we are, so we've become an invisible people, both in our own land and when we go abroad," he says. The "we", I learn, has a double meaning: the brothers are not only talking about their faith community, their nation within a nation, but also the wider Palestinian nation as a whole. Abu Shanab tells me that the Palestinian Christians are not either this or that, but both, just as the rabbi put it at my daughter's bat mitzvah; yet they constantly face accusations and hostilities that come from a need to boil them down to one single identity. When the Israeli army carries out raids on Christian sites such as the Church of the Nativity, hunting for terrorist suspects, the soldiers are apprehensive and taken aback when the brothers make conversation with them in Hebrew, trying to ease the situation so there is still some human connection in the most unhuman of circumstances.

The older Abu Shanab tells me that this unasked-for categorisation has made the Palestinian Christians hold more closely to a collective Christian identity, when once just being "Palestinian" was enough; ethnic or national identities were not always judged against religious affiliation. The wars of the twentieth century have altered the physical and psychological map of the country to which the Abu Shanabs and others like them once belonged, changing the people's own perception of their collective selfhood, seemingly perpetually locked in a conflict not of their making. "Not mine! Definitely not. We've been here for many generations." That made me reflect on my grandmother's story of living in three countries without ever having moved.

The immense difficulties facing Palestinians—of every degree of belief and every religion—prompt them to fold into their day identity performances suited to particular circumstances. I meet other Bethlehemites who claim that their families have been there since the birth of Christianity, and you would not take such claims as wild daydreams: they have more weight than my father's Persian fantasy. The community I meet has always lived in the shadow of the Church of the Nativity, which Christians believe is on the site of the manger where a heavily pregnant Mary and her husband Joseph rested for the night after their long trek from Nazareth. The rest is Christian history. I smile musing on the prejudice of Homeland Security officials, probably from Christian families, sizing up and racially profiling as potential terrorists these brothers from the very birthplace of Christianity.

As we are sitting in the Abu Shanab brothers' restaurant, my companion, Fida, casually remarks that she and her Muslim family might actually be the original Jews! Well, if you did a DNA test, Palestinians might well be ethnically closer to Jews than to white Christian Europeans, she says. But, I counter, if we did worldwide DNA tests, all sorts of revelations may question our understanding of race. It is not DNA that enables many Palestinians to get by in life by passing as Jews, or not correcting assumptions in Israeli workplaces, where many have found employment and escaped poverty in the occupied territories. In Jerusalem, you meet Palestinians working everywhere—in cafes, restaurants, markets, hospitals—and, after a decade living there, I could not always tell whether or not they were Arabs. Most of them speak immaculate Hebrew, and appearance-wise it is easy for many Palestinians to pass as Israeli Jews.

Fida and I leave the Abu Shanabs to speak to a group of musicians, young and unemployed, with aspirations of passage to America—failing that, a pass to Jerusalem. Antonio is a part-time hair-dresser, Karim is an oud player—their names were not among this year's lucky candidates issued with the much-coveted Jerusalem permit. Karim has his own band and plays in a trendy bar called Taboo. Here, it seems, young Bethlehemites break all of Arab society's taboos. The bar is designed as if it were straight out of Soweto, with African masks hanging here and there as beautiful men and women sway to the cool DJ's latest mix, or to live Oriental jazz.

As we watch the dancers, Fida's friends start telling me that, in spite of the wall and other restrictions on their movements, Palestinians are a resilient lot. While there has been some of what they call self-destructive violence from a tiny vengeful minority, most Palestinians—despite lacking the basic rights that even the world's most deprived nations provide to their citizens—just want to move on. Most of the young people I see at Taboo have never been "legally" out of their city. The journey from Bethlehem to Ramallah, which should take half an hour to forty minutes by car, can end up being a couple of hours for a Palestinian through various back roads, crossing minor and major Israeli checkpoints due to the myriad travel restrictions. Many decide not to venture beyond Bethlehem, or to do so as little as possible.

But this is only a strategic show of "laidbackness", Karim tells me: some of these young people have gone everywhere on the Jewish side, even to Tel Aviv. But the recipients of the Jerusalem permits are usually people over 40, women, domestic workers, labourers, the sick needing medical assistance in Israel. They do not stretch to this young crowd.

"So, how do you do it?" I ask.

"Aha!" They tut in unison. "Have you heard of the settler roads?"

Of course I have. I myself have taken them often, to avoid the wall and the major checkpoints where rigorous passport checks by Israeli soldiers are routine.

"Well, when I take you back, we'll drive along one," Fida says. "It's also used by the adventurous Israelis from Jerusalem who want to check out real Arab restaurants or an evening out in a Palestinian bar."

"You are from India?" Karim asks me.

"Well, from London actually."

"Your face looks Indian."

"It does?"

"We see a lot of Indian films."

"Where?"

"On TV—I live in Dheisheh refugee camp; there, everyone has a satellite dish—a window to the world that is walled away from us."

This is not the first time I've found myself appointed by people in the Middle East as a Bollywood ambassador, so I decide to continue the conversation, asking which actors are Karim's favourite. "Amitabh Bachchan," he promptly replies. "He's the best." But he's old, I say. There are many new faces. "I like the Miss World, Ayshwariya Roy," Karim adds. She is very pale, I remark, very un-Indian-looking, with green eyes. "Yes, I know," Karim says, "your face looks more like Amitabh Bachhan's." Oh, I'm flattered, I reply. Or should I not be?

"No, no, I like your dark face." Karim says quickly. "But you know, our men, they like white faces, white women. Many Palestinian women put white powder on their faces to look European, and bleach their hair, to make it lighter, to look blonde."

"And many European women sit for hours in the sun to become brown!" I say.

"I know, I know, but underneath they are white." Karim sounds exasperated suddenly. It's clear what he's thinking: that whiteness is power, and so once you have it, you can play around with it. I can almost hear his unspoken reply: "Don't give me the ludicrous stuff about Europeans trying to look brown—what luxury!"

"How many years have you lived in England?" Karim demands. Most of my adult life, I say. "Your parents are there?" No, they're not. "They're still in India? So you're pretending to be British!" No, I actually feel British! I'm surprised at the stress I put on "feel". Well, Karim muses, "When I am in Tel Aviv, I can also make myself feel Israeli. I even look like one!" His eyes twinkle mischievously, as if he can vanquish the collective Palestinian destiny with whatever trick comes his way, overpowering it through cunning momentary wit. Fida lets out a laugh. They may be displaced from their home, she says, but their ghosts are all there, visiting the houses they left behind, places their people once roamed, among their olive trees and almond orchards.

When she mentions ghosts, she does not say it as a throwaway metaphor, she means the Palestinians' collective spirit.

> Can you imagine, if we always had to wait for those few permits to visit the land where we still have relatives caught in the partition plan who found themselves as the so-called "1948 Palestinians"? Which means all those who were given "Israeli" nationality, while half the people who fled or were left behind the armistice line would need passes to visit their grandparents' backyards and almond groves that are now in the State of Israel.

Fida looks weary as she finishes the long outburst. She is one of those caught-behind-the-line descendants, not a permit-holder. But she too goes back and forth to Israel all the time, to visit her family in the north. Unlike her, her mother and brothers live in an "Arab Israeli" town, Umm al-Fahm. Though the city is overwhelmingly Arab, the family are all on borrowed time, on one-year permits offered and renewed at the discretion of the Israeli Supreme Court. Because Fida's father was working in Kuwait in 1948, he did not receive Israeli citizenship; his children were born stateless. Fida herself used to have a Jerusalem ID, also renewable every year, but that process became so humiliating—filling in forms to prove she is not a security threat—that she doesn't bother with it anymore. And so Fida takes the back routes, "acting" as a settler.

How does one "act like a settler"? Fida promises to show me first-hand, and it turns out she doesn't need to "act" at all. All she has to do to pass as Israeli is just to be herself. She winds down the window and is waved through by young Israeli soldiers. During the first leg of the journey back to Jerusalem, we take the long, "legal" route, through the outskirts of Ramallah. It takes us around two hours, navigating through heavy traffic. She does this all the time, she says. "It would have been better if we had a settler car," she adds as we head for Jerusalem. What's a settler car? "Usually a seven-seater, four-wheel drive," she replies. "For their large families." I realise I have more freedom to move around Fida's ancestral land than she does.

We continue on in my little white car—which at least has the right kind of number plates, yellow with Israeli registration—but we don't follow the usual route, because Fida won't be allowed through without a permit. Known locally as "via Hezme", this route to Jerusalem passes through lots of little, tucked-away Palestinian villages, loomed over by rows and rows of hilltop Israeli settlements, red-roofed and resembling Swiss chalets. They are fortress-like, the red and white dazzling your eyes and brutally destabilising the matt grey-ochre landscape. You feel you are being watched, scrutinised, even if you have not done anything against the legal restrictions on your movements—but of course we have. "How else would I visit my family in Israel, in another country?"

Among the Palestinians passing in their cars every day are many religious women, Fida says, abruptly laughing before turning serious. If you are a Jew, you tuck your headscarf behind your ears; and if you are Muslim, you fold it over your ears. All a Palestinian has to do is to rearrange the fabric. That's the only difference? It's a statement from me, not a question. I know this already, having lived amongst the two communities for almost a decade. Often this headscarf arrangement is the only visible marker of your religion, which—as we learnt from the Abu Shanab brothers—is generally assumed to mark your nationality, and therefore where you can drive.

Of course, if you are caught, and you don't speak Hebrew and can't give the soldiers a good answer as to where you're coming from—a proper hilltop address—then you're in trouble. I know that won't be us. With my number plates, Fida's perfect Hebrew, and her reckless nonchalance in the face of this powerful system, we'll sail through the minor checkpoints along the forbidden settler route. I feel I am the one with a fast-beating heart as we approach Jerusalem. Meanwhile, Fida is casually rambling on

PASSING

about how easy it is for the Palestinians to pass as Israeli, because there isn't an immediate colour barrier. "Our apartness"—I realise she's translated from the Dutch *apartheid*—"is a dark comedy, an administrative board game, where you may 'go to jail' or you may win a hilltop house."

I look out the car window, taking in another eyeful of the white, red-roofed uniformity, looking for a glimpse of seven-seater Jeeps descending into the valley to hit the settler road we are already on. My vision blurs as a barrier manned by soldiers in brown zooms into view. "*Ahlan*," I hear—an Arabic greeting meaning hello, widely used in modern Israel with the "h" unaspirated, so you know when the person pronouncing it is an Ashkenazi Israeli, a Jew of European origin.

"*Manishma*, how are you doing," Fida murmurs, just audible enough, with an aura of fearless casualness.

"*Lé ann?*" Where to?

"*Le Yarushalayim*, to Jerusalem," she answers. They wave us through.

Twenty minutes later, we arrive in the middle of Jaffa Street, West Jerusalem—in Israel. Fida announces that she'll stay the night in the city before going on the next day to northern Israel. She says she has a surprise for me tonight: she's taking me somewhere special to hear some music. We walk into a tucked-away venue at the top of the street, a club popular among young Israelis—and, as it will turn out, young Palestinians. Like Fida, they have braved various settler roads to join both the dancers and the team of DJs. An explosion of electronic music alternates with live oud at one end of the small dance hall, with a back-to-back crowd—Israel and Palestine, Palestine and Israel. There is also a small handful of international peacemakers and foreign hangers-on like me, diving for the night into a live melting-pot of people who, in daylight hours, are caught in a visceral conflict, separated by walls, checkpoints, Jewish settlement belts across the occupied territories, and gun-wielding teenage soldiers defending them.

Suddenly, an apparition: the Palestinians I met earlier that day in Bethlehem, Karim and the others, have waded into the crowded room. They are speaking Hebrew with the perfect modern Israeli accent, walking around indistinguishable from the citizens of the

Jewish State. Fida tugs at my arm to come to the dance floor for a popular song by an Algerian singer. I've been immersed in a bowl of silence, with all the noise going on around me. I am seeing the scene through a thick pane of glass between me and the people in the room.

Moving around me in the dimmed light, swaying and smiling, the secret Palestinians are the ghosts of the displaced. But the scene around me is far from ethereal; it is solid and real, born of defiance at the segregation and half a century of occupation. I stand there transfixed at this riotous extravaganza of identity escape, the community of passers effortlessly impersonating the community they are fighting against.

The day I have described is a typical day for many Palestinians. This stateless nation is used to going in and out of territories and swapping identities as they go, navigating one of the world's longest-running conflicts by carefully yet routinely putting on an Israeli act, tweaking their appearance, mannerisms and language, or else simply playing along with Israelis' assumptions—all in order to be unticked on that racial-profiling list of security threats. Sometimes, as with the crypto-Jews, it must be an active performance; and sometimes, as for the Turkish Armenians, it is an act of silence.

Passing as Israeli often means assimilating into Israeli culture, but it is a temporary state, dictated by administrative constraints. At the same time, it has become an integral part of the community's experience under occupation, part of the way of life and of self-understanding. By constantly confronting—and putting on the identity this requires—the Palestinians remain intimately tied to their history of exclusion and oppression, just as Jews do on the other side of the walls when they tell the Seder story. The Palestinians' longing for Jerusalem is just as legitimate as all dreams of return among displaced people. But when conflict over this shared homeland began in the 1920s, it was not the first time an ancestral home had been contested by two communities amidst an identity transformation.

Black-skinned, White-souled

In our history, communal shifts in identity have been determined by drastic changes in the world's or a country's power structure: mass passing as a response to mass bigotry, when a whole group or people caught in the cracks strives to rise above their perpetually inglorious social status by creating a whole new nation. But what happens when this collective transformation takes place not within the persecuting society, but in an escape away from it, into somebody else's?

As we saw with the crypto-Jews of Iberia, in pre-modern times religion was one's nationality, and in order to belong to a "nation", one usually had to adhere to the majority faith. As definitions and frameworks of identity changed over time, so too did the nature of mass passing. One of the most fascinating examples of the collective passing phenomenon takes us back to race: the mass transfer of freed slaves and other African Americans from the United States to West Africa, starting in 1822; the founding of Liberia in 1847 as the first independent nation-state in Africa; and the new-old identity these settlers adopted when they reached their "homeland".

Liberia was born of a scheme proposed by the nineteenth-century American Colonization Society (ACS), a body of Northern philanthropists and politicians and influential Southern slave-holders like planters. By the time of slavery's abolition and the aftermath of the Civil War in the 1870s, more than 12,000 American-born Africans had been shipped to Liberia to start a new colony of freed slaves. According to ACS records, 4,500 of these were born free, 350 had bought their freedom, and another 6,000 were freed on the condition they would permanently leave America. This last group shows us the true racist purpose behind this supposedly emancipatory and redemptive operation: "The real goal of the society was to rid America of Negros. Liberia was the solution to the 'Negro Problem'. Free Negros threatened slavery and were thought to instigate slave revolt. If they became successful, they might marry white women."[9] Simon Schama explains fear of inter-racial relationships as "a threat to the purity of white womanhood".[10]

As we saw in Chapter 2, miscegenation was the darkest thought on the minds of many whites—even of abolitionists in the North like Thomas Jefferson. Jefferson was wary of the sudden emancipation of the slaves and advocated instead phased eradication of the evil practice. As well as miscegenation, he feared race riots resulting from the slaves' resentment after centuries of inhuman treatment, which he thought would naturally be unleashed on their emancipation. He recommended their relocation to West Africa, supporting the ACS. The same pattern of resettling black people in Africa had happened in the UK in the previous century: when African American loyalists arrived in Britain after defeat in America's War of Independence (1775–83), their bedraggled presence sent shockwaves through the country. The Treasury bore the expense of transporting the destitute veterans to Sierra Leone, with food, clothing and tools to build their settlement. Historians have argued that, although the scheme was sold as "utopian idealism", it was in fact more like an "experiment in social hygiene", supported by diehard British defenders of slavery (not to be abolished for another fifty years), who feared that this black presence would swell the ranks of the abolitionists.[11]

On the other hand, the creation of Liberia as a free home for nineteenth-century African Americans was seen by some of them as a path to redemption, a reverse journey across the Atlantic to reclaim their African heritage. Even after the Civil War, many African Americans who had fought for the Union, both slave and free, found that they weren't really wanted. They were fully aware of the ACS's ulterior motives in ridding America of their "black blood", but they jumped at this opportunity for a new chapter and a recovery of an African identity. By reinventing themselves not as African Americans but as Liberians, and taking that classic step of the identity-transformer—a physical journey to a new life—they might finally find a selfhood they could live with. As George Harris famously says in *Uncle Tom's Cabin*, "I have no wish to pass for an American, or to identify myself with them. It is with the oppressed, enslaved African race that I cast in my lot; and if I wished anything, I would wish myself two shades darker, rather than one lighter."[12]

For many of the 12,000 that arrived from America, Liberia was a spiritual homeland in the same way Israel has been for the Jewish diaspora. Some writers have made this same analogy, connecting these "returnees" with the Zionist vision of the Biblical chosen people arriving in their "homeland".[13] African slaves and their descendants have often found meaning in their collective ordeal by likening it to Old Testament history, the most memorable of the plantation songs inspired by Moses's plea to the Jews' pharaonic slave-masters to "Let My People Go". But this was treading on precarious territory. The idea of Israel—or Jerusalem—as the Jewish homeland, endorsed by the Old Testament, has held the Jewish people together through all their centuries of displacement. But after 400 years of brutal slavery, Liberia for the African Americans was an African beginning, without a remembered African past.

For what is a remembered African past in the Western diaspora? How do you memorialise your roots and lineage after being wrenched from your homeland, separated from your family, sometimes multiple times? Jews who fled the Holy Land and went into exile, and those who had to flee repeatedly after pogroms and inquisitions, generally did so in families and communities, with the expulsion or persecution of their entire people. The ancestors of African Americans were stolen and sold individually to ruthless slave-owners across the ocean. This was broken history of a different magnitude; often a slave in the Americas would not remember or know their own parents, let alone their ancestral heritage.

The settlers who came to Liberia were without an African memory, and—just as the advocates of Zionism failed to take into account the natives of Palestine—they were not prepared when they got off the boat for a land alive with people who had lived there continuously throughout the centuries of imperialism and slavery, people who did have a strong past. The indigenous Liberians—the Kru, the Kpelle and so on—were well endowed with a living history, and they did not want colonisers on their land, regardless of their skin colour. The settlers were black, but they followed the same racist, segregationist legal institutions of the American South from where they came. They settled along the coast while the indigenous tribes were pushed further, deeper into the forest. The Americo-Liberians, as they came to be known, followed the well-trodden path of European colonials before them, and "the problems of hierarchy sundering antebellum America [were] reinscribed in Liberia's American foundations."[14]

Being placed in the continent from which their ancestors had been stolen, in a randomly carved "independent" African spot, the Americo-Liberians had great difficulties in adjusting to their new life in Africa and communicating with the locals, who resented them and did not share their language. The emigrants arrived with views directly influenced by the white settler-colonial mentality, and many showed little understanding that the native population had their own laws and customs, an established system regulating their lives—they really did possess an African "civilisation", steeped in their unbroken African history. As the Americo-Liberians emerged as a colonial elite, they looked down on the indigenous Liberians as African subjects over whom they ruled; they denied them legal rights, and stripped them of human rights including freedom of movement. The conflict that started soon after their arrival germinated and very quickly homogenised the whole nation into the perspective of the coloniser, whose motto was "The Love of Liberty Brought Us Here".

To justify their mission, the Americo-Liberians used the old white European Christian argument. They believed they had the key to salvation, which lay in Protestant civilisation—educating and improving the lives of the natives, this time a black man's burden. The diasporic spirit of togetherness woven by Anansi had been left behind on the plantations. To these settlers, determined to transition to an African life, the "lure of going back to Africa was to be powerful, to be in charge and have power over others."[15] They felt they were claiming something rightfully and always theirs, while the indigenous Liberians saw them as illegitimate claimants to an African identity—as mass passers.

But then, who can blame them? It was not their idea to create the colony. They took the opportunity when it was presented to or forced upon them by white power and its racist export scheme. Like the native Liberians, the community of Americo-Liberians were also a group of racialised people, unwanted in their land of birth and now trapped on the wrong continent, rejected by their ancestral Africa. The indigenous resisted these black-skinned, white-souled colonials, seeing them as an army of "mimic men" who had no right to identify as African. The literature professor Julia Stern remarks,

> Engaged in a civil war that pits the colonial elite—descendants of nineteenth-century African American slaves—against the descendants of the colonized indigenous African tribes of the area, late-twentieth-century Liberian factions can be seen as playing out the final act of the patriarchal, revolutionary politics at work in *Uncle Tom's Cabin*.[16]

In a way, this nineteenth-century conflict uncannily pre-empted a very contemporary debate, where the right to claim or perform certain identities is fiercely contested. Today, as we will see in Part Four, this "culture war" is often focused on the actions and words of individuals, but the notion of inherently not belonging to an identity you have chosen for yourself has its roots in ideas of community and inheritance. Before closing this part of the book, then, let us look at some more examples of individuals who have entered the treacherous waters of contested or heavily guarded identity as a means of achieving not just personal redemption, but membership of a new group, a new people—from the boys' clubs that have excluded women, to colonisation of the mind.

10

MINDSETS OF BELONGING

SOCIO-CULTURAL PASSING

Perhaps the single most complex type of passing is what I call socio-cultural passing: inhabiting a culture, social identity or language other than the one you were born with. In Chapter 13, we will explore the idea of socio-culturally passing "down", in other words engaging in cultural appropriation; here we are talking about the standard direction of true passing: from an underprivileged culture or class to one of dominance. We've already met various figures who could be described as socio-culturally passing in service of their overall "disguise"—Anatole Broyard's echoing of racist ideas, Brandon Teena's exaggerated masculinity, Chris Gunness's quiet toleration of the jokey homophobia in his office, Balram Halwai's ostentatious and materialistic lifestyle. But there are also many socio-cultural passers who have no other disguise beyond their imitation of, or integration into, a cultural or social world.

For these passers, there is usually no clear divide between their past or origins and the performance of their current or future identity, because shifting towards the dominant culture or mainstream society is not a sudden decision, but usually a gradual process, for some dating back to early childhood. The socio-cultural passer has long internalised the social or cultural values and outlook that they embrace, in some ways seeing this as an alternative to "real" passing—assimilating rather than infiltrating. There is a blurring, a strip of no man's land when the shifter of identity is being regenerated as a new person with an adopted soul, a different place in the world or a fresh way of seeing it. Although other types of passing involve more obvious physical disguises, here too is the fear of being caught out as a misfit; the insecurity around being considered unsuitable can take over the non-native member of a culture or class.

What this tells us, and what the stories below will show, is that our conditions at birth still inform not just our lives, but how others see us today—despite supposed landmarks of progress like universal suffrage regardless of class, gender or ethnicity. As we will see, what has changed is how difficult or easy it is to move away from these "origins" into a new belonging—at least temporarily.

When it comes to class, the new social and cultural persona is intended not just to free the individual, but to become a legacy for their progeny—replacing a low-born inheritance with a new one. In societies where class is formally tied to another identity, we have seen that this aspiration informs other types of passing too, from South African "playwhites" to the Turkish Armenians to India's caste-passers; but even those who adopt a higher-class persona in and of itself are passing not only in the present but for the future. This means that class-passing stories are sometimes a family affair, and they are often fabulously told by novelists and film-makers, a genre that ranges from sentimental social realism to breath-taking horror—sometimes within the same work.

One such powerful piece of art is Bong Joon-ho's *Parasite*, which became the first foreign-language film to win Best Picture at the Academy Awards in 2020. This captivating Korean film, which is as darkly humorous as Adiga's caste-passing novel *The White Tiger*, follows a working-class, perpetually unemployed Korean family of four. In the course of the film, their tragi-comic story—a spectacularly successful yet short-lived bout of class-passing—turns dramatically dark and violent.

The Kims huddle in a basement flat at the bottom of a dead-end alley, where the only view to the street is through half a window, partially blocked by a clothes hanger drying socks. Because they are in the basement, the Kims' view of the outside is also intercut with the feet of other social misfits and drunks, who urinate against the sunken window. The camera shots of this obscured view onto the world throughout the film serve as a metaphor for the family's existence as the lowest of the low. The miserable Kims—mother, father, son and daughter—spend most of their time holding up their phones while perched on a toilet lid, trying to connect to the unlocked Wi-Fi of a nearby establishment; but soon they will come up with a scheme to improve not only their phone signal, but their circumstances. With brutal resolve, one by one, the four basement-dwellers get themselves hired as employees of a super-rich family in a wealthy area of Seoul, using fake identities that conceal their relation to one another: a university student who can tutor teenagers, a US-educated art therapist, an experienced Mercedes driver and a trained housekeeper. The contrast and interactions between the Kims and their unwitting employers, the Parks, play equally on the prejudice and insecurity of the privileged, and the resentment and inferiority complex of the downtrodden.

There are many uncanny parallels with *The White Tiger*. The Kim family are as ruthless and subversive in their breaking of the class system as Balram, unscrupulous artful dodgers who have a riotous time during their brief foray into the upper-class world, cold-heartedly taking over the Parks' home and lives, their bedrooms and their booze. Remorse, they seem to feel, is a guilt trip created by the oppressor class to maintain the servanthood of the low-born, forever in awe of their master-employers; the four Kims can only enter the physical home and social world of the wealthy Parks by providing personal services to them. While "parasite" typically denotes the working classes, often described by the powerful as scroungers, in Bong's film it is the rich who are shown to feed off the servility or servitude of the poor.

The parody comes from the poor family's unrepentant antics as class-passers; the tragedy comes from the dual realisation that the rich family are the true posers, yet still the ones in control of the system. In the end, it all unravels for these self-proclaimed avengers of inequality; the Kims' class-passing tragically backfires. The audience is left with that old moral, the bleak prognosis of people reaching higher than their allotted rank, who ultimately remain of little consequence. The system is still stronger than random individuals attempting to get even with it. Ultimately, it course-corrects, shaking off the Kims in a violent denouement that restores a horrifying normality to the lives of both families.

Sometimes, though, even if hierarchies can't be dismantled by those they exclude or exploit, they can be played with, to the passer's benefit; and, in the long run, they can lose some of their importance. Next we will look at a kind of socio-cultural passing that is no longer as necessary as it once was.

Mythic Mannish Lesbians

In a time when British women did not have equal rights under law, the dominant and privileged culture was not just one of high class, but of exclusively male high class. We have already seen women passing as men to access opportunity in Chapter 5, but these were women dressing up as men. Others instead retained a woman's identity, but created a "masculine" persona that conformed to the cultural and social gender values of the age. This was not a passing undertaken lightly or without good reason: living openly as an identity-transgressor is no easy life, as the trans figures of Chapter 6 have shown us. The socio-culturally male-passing women we will meet here adopted masculinity as a protective armour giving them freedom to pursue their queer relationships—a sort of less extreme version of the Bashevis Singer character Pinchosl and Hubert Page in *Albert Knobbs*. It took not only identity confidence, sexual bravery and creative genius, but also high social class to begin with. To see how gender, class and sexuality have been intertwined in these women's cultivations of masculine roles, we shall first look into the true story of Gentleman Jack.

Anne Lister (1791–1840) was a late Georgian diarist and landowner, and a lesbian. Her journals reveal the industrial and aristocratic worlds in which she moved, documenting many social events, but also—more importantly, and more sensationally when they were first published in the 1980s—recounting her seduction of and sexual liaisons with women. She was the female Don Juan of her time, with one sixth of her diary pages—written in code that she devised, a mixture of algebra and Greek letters—containing graphic details of her encounters with married and single women, before she settled down with Ann Walker, a fellow heiress. Throughout these coded pages, Lister tries to make sense of her sexuality, at a time when there was no term available to describe it. She described her identity to one of her lovers by saying that she had her "particular ways".

Unlike many of her friends, Anne Lister did not have to straight-pass; she was openly interested in women. Her class not only gave her greater freedom to pursue her conquests, but formed an integral part of the personality she inhabited in doing so—not just Jack, but Gentleman Jack. As an unusually wealthy and educated woman of her time, she assumed the "liberties and manners of the opposite sex".[1] The entitlement and confidence of her class were essential to society's acceptance of her in what was then seen as a man's sexual role: conquest. Anne had acquired financial solvency and land-owner status through inheritance of her aunt and uncle's Yorkshire estate, Shibden Hall: coal pits, rent from tenants, agriculture. They left the Hall to Anne and not to her sister Marianne precisely because of Anne's sexuality: Marianne was going to marry, and so the property would have left the family, passing into her husband's name and ultimately going to their sons. Lister refurbished and looked after the fifteenth-century house and grounds until her death, as her diaries describe in minute detail. Today Shibden Hall is a museum dedicated to her legendary life, and a site of lesbian pilgrimage.

It was the residents of Lister's tenancy area in Halifax who gave her the title Gentleman Jack, perhaps with a dash of cynical amusement at the idiosyncrasy of the rich—their ladies are even at leisure to dress as men. Lister's lovers called her Fred, and one of her closest married love interests, Mariana Belcombe, described her as having a "masculine appearance", for Lister dressed in tailored black, with a top half resembling men's clothing of her class and time. Her diaries note, perhaps boastfully, "The people generally remark, as I pass along, how much I am like a man".[2] In this unusual and striking outfit, she both visited her tenants and appeared at top-class social gatherings as the landed gentry of her time did, exuding the self-confidence of a "genius" businesswoman, wealthy adventurer and maverick socialite. She obsessively wrote nearly 8,000 pages about her life as a woman of means, from business transactions—including fallouts—to travelling around Europe at a time when women travellers were rare, even meeting the Danish Queen in Copenhagen. Lister's social position and wealth allowed her the freedom she needed to cross back and forth over heteronormative and gender-normative identity lines, in full view of society.

It is important too that Lister was not just a landowner, but an influential industrialist, the owner of a colliery on her Yorkshire land. The nineteenth-century rise of industrial capitalism led to more accessible travel, the emergence of leisure time for lower classes, migration from countryside to towns where people mixed, and a new privileged class of the self-made, or the bourgeoisie. These social upheavals were instrumental in disinhibiting all kinds of marginalised people, including those we would now call gay or queer. They allowed "freer expression because of increased mobility, more tolerance of unconventional behaviour for those whose status is achieved through wealth rather than birth, greater independence through inheritance of moderate but adequate wealth without the necessity of marital or family alliances."[3]

The intersectionality of class privilege and sexual freedom makes Anne Lister's diaries a fascinating study. Her circumstances were such that she was able to adopt the archetype of the social libertine as soon as she became aware of her sexuality. This included in her relationships: Lister played perfectly the part of a serial womaniser, her diaries revealing how she liked to perform the traditional male role as a "giver" of sexual pleasure to her "lady interests", who were often of a lower social status than she was. In Chapter 7 we saw that the Bangladeshi lovers Sanjida and Puja initially hoped that they could continue their relationship in secret, even after Puja had been married to a man; it didn't work out for them, but Anne Lister was not a *mofussil* villager. She had many "straight-passing" lovers, who kept their public marriages intact.

Just as Puja's family believed that Sanjida had brainwashed or drugged her into eloping, Anne was often described as a deviant polluting the heads of innocent women. But, unlike Sanjida, Anne was allowed her freedom: her instinctive understanding of upper-class male culture and society made her socially passable, even with her "open and gentleman-like" flirting—space was made for her sexuality because of her impersonation of male privilege, which was in turn facilitated by her fortune and her excellent home tutoring, at a time when girls were barred from educational institutions. During a visit to Halifax, I had the opportunity to see a selection of the Lister diaries in the West Yorkshire Archives. The following lines, where Lister chooses to quote Rousseau, stuck with me as a timeless reminder of the class-privileged person who confidently and boastfully flouts social norms, delighting in their ingenuity, because they understand those norms and, simply, because they can: "I know my own heart and understand my fellow man. But I am made unlike anyone I have ever met. I dare to say that I am like no one in the whole world".[4]

At the Holy Trinity Church in York, Lister and her long-term partner, Ann Walker, took a private "marriage" vow, just as Sanjida and Puja would do in a Hindu temple 200 years and 5,000 miles away. In both cases society had no word for these women's sexual identity, but Anne was not in doubt. BBC One and HBO's 2019 dramatisation of Lister's life, *Gentleman Jack*, quotes directly from the journals: "I love, & only love, the fairer sex … my heart revolts from any other love than theirs." The script builds on this line, as the diarist, played by Suranne Jones, declares:

> These feelings have not wavered or deviated since childhood. I was born like this. I act as my God-given nature dictates. If I were to lie with a man *that* would be unnatural, that surely would be *against God*. Who made us. Every one of us. In all our richness and variety.[5]

In Britain, attitudes have shifted significantly in the time since Anne's death at the start of the Victorian era. Though queer individuals and scholars would debate the essentialist interpretation given here of her sexuality, mainstream society no longer sees being gay as sinful, and non-hetero sexualities are no longer considered unnatural. The blue plaque commemorating her marriage long described her as a "gender-nonconforming entrepreneur" without mentioning her sexuality; in 2019, it was changed after years of campaigning by gay activists to the following:

Anne Lister
1791–1840
of Shibden Hall, Halifax
Lesbian and Diarist;
took sacrament here to seal her union with Ann Walker
Easter 1834.

* * *

One hundred years after Anne Lister lived, in the first half of the twentieth century, lack of understanding or acceptance of homosexuality still meant that gender and sexuality were often confused or tied together, even in cases where they shouldn't have been. In 1905, Freud described non-heterosexual desire as "inversion" in his essay "The Sexual Aberrations". Traditional sexology, including the well-established Freudian theories, follows a pre-ordained path based on a set of essential, binary gender characteristics—in other words, the idea that homosexuality can be explained as a gender confusion or mismatch within an individual's psychology. This essentialist "science" was put forward, for example, in Otto Weininger's work *Sex and Character* (1903), which makes claims of inherent masculine superiority.

Lesbian leanings have been and are still in many cultures seen as some kind of masculine aberration in a woman "trapped" in the wrong emotional frame. Even in supposedly more open Western societies today, there remains a strange fascination, particularly among straight men, with finding out "which one of the two is 'the man'" in a gay relationship, whether between two men or two women. It seems to comfort society somehow to know that at least gender norms are being upheld in some way.

When the pattern of fixed gender characteristics (including heterosexuality) is challenged, when a woman in her female body, somewhat androgynously dressed, goes for another woman, she is just a "Mythic Mannish Lesbian"—the term coined by Esther Newton in her essay on the lesbian and ultimately gender-nonconforming English author Radclyffe Hall, whose interwar novel *The Well of Loneliness* popularised the concept of sexual inversion beyond medical terminology, depicting a masculine lesbian.

The novel "brought significant social backlash, and the book was eventually brought up on obscenity charges."[6] When it was published in 1928—the same year as Woolf's gender-bending *Orlando*—the word "lesbian" carried negative connotations even among literary circles.

The result of this ongoing homophobia was that the "mannish lesbian" persona so successfully presented by Anne Lister in the nineteenth century continued to have a place in what we would now call queer society, in both fiction and real life. Today we have various terms which might describe this kind of woman—butch, queer or genderqueer, transmasculine—but it is hard for us to know which historical figures might have identified as gender-fluid or trans had they lived today, and which would simply identify as lesbians who had felt the need to inhabit a form of masculinity in order to make their sexuality acceptable.

One lesbian figure to whom the term transmasculinity has been applied by sociologists is Gertrude Stein, one of the most celebrated authors of the early twentieth century, who openly lived with her "wifie", Alice B. Toklas, and who found fame by conforming to the rules and terms of success devised by a patriarchal system. In many ways, Stein and Toklas's relationship—widely known in their 1920s Parisian intellectual circle—mirrored a typical heterosexual married couple's, in its daily routine. Alice liked dresses and cooking, even publishing a cookery book, while Stein liked men's hats. Toklas was not just a typical "wifie": she was strong-willed, managed Stein's creative professional life, and was her equal soulmate. But there was still an obvious imbalance. Stein identified with her male "genius" contemporaries—authors, artists and philosophers who wrote about her, photographed her, painted her, and this informed how she saw her relationship with Toklas. The "marriage" was not unlike the romantic and sexual partnerships of their male peers, for example Picasso and his various muses.

Stein lived out, and perhaps even consciously articulated, "a unique mode of transmasculine *subjectivity* that enabled her copious literary production as well as her relationships with Toklas and her masculine colleagues."[7] She apparently wrote of Picasso, Matisse and herself that "the two men have 'a maleness that belongs to genius. *Moi aussi*, perhaps'."[8] Her too. Stein's early association of genius with maleness points to the way her intellectual life allowed her to act out and normalise her queerness, just as Anne Lister's aristocratic life had done for her.

The trendy Paris salon where Stein and Toklas hobnobbed with painters, Hemingway and other key avant-garde and modernist intellectuals was "a crucial transactional point",[9] where neither gender or sexual orientation, nor ambiguity around these, was a barrier to membership. In the age of Freudian "inversion", queer personas and liaisons were deemed subversive, anti-social; a threat to pre-existing norms of sexuality and gender and the prevailing myth that the two were always bound up together. Gertrude Stein organised her artistic, social and personal life around opposing these rigid ideas.

Stein established herself as a queer artist long, long before the concept would be popularised as we understand it today, and challenged her heteronormative society in her experimental poetry collection *Tender Buttons* (1914), which also explores social ignorance around female and lesbian sexuality. Stein rejected the gender theories of the early twentieth century. She also wrote erotic poetry, an artistic genre generally considered to be masculine. Her "mannish lesbian genius" persona gave her the licence to write fairly explicit visions of sexual desire, and to focus in those scenes on women's bodies and women's pleasure. If women's writing were to be regarded as of any importance at all in the early twentieth century, it would have been unthinkable, or at least socially deviant, for an ordinary straight woman to produce such "obscene" work, of explicit sexual nature, or violence. It was not even acceptable for *men* to portray women having such desires: Stein was writing at the same time as *Lady Chatterley's Lover* was banned and censored in Britain.

Not only was Stein's own work groundbreaking, but she is also believed to have been a key inspiration for Virginia Woolf—living as a woman while married to a man, and loving another woman who sometimes toyed with transmasculinity, Vita Sackville-West. It is believed Woolf, Stein's ideological successor in some ways, drew heavily on her ideas and style to write *Orlando* in a way that would be regarded as experimental and therefore of literary importance, rather than socially and sexually subversive. For Woolf's novel was just as much of a threat to the period's predominant ideas of sexology, inversion and gender essentialism as Stein's work:

> Orlando's shift in sex and gender creates a more ambiguous sexual identity, as Woolf portrays Orlando's attraction to both men and women. Yet, because of Orlando's shift into a female body, her sexuality cannot be defined in terms of gender. This ambiguity challenges Freud's theories and expands the limitations they place on desire.[10]

In a strictly gendered and heteronormative society, those who couldn't conform sexually could seek to dodge the penalties for their transgression by conforming socially and culturally. The more creative among them did so by ingenious plots and storytelling, extraordinary language, and charisma. Woolf's writing would not have been appreciated by her contemporary readers and reviewers had she not created an absurdly strange protagonist with an unrealistic lifespan of three centuries. Orlando is not only an embodiment of both male and female, but lives those three centuries "deemphasising" gender's importance in his/her relationships.[11] He becomes a she without much fuss; no one raises an eyebrow, not even in Constantinople when the British ambassador, Orlando the man, jumps out of his bedroom window in baggy Turkish trousers and transforms into Orlando the woman. The caravan of gypsies she joins do not question her female identity, gender binaries being less set in stone in that society than in Georgian England; although they do become suspicious of her penchant for poetry and solitude. Orlando is the ultimate socio-cultural gender-passer, easily alternating between masculine and feminine "characteristics" and lifestyles, and blurring the boundaries between them.

Stein and Woolf's critical commentary on established social theories of sexuality and gender also deviate from the norm in their style. Orlando is tauntingly subtitled *A Biography*, as if to say that his/her story represents a true reflection of human nature, but many of its elements are fantastical. Meanwhile, Stein's verse verges on the abstract, experimenting with word repetition and opaque, absurd paragraph forms. Just as Anatole Broyard's lifelong white-passing enabled him to escape the label of "Negro author", both Stein and Woolf manipulated society's limited ideas of intellect and artistry to establish themselves as mainstream writers, pushing their way into a culture that was, at the time, decidedly masculine. They created history in shaping the way we think today about gender and sexuality. Here passing is not just escape from; it is also acceptance into.

Old Natives vs New Natives

So far in this chapter, we have explored examples of those trying to escape a pernicious, complex and deeply rooted system of class and gender hierarchies, within mostly ethnically homogeneous societies. But things get much more complicated, and bitterly contested, when performance of class or culture overlaps with racial power structures and legacies of empire.

When members of a historically or currently powerful identity group seek to adopt the culture of a less privileged group, this is called cultural appropriation—we'll get on to that in Part Four. When it comes to cultural minorities, however—in the West, primarily migrants and their descendants—socio-cultural passing can manifest in various forms: integration, acculturation, assimilation, multi-culturalism, code-switching. But there are all kinds of questions that arise from this. Is culture-passing the right way to describe these transitions? Is it possible to call foreigners and cultural minorities who integrate into their host societies culture-passers, or are they simply culture-inhabiters? Passing is only passing if it works: if you understand and express a culture well enough to participate and communicate in it, are you passing *as*, or passing *to*? And does the answer depend on whether you are imitating the dominant culture out of habit or by conscious decision?

In the 1960s, around the time of the American Civil Rights movement and radical social reverberations shaking Europe, it had seemed that a global, feel-good, all-you-need-is-love, hare-krishna-orange-robed, sari-wearing, afro-styling approach would ultimately have the healing power to restore trust between the historically oppressed and the historical oppressor, a trust shattered by 400 years of human tragedy and shame: slavery, colonialism, persecution. In the new age of free love, social reform and forward-thinking dreamers, these hierarchies, divisions and injustices would be replaced with a post-identity world of universality, equality and freedom. But it did not happen. Again in the 1990s, with centre-left governments coming to power in both the US and the UK, there was an emphasis on celebrating multi-culturalism, as if all cultures were treated and accessed equally nowadays. But this was an illusion too—the multi-cultural or post-racial utopia never arrived. If anything, we are more entrenched in identity politics and "clashes of civilisations" now than we were thirty or even sixty years ago.

That said, the goalposts in this supposed "culture clash" have moved. There is an argument, particularly in Western Europe, for saying that complexion is now dissociated from racist categorisation, and that ideas of belonging in the West have transformed from a racial question into a social one, somewhere between culture and class. The majority tribe controlling the rights of the rest is no longer defined by skin colour; complexion-based racism is being pushed back to the talkback section of the *Daily Mail*, whose front pages are more worried about EU migrants. A white British acquaintance who lives on my street has had more of an issue with "the Eastern European foreign labour"—"those Poles who don't even speak English"—than with his Caribbean and Pakistani neighbours who act "proper British" and, of course, speak English "better than the English". I have heard the same sighs of dismay from non-white Britons: first-, second- and third-generation brown and black immigrants sneering at these new outsiders, who may be white, but cannot pass as British.

If you have gone to one of Britain's top boarding schools for boys, married the heiress of a billionaire Indian entrepreneur and worked for Goldman Sachs, you may be brown-skinned, but the white-majority public could not care less if you are elected to run their economy. Britain's Chancellor of the Exchequer since 2020, Rishi Sunak, has seen his class status successfully whitewash what would have stood out and hindered his social mobility not so long ago: his complexion. But what's important to remember about Sunak and others like him is that he still had to overcome the obstacle of racism in the first place; for a white man of exactly the same class background as him, there is no initial challenge to, or question over, his belonging. Britain may have become more inclined to use other or additional criteria to define "them" and "us", but racism is still alive and well in the West.

As we have seen in the opposing cases of the low-class Kim family and the high-class Gentleman Jack, how society treats a member of an outgroup often determines whether or not that individual is driven to culture-passing, or instead to rejecting altogether the dominant social and cultural worldview. As we will see here, the same holds true with regards to migrants and particularly ethnic minorities in the West. We've already seen some evidence of this in Chapter 4: Anthony Ekundayo Lennon's experience of racism led him to reject a white identity, while Barack Obama has built a successful career partly on his ability to inhabit and be accepted into cultural whiteness. And in fact we have already met one socio-cultural passer, all the way back in Chapter 2: Josephine Baker, who understood so perfectly white French attitudes toward black people that her audiences couldn't tell the difference between her parody of them and the real her. This act was her escape route to freedom.

The dilemmas of culture-passing concern all migrants and outsiders, but it is the race question particularly that has never fully gone away: optically non-white people cannot ever tiptoe around the racial perceptions of a predominantly white society. However many generations of your family have lived in the UK, for example, if they are of South Asian origin, your identity will always be qualified as "British Indian" and so on; my second-generation Jewish and Polish friends have been much freer never to look back. Social and cultural transitions won't necessarily require or involve a wholesale rejection or concealment of one's origins, because we generally view social mobility as a legitimate kind of identity transformation. But when such transitions are being undertaken by a person of colour, the equation changes; society does not accept that it is possible to become a different race, as we'll see in Part Four.

The grounding of racial understanding and identification in appearance means that there is only one way around this, for those who cannot visually pass: removing their physical presentation altogether. Many of my non-white friends in broadcasting feel relieved when they hear their "British" voices coming out of the radio—so long as they don't have "strange foreign names", the cultural authority of their voice is safe from being questioned. When I joined BBC radio in my early twenties, I knew many colleagues who paid for private speech lessons to get rid of their "foreign" accent, even though many of them were native English speakers who had grown up in South Asia with English as their first language.

This brings us to one of the most interesting and important films of the late 2010s, based on a true-life account of an African American policeman infiltrating white supremacists—by passing as one himself. Darkly comic like *Parasite*, Spike Lee's *BlacKkKlansman* is based on the officer's memoir; his name was Ron Stallworth and in the 1970s he became the first black detective in the Colorado Springs police department. In the film we see how Stallworth convinced the Ku Klux Klan's Grand Wizard over the phone that he was a diehard white nationalist. He became a card-holding member of the Klan, and worked as an undercover agent within the KKK for nine months, a highly dangerous infiltration mission. He had his certificate of membership framed and displayed in his office. It was signed by David Duke of New Orleans, the Grand Wizard.

It is important to see why this operation worked for Stallworth— he was able to pass as a Klan member because he did not meet Duke face to face. Whenever a real-life meeting was required, he sent his white (Jewish in Lee's film) colleague in his place. All he had to do was speak on the phone in a particular way, culturally and socio-economically passing as white by playing on the prejudices of a racist, speaking in standard US English without an accent popularly associated with African Americans at that time. The KKK chief simply could not fathom that a man as "well-spoken" as Stallworth could be black.

* * *

Ron Stallworth used his socio-cultural white-passing to fight evil, but for some post-colonial critics the real evil is ethnic minorities in the West seemingly pandering to white outlooks, values and behaviours. The Martiniquais-French psychiatrist and philosopher Frantz Fanon's famous 1952 book *Black Skin, White Masks* analyses the post-colonial psyche as an amorphous, timorous state of being tainted by "the black problem". By this Fanon means the lengths to which those of non-white background will go to prove their belonging in white-majority societies, usually the "mother countries" that were historically their own people's slaver or coloniser. In Fanonian language, those with black skin assert a cultural and psychological "white face": a painstaking emulation of social whiteness, from etiquette and ways of communicating to dress sense and appreciation of "white culture". One aspect of this, as in Ron Stallworth's case, is people of non-white backgrounds assuming a "white" language when speaking to white people, but breaking into more natural idioms or tones when with those of their own kind.

This kind of in-person "socio-cultural white-passing" is an invisible process, but it can be as coerced or involuntary as other kinds of identity performance that we have seen in earlier chapters. Being "native" in the West means you have roots that provide authority, whereas "native" in the colonies was a derogatory title for the subordinated nation. Those in the West who belong to former subject peoples consciously and subconsciously navigate the psychology of racism—it is hard to cling to cultural pride and brush off a mentality hostile to your "curry smells", wrongly assuming you to be "angry", and so on, when that mentality is all around you and controlling the society in which you live. Many respond by working out how to suppress in every possible way their otherness, and assimilate as closely as possible into white society. A black adult will change their behaviour in the workplace to avoid being seen as aggressive; the brown kid trying to blend in will complain about dinner and want to eat fish and chips "like the other kids". People of colour with "difficult" "foreign" names will not only resign themselves to a lifetime of mispronunciation, but will accommodate the majority by accepting, or even adopting themselves, anglicised versions. Eventually, they think, the colour of their skin will be overlooked, if only they can signal that they are white in other respects.

Some, particularly from the post-war generation of immigrants from colonies or former colonies, would argue that this is not about buying into white values (and the value of whiteness itself), but about self-preservation. That first generation faced overwhelming legal and social racism; would you have had them risk their lives for the sake of projecting pride in their culture? And today, should people of colour in the West be accused of being "coconuts"—"ethnic" on the outside, white on the inside—simply because they don't want to subject themselves to prejudice and disadvantage?

But the London-based psychoanalyst M. Fakhry Davids thinks the line is blurred, even to the socio-cultural white-passer themselves. Davids, who has written extensively about Fanon's work, took on his Welsh wife's surname in order to appear less foreign and to cover up his Middle Eastern origins from his clients. He could have said or believed that he simply did this to make his life easier, to gain business or avoid losing it. Instead, in his book *Internal Racism*, he analyses the Fanonian observation of the non-white outsider's internalised inferiority—even if putting on a white face starts off as a matter of safety or convenience, it is impossible not to begin identifying with an attitude you have acted in response to.

Why get drawn in, trying to prove that one is not, say, hypersexual/violent, or else succumb to that stereotype? Why not shrug off a racist projection and walk away? [Fanon's] answer is that the relentlessness of these interchanges, in which the black self is constantly denigrated and a tantalizing picture of whites apparently free of your predicament is held out, brings about an inner change in which an unconscious longing to be white is installed in the mind.[12]

Davids says that his attempt to appear British on paper, the "phantasy" of being white, left him with a divided selfhood. As we have discussed in earlier chapters, rupture in the self has been the clearest and most common fallout of the identity performer's pursuit of invisibility and belonging—but, for passers, that tortured division is still necessary and unavoidable, because it offers an escape from a greater torture. For Davids, identification with white culture "sidesteps the pain"[13] of being born into or coming from a culture that has been projected as backward by colonial history, written by the Westerners and/or Westernised.

Another emphatic voice that talked about and offered her explanation for the inherent internalised inferiority of the non-white mind was Toni Morrison. As the famous quote goes:

> the very serious function of racism ... is distraction. *It keeps you from doing your work*. It keeps you explaining, over and over again, your reason for being. Somebody says you have no language and so you spend 20 years proving that you do. Somebody says your head isn't shaped properly so you have scientists working on the fact that it is. Somebody says that you have no art so you dredge that up. Somebody says that you have no kingdoms and so you dredge that up.[14]

Why do those othered because of their skin colour consistently respond to their othering and frame their identity around it? Why does the racialised individual feel, if you believe Fanon and Davids, such a strong need to prove their own worth—the "psychoexistential complex",[15] as Fanon calls it—or, simply, a deep-seated inferiority complex? Why does an Indian or a Jamaican with perfect English feel self-conscious about their or their parents' accent, when an Australian or a Canadian living in Britain thinks theirs is just another official variation of "proper English"? When and how does the mind become susceptible enough to colonial expectations that one is not only imitating the white world, but identifying with it?

In Chapter 2 we encountered the St Lucian poet and essayist Derek Walcott's black swineherd lover, filled with desperation for his unreachable white beloved. Fanon acknowledged the cultural aspect of this anguish and longing:

> Out of the blackest part of my soul, across the zebra striping of my mind, surges this desire to be suddenly *white*.
>
> I wish to be acknowledged not as *black* but *white* ... who but a white woman can do this for me? By loving me she proves that I am worthy of white love. I am loved like a white man ...
>
> When my restless hands caress those white breasts, they grasp white civilisation and dignity and make them mine.[16]

As Davids points out, this acceptance of the superior value of whiteness may not even be conscious:

> Once white identification is in place it cannot but call into question the relative inner peace that flowed from a normal upbringing, since that was achieved in a family milieu now denigrated on account of its blackness. Whether the unconscious wish to be white is enacted or defended against, the wish is now a feature of the black person's mind. The external colonial distinction has been internalized.[17]

In other words, because of racism, colonialism and imperialism, the world is organised around whiteness; white has become the norm against which deviance is defined, and so the question of whether or not one should be socially and culturally white is inherent in the mind of every child of Empire, regardless of how they end up responding to that question. This suggestion of white identification makes its way into the subconscious long before they find themselves among the white majority, because part of white colonisation was the dismantling and dictating of culture in societies that have yet to escape that legacy today.

Today's preoccupations with identity are driven by the same fissures and fusions of global power, connection and displacement as those of Empire's heyday. Take my own sense of belonging, for example. Like M. Fakhry Davids, I am a typical product of the colonies, programmed to think like, act like, eat like and dress like my people's white conqueror. By historical default, I had always felt a connection with Britain, further forged when I was a child by the royal family photos on my grandmother's wall. These pictures were my magic carpet, the friendly ghosts of my ties to Britain. Growing up I could name all the kings and queens of England going back at least to Elizabeth I, in chronological order. Later, as a teenager, I was attracted by other stories of England, its literature, art and continuity. I used to love reciting Caliban's "You taught me language, and my profit on't/Is I know how to curse",[18] only, instead of cursing, I was more drawn to dreaming, reading and writing in English.

It started with my introduction to romantic Raj literature—Rudyard Kipling, Paul Scott's *The Raj Quartet*, Ruth Prawer Jhabvala's entire oeuvre, E. M. Forster's *A Passage to India*. I then moved on to Thomas Hardy, the Brontë sisters—my arrival in England was prefigured by my arrival on the pages of these books. I would imagine the chalky cliffs, the White Horse on an undulating green West Country slope, the Victorians. When I closed my eyes in the tin-roofed, wooden-walled village house where I mostly spent my early years, listening to the song of the rain, I would be transported to the prehistoric stones where Tess was taken by Alec D'Urberville—the eponymous heroes of the Thomas Hardy novel. I was not passing as British, I felt, I was culturally British already; I always held on to a dream that one day I would break free of the prison of my origins and live in this place I already knew so well.

In his 1974 essay "The Muse of History", Derek Walcott poignantly describes this conflict between actual personal experience and the memory of imagination. Those made up of fissured allegiances—whether willing or forced—often long for a mythical wholeness. Perhaps it never existed, even for my pre-colonial ancestors, but we project our fantasies onto a presumed, perfect identity. The memory of imagination becomes so vivid in the mind of the colonised that they almost forget that they have not been to England—or France, or Portugal, or Spain. Walcott writes, "like any colonial child I was taught English literature as my natural inheritance … snow and daffodils … were real, more real than the heat and the oleander" of his native St Lucia, because they "lived on the page, in imagination, and therefore in memory."[19]

I can't speak for all children of the colonised, but in my case this cultural confusion has certainly led to some kind of internalised inferiority or aspiration to whiteness. For example, when I cannot instantaneously tell who composed a piece of European classical music, I experience the outsider's usual self-doubt, fearing that I have a long way to go before I can properly claim a place in my adopted nation. If I played a piece of *raga* to a regular British listener, would they feel ashamed of their ignorance of Indian music? But I would not even ask myself these questions. In fact, I would not like to engage in this debate. I was reborn the day I arrived in London. The past was not history, the past was an annoyance—one that keeps lurking there, threatening to destabilise my new life.

Back in the Bengali *mofussil*, I hadn't had the guts to pass on the Western education that arrived at my door as a descendant of the colonised, and I made it into my own pass to cultural whiteness. The term "native English speaker" is heavy with significance for the children of colonialism: I have appropriated the English language until it pushed aside my own perfectly complex mother tongue, in which I wrote my first novel, but which now vanishes into a distant memory of nursery rhymes sung by my grandmother.[20] Whether or not I cursed like Caliban my inheritance of British domination, English—plus a substantial amount of French thrown in—and my Commonwealth passport opened the door to my migration to the Mother Country, and then a decade of travel and living abroad, in North Africa and the Middle East. My dark complexion and my Bengali roots have been bypassed by my perfect white education.

Afro-Saxons

When I arrived in the motherland gifted me by Empire, I was forced to confront my imagined memory of Britishness, and to find a true belonging somewhere in between. I read and reread Walcott as I tried to embrace what the poet called an "Adamic vision", to make sense of "the enigma of arrival", as V.S. Naipaul described his own passage to England.[21] In the beginning, during my Brixton commune days, I would bask in a kind of Raj romanticism, thinking that I was in London because I had this amazing connection. I had internalised 200 years of British culture until I thought that I had earned my time in England by inhabiting Englishness, both emotionally and intellectually. But I was also still attached to a benign pan-Indian nationalism. Walcott emphatically raises this dilemma in an early poem:

> I who am poisoned with the blood of both,
> Where shall I turn, divided to the vein?
> I who have cursed
> The drunken officer of British rule, how choose
> Between this Africa and the English tongue I love?[22]

Like Walcott, I adore the English language; but these lines speak to a broader conflict of cultural identity. My history too was informed by "the blood of both". Today, I have successfully penetrated the castle of Englishness, and I live close to the landscape of my teenage self's favourite books, in the countryside that I grew up imagining: the big skies of the West Country, the forest beds full of bluebells, the strange and mighty circle of Stonehenge. I have incorporated my Indianness into my British life, and found peace.

But can this continue to be accepted as the natural aspiration of the outsider? Becoming Western? Fanon's *Black Skin, White Masks* says that, for the black man, there is only one destiny: white. That has changed significantly in the new millennium, with the West's ethnic-minority youth proudly asserting their identity and challenging that mindset. But there have always been those among the colonised and racialised who have resisted the culture of white superiority and white normativity, not least Walcott himself. The very act of articulating so beautifully his torn self, caught between the hatred of Empire and the love of English, dismisses the racial and cultural boundary. While Walcott's swineherd lover cannot disguise his stigmatised complexion, he can appropriate the English language and speak the language of the racial supremacists. He may have been taught this tongue by his colonial masters, but he has perfected it.

Earlier I quoted Shakespeare's last play, *The Tempest*, which has long held me in fascination. I see in this drama a resourceful document of colonial discourse. Caliban the slave has his freedom taken by Prospero—the foreign agent who catapulted him from his organic, earthy life into the tumult of the sea, with the white invader-explorer-coloniser's magic that struck him into a slave.

Caliban has learnt English to curse his enslaver, but—and what could be worse?—we do not know the mother tongue in which he had once communicated and written words of love, hate or trivial reflection. Eventually, all those people enslaved and occupied by Empire appropriated the white ruler's language—well enough to ignore its colonial legacy, to write in it, to let their imagination run amok.

Derek Walcott handled "English with a closer understanding of its inner magic than most (if not any) of his English-born contemporaries".[23] His English was one of reconciliation; Walcott did not seek out a language of revenge or recriminations. He addressed both the colonial and the enslaved as a "white ghost and black ghost" who whisper history, but he insisted that his own history was not going to be determined by these ghosts' take on the past, on what they had done and been subjected to. Walcott apologised for this but said it was not up to him to forgive. His memory, which had suffered Atlantic amnesia,

> cannot summon any filial love, since your features are anonymous and erased and I have no wish and no power to pardon ... but to you, inwardly forgiven grandfathers, I, like the more honest of my race, give a strange thanks. I give the strange and bitter and yet ennobling thanks for the monumental groaning and soldering of two great worlds ... you have placed me in the wonder of another, and that was my inheritance and your gift.[24]

These lines sing powerfully for many of the post-colonial generations who, in one time or another, will have committed the act of socio-cultural passing in the land of their former masters. Some of Walcott's contemporaries—post-war Caribbean thinkers and writers in the United Kingdom—used their cultural whiteness or Britishness with far less, or none of, Walcott's agonising. We saw in Chapter 3 how difficult life was for the Windrush generation of new arrivals, and some just wanted a swift ride to invisibility. Some of the light-skinned passed for white, as we saw with the film character Sapphire, while others passed culturally or socially to achieve assimilation. British society was not ready for "native" intellectual equality, so the only way to be treated as something like an equal was to display total allegiance to the West's cultural imperialism.

MINDSETS OF BELONGING

One of my most beloved authors, the Trinidadian V. S. Naipaul, tops the list of cultural passers who internalised and projected Britishness, speaking about his fellow West Indians in a racist language that was incomprehensible to other post-colonial writers at the time. Naipaul, the father of literary metamorphosis, first came to England after World War II on a scholarship to Oxford, along with fellow Trinidadians including the father of Chris Gunness, whose struggle with his racial and sexual identity was explored in Chapter 7. Naipaul moved to London after graduation, worked for the BBC World Service—just as Chris would do thirty years later— and only ever returned to the Caribbean as a "tourist", documenting life in the West Indies and in South America as if the people there were an undiscovered foreign species.

Once again we're reminded of Anatole Broyard as Naipaul describes his fear of being pigeonholed as a West Indian:

> I had never wanted to stay in Trinidad. When I was in the fourth form I wrote a vow on the endpaper of my Kennedy's *Revised Latin Primer* to leave within five years. I left after six; and for many years afterwards in England, falling asleep in bedsitters with the electric fire on, I had been awakened by the nightmare that I was back in tropical Trinidad ... [which] I knew to be unimportant, uncreative, cynical...[25]

Naipaul never showed any remorse for his openly anti-black views. Though I spent my formative years drunk on his literary elixir, his superbly dark analysis of "the enigma of arrival" of the immigrant, I also wanted to ask him why he couldn't see that his comments about his fellow Caribbeans simply amounted to self-mockery. But it was too late when I finally met him: in London, two years before his death, at the funeral of his literary agent Gillon Aitken, who first introduced Naipaul to the English literary limelight (and with whom, of course, this "irascible gentleman" had fallen out at the height of his fame). Naipaul looked frail, in a wheelchair. His bronzed face was darker than that of his literary nemesis, the Afro-Caribbean Derek Walcott. I couldn't help thinking about how, throughout his life, Naipaul had never stopped expressing his internalised white colonial disdain for Africans and black people, in Walcott's words his "repulsion towards Negroes ...

a physical and historical abhorrence that, like every prejudice, disfigures the observer".[26]

It was certainly not easy to turn away from white colonial cultural hegemony. In the isolation of the cold Mother Nation, the Windrush generation came face to face with what Lacan called "a subjective impasse, because the subject is called on to face in it the lack through which he is constituted."[27] In other words, creatives of this community sometimes internalised the mood of the place, the Western assumption that there was no "original" equivalent culture or society in the "before" of the New World. Among them was the Barbadian poet and academic Kamau Brathwaite:

> I found and felt myself "rootless" on arrival in England and, like so many other West Indians of the time, more than ready to accept and absorb the culture of the mother country. I was, in other words, a potential Afro-Saxon.

> But this didn't work out. When I saw my first snowfall, I felt that I had come into my own; I had arrived; I was possessing the landscape. But I turned to find that my "fellow Englishmen" were not particularly prepossessed with me.[28]

Walcott was not the only one who managed to rise and meet this challenge. Naipaul lived, wrote and published in Britain until his death in 2018; Kamau Brathwaite ultimately landed at the other end of their generation's post-colonial white-passing spectrum. Like Naipaul, he first came to England to attend Oxbridge; both graduated in the summer of 1953. Once living in post-war Britain, Brathwaite sought to reassure himself that it made no difference if he was "black or white, German, Japanese, or Jew"; what mattered was the "self-involving vision", in other words cultural Britishness. As a student he devoured Keats, Conrad, Kafka, thinking he had formally passed over into the white literary world. "But the Cambridge magazines didn't take my poems. Or rather, they only took those which had a West Indian—to me, 'exotic'—flavor. I felt neglected and misunderstood."[29] Brathwaite began to realise the Fanonian dilemma he faced.

Even though he believed he had come to possess the English landscape as I have, the British themselves were not particularly impressed by his claim to Englishness and English itself. The host society refused to permit him his own chosen identity as "Afro-Saxon", confining him to the status of "black author". Kamau Brathwaite, at the height of his literary success, chose not to be that black author. He decided that he could not remain in the United Kingdom, because doing so would force him either to give up his West Indian identity, or give up any dream of a British one. He could see no room for someone like him, looking to pass back and forth between cultures. He returned back across the Atlantic, and died a black Caribbean author in his native Barbados in 2020.

* * *

Brathwaite responded to Britain's ongoing racism by taking his writing where he felt it belonged, or could be free. Other Windrush authors responded by creating a new, distinctly Caribbean dialogue with white British society, challenging the notion of internalised whiteness among the colonised by constructing a black British or British-Caribbean identity: "positing an origin, a 'before.'"[30] For these intellectuals, there were opportunities for self-expression through spiritual connections to the ancestral motherland, for rebirth in a new landscape. The sea is history, says Walcott. The new West Indian can shape their new future in whatever form or shape they choose. Many writers of this time on both sides of the Atlantic were described by the Guyanese writer Wilson Harris (1921–2018) as "Anansi artists", for their capacity to remould "disruption, discontinuity, brokenness, and defeat into triumphant new configurations of possibility."[31] Descended from slaves and indentured labourers who had been taken out of Africa and Asia to serve Western powers in the Americas, the Anansi writers now found themselves in a Western world where race dominates every public and private discourse. According to Joyce E. Jonas, Harris argues that the West Indian artist "is working in a limbo—a void *between* two worlds. Surrounded by and exiled from the structures of an alien world view, he must create his own world in this absence, or else be forever a negative, an exiled scapegoat."[32]

These authors embracing the limbo learnt how to transcend their split identity and create great literature, turning disinheritance of the original self into narratives of renewal and reconstruction that could nourish not only their own community in Western societies, but the next generation too. They used their pens to expose the inadequacies of white authority, transgressing the limits it placed on black selfhood. In other words, they absolutely refused to culture-pass as white. Another Trinidad-born author who found himself in the mid-century capital of the declining British Empire was Sam Selvon, an Indo-Trinidadian like Naipaul. In his seminal novel *The Lonely Londoners* (1956), he brought to life a black London, described in creolised Caribbean English, where black people discussed life, hope or the lack of both, in an intimate immigrant world that was facing inward, not looking to white society.

Long before "black culture" became the popular idea it is today, Selvon wrote a rough guide of a possible future for black London. The opening lines of his novel evoke the timeliness and timelessness of the cityscape:

> One grim winter evening, when it had a kind of unrealness about London, with a fog sleeping restlessly over the city and the lights showing in the blur as if is not London, but some strange place on another planet, Moses Aloetta hop on a number 46 bus at the corner of Chepstow Road and Westbourne Grove to go to Waterloo to meet a fellar who was coming from Trinidad on the boat-train.[33]

Reviewers, alarmed at the idea that the Windrush generation simply might not aspire to belong to white society and culture, called *The Lonely Londoners* a tale or example of "colonising in reverse"—a phrase I have heard often in the context of ubiquity of curries in Britain and their unofficial accreditation as Britain's national cuisine. The Barbadian-born British novelist George Lamming described the 1950s immigrations to Great Britain, and the racism that greeted the new arrivals, as "a total alienation of man the source of labour from man the human person."[34] The double-uprooting of the Caribbean slave descendant now migrating to Britain is expressed throughout his debut novel, *In the Castle of My Skin* (1953)—for his title, Lamming tweaked Derek Walcott's powerful couplet.

The novel is set in Lamming's native Barbados, but was written and published after his arrival in a racist, segregated London. The ancestral voice cries out, when the dilution of the African tribes during the Middle Passage is complete, "The silver of exchange sail cross the sea and my people scatter like clouds in the sky when the waters come"; "And strange was the time that change my neighbour and me, the tribes with gods and the one tribe without."[35] Unlike the reserved, shadowy characters of Larsen's iconic Harlem Renaissance novella *Passing* (1929), *In the Castle of My Skin* sketches vivid, well-defined black men and women—"the people"—with clear, beautiful voices, including the character Trumper, who articulates unequivocally his declaration of self-defined belonging: to "The Negro Race".[36] This was a decade before Martin Luther King's March on Washington.

But we should remember that black authors were not the only ones coming from the Caribbean to assert their identity and roots against Britain's imperialism. The Indo-Guyanese writer David Dabydeen, who came to Mother England in the 1960s, penned *Turner*, a verse novella in dialogue with the famous 1840 painting by J.M.W. Turner, *Slavers Throwing overboard the Dead and Dying— Typhoon coming on*. The painter had been a supporter of the British abolitionists and was disappointed that more was not done to enforce the law after it passed. While traditional Turner enthusiasts focus on the colours of his wild fiery sky and his turbulent ocean, Dabydeen uses the very same language and metaphors— Turneresque—to focus on the named subject of the painting. In the preface to his poem, Dabydeen is transfixed by Turner's submerged African head. He says that it, perhaps like African consciousness, "has been drowned ... for centuries. When it awakens it can only partially recall the sources of its life, so it invents a body, a biography, and peoples an imagined landscape."[37]

The Anansi writings of Britain's mid-century Windrush authors are often graciously humorous, populist, presented with a lightness of touch—just the right amount of mockery so that their assault on Western cultural imperialism is transmitted without provoking too much wrath. These British-Caribbean authors specifically wanted to be known as such, to write about Windrush issues, talk about Windrush suffering. The Mother Nation had been exposed as a school textbook fantasy wonderland. They knew that they could only survive and find selfhood amid hostility by recognising and asserting their specific identity, the castle of their darker skin—through pride in not passing as culturally white, in refusing to inhabit the self-deprecating colonised soul; by inventing themselves anew. These writers returned in a modernist fashion Caliban's curse: You gave me the language and my profit on it; I can write my own history, for your audience.

These Anansi artists of the Windrush generation were predecessors to today's ethnic minorities, who are often non-compliant with Western expectations of deference to the white Western norm. They are deconstructing and redefining Fanon's bleak definitions of immigrant and post-colonial identity. The majority doesn't always understand or welcome this growing cultural defiance of the outsider, but perhaps placing it against the widely understood need for a black British identity in the post-war context will make it easier to see the origins of both Western wariness and minority boldness: the brutality of colonialism, the crimes of slavery, the horror of the Holocaust and the violence done to the racialised mind. It is to this clash, and its connection to questions of passing, that we will now turn in Part Four.

PART FOUR

TRESPASSING

11

HEART OF WHITENESS

THE QUINTESSENTIAL REVERSE-PASSING OF RICHARD BURTON

Little did the American authors of the original race-passing literature know that the passing phenomenon would regenerate in the later twentieth and the twenty-first centuries, as a major force sweeping up a much wider range of the social media and other contemporary manifestations of selfhood in the world to come. With this "identity wave" of the recent past has come a wave of argument and debate assertion about the legitimacy of particular identities and identity assumptions. We've started to see this contemporary debate emerge in the previous chapter, and we will come to explore it in greater depth in this final part of the book. In the new millennium, two key ideas of illegitimate identity performance have crystallised: cultural appropriation, a member of the majority's occasional dalliance with a minority culture; and reverse-passing, the act of passing "down" by disguising oneself as a minority.

Before we look at these accusations of identity trespass in today's world, let us look back: our understanding of who can legitimately perform an identity or engage with a culture is always closely linked to contemporary social and cultural values, but also to history. Take the concept of cultural appropriation, which we'll examine fully in Chapter 13—those who refer to this term argue that the use made of minority culture by today's powerful and privileged identity groups is traceable back to the extractive mentalities of colonialism. In the age of empire, European powers not only exploited the literal natural resources of subjugated peoples; they also viewed themselves as entitled to examine, control and even impersonate or take over those peoples' culture. Some white colonials of this mindset, such as explorers and spies, actually went so far as to pass as "natives", learning their language, imitating local behaviour, adopting indigenous clothing and eating habits, assuming fake names and sometimes darkening their skin or otherwise altering their body.

Ethnic minorities who inhabit whiteness, whether literally as in Part One or culturally as in Chapter 10, do not "appropriate" white culture; that term implies exercising power to take something from the disempowered, whereas passers are typically forced into that role because they are disempowered themselves, being othered and marginalised for their skin colour, sexuality, gender identity, caste, class or religion. This compulsion or desperation did not motivate European colonials passing as "natives". Nor were they sincerely identifying with the native culture, as we will clearly see below: on the contrary, they were motivated by their belief in their own superior political or national ideology, and their own superior identity. When the privileged pass for the oppressed, the word for it is reverse-passing.

This kind of passing is not without danger; it can even be fatal, especially in the world of espionage. But "true" passers of the kind we've met throughout this book transform their identity based on a calculation that to keep living in their assigned self would be even *more* perilous. Reverse-passers, on the other hand, freely choose to take on a new identity, and they do it far more easily. Rather than painstakingly building a persona as far as society will allow them, they typically "acquire" this alternative identity from a higher position, and it is not a permanent or an emotional transformation—sincerely embracing this other self would require them to give up their higher-status identity. Reverse-passing is a role and a game, performed by a player. And the best way for us to explore the culture and "identity politics" underpinning this game is to home in on one player who embodies it utterly.

* * *

In the theatre of self-invention, sometimes history's passers beat their fictional counterparts. And one of the most colourful of all real-life passers was the reverse-passer Sir Richard Francis Burton (1821–90), who carved out an enduring persona for himself in the world of colonial identity performance that memorialised names such as T.E. Lawrence. This was an exclusive arena of adventure through passing, reserved for the white Christian European explorer-traveller.

In the course of his colonial career, Burton took on a whole array of "native" identities to facilitate his journeys and escapades around the ever-increasing lands of British influence or control. He started out as an East India Company officer: during his time in 1840s British India, he posed as an Arab-Persian-Indian doctor-trader. Later in life, he was recorded as "the first European to enter Somaliland", before "discovering" the Great Lakes of Central Africa, in 1854–60. But his most famous performance of all was that of 1853, when he posed as a dervish—a wandering Muslim holy man—to gain access to the most sacred of Islamic pilgrimage centres, Mecca and Medina. At that time, Europeans were forbidden from entering both holy cities on pain of death; even today, non-Muslims are not allowed into Mecca, or the Prophet's Mosque in Medina. Burton remains one of a handful of non-Muslims to have performed the sacred ritual of Hajj in Arabia and returned unnoticed, reaching right into Islam's holiest site, the Kaaba at the heart of the Great Mosque.

This reverse-passing adventure smacks of the audacity of the colonial without scruples—not only judging by today's sensibilities, but also to many who heard of it at the time. Critics lambasted the explorer for his "hypocrisy" and contempt for Muslim and Arab culture, despite the immense interest it generated in the Orientalist camp and among fellow adventurers. One contemporary, William Gifford Palgrave, said:

> Passing oneself off for a wandering Darweesh, as some European explorers have attempted to do in the East, is for more reasons than one a very bad plan ... To feign a religion which the adventurer himself does not believe, to perform with scrupulous exactitude, as of the highest and holiest import, practices which he inwardly ridicules, and which he intends on his return to hold up to the ridicule of others, to turn for weeks and months together

the most sacred and awful bearings of man toward his Creator into a deliberate and truthless mummery, not to mention other and yet darker touches,—all this seems hardly compatible with the character of a European gentleman, let alone that of a Christian.[1]

Burton tore this criticism and its author into pieces in the preface to his book recounting his Arabian transgressions, a forensic two-volume account published as *Personal Narrative of a Pilgrimage to Al-Madinah & Meccah*. He called Palgrave's expressions of outrage "Satan preaching against Sin",[2] in turn accusing his accuser, pointing out that Palgrave himself had passed as a native Syrian "quack" and had converted between different denominations of Christianity. Palgrave's attitudes are also those of the Orientalist on a "civilising mission" among the heathens; his objection to Burton's Meccan adventure does not come from today's ideas of identity trespass. The problem was not that one shouldn't infiltrate societies for colonial purposes; Palgrave's problem was with Burton's methods, not his aims. He obviously thought that it was plain blasphemy to pretend to believe in another man's god; not the proper Christian way to go about things. Yet the difference between the two men, as Palgrave makes plain in his critique, is a minimal level of cultural respect for the "natives"; and, of course, any attempt or desire to help them.

Regardless of Palgrave's own reverse-passing sins, it is clear from Burton's very long preface that he did not think there was anything remotely wrong with disguising himself as another faith's holy man in order to visit sacred places, with a view to dressing this up as a great lark, and the faithful he found there as objects of mockery. The reason for this is equally apparent in Burton's writing: he passed as a Muslim and an "Oriental", and thought nothing of it, because he felt entitled to do so. He lived and wrote at the height of the British Empire, with the Crown taking direct control of India from the East India Company in the mid-1800s just a few years after his trip to Arabia. To Burton, infiltrating the holy places of Islam was just another conquest on behalf of the Empire.

The colonial explorer, in his intrepid quest for fame and for a personal narrative of adventure amongst heathens, approached an undiscovered society or place much as climbers view Everest. Burton betrays this sense of thrill and power in his diaries, describing himself as "an Eastern upon the stage of Oriental life".[3] This was an age of celebration of the white man's ego through planting flags, being the first to get to the "virgin lands". The indigenous people already living there were only part of the landscape, to be conquered, colonised, civilised, tricked and trampled in the rush to claim the territory for the Crown.

Burton, bored of his life in India, had offered his services to the Royal Geographical Society of London to visit the eastern and central regions of Arabia in the guise of an Eastern wanderer, "for the purpose of removing that opprobrium to modern adventure, the huge white blot" in the maps of the time, which no one had yet "described, measured, sketched and photographed". All this aligned with Europe's oceanic dreams, dating back to the Portuguese setting sail in the fifteenth century and "discovering" the West African coast. In the same spirit, Burton proposed to conquer the secrets of the "Moslem inner life" in an Islamic country.[4] His passing was an act of colonialism: imperial "discovery" is always followed by imperial "documentation"—and this is always done from a Eurocentric point of view.

We can see clearly in Burton's works the extractive mentality of Empire: getting one's hands on the entire known world, whether it be diamonds, spices, customs or culture—because as a colonialist, a white European Christian, you have the right to do so. Cultural appropriation goes all the way back to this time at the height of Europe's imperial success, as do the research disciplines that would eventually be known as ethnography and anthropology. Burton was one of the most prolific data-collectors in the burgeoning business of European ethnography, and a tremendously successful one. He simultaneously "took" Arab Muslim culture for the British—infiltrating and surveying it, and bringing it home with him in a British interpretation—and, temporarily, took that culture for himself, the impostor dervish, in order to gather his "information" in the first place. All was done in the name of great material progress, sanctioned by the Christian God, and the Empire that placed its faith in Him.

The frenzied European hunger to "discover" and categorise waterfalls, rivers, birds and pockets of "unchartered" land that had forever been known to indigenous peoples reached a fever pitch in the mid-nineteenth century. One of Burton's most celebrated contemporaries was the English explorer and missionary, David Livingstone, who made the "first discovery" of Victoria Falls in 1855 while trekking in the African interior: "It had never been seen before by European eyes".[5] The pre-existence of the waterfall didn't matter: for Europeans, it only existed once it had been named after the Queen, and was only blessed by divine guardians once a Christian man had laid eyes on it. The historian Audrey Farley explains this philosophy:

> In 1901, members of the Zoological Society of London proudly displayed an exhibit of the legendary "African unicorn," sent by Sir Harry Johnston, the British Governor of the colony of Uganda. The animal, which resembled a cross between a zebra and giraffe, had been known to the people of Central Africa for millennia as an "okapi". But like the famous waterfall, it only became real when Europeans could see it. Writing about the okapi and other creatures and "lost cities" on the continent, historian Edward Guimont identifies an "insidious logic at work in nineteenth-century European colonial exploration," according to which "the existence—or *non-existence*—of creatures in Africa could only be proven through European 'discovery.'" Indigenous knowledge only had the potential to demonstrate possibility; it could never demonstrate actuality.[6]

The urge to "demonstrate actuality" was so great in the Victorian world that British explorers effaced and dismissed the wisdom of local inhabitants, who had known their national treasures since the beginning of history and could probably have told the Europeans quite a lot about them. Instead the Victorians themselves went to great lengths to access these places. And if they were closed to outsiders for reasons of piety, they could simply dress as a "Mohammedan" and go there anyway. In observing personally the rituals of Islamic pilgrimage, only possible in his elaborate disguise, Burton verified the "actuality" of the religious rites. This particular white blot was finally surveyed and coloured in.

* * *

So this was the world of Burton. Upon his arrival in India, he learnt to speak fluently all major Indian languages, working as an interpreter for various British officials posted there; he also took significant interest in the "Eastern religions", particularly Islam. But, once it was gathered, Burton decided to use his linguistic, cultural and geographical knowledge to change job: he would become a model colonial adventurer. Soon enough, he grew his hair and beard long, hennaed his hands, and transformed into a half-Arab, half-Persian trader from the Gulf, Mirza Abdullah—Mirza being a Persian name and Abdullah an Arabic one. This juxtaposition of two false identities was carefully maintained by the man quickly becoming a master disguiser, to further confuse those who might have doubted his claims of his race, religion and nationality.

After a period of scouting out his surroundings under his new identity—visits to bazaars, mosques, drug dens, brothels and rich peoples' homes—Burton grew tired of Mirza Abdullah. He wanted to use his expertise for a more rewarding and glorious colonial pursuit. In 1852, he changed persona again and re-emerged dressed as a Sufi called Sheikh Abdullah, a 30-year-old practitioner of traditional medicine. These ruses kept Burton entertained for ten years of service in India. It was only after that decade had elapsed that he proposed an even more exciting ploy to the Royal Geographical Society: a plan to enter Mecca.

In order to complete his disguise and avoid exposure of the kind said to have brought down Pope Joan, Burton had himself circumcised. Given the ubiquity of the hammams—communal same-sex baths—in Arab culture, there would always have been a risk of being given away as a non-Muslim. Burton then went to the "inept" authorities in Egypt to obtain necessary papers for travel to Arabia. On his voyage from Cairo to the Peninsula, he boasted that even the Englishman on board couldn't identify a fellow countryman through his dervish outfit; Burton fooled everyone he came across during his adventure, with his perfect behaviour, command of the vernacular and apparent mastery in performing Muslim prayers and other rituals. Burton then crossed 80 miles of desert on a camel.

By his own account, he was invincible in his passage to Mecca. He reached Medina after a lengthy sea voyage and stayed in that second holiest city of Islam for research, before scouting out safe ways to enter Mecca. For this expedition was not risk-free. Not only had Burton gone to the extreme of circumcision, he had dodged attacks by Bedouins during his camel ride across the desert. His maverick boasting in his written account did not take away the fear he admits he was struck by as he entered the Kaaba; he felt like "a trapped rat."[7] But this did not make his reverse-passing any less an exercise of power. The killing of natives who resisted European colonisation, from New Zealand to Amritsar to North America, is disremembered and almost never apologised for; but if a European settler-explorer succumbed to death during their exploits, they were a "martyr for empire". The disruption posed by some local tribesmen to encroachment on their lives and society, even if it did briefly become an existential threat to Burton, does not compare to the mental and physical jeopardy, often life-long, endured by those passing up.

This is clear in another escapade of Burton's. Soon after his mission to Mecca was complete and his memoir found its way to the publisher, he entered another forbidden city in disguise. This time, it was the fortress of Harar in the Horn of Africa, an ancient port town frequented by Arab slave-traders. Burton wished to present himself as a British envoy to the emir of Harar, but was told that the local people would not tolerate a Christian in their midst. He disguised himself as a Turkish merchant, only changing to British dress and forging his papers after making it into the fortress. Upon receiving a ten-day visitor's permit based on his perfect Turkish disguise, Burton was so thrilled to have duped the emir that he could not resist the temptation to gloat over his accomplishment in his next travelogue: "I was under the roof of a bigoted prince whose least word was death; amongst a people who detest foreigners; the only European that had ever passed over their inhospitable threshold; and … the fated instrument of their future downfall."[8]

During this latest "adventure", Burton's team came under attack by local tribesmen who left one dead and three injured—some seriously. Burton himself managed to escape, but with terrible facial injuries. A lance perforated his upper and lower jaws, leaving him with permanent deep facial scars. Burton was at no lesser risk of being tortured, killed even, than an escaped slave passing as white to reach freedom, a victim of religious persecution pretending to follow the dominant religion, or a transgender person pretending to be cis to avoid harassment or violence.

Burton, like any passer, would be seen if caught as a trespasser into an identity that the society around him felt he had no right to claim. But Burton chose to pass, and to pass down, for the reasons we know. He may have feared exposure, because then the adventure would be ruined; but he dealt with his concern by repeatedly reminding himself that he was only dealing with barbarians; when an "Asiatic official" shouted abuse at him, "*Ruh Ya Kalb*, Go O dog!", and the strike of a horsewhip was threatened, he commented, "British flesh and blood could never have stood *that*."[9] Burton dressed up as a Muslim to enter the Muslim's world and upstage him, oust him, master him. His reverse-passing adventures led him toward triumph and conquest, not escape.

* * *

Burton never forgot what he was in India, Arabia and Africa to achieve: "discovery" in the European colonial sense. The languages he learnt and the Eastern clothing he donned were tools used for a limited and specified purpose: to acquire access, and therefore insight, into the world of "heathenry". Each time the conquest of the barbaric culture was complete and Burton was safely back in Britain, the anchor of civilisation, he swiftly changed back into his Western clothes and his own "native" social status. Away from the chaos of the jungle, desert and unenlightened people, he "hastily" published his narratives, separating himself from the "Oriental" character he had worn by reflecting on his adventures in European colonial terms: memoirs and travelogues that boasted of his talents as a perfect explorer-impersonator-conqueror-ethnographer.

> After my return to Europe, many inquired if I was not the only living European who has found his way to the Head Quarters of the Moslem Faith. I may answer in the affirmative, so far, at least, that when entering the penetralia of Moslem life … my Eastern origin was never questioned…[10]

In fact, as Jeremy Paxman has noted in the *Financial Times*, Burton may not have been the first European of this era to gain access to the Kaaba. But his "conquest" of Mecca was made memorable by his extensive subterfuge, his obsessive note-taking and map-drawing—including on the inside of his long white Islamic robe—and of course his self-glorifying publication of the story.[11] To him, Sheikh

Abdullah, the Sufi dervish and all the others were just a means to an end, a tool to achieve his colonial and personal goals.

In other words, unlike those passing out of necessity, Burton did not suffer from any rupture in the self. Not once did he forget why he was faking the identity of a Muslim man. He never lost control of his act, he never lost sight of his Englishness, he never doubted who he was. Disguise and subterfuge were essential tools of colonial superiority and control, miles apart from the rapid loss of control experienced by many "true" passers and the inferiority complexes often driving them. By contrast, Burton's writing shows his aversion to the East Indian he impersonated, whom he likened to "the fox in the fable", "disagreeably familiar, offensively rude"; he found him "of all Orientals, the most antipathetical companion to an Englishman".[12] To travel to Mecca and Medina, he mastered "three ways of treating Asiatic officials,—by bribe, by bullying, or by bothering them with a dogged perseverance into attending to you and your concerns."[13] Page after page, Burton's memoirs unscrupulously catalogue the backwardness of natives on both sides of the Indian Ocean, and even the climate and landscape strike him as "double dullness"—the same hot winds, heat clouds and fiery sunsets in all the lands of his "conquests" unites non-European peoples, he says, in lethargy and laziness. In contrast with good Protestant industry, work days are "truly orientally lost."[14]

Burton's disdain for the "natives" is shown even in the way he chose to pass for them, entering and journeying through what he described as "the barbarous countries" by faking timidity and subservience. Speaking of his early disguises while working for the East India Company, Burton did not miss the opportunity to trumpet both his and the Empire's cleverness, allowing 50,000 Englishmen to hold 150 million Indians. Describing his experiences of organising his trip to Arabia, he persistently mocks the bureaucracy of the Egyptian foreign office and its "glorious confusion". Throughout his "personal" narrative of his voyage on from Cairo, we repeatedly read of Burton's inner contempt for the behaviour, food, language and clothing of the people he comes across.

One particular target of this contempt were "natives" who tried to pass "up" culturally, in particular the Indians, whom Burton mocked mercilessly: "There were two Indian officers, who naturally spoke to none but each other, drank bad tea, and smoked their cigars exclusively like Britons."[15] The Indians didn't even drink properly the tea they actually grew—this was the view of the English upper class, and their weak attempts at imitating Britishness by smoking cigars in a certain manner made them charlatans. During Burton's travels to Mecca and Medina, he met Khudabakhsh, a "native of Lahore" who spoke Persian and Hindustani. When this man struck up a genial conversation with the travelling dervish, Burton the Englishman started sizing him up, picking holes in his manners to mock him with. At the moment Khudabakhsh invites the "dervish doctor" into his house, Burton can no longer resist ridiculing his unassuming host to his white British readers: "My host had become a civilised man, who sat on chairs, who ate with a fork, who talked European politics, and who had learned to admire, if not to understand, liberty—liberal ideas!"[16]

This hypocritical, one-way attitude around cultural or racial impersonation is one that we will see repeatedly throughout this last part of the book. Burton is clear: Indians cannot successfully pass as Britons, even if they employ the very same methods as he does to impersonate them so brilliantly. Even when they are seemingly "civilised" to perform western etiquette, they will still be caught out and lampooned by the hawk-eyed authority of colonial culture, as nothing more than a bunch of brown natives in European clothing. This is how we know that Burton's passing is very different from that of the marginalised—his is an exercise of privilege and power and an expression of superiority, not a risky quest to attain those statuses against the odds.

But there was one writer of the British Empire for whom the boundaries between brown and white, colonial and colonised, were far less clear-cut. In his case, we will see that even members of the Raj elite could believe in their own act, to the extent that a blurring of their former selfhood left them in a "sunken" place where they didn't quite know who they were. As we navigate the treacherous waters of contested identity, culture wars and power struggles over legitimate selfhoods, trying to separate passing from trespassing, we need to look not only at the reverse-passer who clearly acts in bad faith. We must also examine one who is far closer to the ambiguities and fluidities of all those genuinely caught between identities.

12

SOMETHING OF HIS SELVES

THE PASSING, APPROPRIATING AND IDENTIFYING
OF RUDYARD KIPLING

What am I? Mussalman, Hindu, Jain, or Buddhist?
That is a hard nut.

Rudyard Kipling, *Kim*[1]

The autobiography of Rudyard Kipling (1865–1936), *Something of Myself*, begins with an invocation to "Allah the Dispenser of Events", as the India-born author recounts his early years in the Raj, growing up in Bombay beside the busy waters of the Arabian Sea, with Arab dhows floating by and Parsis walking out to pray to the setting sun. We first meet Kipling walking through a burst of colour at Bombay's fruit market with his Portuguese Catholic *ayah* (nanny); they stop to pray "at a wayside cross". Back home, Rudyard goes over to the other domestic servant, Meeta, who takes him to meet the friendly gods of her Hindu temple. Caste restrictions against non-Hindus visiting the temple did not apply to the underage boy. After a day such as this, ending with Hindi and Marathi fairytales from the *ayahs* and other domestic workers, Rudyard and his younger sister are dressed for dinner with their parents, with their various carers' stern warning, "Speak English now to Papa and Mamma."[2]

Kipling goes on in his memoir to explain that he did indeed speak English when in white British society, but only after translating out of the "vernacular" in which he dreamed and imagined his little world. This world was to pursue him for the rest of his life, with issues of identity featuring prominently in almost all of Kipling's work. So, although George Orwell called him a "prophet of British imperialism"[3] and Edward Said viewed him as a promoter of Orientalism, I could not write about performing identity without drawing on the work of an author who devoted his entire literary life to creating characters—men, boys, and beasts—in multi-coloured personality coats that they put on and took off. Kipling is the creator of Kim, the young Anglo-Indian who moves between Muslim, Hindu and Buddhist identities and, when forced, gets by well enough as a British military cadet in colonial India, being groomed to become a spy. One of Kipling's best-known characters is the boy-wolf, or boy who wanted to be a wolf: the enchanting Mowgli of *The Jungle Book*.

What do these stories tell us about the well-meaning reverse-passer? Can reverse-passing pass as a romantic idea?

The literature professor Jan Montefiore has said, "Kipling always was and always will be a contradictory figure."[4] He has been lambasted for his biased depictions of India, of the Indians and, above all, of the British in India. But it is not straightforward to issue a verdict on the cultural convictions of the writer that Kipling would become, as we shall see. He was much more than Edward Said's prognosis of him as an imperialist obsessed with the white man's burden, and his work is far more complex than the case of Richard Burton. In contrast with Burton's contempt for the "natives" he impersonated, Kipling's reverse-passing British characters, like Kipling himself, fully empathised with the Indian identities they inhabited.

Kipling's struggle to understand what it means to be English, or not to be, runs throughout his writings. His love of the scent and noise of undivided India is manifested over and over again in the characters he created, so faithfully, with outstanding knowledge of the languages and traditions of the land. But Burton too had mastered the cultures of India—what is different about Kipling is why he did so. Whether or not you think Kipling had the right to identify as Indian, he clearly did—his characters get something out of their reverse-passing beyond an immediate material gain, and part of that is an evolution in their own sense of identity. They fully transmogrify into the native characters they are passing as, and embrace the complexities of their new selfhood, living them fully.

SOMETHING OF HIS SELVES

The socio-cultural reverse-passing of Kipling, and the physical passing of his characters, involve the usual anxiety of the trespasser, and a constant struggle with blurring of identities—as with those who pass "up" to a more privileged identity. Burton, as we've seen, experienced none of this confusion: he always remained emotionally distant from the races, religions and cultures he imitated. Kipling's explorations of selfhood and cultural crossings in the pluralist world of British India are in fact writing *against* colonial and Orientalist ideas of rigidly categorised identities. Yet Kipling and his characters are also delusional, believing themselves to identify with a status they are in fact only happy to inhabit temporarily. In that sense, you might say they are not so different from Burton and other Victorian conqueror-explorers after all.

* * *

This is what I wrestle with when I read Rudyard Kipling. If I, a native of the Indian subcontinent, were being cast away to a desert island, between the books by Kipling the imperialist and those by Said the spokesman for the colonised, I would probably take the Kipling. I am challenged by the virility of his prose, fascinated by the self-delusion of his characters, and entertained by his immaculate observations of life among so many categories of people in Indian society. Nowhere is this exploration richer than in his autobiographical novel *Kim* (1901).

One fascinating aspect of Kipling's work is that the novelist too is passing within them, in the various disguises of his characters. Looking at Kipling's birth and life in India, it becomes apparent that his protagonist Kim is based on the writer's younger self. Like Kipling, Kim appears to have a perfect command of Urdu and certain other Indian languages, and speaks English less fluently; like Kipling, he lives in a multi-religious, multi-complexioned, multi-ethnic world. Kim's escape out of British Indian society into an India of formless, fluid identity is not too far from the author's own account of his urge to "go native", described in *Something of Myself*. Right at the start of his memoir, Kipling recalls his return to India at the age of 16, after finishing his years at a rough boarding school in dreary Portsmouth. He confesses that, after his "three or four days' rail to Lahore", where his father had secured him a job, upon arrival "my English years fell away, nor ever, I think, came back in full strength."⁵

A great part of *Kim* involves the adolescent protagonist travelling across India's vast landscape with a Buddhist holy man, the Lama, to reach a mythical body of water. In brownface, Kim seduces a rich Indian maiden who pays for his train ticket, and he boards as the lama's *chela* or disciple. Kipling, narrating as Kim, describes the lama as a man with "yellow" complexion against the "brown" sea of other Indians. But Kim is not truly holding these "natives" at arm's length as Burton does in his writing; so deep is the young man's conviction that he makes himself forget his "white" self, seeing his "real" identity as an "Anglo-Indian" with Irish parents not as his true self, but as his other self. When he is finally thrown off the train—for travelling without a ticket, not for pretending to be Indian—he runs along the carriage, pleading with the "half-caste" ticket master that he is an indispensable companion, the *chela* of the lama; without him, the lama would not be able to survive. The reader here pauses to wonder if the young man in brownface has truly suspended disbelief at his "passing" act. Like many good-faith passers we've met in this book, Kim becomes the act he is putting on.

Kim may not engage in passing under social pressure—that is what makes him a reverse-passer—but it is clear that he passes out of zealous curiosity about his own self and other people's. Increasingly over the course of the novel, we witness his sense of oneness with the multiple identities he assumes, to the extent that he can no longer differentiate his real identity. Kim's selves overlap, and at the end of the narrative he emerges on the other side somewhat delirious, unsure of who he is: "'I am Kim. I am Kim. And what is Kim?' His soul repeated it again and again."⁶

But this is not a negative experience of lost heritage or a sense of betrayal, as we've seen with so many passers in the first three parts of this book. For Kipling, and so for Kim, straddling identities is the whole beauty of being a British Indian. The title *Something of Myself* alone suggests that Kipling felt he had many such selves, and could never be distilled into one alone. This pride in a complex identity is described by Kipling in the powerful poem that opens Chapter 8 of *Kim*:

> Something I owe to the soil that grew—
> More to the life that fed—
> But most to Allah Who gave me two
> Separate sides to my head.
>
> I would go without shirts or shoes,
> Friends, tobacco or bread
> Sooner than for an instant lose
> Either side of my head.[7]

Although Rudyard Kipling has been criticised for his apparent espousal of nineteenth-century ideas of race science and racial hierarchy, particularly in his poem *The White Man's Burden* (1899), it is impossible to ignore his unequivocal celebration in *Kim*, as well as in his other works, of a variable conception of culture, long before dual or fluid identity became fashionable notions.

His characters' fixation with perfect disguise and dissimulation reflects the literary imagination of the late nineteenth century, by which time stories of escaped slaves passing as white had long been published in trans-Atlantic newspapers and featured in many novels, such as *Uncle Tom's Cabin* (1852). Kipling travelled extensively in North America in the 1890s before settling there with his wife; the family lived in New England for most of the decade. These were the years when Kipling was most prolific—he started writing *The Jungle Book* (1894) in his Vermont cottage—and in this period the metamorphosis of the individual, oscillating between assigned and assumed appearances, had become an established theme of American literature. It is not beyond the bounds of possibility that the race-passing of the age may have influenced Kipling's own personal and artistic obsession with identity transformation.

In the second half of the Victorian era, disguising one's identity as defined by the "origins" of birth was a new phenomenon in the English novel, and it heralded a fresh way of looking at established notions of individual and communal selfhood. Kipling's characters led the way for this rethinking of the past in light of the present—in the late-nineteenth- and early-twentieth-century British Empire, that meant questioning the racial status quo, seeking an alternative selfhood in a cautious celebration of ethnic and cultural ambiguity. Kipling's Anglo-Indian characters, just by contemplating the possibility that they could legitimately consider themselves "native", have all gone "deeper than the skin".[8]

Indeed, it seems that Kim—the character who most closely resembles Kipling himself—actually prefers to be "native". In order to escape the claustrophobia of his military school, where he was required to wear English clothes and eat "raw beef" on a platter, he put on the outfit of a Hindu boy. He "yearned for the caress of soft mud squishing up between the toes, as his mouth watered for mutton stewed with butter and cabbages, for rice speckled with strong-scented cardamoms, for the saffron-tinted rice, garlic and onions, and the forbidden greasy sweetmeats of the bazars."[9] Later on, when he is made to join the British intelligence services, he agrees to do so only to be able to continue living an Indian life, as his disguise will now become officially sanctioned. In the course of the novel, Kim becomes so accustomed to passing as Indian that his English identity represents a constraint on his freedom of movement, and he seeks every opportunity to break free and "escape into great, gray, formless India". But "Meantime, if the Sahibs were to be impressed, he would do his best to impress them. He too was a white man."[10]

Passing is a process that can confuse what one is passing to or from. Often these become interchangeable, as the lines blur between one's original or assigned identity and one's experience of oneself. "He too was a white man"—as if Kim the character, or Kipling the novelist, almost forgot that he was not in fact Indian. Kipling's writing reflects skilfully what the notion of "passing" exemplifies: ambiguity, multiplicity, the questioning soul. Reading Kipling first as a teenager and again in subsequent years, I have always felt that I was not convinced by the anti-colonial verdict on *The White Man's Burden* as a full testament to who Kipling was. Instead of looking at the poem as a work by a colonialist frustrated by the white man's mammoth task to civilise a barbaric world, it can also be read as a warning to a bunch of conceited white men, drunk with the memory of Empire's glory earlier in the century, to be watchful of all the "pomp of yesterday".[11]

Even if the white characters' multiple "native" disguises may offend some, these stories, and the fact that they were so clearly drawn from Kipling's own life, do demonstrate that the clear-cut, binary and supposedly non-negotiable categories of identity promoted by the race science and imperial ideology of the day were false even for white Europeans born and raised in the shadow of Empire. Kipling's Indian characters are also immensely resourceful; they too can perform identities that are not their own. The Muslim, the Hindu, the Calcutta *babu*, even the Buddhist lama find themselves mirroring the Indian multitudes, alternating or at least empathising with all. Just as Kim is described by his creator, they are all a "Friend of all the World."[12] The selves assumed by these characters are part of their being and belonging to this "most beautiful land"[13] of plurality and diversity, and of their negotiated place within it.

That was the Indian subcontinent before the partition, or before British rule, when faith communities and religious observance were not bifurcated but mixed, and given far less significance, if any, as markers of identity. When the British arrived and became master of all India, they upended centuries of religious pluralism. Shashi Tharoor, author of *Inglorious Empire*, calls this pre-British culture a kind of "fuzziness that existed in Indian social categories between castes, between religions".[14] In this muddled sort of way, communities got along for centuries; and the imperial rulers before the British, the Muslim Mughals, also learnt to get along in this way, inhabiting Indianness.

As we saw in the previous chapter, the British felt that in order to understand you need to categorise; classification of religion and caste were of particular appeal to India's colonisers. One particular example relates to the Muslim kingdom of Avadh, Awadh or Oudh, in the modern Indian state of Uttar Pradesh. The Nawab, Wajid Ali Shah (1822–87), was a Shia Muslim, who presided over Hindu celebrations of Krishnalila, the mythical story of the god Krishna—his romance with his human consort, the milkmaid Radha, and her girlfriends. In the performances, the Nawab's own wives played the parts of the milkmaids, dancing around the god—"that," Tharoor has commented, "was the extent of the kind of syncretism that existed."[15] All this had to go when the British Crown annexed India in 1858.

When Kipling was writing in the late nineteenth and early twentieth centuries, the "fuzziness" of religion and caste still existed, as the British Empire's most famous literary representative vividly portrays. Or, at least, there was a kind of lingering nostalgia in the

Raj for an earlier fuzziness now lost, "overlooked because of the British cut and dry way of doing things" (Tharoor).[16] Kipling's most memorable characters represent what the British would have called "a muddle", an alliance between Hindu, Muslim, Jain, Buddhist or something else. We have already met another prolific Indian writer, Kipling's contemporary, who reflects this ongoing celebration of an Indian idea of fluidity and pluralism: Munshi Premchand, the master of caste-passing stories.

This progression from one identity to another in Kipling's narratives is described by the British imperial literature expert John S. McBratney as "decoding" of a foreign identity and then "encoding" it into one's own performative selfhood.[17] Cultural expectations were racialised by the people of the Raj, who saw Kim behaving like an Indian and assumed he must be one, without realising that he was in fact white. Ellen Craft was similarly assumed by Southern society to be a free white person, because she behaved like one. The native disguises of colonial representatives, whether on the ground or in the stories circulating through the colony, threatened to unsettle not only that individual's personal identity, but also what British or other European imperial identity stood for. And nowhere is this curious racial indeterminacy among a racially empowered people more accurately or deeply portrayed than in Kipling's work.

Kipling's changelings reflect the dilemma of colonial children, who were put under a life-long test of allegiance—whose side should they belong to? Hovering between the two worlds, and watching the line between them gradually vanish, Kim, Mowgli and other Kipling characters all ask the same question: who am I? Their very ability to ask this question shows Kipling's rejection of the notion that he had to choose a side, or that his side was chosen for him at birth. We can argue that, by defying the "colour-coding" that was the norm in European colonies, Kipling's characters broke free of the Orientalist classification of the white man. Kim taunts Mahbub Ali—his spy mentor, who is perpetually puzzled at his young protégé's knack for multiple disguises, demanding, "What am I? Mussalman, Hindu, Jain, or Buddhist?—That is a hard nut."[18]

Kim's hard nut is the antithesis of the nineteenth-century portrait of an Orientalist. Edward Said lays out at least two crucial ideas underpinning the Orientalist mind:

One of them is the culturally sanctioned habit of deploying large generalizations by which reality is divided into various collectives: language, races, types, colors, mentalities, each category being not so much a neutral designation as an evaluative interpretation. Underlying these categories is the rigidly binomial opposition of "ours" and "theirs," with the former always encroaching upon the latter (even to the point of making "theirs" exclusively a function of "ours"). This opposition was reinforced not only by anthropology, linguistics, and history but also, of course, by the Darwinian theses on survival and natural selection, and—no less decisive— by the rhetoric of high cultural humanism.[19]

Said's Orientalist and White Man are interchangeable, transmitting "a sense of the irreducible distance separating white from colored", locked in that place where the natives are objects of study.[20] But although that was generally the case in the hierarchy of colonial and colonised in India, and elsewhere in the world under European imperialism, Kipling's characters transcend this norm. In his work, it is the white man and the native who emerge as interchangeable characters.

By reverse-passing, Kipling's characters represented a curious kind of challenge to the philosophy underlying racist power structures, by embracing new possibilities of social freedom that would be sought a century on by caste-, class- and religious passers of independent India. In the short story "Miss Youghal's Sais" (1887), a British police officer, Strickland, appears in perfect disguise as an Indian *sais* or groom, in order to win the heart of Miss Youghal, whose parents have rejected his advances. His ploy is successful, even once his reverse-passing has been uncovered. McBratney explains:

> In his playing off of Anglo-Indian against Indian identity, [Strickland] mocks the racial essentialism that gives the Briton a clear sense of selfhood. And by subverting the binarism of brown and white, he collapses the hierarchy of color to which Anglo-Indian political authority is pinned. For himself, he achieves a freedom beyond race as great as his trespass is large.[21]

We cannot reflect on Kipling's explorations of identity freedom without going back to the most memorable of his identity performers, Mowgli. Raised by a pack of wolves, Mowgli wants to stop being a "man-cub" and live as a wolf himself. Like Kipling's other books, *The Jungle Book* explores identity, both external and internal, and how the two overlap, or fuse; and how, sometimes, they don't or can't. There is often tension between the two. Although Mowgli is outwardly and physically a human child—a "man-cub"—he feels part of the animal world. But he does not have sufficient features or skills in disguise to truly pass as a wolf. One day he arrives at the human village, having been rejected by the jungle. He realises his heart is locked in the animal world, even though he cannot truly be part of it—a rupture in selfhood we have talked about throughout this book. We hear Mowgli's cry over his failure to belong fully to either side, and his struggle to keep up with his strategic non-dual status, constantly on the verge of being revealed to those who want to harm him—the predators of the animal world, as well as those in the man village who may not trust his story.

Belonging continues to be an important theme in our time, and we now understand it as something that can be not just a fact of birth, but a chosen state; not just a single fixed identity, but a life of multiple spiritual and cultural allegiances. The 2018 film *Mowgli: Legend of the Jungle*, an adaptation of Kipling's collection *All The Mowgli Stories*, has been praised for its faithfulness to the spirit of Kipling's original stories, but the script is modified to deal more explicitly, in twenty-first-century rhetoric, with questions of mixed heritage. The young man-cub tells his wolf-mother, Nisha, that all his life he has only wanted to prove that he belongs to the wolf pack. Nisha assures him that he has, only to be contradicted by Mowgli's mentor in the ways of the jungle, the wise Bagheera, who expresses with dismay his feeling that Mowgli can never quite fit in anywhere: "I thought I could teach you how to belong … I was wrong, Mowgli."

Mowgli defies Bagheera and tells him that, even if his nemesis Shere Khan might bring about his end, he would still not give up hope of belonging to the jungle community. He hops from branch to branch with his friends Bagheera and Baloo, fighting off his official identity as a man-cub. In the end, though, he is exhausted by the effort to shut down part of his identity, like any passer. Just as Kim, at the end of his pilgrimage with the lama, exclaims, "Who am I, I am Kim, who is Kim?", Mowgli cries out on screen, "I am not a man, but neither am I a wolf. Which of you will follow me?"

The film ends with Kaa the Python's closing words on the friction between Mowgli's inner duality and the lack of space for it in the real world: "With the tiger and the hunter now gone, the future shimmered from darkness into light. Mowgli, man and wolf, both and neither, had given the jungle a voice. And for as long as he stood watch, it would speak a lasting peace." Figures both fictional and real who have stepped into the realm of shifting identity may be racked by their plight, but they go on, and they stand watch, maintaining their hybrid selfhood—past and present, black and white, powerful and powerless, man and woman, "both and neither", dual and non-dual. This may be the picture of what constitutes the modern person, but this aspect of identity's prevarication is as old as the dispersal of humanity into all corners of the earth. Leaving aside the relative validity of the particular identities Rudyard Kipling felt he was struggling with, his work is an important articulation of that struggle.

* * *

Even so, reading Kipling, one is reminded of the post-colonial debates around white privilege and cultural appropriation. This attitude of "going native" has its roots in European ethnography—to recap what we've learnt from Richard Francis Burton, a product of colonial social science, extractive in the same way as colonialism was materially extractive of colonies' natural resources. Taking what is not yours for your own benefit, generally without the consent of those who do have ownership over it. When it came to culture, not among those like Burton who breezed into "exotic" lands for a limited, specific mission, but among those like Kipling who were born and raised in the colonies, this manifested as random, impulsive participation in "native" life. Kipling's characters used disguises as "a matter of mastering—of decoding, imitating, and controlling—aspects of another culture" (McBratney again),[22] just as Richard Burton needed to conquer the "white blots" of the British Empire's maps. Kipling's obvious infatuation with Indian culture as he saw it is hard to separate from his infatuation with his freedom to impersonate it.

In "Miss Youghal's Sais", Strickland's passing as a native servant named Dulloo pays off, and has a happy ending. He succeeds in winning the hand of Miss Youghal—whose parents had originally refused to allow their daughter to marry someone from the worst-paid department in India, the colonial police—first by entering his disguise, and then by dropping it when he can no longer act freely within it. One day, while tending the Youghals' horses, Strickland sees a rival suitor of Miss Youghal, a general, take her riding and flirt with her. Strickland becomes jealous and angrily catches hold of the general's bridle, then, "in most fluent English", invites him "to step off and be heaved over the cliff."[23] The good-humoured general bursts out laughing, and tells Miss Youghal's parents to agree to accept the couple.

Yet nobody ever burst out laughing when they discovered that the apparently white person in front of them was, on paper, "Negro". They would be more likely to be lynched. Strickland, Kipling says, put on any disguise "that appealed to him at the time, stepped down into the brown crowd, and was swallowed up for a while"[24]—only ever for a while. His instant reassertion of his British identity (and so his power) when he feels his position is threatened is the very opposite of Irene and Clare's helplessness in the face of racism while Clare is white-passing in Nella Larsen's novella. There is none of that trepidation common to forced passers, who cannot indulge in the "for-a-while" privileges and boastful performance art of Strickland or Kim. The former is a maverick policeman who flaunts his perfect "ability" to know the natives as much as the natives know themselves: "Now, in the whole of Upper India, there is only ONE man who can pass for Hindu or Mohammedan, chamar [a tanner, i.e. an Untouchable] or faquir [wandering holy man], as he pleases."[25] Kim too delighted in presenting himself as a hard nut that even his mentor could not crack.

In this way, Kipling's characters seem to fall after all on the Burton side of reverse-passing; they appear to delight more in the "game" than in an ultimate positive outcome for their passing personas, which is ultimately of little consequence. The risk of failure was not a bleak future of punishment, perpetual poverty, misfortune or loneliness, but simply loss of face. The white British felt safe to pass as Indian, because they knew they could go back to their own "real" identities. For them, the shifting of selfhood simply sets in motion a brief or long-term romantic adventure. Though Kipling may challenge the tenets of the Orientalist in some ways, Orientalism is not only about defending a clear and immutable separation between the white man and the rest; one of the ways in which Orientalism draws that line is through the exoticisation of the rest—a process of othering that is just as objectifying and alienating when it is done "positively", through praise and fascination, as when it is done negatively, through the scorn of Burton and his ilk.

In the post-colonial line of argument, it is a sense of superiority, or an absence of the Fanonian inferiority complex, that gives white individuals or societies the licence to appropriate the culture of the others. It is about the white normativity Reni Eddo-Lodge uses to explain the whitewashed failures of the film industry—seeing whiteness as universal and everything non-white as "other"—which opens a whole world to whites, while placing limitations on people of colour or other minorities. In Kipling's world, the scope for passing is reserved for the privileged—another established critique of the British colonial author. No Indian "native" is portrayed in his vast body of work as passing for an Englishman; we never meet a "brown" person who gets away with pretending to be "white".

Meanwhile, in another echo of Richard Burton's attitudes, those aspiring Indians among Kipling's characters who attempt to pass socio-culturally for British—the Bengali *babu* in *Kim*, for example—are comical figures, despite their perfect command of the English language and their Western clothes. They are seen to be having a go at passing "up", but failing miserably. In fact, the tragi-comic figure of the Bengali *babu* or baboo—a Westernised, fat-bellied Bengali in ill-fitting European garb, self-delusionally looking down on other Indians—has been immortalised in popular Victorian literature, beyond Kipling's work, as a caricatured colonial serf. He is the archetypal native trying to pass as a colonial, and making a disastrous fool of himself. *Kim*'s Calcutta babu is boastful, mocked by others behind his back; his obesity and clumsiness are exaggerated. He is not a person you would want to identify with; he lacks the sympathy of his co-characters, the writer and ultimately the reader. His attempt at assuming Britishness is not an impressive or exciting story of a great feat of passing, but rather a sign that Kipling's writing upholds colonial supremacy, granting enormous respect to his "pretend-Indian" British characters, but none for his "pretend-British" figures. As Said puts it, "[o]nly an Occidental could speak of Orientals"—never the reverse.[26]

Kipling can be read as representing truthfully the themes of passing and identity confusion within limited boundaries—his characters are powerful members of a ruling elite, but even their reverse-passing ultimately cannot shake off the "White Man's Burden" of his own inherent whiteness. In the end, both Kim and Mowgli must face a nagging self-doubt, stuck at a mid-point, having tried and failed to break free of a mono-cultural social hierarchy. A definitive journey into a new permanent identity—which would be natural in a post-colonial reality—in these tales seems inconceivable. Ultimately, Kipling implies, Kim and Mowgli are the victims of their own misplaced selfhood, their identification with another race—Indian, animal—a mistaken and doomed attempt against the way things must be.

Passing in the Empire can only ever be temporary, and it can only ever be a case of colonials, usually men, using cultural Anglo-Indianness to pass down. Regardless of their feeling of oneness with the "native" culture, the British, like everyone else, are ultimately restricted within the racial and social hierarchy. Said described this, too, within his theories of Orientalism: "although a certain personal latitude was allowed, the impersonal communal idea of being a White Man ruled."[27] Whether you see Kipling as a mouthpiece for racist empire arguably comes down to why you think he held this defeatist view and repeatedly illustrated it in his work: whether he thought the unbending nature of race in British India was a just reflection of fundamental differences in nature, or simply a practical reality of society and culture being organised that way, *against* nature.

I personally think that Kipling's writing on identity, self-definition and inner turmoil is too complex to come from a mind that believed human nature could be boiled down to a series of lists describing fixed racial characteristics corresponding to inherent values. But perhaps his love for India, or his idea of India—a love always contained out of duty to the Empire, and only allowed to emerge fully through creations like Kim—blinded Kipling to the inequality of his "theatre of self-invention",[28] which he claimed to associate with the great fluid culture of native India, yet reserved for his British characters.

Today we have a name for this imbalance of power in the adoption or imitation of culture: cultural appropriation. In the next chapter, we'll see how this concept, more than any other, symbolises our ongoing debates with ourselves, both internal and public, around which identities we should or shouldn't claim, and where the lines are drawn between identifying, passing and trespassing.

13

WHO'S PASSING FOR WHO?

THE CURIOUS CURSE OF CULTURAL APPROPRIATION

Appropriately, passing has brought into its fold a multitude of identity transformations in different times and places. But perhaps in the West, at least, identity persecution is no longer the brutal force that once terrorised people into giving up their memories, cultures, communities and understanding of themselves, simply in order to survive. This next phase of the passing narrative was predicted by Langston Hughes in his 1950s short story "Who's Passing for Who?" After so many social revolutions—from the outlawing of many forms of identity-based discrimination and the arrival of universal suffrage, to the decline of religious observance and the rise of global connectivity—are we entering a post-passing world? Has passing passed out?

Here is an interesting twist. Instead of fading into history, ideas of the self, whether or how we can change them, and who gets to define them have become a more insidious subject than ever. In the new millennium, individual and collective passing—and especially trespassing—is a major topic of public debate, including the ethics of identity performance, transfer or self-determination. From across the identity politics spectrum, arguments are constantly put forward—sometimes angrily, sometimes eloquently—as to who can or cannot assume a particular identity, and why. Just as some "blue-blooded" individuals believe that those passing up a class through social mobility could never legitimately identify as high-class, some white Westerners believe that foreigners and people of colour, even subjects of their former empires, can never truly be Western. But, on the whole, such attitudes are considered today to be bigoted; instead, and perhaps for the first time in history, it is those other "natives" who are being scrutinised over the validity of their affinities and projections of identity: white Westerners.

Since the time of Burton and Kipling, the world has become increasingly documented, bordered, and organised around principles of universal citizenship; white Christian empires have fallen, with their physical presence largely withdrawn from colonised lands; and Western society has become more sensitive to the cultural and psychological legacies of an unequal global history. As a result of all this, we see and speak less of the "literal" reverse-passing conducted by the likes of Richard Francis Burton and Kipling's characters. Today's heated debates over who can be what, and how this relates to their background or experience, focus far more often on the social and cultural intrusions represented by Rudyard Kipling himself—it is important to remember that, though his narratives of torn souls may speak to the "mixed-race", Kipling was not himself ethnically Anglo-Indian. His own dilemmas were about identifying with a culture his native society did not believe he should feel part of, because of his race; and our dilemma in reading him today is about whether or not his society was right about that.

In other words, today, a new discourse on cultural appropriation has been brought into our discussions of identity trespass. Particularly in the "melting pot" of the twenty-first-century West, cultural empathy now has to be measured against a political scale; everyday interaction is now an engagement in these power struggles and moral hierarchies based on who we are and what we have lived through—any discussion of social groups or cultural backgrounds is now a step into the arena of contested selfhoods. M. Fakhry Davids, the psychoanalyst and self-confessed victim of internalised whiteness, remarks:

> Today we live in a post-modern global village where, in our day-to-day lives, these "othering" processes are more easily revealed; we are much more readily caught in the act. Flashpoints around such incidents can easily spiral out of control, turn violent and generate new enmity and hatred that fuels the maintenance of polarized us–them categories. These, in turn, can be seized upon

by regressive movements—for instance, contemporary terrorism and its powerful imperialist counterpart...¹

So, what are the limits of cultural give and take? How far will culture wars take the modern world?

* * *

The end of the twentieth century saw a near-dilution of stigma around identity transformation. I remember thinking what a funny term "multi-culturalism" was when I arrived in London in the early 1990s. Like many people at the time, I presumed it was a positive term, something we must all aspire to. All identities and cultures were there for the taking; it was our common humanity that we were celebrating. White "Hare Krishnas" were thronging the streets of London, Notting Hill Carnival was a riotous epicentre of cultural celebration and exchange; lambada skirts, rap music and jerk chicken did not follow a particular colour line. Cultural possessiveness was yet to challenge cultural naivety; cultural appropriation was not on anyone's lips.

The possibility of starting fresh really is in front of us, but not on the terms promoted by those who see accusations of insensitivity or racism as a "snowflake" claim to the "right not to be offended". A post-identity future is not about purity of selfhood, about either assimilating or ghettoising; it is not about an insularity of experience shaped by an assigned identity. It is about the opposite. We are experiencing a fertile season of global interaction, birthing previously unknown social groups and personal identities. We have never had greater cultural familiarity than today, and some who argue against cultural and ethnic ghettoes are not white/Western supremacists, but simply advocates for a world where culture is not a divisive identity; where we can all live together in one great hybrid commune, as in the "multi-culti" vision of the 1990s. But this has been paralleled by endless talk of despair over the loss of "Western Culture"; by open and covert hostility toward immigrants and minorities and particularly the visual symbols of their culture, which make it impossible for them to pass for a certain idea of Europe: the minarets, synagogues, masala, saris, hijabs—and the colour of their skin.

PASSING

I was thinking about this while flicking through Douglas Murray's *The Strange Death of Europe* on a long-haul flight. Murray gives a chilling account of brown and black people's mass invasion of Europe, apparently resulting in "Muslim" spots across the continent, robbing these great nations of their white Christian culture. While Murray and his kind consider their own assertion of cultural identity to be legitimate, they base that identity on the supposed illegitimacy of another culture: in particular, first-plus-generation Muslim immigrants. It's important to note, though, that there are also an impressive number of minorities and migrants among the self-appointed protectors of "Western values". These unlikely soldiers include writers, polemicists and artists of colour or non-Western origin who think that progress means Westernisation, while adhering to non-Western culture means disrespect for your host society. This hatred or fear has been growing in the (post-)Trump, (post-)Brexit world, with increasingly open hostility to outsiders.

As we saw in Chapter 10, the domination of this modern or post-colonial identity binary—are you someone who blends in, or someone who refuses to?—has long forced minority cultures in the West on the defensive. Murray's argument describes what it sees, rather than what put it there in the first place: the colonies, post-colonial broken economies and neo-colonial conflict zones fled by the poor, the ousted and the alienated; the work that white Westerners don't want to do that offers them a living in safer and more prosperous countries. Penned into marginalised neighbourhoods, people of colour—who seem to vex white cultural protectionists the most—try to build an identity from what has been lost through centuries of empire and the culture-passing it forced on their ancestors.

But now, these "bloody foreigners" and their descendants are fighting back. Communities of the enslaved, colonised and disenfranchised, survivors of genocide and fragmented homelands—all are now setting their own terms and conditions. For them, overcoming or leaving behind past oppression of their people doesn't mean folding into the majority; it means drawing something positive from this dark history to assert a new selfhood, emerging stronger from rootlessness. By claiming a cultural tradition, twenty-first century minorities, particularly the younger generation, have declared their right to exist, marked by a cultural barricade: ownership is theirs alone. It is from the flashpoints around the othering process that we see a new battle for self-determination rise.

The irony is that this has become a vicious cycle, as post-millennial cultural self-determination, based on the lived reality of not belonging, is held up by certain Westerners as proof that minorities are not even trying to belong, the strength of each cultural viewpoint feeding the other. While the white nationalists and cultural protectionists wage their anti-outsider war—leave or assimilate—the other side, both those from oppressed communities and Western progressive liberals, level the charge of cultural appropriation. Today, ideas of colour-blind multi-culturalism have faded away. Minorities are not only seeking to reclaim their heritage from its historical adulteration and violation; they are also defending it from the same process in the West today.

While refusing to be absorbed into expectations of cultural homogeneity, these othered Westerners are telling the crypto-colonials, the hidden Orientalists, and, often, the well-meaning but self-uncritical liberals to stop taking elements from their heritage, copying their language, music and aesthetics, out of so-called appreciation for the "ethnic". Though there are regular calls for reparations to make amends for imperialism, no one has yet asked for royalties for present-day cultural appropriation. But cultural figureheads are being publicly questioned and their "cultural empathy" disparaged, from Jamie Oliver selling jerk rice to Ed Sheeran dipping his toe in grime music, to celebrity hairstylist Julien d'Ys, who put a series of white models in cornrow wigs on the runway at Paris Fashion Week 2020, claiming that he had been inspired by the headdress of an Egyptian prince.

There has also been some reviewing of history along these lines: we've seen how critics have condemned Kipling's patronising Englishmen heroically passing as natives. T. E. Lawrence in his Middle Eastern garb is none other than a colonial imposter hiding behind his enthusiasm for Arabs or Arab culture. I wonder if John Howard Griffin's black-passing in the name of research and social justice would still be seen favourably today as an act of brave and noble journalism. Those guilty of cultural appropriation may have had good intentions, their accusers say; they may have wanted to express their solidarity with that culture and its people. But cultural sympathy is in a different spirit from that of cultural appropriation.

Others ask—some disingenuously, some sincerely—why everyone across the world is "allowed" to drink espressos and love French food, while white Westerners are vehemently criticised for adopting elements of ethnic-minority cultures. Why, they ask, can black or brown people wear suits and ties, skirts and blouses, if white people can't have bindis or kimonos "anymore"? Can white Westerners, too, feel offended by accusations of cultural theft? Doesn't putting white culture and other cultures on two different levels simply encourage white normativity and white exceptionalism? If we really want to support minorities, shouldn't we treat all cultures equally?

In 2016, the American author Lionel Shriver caused controversy by saying that no one owns their experience—at least, not exclusively. For her, it is not even a question of cultural sympathy, but merely of cultural borrowing and lending as a natural artistic practice. I asked her about this in 2019, and she reiterated that she would always advocate breaking the boundaries of personal experience, because this is what a novelist, a historian, an explorer or traveller does instinctively. A self-described "cultural rebel", she feels that there is now widespread self-censorship of what she sees as an innocent, even enlightened, mutual sharing of knowledge and culture. "[The concept of] cultural appropriation is not in the interest of any fiction writer, to have this artificial and irrational constraint put on their imaginations," Shriver told me. "I am a bit disconcerted that so many novelists keep quiet on this issue, or even lend this concept some credence."[2]

One writer of colour who has not been afraid to express her disquiet is Bernardine Evaristo, who became the first black woman to win the Booker Prize in 2019. She told *The Times* that she too thinks "the whole idea of cultural appropriation is ridiculous".[3] Evaristo refuses "to construct some kind of character who's going to appease everybody" just for the sake of upholding a principle, while Shriver argued in my discussion with her that "The purpose of art is not to create more goodness in the world. The purpose of art is to create more good art." In other words, both Shriver and Evaristo are defending their right to write as novelists, not as social reformers. I asked Shriver how she felt about the concept of an author "passing" as their narrator; she replied that this was exactly what good writers did. "Fiction writers are impressive when they get beyond their own experience and successfully enter the expressions of people who are very different from them. Therefore they are able to put together a story that is a plausible simulacrum of real life."[4] Only writing within your own experience is "myopic", she told me. Evaristo agrees: staying in one's own cultural or racial lane, she argued, "would mean that I could never write white characters" either.

But, again, not all experiences are equal. The idea that all cultures are equally for the taking is what leads culture warriors to cry hypocrisy if a Nigerian-origin Westerner is allowed to set a book in Europe, while a white Western author is not supposed to write a story about a Yoruba family. This seems a logical objection in theory. But this perspective completely ignores an important fact: how such writers came to speak the Western language, both culturally and literally, in the first place. For so many of us around the world, this is the language in which we write and dream, shop and post on social media, curse and tell off our children. The British Empire's cultural export, inherited by American global capitalism, has been so successful and widespread that English no longer belongs to any one race or nation or group or creed. Our ancestors had no choice about the arrival of Western culture on our shores, and we, their descendants, had no choice about the links forged by Empire that have brought us or our parents to Western shores today. The renowned author Jhumpa Lahiri felt so caught between her native Bengali and the English of Empire that she felt compelled to learn and write in Italian, a language without historical baggage complicating her identity.

Children of the old colonies cannot "appropriate" Western culture; it has always been part of their heritage. Those who try to appropriate the experience of another culture or tradition do so from their own culture's privileged position. Minorities can only *adopt* a majority culture, and the word used for this is assimilation—an explicit requirement for belonging in the West. Assimilation implies understanding and accepting the majority culture, whereas the main argument against cultural appropriation is that it mimics other people's customs *without* understanding their historical context. A black British person, or one from a former British colony, does not have to do any research to understand whiteness or Britishness. Bernardine Evaristo is partly of Yoruba heritage, but she lives in a default-white culture; Lionel Shriver would have much further to go to see the world from a Yoruba perspective.

The fact is, while intellectuals and creatives do exist who are truly willing and able to defer sensitively and respectfully to the knowledge and experience of a minority culture, and portray this without reframing it through a white lens, most cultural appropriation does not have this mentality. Anyone can throw a "Mexican party" full of fajitas and sombreros; but very few outsider fans of Tex-Mex will be aware that fajitas traditionally come from the beef off-cuts given to Mexican cowboys on Texas ranches, by often-exploitative ranchers who didn't think the Latinos were worth better than trimmings that would otherwise have been thrown away.

"Mexican parties" and so on represent a selective sampling of culture, which can therefore never be a sincere appreciation. That is why cultural appropriation and ongoing cultural intolerance sit side by side. Today's minorities say: you like our trappings, but you don't like us; you can't eat fajitas and build the wall; you can't love my hummus and laugh at my headscarf. Beyond the historical power imbalance in cultural interaction, this is why experience matters when using the symbols of another heritage. If you don't know what they mean, how could you possibly be confident you're not being offensive?

If colonialism had not happened, perhaps the world would have followed the same natural progression in cultural understanding as it has in scientific understanding—a gradual, upward evolution into a voluntary, amicable sharing of knowledge and skills, without the battle of whose culture is superior and whose is off-limits. But the history we're living with is the West's colonial rule over other nations it considered inferior; and isn't it a more plausible explanation that racism and cultural imitation coexist in today's white-majority societies, not as a confusing contradiction between respect in some contexts and disrespect in others, but in fact as two products of the same disregard?

Optics

This doesn't have to mean that cultural appropriation always comes from bad intentions or attitudes. Cultural reverse-passing can simply arise out of callousness or naivety—for example, in the vexed case of fancy-dress parties. I asked Lionel Shriver if moonwalking at a Michael Jackson party might be allowed, but blackening the face would be taking it too far. She agreed with both statements. Again what matters is context: blackface, or adopting any visible elements of African heritage, will bring to mind a painful chapter in Western history. People who co-opt these symbols playfully are not exonerated by their casual approach; it simply makes them disrespectful of history and its legacy.

America has a long and ignoble history of white performers darkening their skin as part of a costume, specifically in order to mock and dehumanise black people. In minstrel shows, white performers—mostly from poor backgrounds—would blacken their faces, usually with shoe polish or burnt cork, put on tattered, dirty clothes and appear on stage in grotesque body-twisting and limb-flinging acts to mimic black slaves on the Southern plantations. According to the Smithsonian National Museum of African American History and Culture, these blackface performers "characterized blacks as lazy, ignorant, superstitious, hypersexual, and prone to thievery and cowardice."[5] This was presented as comedy. The first minstrel shows were performed in New York in the 1830s, and continued throughout the nineteenth century, perpetuating their caricatures.

One particular performer from the birth of minstrelsy, Thomas Dartmouth Rice, was known as the "Father of Minstrelsy". His blackface creation, "Jim Crow", became hugely popular all over North America; its legacy led to the infamous *Jump Jim Crow* song. Based on this original model, other characters were created, becoming a core part of popular culture and entertainment; the shows stirred particular curiosity in the Northern and Midwestern cities, where African American faces were not as common as in the South. Even in the twentieth century, Broadway and Hollywood continued to put on blackface shows, perpetuating the stereotyped image of the slave long past abolition. Many show-goers, who were usually white, inevitably thought: if the blacks are so dull-witted, why should we take the civil rights movement seriously? Surely these animal-like simpletons shouldn't be allowed to vote? These shows were not simply a theoretical offence of cultural intrusion; they had a deep and lasting impact on attitudes. Minstrelsy, with blackface at its heart, codified blackness as a farce and black people as subhuman, transporting these ideas into the white and also the middle-class black psyche.

In Britain, blackface was quickly taken up by London around the 1840s, and retained its cultural importance into the 1970s, even after it had died down across the Atlantic. In Britain too minstrelsy specialised in racial mockery, portraying "a stereotypical depiction of African-American people and their vernacular cultures as these had developed within the system of British slavery and its historical continuations."[6] But there was one important difference: in North America, minstrelsy had flourished as part of "commoner" culture, aimed at working-class men. Yet soon after its introduction in Britain, it was given a facelift and brought into the drawing-room, allowing the women and children of wealthier families to temporarily shake off the Victorian stiff upper lip and enjoy something loosely deemed "popular culture", the term itself coming into existence in the mid-nineteenth century.

The refinement of blackface in "higher" British society saw its ultimate metamorphosis into fine art. As we will see in the next chapter, it has even been considered Oscar-worthy. The enduring legacy of blackface minstrelsy in Britain, music historians believe, contributed to later white projections and appropriations of blackness, from ragtime to rap: by the early twentieth century, British "minstrelsy met an intense need for what its idea of blackness was about. It didn't matter if this was diluted or distorted, for in greater or lesser degree this was [also] true of later white mediations of black musical culture where a mask wasn't formally worn."[7]

While it is now widely accepted that literal blackface is offensive, it persists in the twenty-first century West. The 2014 film *Dear White People*, now a successful television show, culminates in a black student journalist's horror to find himself at a blackface frat party; before the credits roll, real-life footage is shown of blackface and "Indigenous-face" college parties from around the United States, all from recent years. European progressives like to look upon and speak of this trend in a tone of incredulous moral condemnation, but blackface is closer to home than they might like to realise. In the UK, morris dancing is thought to derive its name from the word "Moorish" and goes back to the turn of the sixteenth century—the time of Othello. To this day, the tradition sometimes incorporates blacked-up dancers. During the Christmastime Saint Nicholas Parade, white people in the Netherlands black up their faces to appear as Zwarte Pieten, or Black Pete. The tradition has continued every year despite outrage from the Dutch black community and a 2015 UN report that said it reflected negative stereotypes of people of African descent, for whom this aspect of white Western culture is a vestige of slavery.[8]

In other words, having some fun in blackface is more than misguided; it is offensive and actively harmful, as the white leader of a Western nation reputed for equality and human rights values has "learnt": Justin Trudeau, Canada's prime minister (2015–). During the 2019 federal election campaign, a photo was published of Trudeau in a bejewelled turban and robe, his face, neck and forearms blackened, having fun at an apparently Arabian Nights-themed party at the private school where he was a teacher. He was 29. The photograph, from the school's 2000/2001 yearbook, shows the blackfaced Trudeau sandwiched between four women, with his right hand resting on the bare upper part of one woman's chest. The whites of his eyes and his teeth glow against his smiling black face, a stark reminder of the minstrel shows, the china figurines of fictional characters such as Little Black Sambo, Golly Wog, Uncle Tom, Blackamoor—all exaggerated caricatures. One can't help wondering what was going through Trudeau's mind; apart from anything else, Arabia is not exactly where black people are typically from. Again, to those who say that nobody has a monopoly on cultural experience, ignorance seems a pretty good argument to the contrary.

It got worse: it seemed that this episode had not been the first time. Two more pictures appeared, this time from the 1990s: in one Trudeau is wearing an afro wig, trying to impersonate a black singer; in another, his face is darkened again to the blackest shade, and he is making crazy hand gestures that would not be out of place at a Jim Crow show of the nineteenth century. Minstrels would often stick out their tongues as part of their act, highlighting their animal-like idiocy and showing that even their tongues had been blackened; one of the photos shows that Trudeau went to this length too. After the scandal broke, the prime minister offered a sheepish apology that he was sorry, he should not have done it: "I should have known better and I didn't."[9]

He surely should have. As the son of a former prime minister, a man of nearly 30 and a teacher, Trudeau cannot possibly have had an excuse not to be informed of North America's long and painful history of slavery and legal racism. When he was asked by journalists if he thought his blackface act was racist, he absurdly replied, "Yes it was. I didn't consider it racist at the time, but now we know better."[10] It is reprehensible that someone of Trudeau's position can claim he did not know in 2000 that blackface was a racist act that dehumanised black people. He said "at the time" as if this had happened in some age long past; if theatrical blackface was already controversial when it won Laurence Olivier an Oscar in 1965 (see Chapter 14), Trudeau's lack of simple historical knowledge at the turn of the millennium is a bafflingly lame excuse.

If he didn't know it was racist at the time to paint his body in black tar, what did he think it was? Just naive exhibitionism? In this vein, some critics have pointed out another photo of the Canadian prime minister: he, his wife and children in Indian clothes, their palms together in the act of praying, at the Sikh Golden Temple in Amritsar during an official visit to India. This 2018 scene was viewed in new light after the blackface pictures emerged the following year, with newspaper columnists seeing Trudeau's apparent habit of "playing dress-up" with an over-the-top sartorial extravaganza as a running sad joke. How many times does the world have to see a white Western leader appearing in the "national" costumes of those the West has colonised and left with a brutal history? Amritsar carries the memory of a particularly bloody imperial legacy: the Jallianwala Bagh massacre of spring 1919, when British colonial troops opened fire on 10,000 unarmed men, women and children. Trudeau should have known better than to enter this temple, of all temples, and pretend to pray like the Sikhs.

India still awaits apology from Britain for the massacre. We can agree that Amritsar is not directly Trudeau's or his government's legacy; but Canada remains a Commonwealth realm, with the British monarch as its head of state. As a white settler dominion of the Crown, Canada profited from the spoils of slavery and Empire just as Britain itself did. Trudeau's "friendly" gesture at the Sikh temple was also very much a self-interested one; he wanted to appease the important Sikh voter bloc back home. He is known to have boasted that he has more Sikhs in his cabinet than his Indian counterpart Narendra Modi.[11] No wonder Modi did not turn up to greet him at the airport as he emerged with his family gesturing the "namaste" sign—palms together, heads bowed. The Indian prime minister was no emir of Harar to be fooled by a white man's condescending disguise.

With Trudeau's resplendent festive wardrobe, a different "Bollywood-themed" outfit at every social engagement, his Indian hosts—after an initial period of amusement—started to feel uneasy, then incredulous. The national press reported that Trudeau was too flashy even for an Indian. The former chief minister of Jammu and Kashmir, Omar Abdullah, tweeted, "Is it just me or is this choreographed cuteness all just a bit much now? Also FYI we Indians don't dress like this every day sir, not even in Bollywood."[12] Over the course of Trudeau's visit, Indians began suspecting they had a possible Orientalist-cum-opportunist on their hands. In an op-ed for *The Washington Post*, the columnist Barkha Dutt agreed: "all that charisma and cuteness seem constructed, manufactured and, above all, not serious."[13]

It is this—not being serious, not having any true understanding of or appreciation for the culture being hijacked—that shows clearly when something is legitimate or well-founded cultural assumption, of the kinds we saw in Chapter 10, versus when it is cultural (mis)appropriation. For Trudeau, *posing* as an Indian for a week was a matter of political strategy. For a Middle Eastern refugee or South Asian migrant worker in Canada or elsewhere in the West, *passing* as a Westerner would be a matter of aspirational belonging—and, for some cultural protectionists, a condition of their right to live in peace.

The "cuteness" was not enough, and Trudeau's non-meeting with Narendra Modi was widely reported as a snub. The Canadian PM was by no means fazed when faced with the media backlash, but his political games backfired. He has been undone multiple times by his clumsy cultural and visual stereotyping of peoples whose history, it appears, he has not grasped.

* * *

Trudeau's "Sikh moment" is a perfect example of someone believing or claiming to be showing respect and admiration for a less privileged culture, when in fact they are drawing benefit from it. I keep hearing the word "appreciation" from my self-proclaimed colour-blind white friends refusing to explore the concept of cultural appropriation. In the case of Trudeau at Amritsar, the benefit of his cultural reverse-passing—had it worked—would have been political capital; among other public figures, the gains of cultural appropriation can be financial. The German model Martina Big turned herself black with tanning injections, grossly enhanced her breasts, and now wants to have an "African nose" to match her new skin tone. She is not alone, but one of an entire collection of "blackfishers"—a term describing a white social media personality, usually a woman, who appropriates a look perceived to be black, using hair products, skin dye, extensive make-up and, in some cases, surgery to change their appearance.

This focus on the need for a particular body deemed to represent blackness recalls disturbingly the physiological "criteria" of blackness and Africanness that were used to make rulings on race in the apartheid courts. The Birmingham-based influencer Aga Brzostowska, who has been labelled a "blackfisher", went through extreme sun-tanning to adopt the appearance of African heritage, has braided her hair, and made her hips and thighs curvy through "hard work in the gym". She told the BBC she does not see anything wrong with her artificial enhancements of her so-called "black" look, viewing it as an extension of her natural physique—referring to her olive skin tone and "full lips". She commented, somewhat brazenly, "I didn't really think much of it. I really appreciate the culture and I really just love the look—that was literally it."[14]

But "appreciating" is not enough, and especially when you "don't think much" about it, there is a fine line between appreciation and appropriation. Blackfishers who alter their body, sometimes permanently, are extreme examples, but they are not alone in feeling that they are justified by their "positive vibes" toward the identity they're invading. When Coldplay's Chris Martin appeared to emulate Muslim dawn prayers during a 2018 sunrise concert in the Jordan Valley, briefly prostrating himself, I could sense the same unease amongst Muslims and non-Muslims alike as had surrounded

Trudeau's costume tour of India; many were suspicious of the band's sudden affinity for Islamic practices just as they were promoting a new album in the Middle East.[15] In this context, I cannot help but quote Aga Brzostowska the blackfisher, who defended herself by pointing out: "Why would I stop doing something that's benefitting me or that I enjoy doing?"

"Benefitting me" is precisely the attitude being decried by blackfishers' black critics—some of whom are trying to build their own platforms as social media influencers with a genuine offer of black culture. Throughout history, being black in the West has been frowned upon; it cannot be acceptable that black has become suddenly fashionable because a handful of whites are race-faking with personalised, offensive versions of what they think "black culture" is, packaging a brand for general consumption and their own popularity and enrichment. They inhabit their illegitimate blackness not secretly like a passer, but in full media glare, trying to outperform each other.

In Chapters 2 and 3 we saw how "racial" features have been categorised and weaponised to control the rights and status of non-white people around the world. In many workplaces in the twentieth- and twenty-first-century West, black women have not been allowed to wear their hair naturally, in an afro or braids; it is only just starting to become acceptable for employees not to go through the painful, expensive and time-consuming processes of relaxing or weaving their hair. Passing as white, or "as close to white as possible", is only necessary because of ongoing prejudice against those who don't "look" white, and—just like passing as straight, or higher-class—it is a bodily discipline to be perfected through meticulous, patient observation of the high-value identity and its appearance. When white Westerners put their hair in dreadlocks or cornrows, they unthinkingly dismiss the trauma and historical danger of those experiences, and the impossibility for most today of escaping racialisation.

Spectrums of Othering

Ordinary people "trying on" aspects of visual blackness are not the typical faces of an oppressor class. But today we are living through a highly explosive, hyper-sensitive phase in the history of identity, with everyday actions and choices called into question too. I was on the Tube in London three Halloweens ago when, amongst a carriage full of people in costumes, I saw a white teenager in an afro wig. I asked who he was dressing up as. Stupid question, his expression seemed to say. A second later, after his initial shock, he boldly replied, "Michael Jackson!"

What was I supposed to make of it? I looked around at the many black and racially ambiguous faces. I saw amusement on some and indifference on most. I was going to ask the young man some more questions, but his absolute determination to physically exhibit his adoration for the King of Pop was clear. Should he be expected to bear the historical guilt for his presumed ancestral connection to a terrible episode in history, just because he is white? Do we have the right to tell him, no, you cannot wear that wig? Besides, it had not occurred to me to question myself just one evening earlier, when I had dressed my own 6-year-old to go to a Michael Jackson party. I got him a *Thriller* outfit, and I was going to buy him an afro wig, but could not find one. Political correctness had not remotely been on my mind. Now, on the Tube, I felt confused. This white teenager seemed as obsessed with Michael Jackson as my son was. Why should there be one set of rules for him, and another for my boy? Did I think that, as non-whites, my son and I couldn't be accused or guilty of cultural appropriation?

I probably justified it to myself by thinking that I had absolutely no legacy to bear for historical injustices committed against Africans; that wasn't the doing of my ancestors, in the last 400 years or ever. Yet ethnic-minority public figures have not been exempt from the accusation. In 2019, celebrity chef Padma Lakshmi wore her hair in cornrows to judge an episode of an American cookery show. A brown-skinned woman of south Indian origin, perhaps she thought she was cleared of the possibility of cultural appropriation, just as I hadn't thought to connect that accusation to the idea of my son in an afro wig. She woke to a media backlash the next day. Kim Kardashian was called "the face of cultural appropriation in America" on social media after appearing at a public event with braids typical of the West African Fulani people. Kardashian is white, but she has a black husband and biracial children. In a post-braid interview, she said that she'd meant no offence: "in no way am I ever trying to disrespect anyone's culture by wearing braids. If anything, my daughter was so excited to see me get matching braids with her. [When] we did her hair in these braids, she was so excited."[16]

We can't know what attitudes lie in the conscious or subconscious minds of these or any other celebrities accused of trespassing into another racial identity. But it's worth coming back to the concept of internalised racism explored in Chapter 10. It is institutional, structural, a stealthy yet powerful force, and it does not discriminate racially. M. Fakhry Davids has described historical racist organisation of society as a stable structure in the mind of a Western adult today, occupying the same "primitive terrain".[17] Liberal white families tell their children that colour doesn't matter, but those children, as they grow up into adults, see that it has been a lie all along. Internalised racism can surface among white people in a patronising pat-on-the-back and loaded comment to a brown-skinned stranger in a swimming pool changing area: "Oh, but you and I have a special bond!" That conspiratorial "but" is an eloquent override of the otherwise unspoken nature of things—the separation between those racialised differently. It links the former white colonial with the European-educated formerly colonised. Britain and India have a special relationship, giving you the right to approach me and tell me that we are connected.

I have often been that brown person at the pool, and there can be internalised racism in a brown person's response too. Should I be ashamed now of what I felt in the 1990s—that I was lucky to have been from the Jewel in the Crown and not from the un-special home islands of many Windrush arrivals? I have seen throughout my life in Britain that people of South Asian origin undoubtedly feel on a higher step of the West's racialist hierarchy than people of Afro-Caribbean origin. Both race science and the international order have explicitly ranked racialised peoples differently, for instance in the statuses assigned to League of Nations mandates after World War I: Middle Eastern colonies inherited from the defeated Ottoman Empire had Class A status, placing them above the former German colonies in sub-Saharan Africa, which were considered less advanced and designated Class B or C.

The gradation is too obvious. The stereotypically brown-skinned Asian is a shorter stretch away from whiteness than the black-skinned African; the "olive" Middle Easterner, even closer. This is as literal at it gets, a pecking order continually woven into the system by those who run it and those who are run by it. We saw in Chapter 3 how hierarchies of complexion have been used to divide and rule individual non-white communities. "[A] lifetime of subtle marginalisation and othering", as Reni Eddo-Lodge puts it, continues to affect both the unwitting racists and the victims of racism.[18] Like "colour" itself, othering is a spectrum, not a binary. And, yes, that means that sometimes even non-white people can be guilty of cultural appropriation.

The Eternal Martyrdom of Rachel Dolezal

The idea of one marginalised group dabbling in the culture of another raises some more complex questions. It's clear-cut when reverse-passers and cultural appropriators are of an obviously, officially and extravagantly privileged and powerful identity, and helpfully spell out their racial disdain, like Richard Burton. And when there is a clear intent or opportunity to exploit the "borrowed" culture for personal gain, in the form of public image or financial revenue, it's still fairly easy to work out that there are problematic dynamics at play. When the actor is white and the culture they're operating in is not, that makes things simpler too. But what happens when cultural appropriation is less straightforward? When it is not solely appropriating culture for gain, or even an outsider "appreciating" a culture they recognise is not their own, but involves *identifying* with that culture—what are we to think of the legitimacy of that identity? It's time to come back to the Kipling quandary.

Rachel Dolezal was president of the National Association for the Advancement of the Colored People (NAACP) in the predominantly white town of Spokane, Washington state. She let everyone believe that she was black. But the true story got out in the summer of 2015, when her white parents revealed to a newspaper that their 37-year-old daughter was just a regular white American, whose only experience of blackness was through her black foster siblings. The outcry from all directions following the news of Dolezal's extraordinary subterfuge was deafening. She was viciously vilified in the media, socially shamed, and ostracised by her birth family, her friends and many former supporters and admirers. Her position as a campaigner was taken away from her. African-Americans accused her of stealing African cultural heritage, including the box braids that she had been wearing since she had started passing as black halfway through life. She had lied to the NAACP chapter committee that had elected her to lead them.

But Dolezal didn't see it as lying. Despite the tornado of bad publicity since her "outing" by her parents, she refused to back down, and still lives with her choices today, changing her name to something more "African" and making a living by braiding African hair—a skill she taught herself while passing as black. Though it has incensed many people, her transition, legitimate or not, was permanent. Her media appearances have been unrepentant: "If people feel misled or deceived, then sorry that they feel that way, but I believe that's more due to their definition and construct of race in their own minds than it is to my integrity or honesty…"[19]

One can argue there is some truth in this comment, in the sense that Dolezal successfully made herself look sufficiently black for white and black alike to take her as African American, and so likely experienced racism. Several times before her unmasking, she called police to report intimidation by white supremacists against her activism for the Black Lives Matter movement—these reports may not have been false. Anthony Ekundayo Lennon's story has shown that racists won't ask to see your family tree or your grandfather's birth certificate before attacking you for looking black to them. Like all race-passers, Rachel Dolezal has exposed the fiction of race as a biological or inherent fact: she has shown it once again to be only skin-deep, based on visual impressions and appearances.

Dolezal's mistake, however, is to believe that because race doesn't mean what racists think it does, race therefore doesn't mean anything unchangeable at all. She told *Vanity Fair* that her black appearance is "not a costume", but a reflection of an identity she has spent a life "negotiating"—a word typically used by those of biracial heritage, which Dolezal is not—through many years of research into and internalisation of African American history and culture.[20] Implicit in this defence is a suggestion that Dolezal knows more about black heritage in America than many people deemed black from birth probably do, and so perhaps she even has *more* right to claim blackness for herself. Dolezal made clear in the same interview that she does not believe blackness is owned by any particular people: "You can't just say in one sentence what is blackness or what is black culture or what makes you who you are."[21] She explained to the world that she believes in "transracialism": a feeling of being born into the "wrong race", as transgender people may feel they have been born in the wrong body—the opposite of transracialism being the tyranny of cis-racialism.

It is true that many black people are deeply frustrated by attempts, by both black and white, to homogenise their experience or identity. But the problem with "transracialism" is that these fluid states of racial being cannot be claimed by people who are not mixed-race; they cannot be claimed by those society has labelled black. Many distinguished commentators have expressed irritation that Dolezal's philosophy has carried enough weight (or interest) in the media to produce a dialogue, leading us to engage in a debate about "feeling black" versus "feeling white" when the two are, for obvious historical reasons, not comparable. When Dolezal reiterated in a defiant talk show appearance after her fall from grace that "I identify as black", the bemused host, the black comedian Loni Love, told her that she couldn't be, because she couldn't reverse herself.[22] Even if Dolezal never intended to "go back" to living as white, she still could if she needed to, and that was known to her when she began to start passing; she could never truly understand the lack of freedom that comes with knowing the world will always see you as black first. This ongoing black struggle, universal despite all the individuality of black people, is vocalised powerfully by the Zambian-born Australian rapper, Sampa the Great. The refrain of her song *Final Form* identifies that imposed, rigid, simplifying and generalising label simply as "melanin".

Rachel Dolezal's defence is that she wanted to be worthy of belonging to African American identity; so how could she have anything to do with a Richard Burton-type figure? This recalls the contested ownership of "native" culture in the case of Kim and his creator, Rudyard Kipling. But another way of looking at it is that she wanted to *own* African American identity, to take it and keep it and make it hers: a mentality closer to Burton's than she might like to accept, and not obviously consistent with the inferiority complex and identity anxieties that often result from the experience of racism. For many, Dolezal's trespass is easy to expose as such: she has hankered after blackness as her raison d'être, as what Doreen St. Félix characterises as her "eternal martyrdom";[24] but had she known what it was like to grow up in America as black, if she had experienced for herself what it is to be black—in all of its pain as well as its glory—she surely would not have found "eternal martyrdom" an appealing selfhood. She might have seen that her "sacrificing" herself and her whiteness to the eternal black struggle was not all about solidarity; that it was maybe more like a saviour complex—albeit a deeply troubled one—than a case of mistaken identity.

* * *

What Rachel Dolezal bizarrely failed to take into account was that racial bias doesn't have to be linked to a calculated attempt to look down on a particular race. It is born of and perpetuated by a real-world, present-day freedom specific to whiteness (though not experienced equally by all whites), and arguably it is also born of a historical sense of entitlement. Dolezal's "genuine passion" for African-American culture and her work for racial justice was not the point. Progressive whites often refuse to be described as having an unconscious racial bias, they feel it is a damning accusation, and their sense of self-defence appears stronger than their duty as individuals to own up to historical injustices and their legacies in today's world.

To address this, say those who cry cultural theft, is far more important and would be far more welcome and convincing than momentary, impulsive exhibitions of love for "ethnic" culture. Cultural minorities in the West are now demanding: do not hide behind your neo-ethnographic interest in us, your wishy-washy universalism, your sharing of and partaking in our heritage because you love us so. Love has nothing to do with erasing racism. Racial bias must be forensically and rigorously dealt with—addressed, marked and rooted out. Before we can all live together in an all-you-need-is-love world, years, decades will be needed for collective self-reflection, admission of historical wrongs, shame and guilt. Only then can the case of cultural appropriation be closed.

Whitewashing the ills of racism by looking away and confining them to a past that has nothing to do with us is the same as saying we can just overlook sexist or homophobic attitudes as a somehow separate, contained and fundamentally exceptional section of our society: "Oh, these are just old-fashioned people!" As Reni Eddo-Lodge emphasises,

> Not seeing race does little to deconstruct racist structures ... We must see who benefits from their race, who is disproportionately impacted by negative stereotypes about their race, and to who [sic] power and privilege is bestowed upon—earned or not—because of their race, their class, and their gender. Seeing race is essential to changing the system.[25]

When the past is a Pandora's box full of mass exploitation and violence, it is only right that the present must try to address it and repent. Still, it is not as simple as issuing an apology and being exonerated. There is a wrong way for white liberals to accept or acknowledge responsibility, one that is preoccupied with its own virtue, homogenises members of a community, and plays into the condescending saviourism that perhaps informed Rachel Dolezal's chosen black role (as a racial justice warrior). M. Fakhry Davids remarks:

> In a race awareness group a white woman insisted that today white people must accept and tolerate black hatred since they bear collective responsibility for the sins of colonialism ... Black anger and hatred towards whites was to be expected and she understood terrorism, corruption in Third World governments, blacks cheating the social welfare system in Europe and so on as manifestations of it. The idea was that this had to be tolerated as a natural consequence of colonial injustice—an eye for an eye, a tooth for a tooth! Racist projection is, of course, a very personal way of colonizing someone else.[26]

An outpouring of misguided self-flagellation and overly sweeping tragic accounts of modern-day "noble savages" will not make good the centuries of ongoing injustice. The rage of the "terrorist" is not to be understood as a parent perceives an upset, unruly child or a heroic avenger. Instead of looking to speak for people of colour and decide on a narrative about their experience of their identity, white

Westerners will have to look to themselves, and consider how history and politics can explain their own behaviours, motivations and relationship to identity. Those who want to embrace and adopt minority culture must consider whether or not they belong to the traditional ruling class that invaded, enslaved, colonised and racialised people still assigned "other", whether they themselves benefit from belonging to that group today, and how they can work to ensure that historic wrongs and white supremacy do truly become a thing of the past.

On a national level, the closest example I can think of for such an undertaking is Germany's work of atonement and prevention for Nazi crimes during WWII, with an education programme that does not shy from teaching ugly history and a policy of accepting accountability for past horrors—including by continuing to offer citizenship to those displaced or persecuted by the Nazi regime and their descendants. While cultural majorities and historically oppressive groups could certainly show more self-awareness, and work harder to direct their energies toward real change in society's power structures, these are systemic, institutionalised problems that cannot be solved by individuals alone. Though hate crimes and far-right politics were on the rise in Germany throughout the 2010s, Germany's example has been much lauded when compared against what (if anything) the British have done to atone for the Empire, for instance.

The rage and the pain of openly discussing identity crimes should help open new avenues of self-reflection—not just for the former perpetrators, but also for the former victims. Together we would then be entitled to move away from the "prison"—let us call it experience—of our old self and embrace a new being. Only then could Rachel Dolezal call herself black and frizz her hair into a 4a, 4b or 4c.[27] Aga the blackfisher could darken her skin to the blue-black of Kali, Martina Big could be "African", my Brixton flatmates could call themselves black—only in a different world, where ethno-cultural injustice has been resolved. Throughout this book, we have seen passers liberate themselves from their assigned labels—at least in some ways, at least for a while—by considering a collective and individual memory of suffering and grafting onto it a new understanding of self. If we want to overcome impositions, hierarchies and oppositions of identity, we must first address their murky heritage.

14

REPRESENT

PASSING AND APPROPRIATION IN THE PERFORMING ARTS

It is increasingly clear that, for many in the West, reverse-passing, whether "literal" in the form of disguising oneself as a lower-status identity or in the subtler offences of cultural appropriation, will no longer stand. Yet there is one particular realm, in which we all participate, where both reverse-passing and cultural appropriation continue to thrive: the performing arts. The charge-sheet against theatre, television and film includes the lack of representation of minorities, due to exclusion of both their experiences and their members from dramatic storytelling; but an important part of this process of exclusion is the widespread phenomenon of "pass-casting".

There are two sides to pass-casting, which will be taken together in this chapter. Firstly, an act of cultural appropriation at the moment of creative decision-making and story-telling. This typically involves subversion of an existing narrative, whether fictional or historical, such that it is bleached of all minority identity and rerouted for the "mainstream"—for instance, a person or community of colour being rewritten during the dramatic adaptation as white, or rewritten "neutrally" (also white). Secondly, an endorsement of reverse-passing at the moment of casting: allowing a character to remain a minority in the script, but then hiring a dominant-group or privileged-identity actor to play the role. This applies not just to white actors being given non-white parts, but also straight and cis actors portraying queer characters; an upper-class elite being prioritised even for working-class parts; and, in some parts of the world, members of one faith community finding themselves shut out of the business unless they can and do impersonate another religion, on screen and in real life.

As we will see, these various arenas in the battle over who has the right to present themselves as what in our performance culture reveal how the complex morality of this question shifts with the winds of social and political change. Yet somehow, amidst the growing outcry against dominant groups performing the identities of the dominated, society continues to largely overlook—and frequently, as we shall see, reward—inappropriate identity transfer and identity imitation, so long as it is done in the name of professional performance art. This feels like a fitting place to end our journey through identity transformation and identity trespass: is acting the last acceptable form of reverse-passing?

Whitewashing

From Pope Joan to *Parasite*, passing has always been, and remains, a popular cinematic theme. Since the term's explicit appearance in popular culture—in the race novels of the early twentieth century—the theme has been extensively explored in cinema from both sides of the Atlantic as well as Bollywood, telling not only ordinary people's stories but also the thrilling adventures of journalists, detectives and forbidden lovers. Yet cinema's apparent obsession with the passer's search for belonging and inclusion is ironic, given that mainstream film-making has consistently failed to represent the voices and stories behind different identities. In the West, in both the characters being depicted and the people chosen to play them, the art and entertainment world remains predominantly white, straight, cis and upper-class. In Bollywood, the world's largest film industry, the norm for characters and the actors who portray them is Hindu and upper-caste—and the gender or sexuality questions rarely even come into it.

This problem of representation—particularly around race—actually goes back to early passing films themselves. While Hollywood has sporadically tried to display progressive sentiments by making "social problems" films, these ultimately do not amount to a major representation of racism or racialised people in the film industry or in wider America. Hollywood's first narrative feature on the theme of racial passing was 1934's *Imitation of Life*. The film, based on Fannie Hurst's novel, follows an African American housekeeper, Delilah, distancing herself from her light-skinned daughter Peola in order to ensure a "white" life for her. Fredi Washington, a black actor, played Peola, and the two younger versions of Peola were also portrayed by African Americans—making *Imitation of Life* the only film of the period with a light-skinned black actor in the white-passing role.

This truthful casting choice hit a raw nerve. The passing films of early Hollywood showed black characters lucky enough to have light complexion breaking free of social stigma and poverty. But they were usually played by white actors passing as fair-complexioned and mixed-race—mainly because, if a sexual relationship was shown on screen between a white character and a black character passing as white, the film-makers could be charged with promoting miscegenation, forbidden at the time. White-passing itself was also a criminal offence in many states, in an age when it was commonly believed and accepted that ideas explored in art should be limited to the bounds of morality in society. In a well-documented 1924 court case, a white man, Leonard Rhinelander, filed a lawsuit against his own wife, Alice Jones, who was legally classified as black but had been using her light skin to hide the fact. He accused her of falsely identifying as white and taking advantage of his ignorance of her "true" blackness.

Unsurprisingly, then, when the file for *Imitation of Life* landed on the desk, the Production Code Administration, the body responsible for enforcing moral—including racial—correctness in American cinema, warned Universal Studios about "the action of the negro girl appearing white",[1] which demonstrated a little too easily the fiction of race. With *Imitation of Life*, as the media scholar Karen M. Bowdre explains, "this 'white' looking character ... had a Black mother. Her physical body (and by extension the bodies of other Blacks who are not easily discernible racially) was central to the PCA's anxiety regarding this film."[2] Though passing narratives were clearly based on a real-life phenomenon, they could somehow be safely confined to art and entertainment so long as no real-life audience had to accept an African American actor as any kind of white—so long as only white actors were depicting passing, it could be implied that nobody with that one drop of black blood could ever get away with it.

The script-writer, William Hurlbut, made various compromises to get the film past the censors. Firstly, *Imitation of Life* made sure that the white-passing character to be played by Washington was not likeable. Peola is presented as a liar, a manipulator fooling the white establishment, even as a child—in her all-white classroom, she does not correct the students and teachers who think she is white. When she is caught lying, the stereotype of the deceitful black race is implicitly confirmed to what would have been a largely sympathetic audience. The greatest fear around anything threatening the clear separation of races was miscegenation, and so, although beautiful, Peola must absolutely not be sexualised. She was no more than a "tragic mulatto"—like Clare Kendry of Larsen's *Passing*—this was a type of blackness the audience was familiar with and could understand, showing her white-passing as misguided rather than legitimate.

Similarly, Peola's hapless mother Delilah was characterised as a Southern mammy figure, the archetypal devoted black caretaker of white families. She was portrayed as a character to be pitied for the curse of her blackness, yet applauded for her virtues. The film's other black characters are not portrayed any more favourably, or with any greater sense of agency and complexity. Finally, the version of the film that won the PCA's approval for release shows Peola coming to regret her transgression into whiteness, with a significant death framing the film's overall moral that no good can come of such aspirations—a message that would be echoed a quarter-century later in the 1950s British tragedy *Sapphire*. The strong suggestion at the film's end is that Peola is going to stop passing and resume her black identity. Yet the 1933 novel on which the screenplay is loosely based makes a bolder statement. In Fannie Hurst's source material, Peola does not return to her mother; she continues to pass as a white woman.

Despite these careful attempts to adapt the story, "Washington's portrayal is so effective and unsettling that Hollywood did not cast Black women in passing roles in the future."[3] Hollywood was never really a platform for promoting racial equality or social reform, and passing films of the Golden Age depicted their black characters as impersonating something they could not be. Nor did these films break the stereotype that white was the default complexion for main characters, which still continues today. British and American productions cast white actor after white actor in roles that were meant for and written for non-white artists, putting them in blackface and yellowface, or simply passing no comment on the sudden racial transformation of the character. The Hollywood Cleopatra is blue-eyed and white. The Japanese Mr Yunioshi in *Breakfast at Tiffany's* is a grotesquely bucktoothed Mickey Rooney.

This was not just an American problem. In 1965, Laurence Olivier's performance as Othello saw him nominated for an Oscar, elevating racial stereotyping, reverse-passing and appropriation of black perspectives to high culture. At the height of the American Civil Rights movement, at a time when Sidney Poitier was celebrated as a prominent black actor (who had won an Oscar himself in 1964), Sir Laurence's Othello—pitch-black, with curly African hair and watermelon red lips—is incomprehensible. The then *New York Times* film critic, Bosley Crowther, wrote that the lead character's racialised make-up "immediately impels the sensitive American viewer into a baffled and discomfited attitude."[4] The blackface was all the more deplorable because an earlier version, the Orson Welles picture from 1951, had the sense to forgo it, with Welles instead appearing slightly tanned.

This approach would be taken thirty years later for *Gandhi* (1982), another blockbuster that won several Oscars, including for Ben Kingsley's portrayal of the Mahatma. At least Kingsley's father was of East African Indian origin. But Kingsley, who was born and raised in northern England, has a white mother and a white complexion, and is usually cast as white, had to wear brownface and put on an accent often used mockingly by racist whites in order to "pass" as the Indian national hero. At the time Kingsley was cast, Bollywood was thriving, with plenty of world-class actors, Indians born and bred, who would have been perfect candidates for the leading role. But actors of colour continued to be overlooked for real-life characters of colour even in the new millennium. Instead of casting a mixed-race actress, Angelina Jolie was chosen for the 2007 film adaptation of the memoir *A Mighty Heart* by Mariane Pearl, a woman of Dutch Jewish and Afro-Cuban Chinese origin. Blackface was thankfully unthinkable at this point, but Jolie had to wear a jet-black, tightly curled wig for the role. Rachel Dolezal, the real-life black-passer, has also been vilified for "hair crimes" in pursuit of visible blackness; Jolie was nominated for the Best Actress Golden Globe.[5]

In those two cases, the source material was history, but the casting of white actors in non-white roles is common with adaptations of fictional literature too. In the 2003 film adaptation of Philip Roth's *The Human Stain*, the story of a racially black professor living as white and Jewish, Anthony Hopkins played the lead, passing as the passer. In other cases, the original or intended ethnicity of a character was simply swept aside. To give another Angelina Jolie example, she played Fox in the 2008 adaptation of the comic book series *Wanted*. The character had been written for an African American woman, and was apparently inspired by Halle Berry. Even in the 2010s the whitewashing continued, of both original fictional characters and those adapted from non-white stories.

Nor was this whitewashing confined to black characters. In Ridley Scott's preposterous Old Testament adaptation, *Exodus: Gods and Kings* (2014), a Middle Eastern Moses and Egyptian Ramesses II are respectively played by Christian Bale and Joel Edgerton, both Caucasian. In 2015, Emma Stone played a woman of Chinese and Hawaiian heritage in *Aloha*. In Disney's *The Lone Ranger* (2013), Johnny Depp painted his face with stripes and wore a wig of long, straight black hair to play a Native American character. Depp claims he has some Native American heritage, but that is a laughable excuse, like me saying that, with my 7.2% Chinese DNA, I can audition for Chinese parts, despite never having been mistaken for a Chinese person and never having experienced Chinese culture from the inside. The passers we have met throughout this book have shown a keen understanding of the need to observe, adopt and inhabit, the mindset and the meaning of their new identity and its culture; this is what has enabled them to feel a legitimate member of that community, or an authentic self-identifier. Yet white actors, and the people casting them, seem to expect that non-white lives are just costumes to be put on and taken off at will, with no deeper meaning behind them. Once again, mainstream society forgets that race is not about skin colour.

* * *

The role of racism in whitewashed casting is clear when you look at the debate being had around it. Some argue that such transgression of racial or ethnic lines in the performing arts should not be a cause for concern—that that's what actors do, they impersonate somebody they are not. But it is not a two-way process; not even now, as we enter the third decade of the twenty-first century. After centuries of white Othellos, when will there be a black Hamlet or Macbeth on the silver screen?

If we can't even cast people of the right background to play actual living or historical people, the industry certainly isn't ready to leave race out of casting for characters who are fictional. There was considerable uproar in the tabloid talkback sections at the suggestion of Idris Elba as James Bond. Everyone from comedians to journalists to Daniel Craig himself has said that James Bond is centrally and fundamentally a "misogynist", and so a female James Bond might not make much sense—but even when a character is not inherently tied to white patriarchal norms, there is still an uproar if any attempt is made to portray them outside those limits. We saw this when Jodie Whittaker became Doctor Who in 2017—a role exclusively played by men since 1963.

When non-white roles aren't going to white actors, they are being kept off the screen and stage altogether. Not only do white actors play important non-white characters (and win Oscar after Oscar for them), in most films made in the West, the original roles are written for their complexion too. Most screenplays expect that lead (or any) characters will be white, unless it is specified that they are not. This is because the industry considers white "normal", and anything else the deviation: films about people of colour are "non-white stories", but films about white people are just "stories". In *Why I'm No Longer Talking to White People About Race*, Reni Eddo-Lodge observes, "It is in film, television and books that we see the most potent manifestations of white as the default assumption. A character simply cannot be black without a pre-warning for an assumed white audience."[6]

Given the assumed whiteness of the audience, film-makers and funding bodies also make a second assumption: they fear that making characters of colour the leads would alienate the audience, risking a box office flop. But both of those assumptions are false. When specific characters have been created explicitly for non-white actors, the films have been a hit among audiences of all complexions. In the 2018 American superhero film *Black Panther*, "a big geopolitical action adventure",[7] based on a Marvel Comics character, the cast is explicitly black, the film imagining a world where an African nation has become technologically advanced and powerful. *Black Panther* took a staggering $1.34 billion at the box office, making it the ninth highest-grossing film of all time. Released in the same year but on a much smaller budget, another tremendously successful example of all non-white casting is *Crazy Rich Asians*, set in Singapore, which took $240 million and became the highest-grossing romcom in over a decade.

Why does representation matter? Because white normativity in culture passes down white normativity to the people who consume it. Eddo-Lodge talks about her yearning as a little black girl relating to the white heroes of popular culture, as she realised she would never turn white. Many of us as little girls, growing up in the shadow of Western fairy tales like Sleeping Beauty and Rapunzel, inadvertently internalise the fiction of our colour-blind wonderland, trying to identify with a white Alice; if not fairytale and Disney princesses, then amazingly free and wild spirits like Laura of *Little House on the Prairie*. In the early 1980s, when I watched every episode of *Little House*, I remember insisting on having my hair arranged in two plaits before school. Every summer when I went to my grandmother's village and walked through submerged paddy fields, my legs covered in water leeches, my long dark plaits flying in the wind, I dreamt of being the blonde, white Laura as I crossed the watery meadow—my own prairie.

Was I truly colour-blind, or was I accepting the idealisation of whiteness? I sometimes wonder what I would have thought had Laura been played by a little black girl with her hair in cornrows. It's hard to imagine. Whiteness has been accepted as the default complexion even when there are no visual arts involved, as we saw with the development of the two-part play *Harry Potter and the Cursed Child*, which premiered in 2016 with the black British actor Noma Dumezweni in the role of the adult Hermione Granger. J.K. Rowling tweeted in support of a black Hermione, stressing that "White skin was never specified" for the character, and condemning any racist hijacking of her creation. All Rowling had ever said in visual description of Hermione, she pointed out, was that the young witch had "brown eyes [and] frizzy hair" and was "very clever".

Many of Harry Potter's non-white fans were relieved to see Rowling's tweet supporting the "colour-blind casting" of *Cursed Child*. However, given the nature of the problem—a universally assumed default whiteness—the argument that "I never said she *wasn't* black" fell short for some. This position ensures white visualisation by omission, even if it doesn't intend to—as borne out by the two book cover designs depicting Hermione white, presumably approved by Rowling. Writing in *The Guardian* in the wake of the furore, the columnist Chitra Ramaswamy, who is of South Asian origin, stated that she had never imagined Hermione as a black or Asian girl. Passive non-engagement with questions of race does not defeat racism. "Not that it matters what Rowling envisaged," she added. "We don't need Shakespeare to have imagined Hamlet as a black man (or, indeed, a woman) to do so ourselves."[8]

Where there is actually evidence that Hermione could excite and inspire Rowling's non-white readers, Ramaswamy pointed out, this is not anything to do with her physical appearance—basing an argument about her race, even one in support of her blackness, only feeds into the fiction of race science. In fact, the potential for young readers of colour "starved of black and Asian characters in mainstream culture" to identify with Hermione comes from Rowling's rejection in the *Harry Potter* series of any inherent characteristics or hierarchies of race. As Ramaswamy reminded readers, perhaps now accustomed to the diluted film version of the character, Hermione is a civil rights activist, "who campaigns for an end to the enslavement of elves."[9] What's more, in the enchanted world of Harry Potter, one's "blood status" and prejudice toward those not of "pure" wizarding stock—including both Harry and Hermione—is a central theme. The moral integrity and magical prowess of these heroes have nothing to do with their heritage. Hermione, the most important Muggle-born character, is an exceptionally gifted witch. In her portrayal of evil wizards obsessed with bloodlines that have long since become muddled, J.K. Rowling has exposed racism and the fiction of race to young people across the world.

So there are signs of progress. Role switches allowing actors of colour to play traditionally white or assumed white roles have happened in a small number of modern theatre productions in recent years, both in London's West End and on Broadway, and it has made the stage a far richer medium, more reflective of diversity. *Harry Potter and the Cursed Child* is just one example—one of the most talked about, critically acclaimed and artistically inventive shows to premiere in recent years has been the musical *Hamilton*, created by and originally starring Lin-Manuel Miranda, who is of Puerto Rican descent. The show, which opened on Broadway in 2015, tells the story of Alexander Hamilton, a mixed-race immigrant who is one of America's founding fathers; the cast is not white. In 2016, the UK's National Theatre—the heart of the British cultural establishment—staged a new production of Peter Shaffer's 1979 play *Amadeus*, with British-Tanzanian actor Lucian Msamati playing the Italian composer Antonio Salieri. The cultural significance of a black actor in a classical composer's role also extended to a symbolic acknowledgment of history's neglect of black composers.

Hollywood is falling behind. But, based on the popularity of the #OscarsSoWhite movement, and in light of the increased portrayal of our diverse society in modern theatre, the world's biggest entertainment industry may soon follow suit. When Jordan Peele's critically acclaimed race horror *Get Out* hit cinemas in 2017, the veteran African American actor Samuel L. Jackson said that the film's British star, Daniel Kaluuya, should not have played the lead role, because Kaluuya could not authentically portray the experience of an African American, which was fundamentally different from that of a black British person. There was also some sense, in the ensuing debate, that life is hard enough for African American actors without black British counterparts arriving on their shores in search of work. We've already come across this idea that there is limited space afforded black stories and artists, and that it's therefore unacceptable for questionable claimants to take up any of that space: in the case of Anthony E. Lennon.

While opinion has been divided on all these questions, the very fact of the fierce and open debates around both Jackson's comments and Lennon's place in black theatre seems to suggest that the conversation about diversity and representation—among audiences and industry figures—has today become both widely accepted and deeply nuanced, perhaps to the point that black actors can even argue among themselves as to who should be playing which kind of black character. Popular opinion against the whitewashing of the performing arts has won the day on at least one big-budget production: Disney's live-action remake of *Mulan*, based on the Chinese legend about a young woman passing as a male soldier in the imperial army to save her frail father from having to fight. The 2020 drama (released straight to streaming amid coronavirus restrictions) cast Liu Yifei, a Chinese American, as Mulan, after a petition amassed over 100,000 signatures, pleading with Disney not to cast white actors in the film. It is telling that this wasn't a wave of outrage prompted by a miscasting; this was an audience, so used to and fed up of whitewashing on screen, demanding representation pre-emptively, before the cast had been announced.

Television, too, is starting to rethink its racial assumptions. In June 2020, in the wake of renewed Black Lives Matter protests following the killing of George Floyd, cartoon shows including *The Simpsons* and *Family Guy* announced that they would no longer use white voice actors for non-white characters, several years after the argument first emerged around the *Simpsons* character Apu, voiced by the Jewish American actor Hank Azaria. And, in another response to the post-Floyd movement, one that can't help but contribute to long-term, structural change in the performing arts, the Academy of Motion Picture Arts and Sciences—the Oscars voting body—announced an expansion by more than 800 new members. Almost half were women, many were young and international, and a third were industry professionals of colour. One would like to think that perhaps change is coming at last.

Here and Queer?

The movement for an end to passing in film, television and theatre has largely focused on racial representation, given that these are visual arts. But identity norms in these cultural scenes aren't just limited to whiteness. Lack of LGBTQ representation in casting shows that heteronormativity is just as pernicious in showbiz as white normativity. Mainstream acting in the UK today is overwhelmingly dominated by a particular class, regardless of the socio-economic identity or experience being portrayed. Finally, in

Bollywood religious identity has been just as linked to social privilege as class, sexuality and race on Western screen and stage. In every one of these cases, as with race, we can see how historical transformations of attitudes and statuses have impacted on the levels of representation—or misrepresentation—in the performing arts. It's worth looking briefly at each of these questions in turn.

More often than not, we see straight and cis actors cast in gay and trans parts. And, as with the racial miscastings we've explored above, often this on-screen passing has led to critical acclaim from within the industry. In Chapter 6 we met the American transphobic-murder victim Brandon Teena. He was played in the dramatisation of his life *Boys Don't Cry* by the cis actress Hilary Swank, who won an Oscar for her performance. We also met a British film character, the trans woman Dil in *The Crying Game*, who was played by the androgynous male actor Jaye Davidson; he was nominated for an Oscar. And we met the Danish transgender artist Lili Elbe, played by Eddie Redmayne in *The Danish Girl* (2015); again, Redmayne was nominated Best Actor for his portrayal.

Many LGBTQ activists found the casting of *The Danish Girl* in particular to be a disappointing reflection of the film industry's notorious biases. The queer and trans communities are certainly more supported today than they were when *Boys Don't Cry* was in cinemas in 1999, and Redmayne's casting was made even more objectionable by the fact that Redmayne's character was not only a real historical figure but a pioneer and icon, one of the world's first recipients of gender reassignment surgery. Campaigners likened the decision to a white actor being cast in blackface as Martin Luther King Jr. Redmayne, when asked why he had accepted the role, told *The Telegraph* that, although he agreed it was valid to question why a trans actor hadn't been chosen for the part, "one of the complications is that nowadays you have hormones, and many trans women have taken hormones." To play the first part of the story as a biological male—the artist Einar Wegener, transitioning to Lili Elbe—Redmayne argued, "you'd have to come off the hormones, so that has been a discussion as well. Because back in that period there weren't hormones."[10]

Needless to say, this defence was dismissed as farcical by the LGBTQ community. A Change.org petition was started in response to the perceived absurdity of Redmayne's comments, saying that if Redmayne was truly motivated by this concern for trans actresses' welfare, then to play the part in a really pro-trans way, he must first experience the sex-change surgery himself, to add authenticity to his role.[11] But Redmayne is not the only actor in a queer role that could have been portrayed by actors who actually identify with the character's gender and or sexuality. We have met the lesbian and gender politics pioneer Virginia Woolf; in 2003, Nicole Kidman won the Academy Award for Best Actress for playing the writer in *The Hours*. In 2004, the award went to Charlize Theron for her role in *Monster*, a biopic of the bisexual serial killer Aileen Wuornos. In 2006, *Brokeback Mountain* won three Academy Awards, with both Jake Gyllenhaal (Jack) and Heath Ledger (Ennis) nominated for their roles. And in 2008, Sean Penn won Best Actor for his role as gay rights activist Harvey Milk, California's first openly gay elected official. None of these critically acclaimed actors is known ever to have been in a non-hetero relationship or to have expressed a non-hetero sexual identity.

Despite growing awareness and outrage in the 2010s, there hasn't been much serious effort to rectify the problem in Hollywood. In 2018 Mahershala Ali played the gay pianist Don Shirley in *Green Book*, and Rami Malek played Queen's bisexual front man Freddie Mercury in *Bohemian Rhapsody*. Both men won Oscars for their performances. In *The Favourite* (also from 2018), Olivia Colman plays Queen Anne of Great Britain, pursuing passionate love affairs with two women played by Rachel Weisz and Emma Stone. Again, all three actors were nominated for Oscars, with Colman winning Best Actress. None of these actors are known to be queer.

The pattern is mirrored in television too. To give just one prominent example of the failure to provide opportunity to queer actors when the role is queer: Dr Arizona Robbins of the ABC drama *Grey's Anatomy*, one of the first and highest-profile gay characters on the American small screen (2009–18). Like many things about Shonda Rhimes's medical drama (which is written "colour-blind" and has always had an ethnically diverse cast), the creation of this character and her positive depiction in a long-term gay relationship were pioneering; but it seems the progress couldn't be stretched as far as actually finding an openly lesbian actor for the part. The representation and minorities lobbies are often forced to take what they can get; in the case of Rami Malek as Freddie Mercury, the "straight-washing" was somehow felt to be cancelled out, or at least compensated for, by the fact that the Parsi-Indian rock star was at least being played by an actor of colour (though one of Coptic Egyptian heritage).

Though true representation hasn't yet arrived, there are starting to be more opportunities for queer actors. At the very least, change appears to be coming much faster for gay and trans roles than with the glacially slow elimination of whitewashing. The speed with which things are evolving and improving seemingly reflects the great strides made in visibility and acceptability of queer identity in a relatively short space of time, before and after the turn of the millennium. In the 2018 Joel Edgerton biopic *Boy Erased*, about a boy's "gay conversion" therapy to correct his homosexual tendencies, the lead character is played by Lucas Hedges, whose gender and sexual fluidity is public knowledge. He has often said that he recognises himself as existing on the queer spectrum: "Not totally straight, but also not gay and not necessarily bisexual."[12] In television too, gay, trans and gender-queer visibility increased dramatically in the 2010s: Samira Wiley, who's openly lesbian, has had key gay roles in the era-defining dramas *Orange is the New Black* and *The Handmaid's Tale*, while since 2017 Asia Kate Dillon has been playing America's first non-binary television character, Taylor Mason in *Billions*.

The performing arts medium where queer representation is most visible is definitely theatre, which has always been a faster-moving, more inclusive and more progressive space than film and television, as we've already seen when it comes to ethnic diversity. This is partly because of a greater willingness to cast representatively. In 2017, for instance, the Liverpool Everyman staged its own inclusive production of *Romeo and Juliet* with gay lovers, keeping the original title, but with Juliet becoming Julius, and the Capulets a family of colour, while Romeo remained white. "[W]ith a few trims and changing 'she' to 'he' and 'mistress' to 'master', I felt like I'd unearthed something really exciting in that play," said director Nick Bagnall.[13]

But for the performing arts to be truly inclusive and welcoming, some critics say, progress can't be limited to rewriting and "bending" old "straight" narratives. We need new stories, ones that are diverse by nature, and theatre is starting to wake up to the need for original

Fig. 26: Unrepentant reverse-passer and champion of colonial "discovery" Richard Francis Burton, disguised as "Mirza Abdullah", 1848.

Fig. 27: The Anglo-Indian protagonist of Kim (1901)—a semi-autobiographical foil for complex cultural "appreciator" Rudyard Kipling—achieves enlightenment as he "transcends identity".

Fig. 28: Canadian Prime Minister Justin Trudeau and family playing dress-up on a visit to the Golden Temple at Amritsar, 2018.

Fig. 29: "I didn't consider it racist at the time, but now we know better": Justin Trudeau in blackface, January 2001.

Fig. 30: The painful origins of blackface—Thomas D. Rice, the famous Jump Jim Crow minstrel, c. 1932.

Fig. 31: Loving the look? Martina Big, 2017, a "blackfisher" who physically changes her appearance to match stereotypes of an African-origin physique.

Fig. 32: Rachel Dolezal, of white origin but "identifying as transracial", at a black rights rally before her outing, 2015.

Fig. 33: The mixed-race actor Fredi Washington (right) in *Imitation of Life* (1934)—a rare, and apparently alarming, casting of an African American in a white-passing role.

Fig. 34: The white actor Mickey Rooney as the caricatured Japanese man, Mr. Yunioshi, in *Breakfast at Tiffany's* (1961).

Fig. 35: Helena Bonham Carter filming *The King's Speech* in 2009. Bonham Carter has played across the class spectrum during her career, yet there seem to be no opportunities for actors of working-class background to play royalty.

Fig. 36: Bollywood actors Nargis (left) and Dilip Kumar (right) as their Hindu characters in *Andaz* (1949). Communal prejudice in India's film industry forces Muslim actors to take on stage names and Hindu parts.

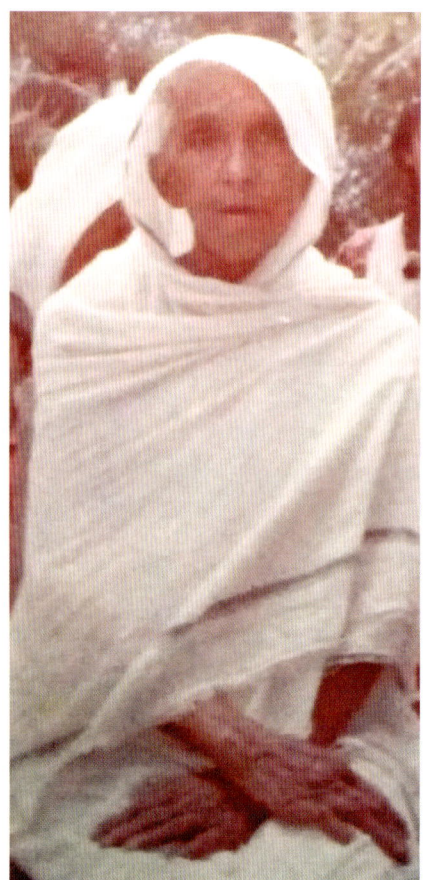

Fig. 37: The author's grandmother, whose nationality changed three times in her lifetime without her ever leaving home.

Fig. 38: The author's father (self-portrait), among the Hindu gods in Pushkar.

queer (and queer-authored) roles. A quick look at premieres of the late 2010s gives us an impressive roster. &*Juliet*, an alternative, musical take on the Shakespeare tragedy, opened in 2019, dazzling the West End with a feminist celebration of sexuality across all spectrums. Rather than simply "modify" Shakespeare's original dramatis personae, new characters were introduced—from a sexually active older woman to a pansexual friend. There also appears to be more space for explicitly queer source material to make it to the stage. A new musical, *The View UpStairs*, premiered off Broadway in 2017, telling the story of the 1973 arson attack on the New Orleans gay bar UpStairs Lounge. The show was praised by *Entertainment Weekly* as "a moving homage to LGBT culture past and present";[14] it has since transferred to the Soho Theatre in London.

So it may be that, particularly on stage, important roles are finally starting to be both here and queer. However, what is at stake is a vicious cycle. The issue with passing as performance art is that it always seems to be one-way, with actors from the privileged group taking on roles from marginalised communities, but never the other way around. There are too few "out" queer actors playing straight or cisgender characters; maybe partly because there are too few mainstream actors "out" full stop—unsurprisingly, given how hard it seems to be to get cast even when the parts are there. When queer actors *are* platformed, they are generally cast in gay or trans productions, which can lead to a perverse double bind when it comes to recognition of their seriousness or talent: the audience may think the role came naturally to them due to their sexual or gender identity, whereas—to judge by the BAFTAs, Academy Awards and Golden Globes being dished out—they are more likely to be impressed by a straight or cis actor in a gay or trans role, further validating that casting.

The only answer is to do it all: platform new queer stories *and* find ways to make formerly exclusive ones more representative; cast queer actors in those queer stories, *and* open more roles to them beyond this.

One-Way Traffic

It is easy when talking about these issues of appropriation and homogeneity to rail against "Hollywood", given everything that this hyper-commercial, old-school world represents. But when it comes to socio-economic passing as art, Britain—world capital of class—is of course a serious offender. On both screen and stage, actors of middle- or upper-class origin are consistently, and increasingly, cast in working-class roles, putting on the relevant accent, mostly badly. In the West End, the same rotating network of overwhelmingly class-privileged stage actors are cast in musical theatre, despite the genre's love of working-class struggle—think *Billy Elliot*, *Les Misérables*, *Oliver!*, *The Fiddler on the Roof*.

You may say, that's what actors do, they train to play parts they don't have experience of; the success of an actor is based on how believably they perform their parts. But, once again, that argument is nullified by the one-way traffic of passing as art. Helena Bonham Carter, perhaps the actor working in Britain and Hollywood today of the highest family pedigree, puts on a Cockney accent—to caricatured effect—as Mrs Lovett in the film adaptation of *Sweeney Todd: The Demon Barber of Fleet Street*, but she is also the one who gets the call for the trans-Atlantic television sensation *The Crown*. There's Helena Bonham Carter again, this time playing her own aristocratic class as Princess Margaret. We've examined this hypocritical, one-way justification for cultural impersonation throughout this last part of the book.

What's curious about the question of class-passing by British actors is that, while queer and non-white representation is now, very slowly, getting better, the trend seems to be the reverse when it comes to socioeconomic representation. Once upon a time we had Anthony Hopkins, Michael Caine, Helen Mirren, Julie Walters—all of them had distinctly working-class upbringings; and even those from slightly better-off families (Judi Dench, Ian McKellen) were still from modest, truly middle-class origins. In the twenty-first century, acting opportunities appear to have been hijacked by actors from exceptionally privileged backgrounds, with the younger generation of A-listers typically represented by Eddie Redmayne (who was at Eton with Prince William), Benedict Cumberbatch (a distant cousin of Richard III), Emily Blunt (from a family of MPs and army officers) and Carey Mulligan (inspired and supported to become an actor by a visit to her private school from Julian Fellowes).[15] There are still exceptions, but the trend is remarkable, and remarked upon by those ever-rarer exceptions: one of the few professions that has always, for centuries, been open to people from disadvantaged backgrounds is today becoming less and less diverse.

It's the same story in Bollywood. In the early days, acting attracted those of poor and modest origins: Mithun Chakraborty, for example, was involved in underground militant Marxism before coming to rule Bollywood in the 1980s. In the twenty-first century, however, prominent stars tend to come from rich, established Bollywood dynasties like the Bachhans, Kapoors, Khans and so on. What does all this say about changes in class identity and representation in the performing arts? Is it possible that, now there is no longer any social stigma attached to the acting profession, the upper classes have sought and managed to reclaim the industry from the underprivileged and reprocess it as a prestigious art? With widening inequality in both Indian and British society, is class identity coming to rule access to screen and stage in the way that racial and sexual identity long shut out the marginalised?

* * *

As we've just touched upon, actors passing due to the marginalisation of minority identities is not just a problem in the Western performing arts. Perhaps nowhere has the history of identity politics penetrated more subtly than into the Indian film industry and its attitudes towards religion. Faith communities are less obviously tied to social hierarchy in the West today, and so the religion of an actor versus that of their character has not been so fraught or contested a question in Hollywood's debates around representation. In Bollywood, however, it has been a major aspect of passing as acting. In Chapter 8 we saw how the violence of the partition of India led to communal strife and ongoing identity changes, and this has included the world of cinema. But, interestingly, Bollywood has not seen actors from the majority Hindu community sweeping up roles that should belong to Muslims. Instead, Muslims (a large minority in independent India) have made their way into the industry traditionally by passing as Hindu—not in their roles, but in real life.

In the early days of Bollywood casting, Muslim actors usually adopted Hindu screen names. Among the most prominent such

"Hindu-passers" from Bollywood's Golden Age were Muhammad Yusuf Khan (1922–), who worked as Dilip Kumar; Mumtaz Jehan Begum Dehlavi (1933–69)—her stage name was Madhubala; Hamid Ali Khan, alias Ajit (1922–98); Mahjabeen Bano (1933–72), who worked as Meena Kumari; the popular comic actor Jagdeep (1939–2020), who began his career as a post-war child actor, and who was in fact Syed Ishtiaq Ahmed Jaffrey; and Johnny Walker (1926–2003)—if it wasn't a Hindu name, it had to be Western or something else "non-Muslim"—who was born Badruddin Jamaluddin Kazi.

The next era in the history of Bollywood passing is symbolised by the journey of Sanjay Khan, a prolific Hindi film and television actor, director and producer. In the beginning of his career, Shah Abbas Khan, born in 1941 to a Pathan Muslim family in the north, started off with the screen name Sanjay—a typical Hindu name. Following his appearance in a number of successful 1960s films such as *Dosti* and *Dus Lakh*, he affixed his surname Khan to Sanjay, projecting a hybrid identity. Gradually, Muslim actors started to appear in major roles under their own Muslim names, most famously Shahrukh Khan, who has portrayed Hindus in countless lead roles. It can be said that Dilip Kumar probably started the whole "Khan craze" in Bollywood—since the 1990s, we have had a series of Khans in lead character roles, notably Shahrukh Khan, Aamir Khan, Salman Khan, Saif Ali Khan and Irrfan Khan.

It may appear, then, that the olden days of religious passing have passed out of Indian cinema. But while this may be true in terms of opportunities for Muslim actors, freeing them from the need to hide their faith or heritage with a pseudonym, the opportunity they have accessed has been to play Hindu heroes. The portrayal of Muslims in Indian cinema is still mired in populist prejudice. The scholar Rachel Dwyer explains, "Muslim characters in Bollywood, as it has been known since the 1990s, are doomed to minor roles fated simply to represent their community and conform to a series of well-established stereotypes."[16] The list of common tropes that serve as "Muslim parts" will be familiar to any black actor trying to make it in the West: best friend or loyal sidekick to the main character (an upper-caste Hindu), gangster-terrorist… Then there are the Indian particularities: fundamentalist Muslim, Pakistani spy and, of course, when it comes to the period dramas that Bollywood loves as much as the British, the archetypal Mughal Emperor for male actors, and for the women his dancing girl—a courtesan.

It seems that, in terms of respectful casting, the difference between Bollywood and Hollywood comes down to the fact that, in Western cinema, actors from privileged or dominant backgrounds are lining up to be cast as a minority. On the rare occasions when a "desirable" Muslim part is on offer—a Mughal emperor, or a tax-collector under the Raj—Hindu actors have typically been there to snatch it up. But on the whole, sympathetic Muslim stories just don't get written and told in Bollywood. In Indian cinema, the communal trauma of partition and of resurgent Hindu nationalism have meant that Muslim characters have simply never been seen as desirable parts, and so there is no fight over them between Muslim and Hindu. With rare exceptions, there's only one way for Muslim actors in Bollywood to make it, and that's competing with the privileged identity group for Hindu roles—the only good ones around.

* * *

On the surface, with their differing stages of advancement and their various levels of debate, these tales of actors performing different types of identity can seem like separate, individual battles, and that's often how they're fought. With women now a key part of the acting industry across the world, we're well past the era of gender impersonation for cis characters; yet whitewashing in casting and adaptation is still far more acceptable than it should be, and straightwashing and cis-washing also remain a problem. Similarly, we may no longer have blackface, but we still have black characters being "turned white" as they jump from the pages of fiction or history onto stage or screen. And, while actors passing is becoming less tolerated in terms of queerness and ethnicity, it is seemingly more prevalent than ever when it comes to class.

But the controversies around representation in the performing arts bring us back to the same debates we have seen emerge throughout this last part of the book: whose identity is valued; how this affects the legitimacy of an identity-performing enterprise; how that can change over time with the tides of history; and how cultural representations can, in turn, influence social attitudes. Who gets to tell stories, and who gets to tell their *own* story? And what world can we build if we broaden the answer to those questions?

And so, with this most current of all chapters in humanity's long saga of identity negotiation, we come back to Anansi. Those dispossessed of their history and of their place in society and culture can look to the master-weaver, the artful shape-shifter, and consider how we might yet spin a better yarn.

EPILOGUE

A PREQUEL TO PASSING

For those with an ambiguous, fluid, evolving or changed identity, the reality of appearance still decides how they will be identified by others, and how they could choose to present themselves publicly. Most of the stories in this book have been of passers who make a choice to begin living another life, at least in certain spaces; but passing can also be an act of passing over in silence an identity that is not visually, and therefore doesn't have to be, specified. A feminine-looking gay woman may decline to declare publicly that she is not straight; a Geordie or Cockney broadcaster may always keep their original accent buried under the layers of BBC English; and Middle Easterners, those with part-African ancestry and anyone else who could be described as "olive", "tanned" or "Mediterranean" may not correct strangers' assumptions that they are southern European.

As for me, I have often let people think I was native Brazilian; when travelling in Cuba, people asked if I was of Indigenous Indian origin, and I obliged with an ambiguous response. Those identities aren't necessarily more privileged than my real heritage, but for many, it is just too burdensome to go into discussions of race and origins every time they come up—especially when there is not going to be a straightforward answer to the question. In my own life, the most hated inquiries from strangers have always been about where I am "from", what religion I believe in, and what faith I was brought up in. The first query always leads to another, and another.

It is tiresome. If you were white in the West, even a first-generation immigrant, you would never face this "friendly" inquisition on a daily basis without even opening your mouth. Sometimes, when I've refused to reply, people have told me they're only showing interest in me and my culture. But the problem is, I want to be invisible in public, just like any white person, especially at the grocery store, on the train, at a drinks party, at the swimming pool. I do not want "interested" people constantly assessing my exotic "origins". Passers may be performers, but they are not attention-seekers; they are simply looking for peace in relation to their identity and how others perceive it.

Besides, after most of my adult life lived far from my place of birth, where do I really, "originally" come from? Do you come from where you were born, where your remembered ancestors had lived, or where you have resettled, studied, raised your family, worked? Are my origins always those of my distant forebears? What about the roots of my own life? Strangers, especially white ones, seem to find it easy to be confident about what is meant by where I'm "from"; yet I myself don't find that a simple question at all. As Derek Walcott said: "To know *where* you are, but not *who* you are; to struggle with the present while still not being able to fully comprehend the past—this, too, is a form of exile."[1]

I cannot draw a true closure to this book without some final reflections on the fictions of identity. I should explain where my first, original impulse to write a book on passing came from. One key inspiration has been Ruth Prawer Jhabvala's memoir, *My Nine Lives: Chapters of a Possible Past*. That title, like Kipling's *Something of Myself*, reads like a warning about the subjectivity of any account of selfhood. Jhabvala chose her readers to be the judge of its veracity, opening the book with an "Apologia": "These chapters are potentially autobiographical: even when something didn't actually happen to me, it might have done so. Every situation was one I could have been in myself, and sometimes, to some extent, was."[2]

Jhabvala (1927–2013) was born in Germany to Jewish parents and came to England fleeing the Nazis in 1939. Most of her father's side of the family perished in the Holocaust. She married an Indian-Parsi architect, Cyrus Jhabvala, and moved to Delhi in 1951, where she lived until relocating to the United States in the 1970s. Jhabvala wrote endlessly—novels, short stories and Oscar-winning film scripts (*A Room With A View*, *Howards End*). Her books indulge in the theme of disinheritance. In a 1979 public lecture given in Edinburgh, Jhabvala said: "I stand before you as a writer without any ground of being out of which to write: really blown about from country to country, culture to culture, till I feel—till I am—nothing ... As it happens, I like it that way."[3]

I too tend to think that every situation I am or have been in since early childhood could have been determined otherwise. I have lived a life in this fuzziness between actuality and invention of belonging, a place travellers, migrants, explorers and passers are well used to. In the absence of an obvious, continuous personal history I could identify with, I have assumed different selfhoods at various stages, When I am in a Hindu temple, I fully carry that cultural connection; likewise, my heart sways with the swaying heads in a synagogue. In both places I have felt I was, or I could have been, one or the other. Throughout my life and everywhere I have lived, I've found myself able to slide into what best suited the situation. This wasn't just about conforming, though that's a necessary part of it: the apparent ease with which I could perform specific cultural behaviours must have been influenced by an innate impulse that I could instantly invoke. I have been trying to understand this impulse in the context of identity, both assigned and assumed.

Only, in my case, the assigned and the assumed have often become blurred by self-doubt. This is what Jhabvala's memoir explores and validates; most of us carry defining memories within us that could just be chapters of possible pasts—and we've seen throughout this book how roots, whether real, imagined or reformulated, are central to our understanding of ourselves. We evoke, recall and invent on gossamer wings of memory, convincing ourselves of our identity first and foremost.

The most haunting moment of John Howard Griffin's identity transformation was when the journalist looked in the mirror of his clinically darkened face and found it difficult to believe he had a white family somewhere safe and sound in a white American town: "the reflections led back to Africa, back to the shanty and the ghetto ... Suddenly, almost with no mental preparation, no advance hint, it became clear and permeated my whole being."[4] Sophie Green spoke about her wonderful mother, who helped fill in the complex gaps in memory from when she was seen by society as a little boy: "My mother would always refer to my child self when speaking to others as, 'Oh, when *she* used to do that, or, when *she*, Sophie, was little', and so on ... she would never use my birth name even when talking about my childhood." I was never told what that boy's name was. Sophie categorically avoided that question, as if it was a faulty link to life's spam folder. All the unwanted and infected records on the selfhood of suffering can rest there for ever.

Identity is shaped by filtered memory, and it must be guarded against contamination. But even among passers, the story or stories of one's self are not a seamless, one-way narrative; never black or white, but rather a conflict between insularity and invisibility. Between fatalism and demurral. The London-based Irish theatre director, Anthony E. Lennon, did not set out to present himself as black. He just found himself perceived that way, and then chose not to identify as white. During synagogue services, worshippers have often assumed I was Jewish by faith, when I was attending as a member of a culturally Jewish household. I have even been described by one news agency as a Jew "with Indian roots",[5] but I've never presented myself as a Jewish writer. I did not protest or send a complaint. On reflection, I must say, it even felt good.

My fluid relationship with identity surely goes back to my father's. What I always believed to be his story might have been a later reconstruction of the stories I grew up hearing, or believed I was hearing. Based on these, I sketched out a possible tale of my ancestors' religious and caste-passing. I must issue a disclaimer here that the story I claim to be my father's may not be claimed by my siblings; but that is okay. Ruth Prawer Jhabvala opens *My Nine Lives* with a riddle that I am all too familiar with: "I may not have outgrown the common childish fantasy that one's real parents are someone different, somewhere else. Or I may have been trying out alternative destinies—this time not, as usual, for fictional characters but for myself."[6]

Jhabvala says that, regardless of how people imagine their parents, their origins, and the places or situations, "always seem to work themselves out … as though characters really were fate."[7] The framework of an autobiography containing many lives, like Jhabvala's, my father's or my own, is usually a mix of basic historical truth fleshed out by imagination and subjective memory. The legend of my family's origins worked its way into the fabric of my father's fate and mine—so what does it mean to say that it's not "real"?

My childhood was spent sometimes amid dust-storms, but mostly in flooded, rain-ravaged landscapes typical of the Bengal

EPILOGUE

Delta, its citizens grateful for survival amid extreme climatic mood swings. The fight against nature has always been so time-consuming that the villagers often did not resist outsiders among them in the same way as those in a securely fortified place would have. Our land has always welcomed strangers, my grandmother would often say. This embrace of "others" and the ancient Indian fatalism went hand in hand, and often stopped the people from properly recording their history—what was the point, when there were always possibilities of landslides wiping the slate clean, and there were always outsider cultures and societies passing through the land? Reality itself was like a landslide, in my family and other lives of the Delta I saw growing up. One moment it was there, the next there was no sign of it—just like Orlando waking up as a woman, looking in the mirror, and walking to the bath in her new selfhood. All that was left was the fast-flowing current of the shoreless rivers.

I may have indulged in "childish fantasy" about who my ancestors were, but at the same time, I have been reinventing myself in four different countries since leaving my ancestral home. As well as the multiple changes of geography, I have also seen a number of personal metamorphoses—I have been an atheist, a communist, a Hindu, a rationalist, a sceptic, a Jew and back to all of these, except perhaps communist and atheist. Each of my identities was as true as the rest. Jhabvala's "memoir" could not have been closer to my heart: I carry many possible pasts within me, and I believe this is what makes us who we are. A memoirist never lies, in the same way as a true passer is never faking. Both are on a mission of self-definition, a quest for identity. Ultimately, it is about belonging, finding peace with oneself.

Some may never find it. My father expressed his duality in a series of speculative mutterings about his past. I believed in all of them. In mid-century passing films like *Imitation of Life*, the identity-changer was often portrayed as a liar, but this tall, light-skinned Bengali surrounded by whispers about his many selves was a most intriguingly honest person. His visceral self-doubt created an insular existence for himself, and it is no surprise that he died alone. Those caught between identities usually do. Anatole Broyard died with his secret; Nella Larsen also died alone, unceremoniously and without answers. For Brandon Teena, and the fictional Jack Twist, discovery was death. Is this because, at the end of their lives, those with assumed selves are finally displaced by an onslaught of memories from a possible past? Kafka's cockroach remembering he was once Gregor Samsa? When an old self leaves the body, and the new enters, the body in turn is left with the question regarding *what* it is. Is it really white, is it black, is it Muslim, or is it Hindu? How could the answers be found in the body and the blood, when they have not changed?

At the same time, Jhabvala's *My Nine Lives* is also a euphemism for the endurance and perpetuity of selves of those who break away from their assigned identity. Like a cat, somehow they always land on their feet. My and my father's combined lives would easily exceed nine. I did not inherit, or chose not to, the Persian or Middle Eastern legacy that had permeated many souls in our part of India, including a section of my family. I rejected it in favour of my ancestral Hinduism. But, as one of my nine lives would have it, later in life I would curiously find myself embracing another faith from loosely the same geographical region as the Persian elements I hadn't absorbed.

Like the jazz rhythms that connected black Americans to Africa, for me the Shabbat candles on a Friday night rekindled memories of oil lamps floating away on a Ganges tributary for *arti*, the evening ritual of my childhood, the invocation of the gods. I learnt to sway with the believers of another ancient religion, to sing their songs. My heart feels the tingle of community spirit when I join in these rituals, I feel a sense of belonging.

Belonging is not just a visual compatibility. It is a code. To crack it, one needs to key in the necessary set of social and cultural hieroglyphics. I have learnt several different ones, and applied them as needed; as felt right. This was just what my father did, his stories of his possible lives colouring my childhood and the years thereafter with a rainbow of emotions, a chronicle of fables. I delighted in them, believed in all of them, and may have invented some more. This way, my father's larger-than-life character has never lost its brilliance in the burning glare of life's ordinary truths.

* * *

EPILOGUE

I have come to a dusty little car-free town on the outskirts of the western Indian desert. Pushkar is where the youngest of my siblings has settled; she runs a small inn above her home. It is a kind of writer's and peace-seeker's retreat, a short walk from the quaint market, nestled in the valley of the Aravali mountain range. I have come here to finish the last section of the book.

Mallika brings me ginger tea in the morning, and asks what my book is about.

"It's about passing," I tell her.

I watch her deep bronze face—it used to be *halka shyam*, light brown, but the harsh sun of this part of India has darkened it over the years. I can't tell from her withdrawn expression and her distant eyes if she has understood what I am writing about. I realise from her unmoving gaze that she is looking through me, at some object behind me, something that would absorb her confusion. We all inherited this knack from our father; when faced with a puzzle, we know how to wait for the answer to come to us, rather than reveal our unfamiliarity. Mallika is watching the dawn rise from behind the ridge of the Aravali. Her face becomes lit by the red of the sky. She is confused, and asks me what exactly "passing" means. Is it death? Whose death? Father's? Passing to a different world? The passing of time? Passing through a place?

I tell her, it is about identity. She waits for more. Now her eyes are focussed, the dawn reflected in her eyes as two red dots, like the red-eye in our father's first colour photographs. It is about passing from one identity to another, I say. Usually from the identity you were given at birth, by society, to an identity you choose or are forced to choose because of circumstances. She smiles. I know what she is thinking. I have plenty of material of that nature in our own family. I tell her that I wanted to begin at the beginning, but there is no beginning; human beings have always passed, in all areas of identity that existed, since the dawn of history.

Mallika gives me a quizzical look. She gets up suddenly and heads back down to the main house. It is time for the morning *arti*. And it is a particularly auspicious day.

It is the Monday before Vijayadashami—the culmination of the Durga Puja festival, with much fasting and ritual cleansing to do. Durga Puja ends on the tenth day of the month in the Hindu lunar-solar calendar; Vijayadashami means Victory on the Tenth Day. It marks the moment when *dharma*—the religion or code of life, goodness in humanity and so on—emerged victorious after the gods' defeat of the demons. The many-armed goddess Durga had been sent down to Earth by the principal gods, who gave her a deadly weapon to hold in each of her hands. With them, she could vanquish Mahishashur, the buffalo form of a demon known for shifting shape in pursuit of evil. Durga herself is an amalgam of the powers and goodness of the Hindu Trinity—Brahma, Vishnu and Shiva, the Creator, Preserver and Destroyer respectively; they took a female form to rid the world of this evil passing as a buffalo. When the battles were fought and won, peace was restored to Earth, and it was time to say goodbye to the necessary incarnations of gods and monsters.

On Vijayadashami, worshippers set out to join a colourful procession carrying a clay form of Durga, her children by her side, and the murdered Mahishashur at her feet. He is pierced through the heart by the goddess's holy *trishula* (trident); his disguise thus revealed, the buffalo head has miraculously transformed into a demon face with exaggerated humanoid features. His cold, dead eyes are half-closed. The worshippers arrive at a river or water source, to immerse the whole clay battle scene until it melts away. The following year, they will recreate the battles and disguises all over again—the identity cloaks of the gods pursuing their divine mission to save humanity, and those of the demons trying to destroy the sacred order of the universe—and once again they will wash it all away in the immersion rites at the water.

Clay, transient by nature, is the symbol of brevity, an ego-busting agent against a mindset stuck in the material world—once submerged in water, the god and the demon both dissolve into non-existence. In the *Rig Veda*, the first line of the Hymn of Creation goes, "In the beginning, there was neither existence nor non-existence". At the end of Durga Puja next year, the perpetual cycle of incarnations will repeat; the grand masquerade for control, conquest and profit will climax on Vijayadashami. Hindu destiny is full of unremitting crossings into new identities, temporary states of being in a world of constant renewal and change: gods, monsters and humans are all subject to this cosmic locomotion.

EPILOGUE

I have been observing the religious fast. Writing on an empty stomach is a strange experience. I have not done that before. But abstaining from eating for the Hindu gods is not the only fast I will be observing, as it turns out. The Durga Puja has curiously coincided with the 24-hour Jewish fast of Yom Kippur, a sudden and fleeting link between the religions and cultures I straddle. I follow Mallika downstairs to the *puja mandap*—a small white marble temple in the corner of the living room, housing a pantheon of household gods. She asks me if I want to perform today's *arti*, since I've been the "holy" one—by double-fasting, she says, laughing. I go to the *mandap*, fill up the copper pots with water. I light the oil lamps, wave them around the gods. I put them down next to a happy-faced Ganesha, one of Durga's children. I smile as I always did when I was a child, looking at the exaggerated pot belly of the elephant-headed god.

Only then do I realise that there is another face, peering from the semi-darkness of the tiny pantheon. It is a laminated black-and-white photo. The face is extremely handsome, and long; the dark eyes, framed by spectacles, are piercingly vivid, and the smile is alive with intrigue and mystery. I realise it is my father in black and white, sitting amidst Durga's colourful children: to his left, the pot-bellied Ganesha, god of wellbeing; to his right, Lakshmi, the goddess of wealth; and in front of him, hiding him from view until this moment, is the goddess of knowledge, Saraswathi.

I cannot find words to describe the emotions rioting inside me. I remember this picture, when it was taken and how it was developed, in my father's own private darkroom. The photo was shot in auto-capture; he had arranged his Yashica camera on the bookshelf in his office. The camera he bought after the death of his first-born, whose little life came abruptly to an end before he could take any pictures of her. Photography had been his obsession ever since, he was adamant that he wouldn't let life pass him by without leaving a snapshot to be processed in his lab. He had set the camera to a five-second timer and hurried behind his glass-top desk, only to realise there was an intrusion in the frame, an unwelcome object—a paperweight atop a pile of office files. He stood up, went around the other side of the desk, quickly removed the pile, and came back to the chair to pose. The camera took the shot before he could sit down properly.

Like many things in my father's life, this used to puzzle me. Why had he chosen that pose, and why did he never retake the shot? Film rolls were expensive, and he possibly did not want to waste a photo. But it is still curious that he decided to use this photo for all his official needs. He made several copies of it. Perhaps this is not remotely linked, but I cannot help thinking that he probably memorialised the caught-in-the-wrong-moment pose because it summarised his life. Here he is among the household gods, hanging in the awkward, sunken space of neither sitting nor standing—just like the lives that he lived, and the death that he most likely chose for himself.

As I return the smile on his face amongst the Hindu gods, I tell him, look at your progeny. They, like you, have never ceased crossing between multiple identities. They have even done better—they have mastered the art, and performed it so well that each new metamorphosis of their lives has appeared more authentic than the previous one. There has never been a false self—all the transformations have sat well, and they have carried them through effortlessly; they still do. Here is my Bengali sister, in her Marwari outfit, her nose-ring and her bronzed Rajasthani skin, preparing for Vijayadashami, while I am observing a Jewish fast, offering oblation to the Hindu gods.

My father has travelled a long way: from the waterlogged Bengali village to this dusty religious town, with its cowbells and temple songs, amidst mountains of primordial purity. He has claimed his place among the mischievous gods whose very essence is informed by their ability to incarnate. His many lives have constellated into the small household pantheon in the living room of his youngest child, in a little holy town dedicated to the god of all creations, the Lord Brahma. The *swayambhu* (self-born) four-headed god is also the author and reciter of the Vedas, the four ancient texts of Hinduism— one delivered from each of his four mouths. He is the Hindus' Anansi, our shape-shifting story-teller. My father, a marvellous murmurer of stories himself, has at last found his place and his peace, in the only town in India celebrated as the abode of Brahma. The "self", like a clay god, melts out of its shape, then enters and spreads into a new form. And it is never just an exile. Each transformation is a chosen home, re-envisioned by us.

NOTES

INTRODUCTION

1. Nicole Rousseau, "Passing". In G. Ritzer (ed.), *The Blackwell Encyclopedia of Sociology*, (15 February 2007), https://doi.org/10.1002/9781405165518.wbeosp006
2. The names of my Brixton housemates have been changed.
3. "Mofussil" is the anglicised version of the original Persian *mufassal*, meaning outside of an urban centre. The term, which is still widely (and somewhat negatively) used in the Indian subcontinent to describe rural areas or people, historically referred to the regions of India outside the main power bases of the East India Company: Calcutta, Bombay and Madras. My father frequently used the term to describe our home in "little mufassals".
4. William Shakespeare, *The Tempest*, (Oxford: Oxford University Press, 2001), Act 1 Scene 4, lines 396–402.
5. Allyson Hobbs, *A Chosen Exile: A History of Racial Passing in American Life*, (Cambridge, MA and London, UK: Harvard University Press, 2014), p. 6.
6. Ibid., p. 269.
7. BBC News, "Dutchman, 69, brings lawsuit to lower his age 20 years", (8 November 2018), https://www.bbc.co.uk/news/world-europe-46133262
8. Jessica A. Krug, "The Truth, and the Anti-Black Violence of My Lies", Medium, (3 September 2020), https://medium.com/@jessakrug/the-truth-and-the-anti-black-violence-of-my-lies-9a9621401f85

1. ANANSI'S WEB: REBIRTH IN CHAINS AND THE DAWN OF PASSING

1. Flora Illes and Theo Meder, "Anansi comes to Holland: The trickster spider as a dynamic icon of ethnic identity", (trans. into English by Mereie de Jong), *Quotidian*, vol. 02, no. 01, (2010), (pp. 20–63), pp. 20–1, http://www.quotidian.nl/www.quotidian.nl/vol02/nr01/a02.html
2. Derek Walcott, "The Muse of History" (pp. 1–28), p. 7. In Orde Coombs (ed.), *Is Massa Day Dead?: Black Moods in the Caribbean*, (Garden City, NY: Anchor Books, 1974).

3. Interview with Hilli Arduin, professional storyteller of Anansi stories. Recorded by Flora Illes, (Amsterdam, 2008). Cited in Illes and Meder, (2010), p. 29.
4. Benjamin G. Dennis and Anita K. Dennis, *Slaves to Racism: An Unbroken Chain from America to Liberia*, (New York: Algora Publishing, 2008), p. 9.
5. Monica Anderson, Skye Toor, Lee Rainie and Aaron Smith, "2. An analysis of #BlackLivesMatter and other Twitter hashtags related to political or social issues", part of the series "Activism in the Social Media Age", *Pew Research Center*, (11 July 2018), https://www.pewresearch.org/internet/2018/07/11/an-analysis-of-blacklivesmatter-and-other-twitter-hashtags-related-to-political-or-social-issues/
6. Pernille Ipsen, *Daughters of the Trade: Atlantic Slavers and Interracial Marriage on the Gold Coast*, (Philadelphia, PA: University of Pennsylvania Press, 2015), p. 30.
7. Ibid.
8. C. A. Burland, *The Exotic White Man: An Alien in Asian and African Art*, (New York: McGraw-Hill, 1969), p. 21.
9. Peter Frankopan, *The Silk Roads: A New History of the World*, (London: Bloomsbury, 2016), p. 117; Andrew Lawler, "Kinder, Gentler Vikings? Not According to Their Slaves", *National Geographic*, (28 December 2015), https://www.nationalgeographic.com/news/2015/12/151228-vikings-slaves-thralls-norse-scandinavia-archaeology/
10. Abbot Emerson Smith, *Colonists in Bondage: White Servitude and Convict Labor in America, 1607–1776*, (Chapel Hill, NC: University of North Carolina Press, 2012), revised edn., first published in 1947, pp. 3–5.
11. This remark is not intended as an apologia of slavery, but many Africanists and laypeople of African descent reject the "Orientalising" tendency of popular history to portray Africans as universally helpless victims of the European slave trade, without any agency of their own.
12. Advertisement from the *Columbus (GA) Inquirer* placed by the planter Zachariah Booth, (9 February 1833). Cited in Martha J. Cutter, "Why Passing Is (Still) not Passé after More Than 250 Years: Sources from the Past and the Present", (pp. 49–67), p. 52. In Mollie Godfrey and Vershawn Ashanti Young (eds.), *Neo-Passing: Performing Identity after Jim Crow*, (Champaign, IL: University of Illinois Press, 2018).
13. William Craft, *Running a Thousand Miles for Freedom; Or, the Escape of William and Ellen Craft from Slavery*, (London: William Tweedie, 1860), digitised edn., p. 29, https://books.google.co.in/books?id=C50TAAAAYAAJ&source=gbs_navlinks_s
14. Ellen M. Weinauer, "A Most Respectable Looking Gentleman: Passing, Possession, and Transgression in Running a Thousand Miles for Freedom", (pp. 37–56), p. 38. In Elaine K. Ginsberg (ed.), *Passing and the Fictions of Identity*, (Durham, NC: Duke University Press, 1996).

15. Craft, (1860), p. 72.
16. Ibid., pp. 2–3.
17. Ibid., p. 52.
18. Ibid., p. 60.
19. Marjorie Garber, *Vested Interests: Cross-Dressing and Cultural Anxiety*, (New York: Routledge, 2011), new edn., p. 286.
20. Harriet Beecher Stowe, *Uncle Tom's Cabin*, (Ware, UK: Wordsworth Editions, 1995), new edn., p. 99.
21. Ibid., p. 400.
22. Advertisement from the Annapolis *Maryland Gazette*, (20 October 1763). Cited in Martha J. Cutter, "'As White as Most White Women': Racial Passing in Advertisements for Runaway Slaves and the Origins of a Multivalent Term", *American Studies*, vol. 54, no. 04, (2016), (pp. 73–97), p. 89.
23. Julia Stern, "Spanish Masquerade and the Drama of Racial Identity in *Uncle Tom's Cabin*", (pp. 103–30), pp. 105–6. In Ginsberg (ed.), (1996).
24. Stowe, (1995), pp. 100–1.
25. Harriet Beecher Stowe, "The Woman Question", *Hearth and Home*, (7 August 1869), pp. 520–1. Cited in Melissa J. Homestead, *American Women Authors and Literary Property, 1822–1869*, (Cambridge: Cambridge University Press, 2005), p. 29.
26. See: Roy Morris Jr., "Introduction". In David B. Sachsman, S. Kittrell Rushing and Roy Morris Jr. (eds.), *Memory and Myth: The Civil War in Fiction and Film from Uncle Tom's Cabin to Cold Mountain*, (West Lafayette, IA: Purdue University Press, 2007), p. 8.
27. Craft, (1860), p. 79.
28. Ibid., p. 54.
29. Stephanie Pocock Boeninger, "'I Have Become the Sea's Craft': Authorial Subjectivity in Derek Walcott's *Omeros* and David Dabydeen's 'Turner'", *Contemporary Literature*, vol. 52, no. 03, (2011), (pp. 462–92), p. 469.
30. George Herbert, "Doomsday", from *The Temple*, (1633).

2. THE CASTLE OF YOUR SKIN: REWRITING THE PAST IN JIM CROW AMERICA

1. Henry Louis Gates, Jr., "White Like Me", *The New Yorker*, (10 June 1996), https://www.newyorker.com/magazine/1996/06/17/white-like-me
2. Hobbs, (2014), p. 14.
3. Derek Walcott, *Epitaph for the Young: XII Cantos*. Cited in Bruce King, *Derek Walcott: A Caribbean Life*, (Oxford: Oxford University Press, 2000), p. 68.
4. Derek Walcott, "A Far Cry from Africa", from *Selected Poems*, (New York: Farrar, Straus and Giroux, 2007), line 27.

5. Robert P. Stuckert, "African Ancestry of the White American Population", *Ohio Journal of Science*, vol. 58, no. 03, (1958), (pp. 155–60), p. 159.
6. Ibid.
7. Mark Twain, *Pudd'nhead Wilson*, (Cambridge, MA and London: Harvard University Press, 2015), revised edn., p. 15.
8. Thomas Jefferson, (14 March 1815). Cited by Hobbs, (2014), p. 10, and elaborated upon in the notes, p. 282.
9. Madison Grant, *The Passing of the Great Race*, (Abergele, Wales and Indianapolis, IA: The Palingenesis Project, 2012), first published in 1916, p. 15.
10. Malcolm X and Alex Haley, *The Autobiography of Malcolm X*. Cited in Adrian Piper, "Passing for White, Passing for Black", (pp. 234–70), p. 256. In Ginsberg (ed.), (1996).
11. Toni Morrison, "Making America White Again", *The New Yorker*, (14 November 2016), https://www.newyorker.com/magazine/2016/11/21/making-america-white-again
12. Ibid.
13. Hobbs, (2014), p. 8.
14. Adrian Piper, "Passing for White, Passing for Black", (pp. 234–70), p. 248. In Ginsberg (ed.), (1996).
15. Zoë Wicomb, *Playing in the Light: A Novel*, (New York: The New Press, 2006), p. 5.
16. James Weldon Johnson, *Autobiography of an Ex-Colored Man*, (Mineola, NY: Dover Publications, Inc., 1995), new edn., p. 90.
17. Hobbs, (2014), p. 18.
18. Countée Cullen, "Heritage". Cited in Nella Larsen, *Passing*, (Mineola, NY: Dover Publications, Inc., 2004), frontmatter.
19. Piper, (1996), p. 245.
20. Johnson, (1995), p. 94.
21. Nella Larsen, *Passing*, (Mineola, NY: Dover Publications, Inc., 2004), p. 78.
22. Hobbs, (2014), p. 15.
23. Larsen, (2004), p. 61.
24. See: Gayle Wald, "Mezz Mezzrow and the Voluntary Negro Blues", *Crossing the Line: Racial Passing in Twentieth-Century U.S. Literature and Culture*, (Durham, NC: Duke University Press, 2000).
25. Josephine Baker, "Speech at the March on Washington", (1963). Available from: *BlackPast*, (3 November 2011), https://www.blackpast.org/african-american-history/speeches-african-american-history/1963-josephine-baker-speech-march-washington/
26. Morgan Jerkins, "90 Years Later, the Radical Power of Josephine Baker's Banana Skirt", *Vogue*, (3 June 2016), https://www.vogue.com/article/josephine-baker-90th-anniversary-banana-skirt

27. Ibid.
28. Josephine Baker, "Speech at the March on Washington", (1963). Available from: *BlackPast*, (3 November 2011), https://www.blackpast.org/african-american-history/speeches-african-american-history/1963-josephine-baker-speech-march-washington/
29. Jerkins, (3 June 2016).
30. John Howard Griffin, *Black Like Me*, (New York: New American Library, 2003), new edn., p. 4.
31. Ibid., p. 11.
32. Ibid., p. 10.
33. Ibid., p. 72.
34. Ibid., p. 68.
35. Ibid., p. 11.
36. Ibid., p. 104.
37. Gates, (10 June 1996).
38. Cited in Gates, (10 June 1996).
39. Shirley Broyard married a prominent NAACP figurehead, Franklin Hall Williams (1917–90). Williams served as the first black US representative to the United Nations Economic and Social Council and was later appointed US Ambassador to Ghana under President Lyndon B. Johnson.

3. THE CHAMELEON DANCE: HIERARCHIES OF COMPLEXION

1. Sarah Yates, "Zoë Wicomb's Playing in the Light: Home, Homesickness, and Race as Place", *WritingThreeSixty*, vol. 04, no. 01, (2018), (pp. 86–93), p. 89.
2. Ibid.
3. Mahmood Mamdani, "What is a Tribe?", *London Review of Books*, vol. 34, no. 17, (13 September 2012), https://www.lrb.co.uk/the-paper/v34/n17/mahmood-mamdani/what-is-a-tribe
4. Suren Pillay, "Being coloured and Indian in South Africa after apartheid", Africa is a Country, (21 June 2018), https://africasacountry.com/2018/06/being-coloured-and-indian-in-south-africa-after-apartheid
5. Hobbs, (2014), p. 21.
6. Nelson Mandela, *Long Walk to Freedom*, (London: Abacus, 1995), p. 175.
7. Zoë Wicomb, *Playing in the Light: A Novel*, (New York: The New Press, 2006), p. 121.
8. Michael Chapman, *The Paperbook of South African English Poetry*, (Johannesburg: Ad. Donker, 1986).
9. Wicomb, (2006), p. 151.
10. William G. Proctor, Jr., "Slavery in Southwest Georgia". Cited in Martha J. Cutter, "Why Passing Is (Still) not Passé after More Than 250 Years:

Sources from the Past and the Present", (pp. 49–67), p. 52. In Mollie Godfrey and Vershawn Ashanti Young (eds.), *Neo-Passing: Performing Identity after Jim Crow*, (Champaign, IL: University of Illinois Press, 2018).
11. Wicomb, (2006), p. 5.
12. Ibid., p. 2.
13. Ibid., p. 13.
14. Rabindranath Tagore, *Krishnakali*. Author's translation from the Bengali.
15. Edward Telles and the Project on Ethnicity and Race in Latin America (PERLA), *Pigmentocracies: Ethnicity, Race, and Color in Latin America*, (Chapel Hill, NC: The University of North Carolina Press, 2014), p. 9.
16. AP News, "136 variations of Brazilian skin colors", (8 July 2014), https://apnews.com/692538d8883a4d20842425d1d265b862
17. Hobbs, (2014), p. 22.
18. Cleuci de Oliveira, "Is Neymar Black? Brazil and the Painful Relativity of Race", *The New York Times*, (30 June 2018), https://www.nytimes.com/2018/06/30/opinion/is-neymar-black-brazil-and-the-painful-relativity-of-race.html
19. Cleuci de Oliveira, "One Woman's Fight to Claim Her 'Blackness' in Brazil", *Foreign Policy*, (24 July 2017), https://foreignpolicy.com/2017/07/24/one-womans-fight-to-claim-her-blackness-in-brazil/
20. De Oliveira, (30 June 2018).
21. De Oliveira, (24 July 2017).
22. *Time Out*, "Sapphire", n.d., https://www.timeout.com/movies/sapphire
23. Ann Ogidi, "Sapphire (1959)", n.d., BFI Screenonline, http://www.screenonline.org.uk/film/id/440288/index.html

4. MISTAKEN IDENTITY: LIVING IN RACIAL NO MAN'S LAND

1. Wicomb, (2006), p. 107.
2. Zoë Wicomb, "Shame and identity: the case of the coloured in South Africa", (pp. 91–107), p. 92. In Derek Attridge and Rosemary Jolly (eds.), *Writing South Africa: Literature, Apartheid, and Democracy, 1970–1995*, (Cambridge: Cambridge University Press, 2011).
3. Bliss Broyard, *One Drop: My Father's Hidden Life—A Story of Race and Family Secrets*, (New York: Little, Brown and Company, 2007), p. 67.
4. Ibid., p. 69.
5. Ibid., pp. 68–9.
6. Johnson, (1995), p. 8.
7. Ibid., p. 34.
8. Anthony Ekundayo Lennon, "Yes I have white parents, but I have African ancestry too", *The Guardian*, (10 November 2018), https://www.the

guardian.com/commentisfree/2018/nov/10/white-parents-african-ancestry-anthony-ekundayo-lennon

9. Trevor Phillips, speaking to *The Telegraph*. In Martin Evans, "White actor who identifies as black criticised for winning place on scheme for Bame candidates", *The Telegraph*, (4 November 2018), https://www.telegraph.co.uk/news/2018/11/04/white-actor-identifies-black-criticised-winning-place-scheme/

10. Simon Hattenstone, "Anthony Ekundayo Lennon on being accused of 'passing' as a black man", *The Guardian*, (7 September 2019), https://www.theguardian.com/world/2019/sep/07/anthony-lennon-theatre-director-accused-of-passing-as-black-interview-simon-hattenstone

11. Lennon, (10 November 2018).

12. Cedric Barber, speaking to David Olusoga, in "The White Descendants of the Black Georgians", (8 November 2016), https://www.bbc.co.uk/programmes/p04flzdc. Clip from "Black and British: A Forgotten History", episode 1: "First Encounters", BBC, (9 November 2016).

13. I am spending the first months of C19 lockdown in a converted barn near Cirencester, in the English county of Gloucestershire. When I look out of my window, I see the vast Bathurst estate and often wonder how much of it was acquired with the proceeds of the Atlantic slave trade.

14. Mark Brown, "Theatre boss defends controversial appointment on BME directors' scheme", *The Guardian*, (8 November 2018), https://www.theguardian.com/world/2018/nov/08/theatre-boss-defends-controversial-appointment-on-bme-directors-scheme

15. Samira Kawash, "The Autobiography of an Ex-Coloured Man: (Passing for) Black Passing for White", (pp. 59–74), p. 63. In Ginsberg (ed.), (1996).

16. Doreen St. Félix, "The Profound Presence of Doria Ragland", *The New Yorker*, (21 May 2018), https://www.newyorker.com/culture/annals-of-appearances/the-profound-presence-of-doria-ragland

17. Ibid.

18. Ibid.

5. MALE LIKE HER: IMPERSONATING THE "OPPOSITE" SEX

1. Garber, (2011), p. 72.

2. William Shakespeare, *Twelfth Night*, (London: Penguin Books, 2005), new edn., Act 1 Scene 4, lines 30–6.

3. Karen Frost, "Women's History: 'Passing' in a Man's World", AfterEllen, (26 March 2020), https://www.afterellen.com/people/533493-womens-history-passing-mans-world

4. Virginia Woolf, *Orlando: A Biography*, (Ware, UK: Wordsworth Editions, 1995), new edn., p. 75.
5. Yaron Druckman, "Barak in drag: The daring operation to kill Arafat's deputy", *Yedioth Ahronoth*, (18 April 2014), https://www.ynetnews.com/articles/0,7340,L-4509923,00.html
6. Valerie Rohy, "Displacing Desire: Passing, Nostalgia, and Giovanni's Room", (pp. 218–33), p. 226. In Ginsberg (ed.), (1996).
7. See: Nick Duffy, "Watch: Eddie Izzard perfectly explains his gender—while getting his nails done", *Pink News*, (15 March 2016), https://www.pinknews.co.uk/2016/03/15/watch-eddie-izzard-perfectly-explains-his-gender-while-getting-his-nails-done/
8. Garber, (2011), p. 10–11.

6. THE WILD SIDE: SLIPPING BETWEEN GENDERS

1. Elaine K. Ginsberg, "Introduction: The Politics of Passing", (pp. 1–18), p. 2. In Ginsberg (ed.), (1996).
2. Kimberly Peirce. Cited in Stephanie Fairyington, "Two Decades After Brandon Teena's Murder, a Look Back at Falls City", *The Atlantic*, (31 December 2013), https://www.theatlantic.com/national/archive/2013/12/two-decades-after-brandon-teenas-murder-a-look-back-at-falls-city/282738/
3. Jeffrey Eugenides, *Middlesex*, (London: Bloomsbury, 2011), paperback edn., p. 477.
4. Ibid., p. 3.
5. Ibid., p. 442.
6. Ibid., p. 332.
7. Ibid., p. 446.
8. Ibid., p. 449.
9. Ibid., p. 211.
10. Author interview with Sophie Green, (Liverpool, January 2020).
11. Jonathan Jones, "April Ashley: from Vogue lingerie model to transgender icon", *The Guardian*, (26 September 2013), https://www.theguardian.com/artanddesign/jonathanjonesblog/2013/sep/26/april-ashley-transgender-liverpool-exhibition
12. Virginia Woolf, *Orlando: A Biography*, (Ware, UK: Wordsworth Editions, 1995), new edn., pp. 67–8.
13. Garber, (2011), p. 15.
14. Jan Morris, *Conundrum*, (London: Faber & Faber, 2010), ebook edn., p. 122.
15. See: Halina Watts, "Caitlyn Jenner refuses to talk about gender reassignment on I'm A Celeb 'out of respect'", *The Mirror*, (9 November 2019),

https://www.mirror.co.uk/3am/celebrity-news/caitlyn-jenner-refuses-talk-gender-20851468
16. See: Germaine Greer, *The Whole Woman*.
17. Garber, (2011), p. 11.
18. Julie McCarthy, "A Journey Of Pain And Beauty: On Becoming Transgender In India", NPR, (18 April 2014), https://www.npr.org/sections/parallels/2014/04/18/304548675/a-journey-of-pain-and-beauty-on-becoming-transgender-in-india
19. Ibid.

7. NOBODY'S BUSINESS BUT OURS: PASSING IN AND OUT OF THE CLOSET

1. Annie Proulx, "Brokeback Mountain", *The New Yorker*, (6 October 1997), https://www.newyorker.com/magazine/1997/10/13/brokeback-mountain
2. Eric Patterson, *On Brokeback Mountain: Meditations about Masculinity, Fear, and Love in the Story and Film*, (Lanham: Lexington Books, 2008), p. xxxi.
3. Proulx, (6 October 1997).
4. Ibid.
5. Patterson, (2008), p. 232.
6. Ibid.
7. Proulx, (6 October 1997).
8. Joe Morgan, "Bangladesh lesbian couple threatened with life in jail for getting married", *Gay Star News*, (25 July 2013), https://www.gaystarnews.com/article/bangladesh-lesbian-couple-threatened-life-jail-getting-married250713/
9. Lipika Pelham, "Arrested after falling for another woman", BBC News, (28 January 2016), https://www.bbc.co.uk/news/magazine-35412388
10. Cited in Lipika Pelham, "Arrested after falling for another woman", BBC News, (28 January 2016), https://www.bbc.co.uk/news/magazine-35412388
11. Isaac Bashevis Singer, "Disguised", *The New Yorker*, (15 September 1986), https://www.newyorker.com/magazine/1986/09/22/disguised
12. Nathan Englander to Deborah Treisman, "Nathan Englander Reads Isaac Bashevis Singer", *The New Yorker* fiction podcast, (10 April 2009), https://www.newyorker.com/podcast/fiction/nathan-englander-reads-isaac-bashevis-singer
13. Raja Halwani, "Outing and Virtue Ethics", *Journal of Applied Philosophy*, vol. 19, no. 02, (2002), (pp. 141–54), p. 146.
14. Singer, (15 September 1986).
15. Daniel Silvermint, "Passing as Privileged", *ERGO: An Open Access Journal of Philosophy*, vol. 05, no. 02, (2018), (pp. 1–44), p. 8.

16. Ibid.
17. Patterson, (2008), p. 178.
18. Author interviews with Christopher Gunness, (London and Ewen, Gloucestershire, June and August 2020).
19. Ibid.
20. Ibid.
21. Ibid.

8. BORN AGAIN: SHIFTING RELIGION AND CASTE

1. Kazi Nazrul Islam, *Bright As The Crimson Sun*. Author's translation from the Bengali.
2. H. Beverley, *Report on the Census of Bengal 1872*, (Calcutta: Secretariat Press, 1872), p. 132. Cited in Richard M. Eaton, *The Rise of Islam and the Bengal Frontier, 1204–1760*, (Berkeley and Los Angeles, CA: University of California Press, 1996), p. 120.
3. Patrick Cockburn, "While Muslims are being murdered in India, the rest of the world is too slow to condemn", *The Independent*, (28 February 2020), https://www.independent.co.uk/voices/delhi-riots-news-narendra-modi-muslims-hindus-jammu-kashmir-trump-a9365376.html
4. Ibid.
5. See: Meryl Sebastian, "My Wife Is Hindu, I Am Muslim, My Kids Are Hindustan: Shah Rukh Khan", *Huffington Post*, (27 January 2020), https://www.huffingtonpost.in/entry/srk-dance-plus_in_5e2ea8cbc5b6779e9c369f13
6. Aravind Adiga, *The White Tiger*, (London: Atlantic Books, 2008), p. 37.
7. Robert Guest, "A tale of two sisters: Japan's untouchables emerging from centuries of scorn", *Far Eastern Economic Review*, (9 July 1992).
8. Author interview with Yae Wallis, (Ewen, Gloucestershire, August 2020).
9. W.G. Beasley, *The Meiji Restoration*, (Stanford, CA: Stanford University Press, 1972), Kindle edition.

9. HIDDEN NATIONS: COLLECTIVE PASSING

1. Kenji Yoshino, *Covering: The Hidden Assault on Our Civil Rights*, (New York: Random House, 2007). Cited in Silvermint, (2018), p. 10.
2. Yoshino, (2007), p. 18. Cited in Silvermint, (2018), p. 10. Yoshino and Silvermint are referring to Erving Goffman's definition of "covering" in *Stigma: Notes on the Management of Spoiled Identity*, (New York: Simon & Schuster, 1963).
3. Avedis Hadjian, *Secret Nation: The Hidden Armenians of Turkey*, (London: I.B. Tauris, 2018), p. 2.

4. Raffi Khatchadourian, *The New Yorker*. Endorsement of Avedis Hadjian, *Secret Nation: The Hidden Armenians of Turkey*, (London: I.B. Tauris, 2018), frontmatter.
5. This strategy was known as the *Action Portuguesia*. Leah Goldstein, "Fate and Identity: 'Non-Jewish Jews' during the *Shoah*", *Yad Vashem Jerusalem*, vol. 78, (October 2015), pp. 12–13.
6. Leo W. Schwarz, "Introduction". In Leo W. Schwarz (ed.), *Memoirs of My People: Jewish Self-Portraits From The 11th to the 20th Centuries*, (New York: Schocken Books, 1963), p. vii.
7. "Life in Lombardy", from the memoir of Leone Da Modena. In Schwarz (ed.), 1963, p. 75.
8. V. S. Naipaul, *The Middle Passage*, (London: Picador, 2001), revised edn., p. 20.
9. Benjamin G. Dennis and Anita K. Dennis, *Slaves to Racism: An Unbroken Chain from America to Liberia*, (New York: Algora Publishing, 2008), p. 10.
10. Simon Schama, *Rough Crossings: Britain, the Slaves and the American Revolution*, (London: BBC Books, 2005), p. 185.
11. Ibid.
12. Stowe, (1995), p. 400.
13. Dennis and Dennis, (2008).
14. Stern, (1996), p. 121.
15. Dennis and Dennis, (2008), p. 31.
16. Stern, (1996), p. 130.

10. MINDSETS OF BELONGING: SOCIO-CULTURAL PASSING

1. Rictor Norton, "Anne Lister: The First Modern Lesbian", *Lesbian History*, (1 August 2003), updated 13 June 2008, http://rictornorton.co.uk/lister.htm
2. Anne Lister journal, 28 June 1918, reference: SH:7/ML/E/2, West Yorkshire Archive Service. Available online at West Yorkshire Archive Service, "Anne Lister", *Catablogue*, n.d., https://wyascatablogue.wordpress.com/exhibitions/anne-lister/
3. Norton, (1 August 2003).
4. Anne Lister journal, 29 January 1821, reference: SH:7/ML/E:4, West Yorkshire Archive Service. Available online at West Yorkshire Archive Service, "Anne Lister", *Catablogue*, n.d., https://wyascatablogue.wordpress.com/exhibitions/anne-lister/
5. Sally Wainwright, script for "Gentleman Jack: Episode 5", Lookout Point, (30 August 2018), p. 43. Available at: http://downloads.bbc.co.uk/writersroom/scripts/gentleman-jack-ep5-shooting-script.pdf
6. Jillian P. Fischer, "'The Sister Was Not a Mister': Gender and Sexuality in

the Writings of Gertrude Stein and Virginia Woolf", *Lawrence University Honors Projects*, vol. 50, (2013), p. 10, https://lux.lawrence.edu/luhp/50

7. Chris Coffman, "Gertrude Stein's Transmasculinity", (10 September 2018), https://euppublishingblog.com/2018/09/10/gertrude-steins-transmasculinity/
8. Cited in Coffman, (10 September 2018).
9. Coffman, (10 September 2018).
10. Fischer, (2013), p. 7.
11. Ibid., p. 9.
12. M. Fakhry Davids, *Internal Racism: A Psychoanalytic Approach to Race and Difference*, (London: Red Globe Press, 2011), p. 110.
13. Ibid., p. 113.
14. Toni Morrison, "A Humanist View", transcript of speech given at Portland State University, (30 May 1975), p. 7, https://www.mackenzian.com/wp-content/uploads/2014/07/Transcript_PortlandState_TMorrison.pdf (Itals in original).
15. Frantz Fanon, *Black Skin, White Masks*, (London: Pluto Press, 2008), revised edn., p. 5.
16. Ibid., p. 45. (Itals in original).
17. Davids, (2011), p. 113.
18. William Shakespeare, *The Tempest*, (Oxford: Oxford University Press, 2001), Act 1 Scene 2, lines 362–3.
19. Derek Walcott, "The Muse of History", (pp. 1–28), p. 25. In Orde Coombs (ed.), *Is Massa Day Dead?: Black Moods in the Caribbean*, (Garden City, NY: Anchor Books, 1974).
20. Lipika Pelham. A slightly altered version of this passage first appeared in "Tale of the Modern Refugee", *Tikkun*, (15 August 2019), https://www.tikkun.org/tale-of-the-modern-refugee
21. V. S. Naipaul, *The Enigma of Arrival: A Novel in Five Sections*, first published in 1987, (New York: Viking Press, 1987).
22. Derek Walcott, "A Far Cry from Africa", from *Selected Poems*, (New York: Farrar, Straus and Giroux, 2007), lines 26–30.
23. Robert Graves, cited in Orde Coombs, "Introduction", in Coombs (ed.), (1974), p. xv.
24. Walcott, (1974), p. 27.
25. Naipaul, (2001), p. 34.
26. Derek Walcott, "The Garden Path: V.S. Naipaul", in *What the Twilight Says: Essays*, (London: Faber & Faber, 1998), p. 132.
27. Jacques Lacan, *Feminine Sexuality*. Cited in Valerie Rohy, "Displacing Desire: Passing, Nostalgia, and Giovanni's Room", (pp. 218–33), p. 229. In Ginsberg (ed.), (1996).
28. Edward Brathwaite, "Timehri". In Coombs (ed.), (1974), p. 32.

29. Ibid.
30. Rohy, (1996), p. 229.
31. Joyce E. Jonas, "Carnival Strategies in Lamming's *In the Castle of My Skin*", *Callaloo*, no. 35, (1988), (pp. 346–60), p. 347.
32. Ibid. (Itals in original).
33. Sam Selvon, *The Lonely Londoners*, (London: Penguin Books, 2006), revised edn., p. 1.
34. George Lamming, "Introduction" to the 1983 edition of *In the Castle of My Skin*, (New York: Schocken, 1983), p. xi.
35. George Lamming, *In the Castle of My Skin*, (London: Longman Pearson, 1987), p. 202.
36. Ibid., p. 287.
37. David Dabydeen, *Turner: New and Selected Poems*, (Leeds: Peepal Tree Press, 2002), new edn., p. 7.

11. HEART OF WHITENESS: THE QUINTESSENTIAL REVERSE-PASSING OF RICHARD BURTON

1. William Gifford Palgrave, *Narrative of a Year's Journey through Central and Eastern Arabia*, vol. 1, (London and Cambridge: Macmillan and Co., 1865), digitised edn., pp. 258–9.
2. Richard F. Burton, "Preface to the Third Edition", *Personal Narrative of a Pilgrimage to Al-Madinah and Meccah*, vol. 1, (Frankfurt am Main: Outlook Verlag GmbH, 2019), digitised edn., first published in 1855, p. 5.
3. Burton, (2019), p. 12.
4. Ibid., pp. 10–11.
5. David Livingstone, *Missionary Travels and Researches in South Africa*, (New York: Harper & Brothers Publishers, 1858), digitised edn., p. 558, https://books.google.co.uk/books?id=P-0MAAAAIAAJ&source=gbs_navlinks_s
6. Audrey Farley, "Tripping to Enlightenment? Science, Religion, and Psychedelics", *Marginalia, Los Angeles Review of Books*, (7 June 2019), https://marginalia.lareviewofbooks.org/tripping-enlightenment-science-religion-psychedelics/
7. Richard Burton, *Personal Narrative of a Pilgrimage to Al-Madinah and Meccah*. Cited in Jeremy Paxman, "Richard Burton, Victorian explorer", *Financial Times*, (1 May 2015), https://www.ft.com/content/357140e4-eeaf-11e4-a5cd-00144feab7de
8. Isabel Burton, *The Life of Captain Sir Richard F. Burton*, vol. 1, (Frankfurt am Main: Outlook Verlag GmbH, 2020), digitised edn., first published in 1893, p. 236.
9. Burton, (2019), p. 23. (Itals in original).

10. Ibid., p. 6.
11. Paxman, (1 May 2015).
12. Burton, (2019), p. 33.
13. Ibid., p. 23.
14. Ibid., p. 24.
15. Ibid., p. 31.
16. Ibid., p. 33.

12. SOMETHING OF HIS SELVES: THE PASSING, APPROPRIATING AND IDENTIFYING OF RUDYARD KIPLING

1. Rudyard Kipling, *Kim*, (Mineola, NY: Dover Publications, Inc., 2005), new edn., p. 114.
2. Rudyard Kipling, *Something of Myself and other Autobiographical Writings*, ed. by Thomas Pinney, (Cambridge: Cambridge University Press, 1990), p. 4.
3. George Orwell, "Rudyard Kipling", *All Art is Propaganda: Critical Essays*, (Boston, MA: Mariner Books, 2009), first published in 1942. Available from: https://orwell.ru/library/reviews/kipling/english/e_rkip
4. Jan Montefiore, Professor of Twentieth Century English Literature at the University of Kent, speaking to Melvyn Bragg. In Luke Mulhall (producer), "Rudyard Kipling", *In Our Time* podcast, BBC Radio 4, (16 October 2014), 41:15–41:19, https://www.bbc.co.uk/sounds/play/b04l3852
5. Kipling, (1990), p. 25.
6. Rudyard Kipling, *Kim*, (Mineola, NY: Dover Publications, Inc., 2005), new edn., p. 225.
7. Ibid., p. 105.
8. Rudyard Kipling, "Miss Youghal's Sais", *Plain Tales from the Hills*, (London: Aziloth Books, 2011), p. 19.
9. Ibid., p. 100.
10. Kipling, (2005), p. 76.
11. Rudyard Kipling, "Recessional", (1897), line 15. Available online: https://www.poetryfoundation.org/poems/46780/recessional
12. Kipling, (2005), p. 37.
13. Ibid., p. 117.
14. Shashi Tharoor, speaking to Nilanjana Roy. "Inglorious Empire", *AfterWords* podcast, Hurst Publishers, (9 March 2020), 17:28–17:33, https://www.hurstpublishers.com/afterwords/
15. Ibid., 14:23–14:42.
16. Ibid., 17:35–17:38.
17. John S. McBratney, "Passing and the Modern Persona in Kipling's Ethnographer Fiction", *English*, vol. 03, (1998), p. 35.

18. Rudyard Kipling, *Kim*, (Mineola, NY: Dover Publications, Inc., 2005), new edn., p. 114.
19. Edward W. Said, *Orientalism*, (London: Penguin Classics, 2019), new edn., first published in 1978, p. 227.
20. Ibid., p. 228.
21. McBratney, (1998), p. 37.
22. Ibid., p. 34.
23. Kipling, (2011), p. 21.
24. Ibid., p. 20.
25. Ibid., p. 19.
26. Said, (2019), p. 228.
27. Ibid., p. 227.
28. McBratney, (1998), p. 44.

13. WHO'S PASSING FOR WHO? THE CURIOUS CURSE OF CULTURAL APPROPRIATION

1. Davids, (2011), p. 231.
2. Author interview with Lionel Shriver, (telephone, March 2020).
3. David Sanderson, "Booker winner Bernardine Evaristo writes off 'cultural appropriation'", *The Times*, (3 December 2019), https://www.thetimes.co.uk/article/booker-winner-bernardine-evaristo-writes-off-cultural-appropriation-bklfsqhgk
4. Ibid.
5. Smithsonian Museum, "Blackface: The Birth of An American Stereotype", https://nmaahc.si.edu/blog-post/blackface-birth-american-stereotype
6. Michael Pickering, *Blackface Minstrelsy in Britain*, (Abingdon, UK and New York: Routledge, 2016), new edn., p. 3.
7. Ibid., p. xii.
8. Somini Sengupta, "U.N. Urges the Netherlands to Stop Portrayals of 'Black Pete' Character", *The New York Times*, (28 August 2015), https://www.nytimes.com/2015/08/29/world/europe/zwarte-piet-netherlands-united-nations.html
9. BBC News, "Justin Trudeau: New video of Canada's PM in blackface", (19 September 2019), https://www.bbc.co.uk/news/world-us-canada-49758613
10. Anna Purna Kambhampaty, Madeleine Carlisle and Melissa Chan, "Justin Trudeau Wore Brownface at 2001 'Arabian Nights' Party While He Taught at a Private School", *Time*, (18 September 2019), https://time.com/5680759/justin-trudeau-brownface-photo/
11. *Daily Mail*, "Canada's PM Trudeau jokes he has more Sikhs in his Cabinet than Modi", (13 March 2016), https://www.dailymail.co.uk/indiahome/article-3490583/Canada-s-PM-Trudeau-jokes-Sikhs-Cabinet-Modi.html

12. Omar Abdullah, (21 February 2018). Available from: https://twitter.com/OmarAbdullah/status/966218016286441472
13. Barkha Dutt, "Trudeau's India trip is a total disaster—and he has only himself to blame", *The Washington Post*, (23 February 2018), https://www.washingtonpost.com/news/global-opinions/wp/2018/02/22/trudeaus-india-trip-is-a-total-disaster-and-he-has-himself-to-blame/
14. Kameron Virk and Nesta McGregor, "Blackfishing: The women accused of pretending to be black", BBC News, (5 December 2018), https://www.bbc.co.uk/news/newsbeat-46427180
15. Coldplay, 'Everyday Life Live in Jordan—Sunrise Performance', 21 November 2019, 1:36, https://www.youtube.com/watch?v=NFf2VFREkZo
16. Sara Tan, "Kim Kardashian Tells Us Why She Wore Fulani Braids To The MTV Movie Awards—EXCLUSIVE", Bustle, (20 June 2018), https://www.bustle.com/p/kim-kardashian-explains-why-she-wears-fulani-braids-despite-all-the-internet-backlash-9505337
17. Davids, (2011), p. 82.
18. Reni Eddo-Lodge, *Why I'm No Longer Talking to White People About Race*, (London: Bloomsbury Publishing, 2017), p. 86.
19. Allison Samuels, "Rachel Dolezal's True Lies", *Vanity Fair*, (19 July 2015), https://www.vanityfair.com/news/2015/07/rachel-dolezal-new-interview-pictures-exclusive
20. Ibid.
21. Ibid.
22. See: Doreen St. Félix, "'The Rachel Divide' Review: A Disturbing Portrait of Dolezal's Racial Fraudulence", *The New Yorker*, (26 April 2018), https://www.newyorker.com/culture/culture-desk/the-rachel-divide-review-a-disturbing-portrait-of-dolezals-racial-fraudulence
24. Ibid.
25. Eddo-Lodge, (2017), p. 84.
26. Davids, (2011), p. 49.
27. To learn more about African hair textures, see: https://blacknaps.org/know-your-hair-type/

14. REPRESENT: PASSING AND APPROPRIATION IN THE PERFORMING ARTS

1. Production Code Administration file, (memo dated 9 March 1934). Cited in Karen M. Bowdre, "Passing Films and the Illusion of Racial Equality", *Black Camera*, vol. 05, no. 02, (2014), (pp. 21–43), p. 23.
2. Bowdre, (2014), p. 23.
3. Ibid., p. 29.
4. Bosley Crowther, "The Screen: Minstrel Show 'Othello': Radical Makeup

Marks Olivier's Interpretation", *The New York Times*, (2 February 1966), https://www.nytimes.com/1966/02/02/archives/the-screen-minstrel-show-othelloradical-makeup-marks-oliviers.html

5. Mariane Pearl had requested Jolie for the role, telling *Time Magazine:* "I have heard some criticism about her casting, but it is not about the color of your skin. It is about who you are. I asked her to play the role—even though she is way more beautiful than I am—because I felt a real kinship to her. She put her whole heart into it, and I think she understood why we should do this movie." See: Carolyn Sayre, "10 Questions for Mariane Pearl", *Time Magazine*, (21 June 2007), http://content.time.com/time/magazine/article/0,9171,1635834,00.html
6. Reni Eddo-Lodge, (2017), p. 135.
7. Kevin Feige, President of Marvel Studios.
8. Chitra Ramaswamy, "Can Hermione be black? What a stupid question", *The Guardian*, (21 December 2015), https://www.theguardian.com/books/shortcuts/2015/dec/21/hermione-granger-black-noma-dumezwani-harry-potter-cursed-child
9. Ibid.
10. Kat Brown, "First picture of Eddie Redmayne as transgender painter Lili Elbe", *The Telegraph*, (27 February 2015), https://www.telegraph.co.uk/culture/film/film-news/11439214/First-picture-of-Eddie-Redmayne-as-transgender-painter-Lili-Elbe.html
11. Change.org petition to Eddie Redmayne, "Undergo Gender Confirmation Surgery to add authenticity to your role in 'The Danish Girl'", https://www.change.org/p/eddie-redmayne-undergo-gender-confirmation-surgery-to-add-authenticity-to-your-role-in-the-danish-girl
12. Ryan Gilbey, "Playing it straight: should gay roles be reserved for gay actors?", *The Guardian*, (14 January 2019), https://www.theguardian.com/stage/2019/jan/14/gay-roles-actors-assassination-gianni-versace-bohemian-rhapsody
13. Ian Youngs, "Juliet becomes Julius in Shakespeare's love story", BBC News, (1 June 2017), https://www.bbc.co.uk/news/entertainment-arts-39998329
14. Isabella Biedenharn, "The View UpStairs: EW stage review", *Entertainment Weekly*, (2 March 2017), https://ew.com/theater/2017/03/02/the-view-upstairs-review/
15. Andrew Pulver, "A special intensity: how Carey Mulligan quietly grabbed Hollywood's attention", *The Guardian*, (4 April 2015), https://www.theguardian.com/film/2015/apr/04/a-special-intensity-how-carey-mulligan-quietly-grabbed-hollywoods-attention
16. Rachel Dwyer, "Top Ten Muslim Characters in Bollywood". In Ziauddin Sardar and Robin Yassin-Kassab (eds.), *Critical Muslim: 5*, (London: Hurst

Publishers, 2013). Available online: https://www.criticalmuslim.io/top-ten-muslim-characters-in-bollywood/

EPILOGUE: A PREQUEL TO PASSING

1. Derek Walcott, *The Castaway*, p. 52. Cited in Robert Elliot Fox, "Derek Walcott: History as Dis-Ease", *Callaloo*, no. 27, (Spring 1986), (pp. 331–40), pp. 334–5. (Itals in original).
2. Ruth Prawer Jhabvala, *My Nine Lives: Chapters of a Possible Past*, (London: John Murray Publishers, 2005), p. vii.
3. Ruth Prawer Jhabvala, "Disinheritance", speech delivered on acceptance of the Neil Gunn International Fellowship Award, (1979). Cited in *The Times*, "Ruth Prawer Jhabvala" obituary, (4 April 2013), https://www.thetimes.co.uk/article/ruth-prawer-jhabvala-8xcq5vf5nf6
4. Griffin, (2003), p. 11.
5. See: Cnaan Liphshiz, "A Yom Kippur tradition in Amsterdam dates back to the invention of electricity", Jewish Telegraphic Agency, (14 September 2017), https://www.jta.org/2017/09/14/lifestyle/a-yom-kippur-tradition-in-amsterdam-dates-back-to-the-invention-of-electricity
6. Jhabvala, (2005), p. vii.
7. Ibid.

FURTHER READING

Poetry

Chapman, Michael, *The Paperbook of South African English Poetry*, (Johannesburg: Ad. Donker, 1986).

Cullen, Countée, *Collected Poems*, ed. by Major Jackson, (New York: The Library of America, 2013).

Dabydeen, David, *Turner: New and Selected Poems*, (Leeds: Peepal Tree Press, 2002).

Walcott, Derek, *Omeros*, (New York: Farrar, Straus & Giroux, 1990).

Fiction

Adiga, Aravind, *The White Tiger*, (London: Atlantic Books, 2008).

Alderman, Naomi, *Disobedience*, (London: Penguin, 2006).

Anthony, Piers, *Race Against Time*, (London: Sidgwick & Jackson, 1974).

Bennett, Brit, *The Vanishing Half*, (New York: Riverhead Books, 2020).

Brugman, Alyssa, *Alex As Well*, (New York: Henry Holt and Company, 2015).

Chesnutt, Charles W., *The House Behind the Cedars*, (Mineola, NY: Dover Publications, 2007).

Ebershoff, David, *The Danish Girl*, (London: Weidenfeld & Nicolson, 2015).

Eugenides, Jeffrey, *Middlesex*, (London: Bloomsbury, 2011).

Everett, Percival, *Erasure*, (Hanover, NH: University of New England Press, 2001).

Faulkner, William, *Light in August*, (London: Vintage Classics, 2000).

Feinberg, Leslie, *Stone Butch Blues*, (New York: Alyson Books, 2004).

Gino, Alex, *George*, (New York: Scholastic Fiction, 2015).

Girard, M-E, *Girl Mans Up*, (New York: HarperTeen, 2016).

Gregorio, I.W., *None of the Above*, (New York: Balzer + Bray, 2015).

Hurst, Fannie, *Imitation of Life*, (Durham, NC: Duke University Press, 2004).

FURTHER READING

Jhabvala, Ruth Prawer, *My Nine Lives: Chapters of a Possible Past*, (London: John Murray Publishers, 2005).

Johnson, James Weldon, *Autobiography of an Ex-Colored Man*, (Mineola, NY: Dover Publications, Inc., 1995).

Jones, Patricia A., *Passing*, (New York: Avon Books, 1999).

Kipling, Rudyard, *Kim*, (Mineola, NY: Dover Publications, Inc., 2005).

———, "Miss Youghal's Sais", *Plain Tales from the Hills*, (London: Aziloth Books, 2011).

Lamming, George, *In the Castle of My Skin*, (London: Longman Pearson, 1987).

Larsen, Nella, *Passing*, (Mineola, NY: Dover Publications, Inc., 2004).

Le Guin, Ursula K., *The Left Hand of Darkness*, (London: Gollancz, 2017).

Lester, Julius, *The Tales of Uncle Remus: The Adventures of Brer Rabbit*, (London: Puffin Books, 2006).

McLemore, Anne-Marie, *When the Moon Was Ours: A Novel*, (New York: Macmillan, 2016).

Mosley, Walter, *Devil in a Blue Dress*, (London: Serpent's Tail, 2017).

Naipaul, V.S., *The Enigma of Arrival: A Novel in Five Sections*, (New York: Viking Press, 1987).

Rosenberg, Jordy, *Confessions of the Fox*, (London: Atlantic Books, 2018).

Roth, Philip, *The Human Stain*, (London: Vintage Classics, 2019).

Schmatz, Pat, *Lizard Radio*, (Somerville, MA: Candlewick Press, 2015).

Scott, Paul, *The Alien Sky*, (London: Pan Books, 1953).

Selvon, Sam, *The Lonely Londoners*, (London: Penguin Books, 2006).

Shakespeare, William, *Twelfth Night*, (London: Penguin Books, 2005).

———, *The Merchant of Venice*, (London: Penguin Classics, 2015).

———, *Othello*, (London: Penguin Classics, 2015).

Stowe, Harriet Beecher, *Uncle Tom's Cabin*, (Ware, UK: Wordsworth Editions, 1995).

Waters, Sarah, *Tipping the Velvet*, (London: Virago, 2011).

Wicomb, Zoë, *Playing in the Light: A Novel*, (New York: The New Press, 2006).

Woolf, Virginia, *Orlando: A Biography*, (Ware, UK: Wordsworth Editions, 1995).

Non-fiction

Bald, Vivek, *Bengali Harlem and the Lost Histories of South Asian America*, (Cambridge, MA: Harvard University Press, 2015).

FURTHER READING

Beasley, W.G., *The Meiji Restoration*, (Stanford, CA: Stanford University Press, 1972).

Bornstein, Kate, *Gender Outlaw: On Men, Women, and the Rest of Us*, (New York: Routledge, 1994).

——— and S. Bear Bergman, *Gender Outlaws: The Next Generation*, (Emeryville, CA: Seal Press, 2010).

Boylan, Jennifer Finney, *She's Not There: A Life in Two Genders*, (New York: Broadway Books, 2013).

Brathwaite, Edward, "Timehri". In Orde Coombs (ed.), *Is Massa Day Dead?: Black Moods in the Caribbean*, (Garden City, NY: Anchor Books, 1974).

Broyard, Bliss, *One Drop: My Father's Hidden Life—A Story of Race and Family Secrets*, (New York: Little, Brown and Company, 2007).

Burland, C. A., *The Exotic White Man: An Alien in Asian and African Art*, (New York: McGraw-Hill, 1969).

Burton, Richard F., *Personal Narrative of a Pilgrimage to Al-Madinah and Meccah*, vol. 1 and 2, (Frankfurt am Main: Outlook Verlag GmbH, 2019).

Collis, Rose, *Colonel Barker's Monstrous Regiment: A Tale of Female Husbandry*, (London: Virago, 2001).

Craft, William, *Running a Thousand Miles for Freedom; Or, the Escape of William and Ellen Craft from Slavery*, (London: William Tweedie, 1860).

Davids, M. Fakhry, *Internal Racism: A Psychoanalytic Approach to Race and Difference*, (London: Red Globe Press, 2011).

Dennis, Benjamin G. and Dennis, Anita K, *Slaves to Racism: An Unbroken Chain from America to Liberia*, (New York: Algora Publishing, 2008).

Eddo-Lodge, Reni, *Why I'm No Longer Talking to White People About Race*, (London: Bloomsbury Publishing, 2017).

Foster, Gwendolyn Audrey, *Class-passing: Social Mobility in Film and Popular Culture*, (Carbondale, IL: Southern Illinois University Press, 2005).

Frankopan, Peter, *The Silk Roads: A New History of the World*, (London: Bloomsbury, 2016).

Fukuyama, Francis, *Identity: Contemporary Identity Politics and the Struggle for Recognition*, (London: Profile Books, 2018).

Garber, Marjorie, *Vested Interests: Cross-Dressing and Cultural Anxiety*, (New York: Routledge, 2011).

García-Arenal, Mercedes and Wiegers, Gerard, *A Man of Three Worlds: Samuel Pallache, a Moroccan Jew in Catholic and Protestant Europe*, (Baltimore, MD: Johns Hopkins University Press, 2007).

FURTHER READING

Ginsberg, Elaine K. (ed.), *Passing and the Fictions of Identity*, (Durham, NC: Duke University Press, 1996).

Godfrey, Mollie and Young, Vershawn Ashanti (eds.), *Neo-Passing: Performing Identity after Jim Crow*, (Champaign, IL: University of Illinois Press, 2018).

Griffin, John Howard, *Black Like Me*, (New York: New American Library, 2003).

Hadjian, Avedis, *Secret Nation: The Hidden Armenians of Turkey*, (London: I.B. Tauris, 2018).

Halberstam, Judith/Jack, *Female Masculinity*, (Durham, NC: Duke University Press, 1998).

Harvey, Leonard Patrick, *Crypto-Islam in Sixteenth-Century Spain*, (Madrid: Maestre, 1964).

Hobbs, Allyson, *A Chosen Exile: A History of Racial Passing in American Life*, (Cambridge, MA and London, UK: Harvard University Press, 2014).

Horn, Stanley F., *Invisible Empire: The Story of the Ku Klux Klan, 1866–1871*, (Whitefish, MT: Kessinger Publishing, 2010).

Ipsen, Pernille, *Daughters of the Trade: Atlantic Slavers and Interracial Marriage on the Gold Coast*, (Philadelphia, PA: University of Pennsylvania Press, 2015).

Jonas, Joyce, *Anancy in the Great House: Ways of Reading West Indian Fiction*, (Westport, CT: Greenwood Press, 1990).

King, Bruce, *Derek Walcott: A Caribbean Life*, (Oxford: Oxford University Press, 2000).

Kipling, Rudyard, *Something of Myself and other Autobiographical Writings*, ed. by Thomas Pinney, (Cambridge: Cambridge University Press, 1990).

Krog, Antjie, *Country of My Skull*, (London: Jonathan Cape Ltd., 1999).

Lukasik, Gail, *White Like Her: My Family's Story of Race and Racial Passing*, (New York: Skyhorse Publishing, 2017).

Maalouf, Amin, *In the Name of Identity: Violence and the Need to Belong*, (New York: Arcade Publishing, 2001).

McBride, James, *The Color of Water: A Black Man's Tribute to His White Mother*, (New York: Riverhead Books, 1997).

Mock, Janet, *Redefining Realness: My Path to Womanhood, Identity, Love & So Much More*, (New York: Atria Books, 2014).

Morris, Jan, *Conundrum*, (London: Faber & Faber, 2010).

Murray, Douglas, *The Strange Death of Europe: Immigration, Identity, Islam*, (London: Bloomsbury Continuum, 2017).

FURTHER READING

Naipaul, V.S., *The Loss Of El Dorado: A Colonial History*, (London: Picador, 2012).

———, *The Middle Passage: The Caribbean Revisited*, (London: Picador, 2001).

Omi, Michael and Howard Winant, *Racial Formation in the United States: From the 1960s to the 1990s*, (New York: Routledge, 1995).

Patterson, Eric, *On Brokeback Mountain: Meditations about Masculinity, Fear, and Love in the Story and Film*, (Lanham: Lexington Books, 2008).

Pattinson, Juliette, *Behind Enemy Lines, Gender, Passing and Special Operations Executive in the Second World War*, (Manchester: Manchester University Press, 2011).

Phillips, Caryl, *Extravagant Strangers: A Literature of Belonging*, (London: Faber and Faber, 1997).

Piersen, William D., *Black Legacy: America's Hidden Heritage*, (Amherst, MA: University of Massachusetts Press, 1993).

Polakow-Suransky, Sasha, *Go Back to Where You Came From: The Backlash Against Immigration & the Fate of Western Democracy*, (London: Hurst Publishers, 2017).

Said, Edward W., *Out of Place: A Memoir* (New York: Knopf, 1999).

———, *Orientalism*, (London: Penguin Classics, 2019).

Schama, Simon, *Rough Crossings: Britain, the Slaves and the American Revolution*, (London: BBC Books, 2005).

———, *Belonging: The Story of the Jews, 1492–1900*, (New York: Random House, 2017).

Scholinski, Daphne, *The Last Time I Wore a Dress*, (New York: Riverhead Books, 1998).

Schwarz, Leo W. (ed.), *Memoirs of My People: Jewish Self-Portraits From The 11th To The 20th Centuries*, (New York: Schocken Books, 1963).

Souhami, Diana, *Gertrude and Alice*, (London: I.B. Tauris, 2009).

Stanford, Peter, *The She-Pope: A Quest for the Truth Behind the Mystery of Pope Joan*, (London: William Heinemann Ltd., 1998).

Sycamore, Matt Bernstein, A.K.A Mattilda, (ed.), *Nobody Passes: Rejecting the Rules of Gender and Conformity*, (Emeryville, CA: Seal Press, 2006).

Telles, Edward and the Project on Ethnicity and Race in Latin America (PERLA), *Pigmentocracies: Ethnicity, Race, and Color in Latin America*, (Chapel Hill, NC: The University of North Carolina Press, 2014).

Tsuda, Takeyuki, *Strangers in the Ethnic Homeland: Japanese Brazilian Return Migration in Transnational Perspective*, (New York: Columbia University Press, 2003).

FURTHER READING

Vincent, Norah, *Self-Made Man: My Year Disguised as a Man*, (London: Atlantic Books, 2006).

Walcott, Derek, *What the Twilight Says: Essays*, (London: Faber & Faber, 1998).

INDEX

ABC, 303
Abdullah, Omar, 279, 336
Abu Shanab brothers, 195–8, 201
Academy Awards, 94, 114, 276, 278, 295, 297, 301, 303, 305
accents, 111, 156, 181, 222, 223, 225, 311
acculturation, 220
Achilles, 109
'Adamic vision', 228
Adiga, Aravind, 175–6, 210, 211
affirmative action, 77–8, 174
Afghanistan, 171
African Americans
    black nationalism, 45–6
    Black Lives Matter (2013–), 26, 285, 301
    Brown v. Board of Education (1954), 56
    Civil Rights movement (1954–68), 44, 45, 46, 53, 55, 220, 295
    Great Migration (1916–70), 43–4
    Harlem Renaissance (c. 1918–37), 49–52
    Jim Crow period (1865–1965), 41–63, 65, 275, 293–4
    Liberia, migration to, 25, 203–7
    light skinned, 9, 29–39, 41–52, 293
    March on Washington (1963), 53, 55
    marriage, 49
    mixed-race, 3, 49
    One Drop rule and, 44–7, 65, 69, 70, 188
    passing as, 16, 17, 56–60, 108, 190, 271, 284–7
    slavery of, 3, 8, 25, 26, 29–40, 276
    white-passing, 3, 29–39, 41–52, 60–63, 84, 293
Afrikaans, 66
afro hair, 88, 281, 282
'Afro-Saxon', 233
AfterEllen, 107
Ahmadis, 185
Aitken, Gillon, 231
Ajaib Gher, 1
Ajit, 308
Akan people, 23
Albert Nobbs (2011 film), 107–8, 212
Alderman, Naomi, 147
Ali G, 17

INDEX

Ali, Mahershala, 303
All The Mowgli Stories (Kipling), 260
Aloha (2015 film), 296
Amadeus, 300
Ambalu, Shulamit, xv, 83, 93
American Civil War (1861–5), 38, 204, 205
American Colonization Society (ACS), 204–5
American War of Independence (1775–83), 205
amnesia, 39, 48, 57, 62, 72, 230
Amritsar, Punjab, 246, 278–9
Amsterdam, x, xv, 191, 322, 338
Anansi, 8, 23–6, 29, 41, 63, 99, 164, 191, 193, 207, 310
Anansi artists, 233, 235–6
& *Juliet*, 305
al-Andalus (711–1492), 188–93
androgyny, 118, 121, 123, 124, 128, 133, 145, 216, 302
Anne, Queen of Great Britain, 303
apartheid, 11, 47, 65–72, 202
Arab Caliphates, 27
Araújo, Maíra Mutti, 77–8, 88
Arduin, Hilli, 25
Arjun, 164
Armenians, 185–8, 203, 210
arti, 316, 317, 319
Arts Council, 89
Aryan people, 74, 166, 167, 168, 188
As You Like It (Shakespeare), 100
Ashanti Empire (1701–1957), 28, 99
Ashkenazim, 195, 202

Ashley, April, 122, 123–4
Asian Exclusion Act (1924), 180
assimilation, 1, 188, 209, 220, 224, 230, 269, 271, 273
Armenians, 186–7
Jews, 188
Palestinians, 203
socio-cultural passing, 7, 156, 209–36, 248–9, 263–4
Atatürk, Kemal, 187
'Atlantic amnesia', 39, 48, 62, 230
auto da fe, x, 189
Autobiography of an Ex-Colored Man, The (Johnson), 47, 50, 87, 88
Awadh (1732–1859), 257
Azaria, Hank, 301

Bachchan, Amitabh, 199
BAFTAs, 305
Bagnall, Nick, 304
Baháʼí Faith, 185
Baker, Josephine, 53–6, 110, 222
Bale, Christian, 296
Baltimore, Maryland, 32
Bangalore, Karnataka, 175
Bangladesh, 12–13, 135–6, 144–51, 163, 171, 214
Banksy, 194
Bano, Mahjabeen, 308
Barak, Ehud, 109–10
Barbados, 232, 234
Barbary states, 28
Barber, Cedric, 91–2
beauty products, 54, 70, 78, 199
Bedouins, 246
Beirut, Lebanon, 110

346

INDEX

Belcombe, Mariana, 213
Bell, Ellis, 105
Bengal, 12–13, 73, 149, 165–8, 314–15
Benin, 26
Berry, Halle, 296
Bethlehem, 193–200, 202
Beverley, Henry, 167
Beyoncé, 55
Bible, 27, 190, 205, 206, 296
Big, Martina, 280
Big Momma's House (2000 film), 111
Billions, 304
Billy Elliot, 306
biracial people, *see* mixed-race people
bisexual people, 6, 139, 154, 303
Black Like Me (Griffin), 56–60, 108, 190, 271, 313
Black Lives Matter, 26
Black Migration (1916–70), 43–4
black nationalism, 45–6
Black Panther (2018 film), 298
black people, 4–5, 9
    apartheid and, 11, 47, 65–72
    black experience, 14
    cultural appropriation and, 53–4, 275–87
    hair, 88, 281, 282–3, 285, 295–6
    Jim Crow and, 41–63, 65, 275, 293–4
    light skinned, 3, 9, 29–39, 41–52, 293
    mixed-race people as, 3, 4–5, 77–8, 86–91
    One Drop rule and, 44–7, 65, 69, 70, 188
    passing as, 16, 52–4, 56–60, 85–91, 92
    performing arts and, 297–301
    slavery of, 3, 8, 25, 26, 29–40
    white-passing, 2, 3, 29–52, 60–72, 79–82, 293–4
Black Pete, 277
Black September, 110
Black Skin, White Masks (Fanon), 223, 229
blackface, 53–4, 275–9, 295
'blackfishers', 280–81, 289
BlacKkKlansman (2018 film), 222–3
Bloody Sunday (1972), 14
Bloomsbury Group, 125
Blunt, Emily, 306
Bob the Builder, 129
Bohemian Rhapsody (2018 film), 303, 304
Bollywood, 172, 279, 292, 301, 307–9
Bong Joon-ho, 210–11, 292
Bonham Carter, Helena, 306
Book of Deuteronomy, 152
Book of Exodus, 27
Booker Prize, 272
Boston, Massachusetts, 30, 34
Bowdre, Karen, 293
Bowen, Essex, 104
Boy Erased (2018 film), 304
Boys Don't Cry (1999 film), 113, 114, 115, 116, 302
Brahma, 318, 320
braids, 282–3, 285
Brandon Teena Story, The (1998 documentary), 115
Brathwaite, Kamau, 232–3

347

INDEX

Brazil, 65, 72, 75–8, 88, 89, 180–83, 311
Breakfast at Tiffany's (1961 film), 295
Brexit, 270
British Broadcasting Corporation (BBC), 87, 88, 135, 157–8, 215, 222, 231, 280, 311
British Empire, 1, 6–7, 79, 226, 228, 229
   American colonies (1607–1776), 28, 79, 205
   East India Company, 241
   gender morals, 123, 136, 145
   Indian colonies (1612–1947), *see* British India
   race science in, 122, 123
   slavery in, 28, 79, 95, 122, 155, 276
   Trinidad colony (1797–1962), 155, 231
   Uganda protectorate (1894–1962), 244
British Film Institute, 80
British India (1612–1947), 12, 13, 248
   Amritsar massacre (1919), 246, 278
   band parties, 135
   Buggery Act in, 136, 145
   Burton in, 241, 244–5, 248–9
   caste in, 173, 257
   Crown rule established (1858), 242, 257
   hijras in, 133, 134
   homosexuality in, 136, 157
   Kipling in, 1, 251–65
   literature, 1, 227
   Partition (1947), 12, 165
   Penal Code (1862), 157
   religious pluralism and, 257–8
   socio-cultural white-passing in, 248–9, 263–4
   Thuggees, 74
Brixton, London, 1–7, 10, 11, 14, 16, 228, 289
Broadway, 275, 300, 305
'Brokeback Mountain' (Proulx), 140–43, 155, 160
Brokeback Mountain (2005 film), 303
Brontë sisters, 227
Brontë, Emily, 105
Brooklyn, New York City, 61
Brown v. Board of Education (1954), 56
Broyard, Anatole, 17, 60–63, 84–6, 89, 105, 164, 168–9, 209, 219, 315
Broyard, Bliss, 17, 60, 62, 84–6, 90, 93, 164, 168–9, 170
Broyard, Shirley, 62, 86
Brzostowska, Aga, 280, 281
Buddhism, 13, 166, 251, 252, 254, 257, 258
Buffong, Michael, 90, 92
Buggery Act (1533), 136, 145
burakumin, 176–80, 183–4
Burakumin Liberation League, 179
Burton, Richard Francis, 241–9, 252, 253, 261, 263, 284, 286

Caine, Michael, 306
Cambridge University, 232
Canada, 34–5, 277–9

INDEX

Cape Town, South Africa, 71
Caribbean, *see* West Indies
'Caribbean Discourse' (Glissant), 39
cassare, 27
caste, 9, 18, 74, 109, 144, 146, 167, 173–84
   in Bangladesh, 146
   in India, 74, 159, 167, 173–6, 181–4, 210, 251
   in Japan, 176–84
   job interviews and, 174, 179
   marriage and, 174, 178, 179
   performing arts and, 292, 308
Catholicism, 18, 100–103, 189, 196
censuses, 18
Chakraborty, Mithun, 307
Change.org, 302
Chapman, Michael, 69
Charles, Prince of Wales, 95
Charleston dance, 53
Château des Milandes, France, 55
Chile, 75
Chilling Out (1990 documentary), 87–8
China, 170, 175, 176, 192
Chosen Exile, A (Hobbs), 10, 46
'chosen exile', 15
Christianity, 18, 267, 268
   Armenian Church, 186
   Church of the Nativity, 193, 197
   conversion to, 188, 189, 196
   homosexuality and, 149, 152
   Jews and, 186, 189
   Old Testament, 190, 205, 206
   in Palestine, 193–7
   Pope Joan story, 100–103, 245, 292
   slavery and, 27, 39, 40
   in Trinidad, 156
Christmas, 277
Church of the Nativity, Bethlehem, 193, 197
Churchill, Caryl, 102, 103
cigars, 104, 249
Citizenship Amendment Bill (2019), 171
Civil Rights movement (1954–68), 44, 45, 46, 53, 55, 220, 295
'civilising missions', 27, 242
class, 3, 4, 10, 11, 15, 17, 109, 156, 267
   accents, 111
   in *Albert Nobbs*, 107
   in Bangladesh, 146
   Craft and, 30, 31
   Gunness and, 155, 156
   in Hinduism, 74, 174–6
   in India, 74, 159, 167, 173–6, 181–2, 210
   in Japan, 176–84
   job interviews and, 174, 179
   Markle and, 95
   marriage and, 174, 178, 179
   performing arts and, 291, 301, 302
   sexual freedom and, 212–15
   in United Kingdom, 212–15
class-passing, 30, 31, 74, 95, 107, 117, 156, 267
   in India, 174–6, 210
   in Japan, 178–83
   performing arts and, 291, 301, 302

INDEX

Cleopatra, Queen of the Ptolemaic Kingdom, 295
Close, Glenn, 107
'coconuts', 224
code-switching, 156, 220
Coel, Michaela, 90
Coldplay, 280–81
collective passing, 185–208
Colman, Olivia, 303
colonialism, 1, 6–8, 158, 206–7
   divide and rule, 66, 173
   queer people and, 137, 145, 157
   reverse passing and, 241–9
   slavery and, 26–8, 66
'coloured' people, 66–7, 68, 69–70
Commonwealth, 6
Concrete Poem (Chapman), 69
Confucianism, 177
Conrad, Joseph, 232
Conundrum (Morris), 130
cowboys, 274
Craft, Ellen, 30–34, 35, 38–9, 44, 146, 147, 258
Craft, William, 30–34, 36, 38–9, 147
Craig, Daniel, 297
Crazy Rich Asians (2018 film), 298
Creole people, 25, 62
Cross, Donna Woolfolk, 102
cross-dressing, 100, 108, 110–12
Crown, The, 306
Crowther, Bosley, 295
Crying Game, The (1992 film), 131–3, 302
crypto-Jews, 189–91, 196, 203, 204

Cuba, 311
Cullen, Countée, 49
cultural appropriation, 14, 17, 220, 239–40, 243, 261, 267–89
Cumberbatch, Benedict, 306

Dabydeen, David, 235
Daily Mail, 95, 221
Dalits, 173, 174, 183
Danish Girl, The (2015 film), 117, 129, 302
Danse Sauvage, La (Baker), 54, 55
Davids, M. Fakhry, 224–5, 226, 268, 283, 288
Davidson, Jaye, 302
Dear White People (2014 film), 276
Declaration of Independence, US (1776), 47
Dehlavi, Mumtaz Jehan Begum, 308
dekasegi, 180–83
Dench, Judi, 306
Denmark, 213
Dennis, Benjamin and Anita, 25
Depp, Johnny, 296
Deuteronomy, Book of, 152
Dhaka, Bangladesh, 135, 163
Dheisheh refugee camp, Palestine, 199
Dillon, Asia Kate, 304
'Disguised' (Singer), 151–4, 212
Dislocating the Color Line (Kawash), 92
Disney, 296, 298, 301
Disobedience (Alderman), 147
divide and rule, 66, 173
djinns, 147, 149

350

INDEX

DNA (deoxyribonucleic acid), 17, 86, 90–91, 94, 170
Doctor Who, xiv, 297
Dolezal, Rachel, 16, 284–7, 288, 289, 295–6
Doomsday (Herbert), 40
Dosti (1964 film), 308
drag, 110
Duke, David, 223
Dumezweni, Noma, 298
Durga, 74
Durga Puja, 317–20
Dus Lakh (1966 film), 308
Dutt, Barkha, 279
Dwyer, Rachel, 308
dybbuks, 152

East India Company, 241
East Pakistan (1947–71), 12–13
Eddo-Lodge, Reni, 263, 284, 288, 297, 298
Edgerton, Joel, 296, 304
Edo Japan (1603–1868), 176–7
Egypt, 27, 192, 205–6, 245, 248, 271, 296
Elba, Idris, 297
Elbe, Lili, 116, 117, 122, 129, 146, 302
electroshock therapy, 149
Eliot, George, 105
Elizabeth I, Queen of England and Ireland, 227
Empire Windrush, 79
English language, 43, 221–3, 225, 228–30, 273
Entertainment Weekly, 305
equality laws, 18
'eternal martyrdom', 287

eugenics, 44
Eugenides, Jeffrey, 118–20, 128, 129, 135, 146
Evans, Mary Ann, 105
Evaristo, Bernardine, 272–3, 274
Exodus, Book of, 27, 205–6
Exodus (2014 film), 296

fairy tales, 298
Falls City, Nebraska, 113, 117, 148
Family Guy, 301
Fanon, Frantz, 223–5, 226, 229, 232, 236, 263
Far Eastern Economic Review, 178
Farley, Audrey, 244
Favourite, The (2018 film), 303
Fellowes, Julian, 306
feminism, 5, 100, 131
Fiddler on the Roof, The, 306
film, *see under* performing arts
'Final Form' (Sampa the Great), xiv, 286
Financial Times, 247
Floyd, George, 26, 301
football, 129
Foreign Policy, 78
Forster, Edward Morgan, 227
France
    Baker in, 53–5, 222
    Indian colonies (1664–1954), 104
    Revolutionary Wars (1792–1802), 104
    Stein in, 217
    World War II, (1939–45), 55
Freud, Sigmund, 133, 216, 217
Fridge, The (gay nightclub), Brixton, 6

INDEX

Fugitive Slave Act (1850), 30
Fulani people, 282

Gandhi, Mohandas 'Mahatma', 174
Gandhi (1982 film), 295
Ganesha, 319
Garber, Marjorie, 112, 130, 133
Gates Jr, Henry Louis, 61
Gaza, 159, 160
gender, 99–112, 113–37
   children and, 128–9
   confirmation surgery, 116, 122, 124, 128, 130, 134, 302
   dysphoria, 9, 11, 102, 117, 128
   female-passing, 2, 99, 100, 108–11, 116, 117, 120–37, 143–4
   fluidity, 4, 6, 106, 123, 126, 134, 136, 154, 217
   intersex people, 115, 118–19, 133
   male-passing, 2, 99–108, 113–17, 122
   performing arts and, 110, 297
   sexuality and, 117, 121, 216, 217, 218
   third gender, 133–7
   trans people, 9, 18, 112, 113–17, 120–33, 140, 212, 302–3
Gentleman Jack, 212–15
Gentleman Jack (2019 series), 215
gentlemen's clubs, 103–4
George III, King of the United Kingdom, 95
Georgia, United States, 30, 34, 56, 91

Germany, 55, 171, 188, 283, 289, 312
Get Out (2017 film), 300
Ghana, 28
Ginsberg, Elaine, 114
Gladstone, William, 155
Glissant, Édouard, 39
globalisation, 7
Globe, Liverpool, 123
Golden Globes, 305
Golden Temple, Amritsar, 278–9
Goldman Sachs, 221
Google Earth, 179
Grant, Madison, 44
Great Migration (1916–70), 43–4
Greece, Ancient, 99
Greek Orthodox Church, 195
Green, Sophie, 120–31, 143–4, 313
Green Book (2018 film), 303
Greenwich Village, New York City, 61
Greer, Germaine, 131
Grey's Anatomy, 303
'griffes', 44
Griffin, John Howard, 56–60, 108, 190, 271, 313
Group Areas Act (1950), 66
Guardian, 90, 299
Guest, Robert, 178–80
Guimont, Edward, 244
Gunness, Christopher, 155–60, 209, 231
Guyana, 233
Gyllenhaal, Jake, 303

Hadjian, Avedis, 186, 187

INDEX

hair, 88, 281, 282–3, 285, 295–6
Hall, Radclyffe, 216
Halloween, 282
Halwani, Raja, 152–3
Hamilton, 300
Hamilton, Alexander, 300
Hamlet (Shakespeare), 297, 299
hammams, 245
Handmaid's Tale, The, 304
Harar Emirate (1647–1887), 246, 279
Hardy, Thomas, 1, 227
Hare Krishnas, 220, 269
Harlem, New York City, 50
Harlem Renaissance (c. 1918–37), 49–52, 235
Harris, Wilson, 233
Harrison, Benjamin, 47
Harrison, William Henry, 46
Harry Potter and the Cursed Child, 298–9
Harry, Duke of Sussex, 94–6
Harvard University, 130
Hattenstone, Simon, 90
Hattiesburg, Mississippi, 57
HBO, 215
Hearth and Home, 37
Hebrew, 195, 197, 198, 201, 202
Hemingway, Ernest, 55
Henry VIII, King of England and Ireland, 145
Herbert, George, 40
'Heritage' (Cullen), 49
hijras, 18, 133–7
Hinduism, 12–13, 144, 146, 159, 164–8, 171–6, 313, 315–20
 avatars, 74, 164
 in Bangladesh, 146, 148, 163, 215
 caste and, 167–8, 173–6, 181–2, 183–4, 251, 292
 Durga Puja, 317–20
 in India, 12–13, 74, 164–8, 171–6, 181–4, 251, 257, 292
 Islam and, 165–8, 171–2
 jatra, 165
 Kali, 74
 Krishnalila, 257
 Mahabharata, 136, 164
 marriage, 146, 148, 163, 215
 Vedas, 173, 318, 320
Hindustan, 12–13, 172, 249
hip-hop music, 89
Hobbs, Allyson, 10, 46, 48, 51, 68
Hollywood, 9, 275, 292–8, 300
Holocaust (1941–5), 45, 188
Homeland Security, 196, 197
Homer, 109
homosexuality, 4, 5, 6, 9, 16, 107, 124, 139–60, 212–18
 'coming out', 3, 4, 5, 6, 144, 150, 152–3
 'fixing' of, 149, 304
 gender and, 117, 121, 216, 217, 218
 as 'illness', 147, 149, 304
 performing arts and, 303–5
 straight-passing, 139–60
 trans people and, 117, 121
Hopkins, Anthony, 296, 306
Hours, The (2002 film), 303
Howards End (1992 film), 312
Hughes, Langston, 267
Human Stain, The (2003 film), 296
Human Stain, The (Roth), 62

INDEX

Huns, 7
Hurlbut, William, 294
Hurst, Fannie, 293, 294

'I Have a Dream' speech (1963), 55
Iberia, 188–93, 196, 203, 204
identifying, 4, 15, 16
    cultural appropriation and, 240, 265, 268, 284
    gender and, 100
    race and, 85, 226, 240
Iliad (Homer), 109
Imitation of Life (1934 film), 293–4, 315
Immigration Act (1924), 180
In the Castle of My Skin (Lamming), 234–5
indentured labour, 28, 155, 156, 158, 233
India
    Bollywood, 172, 279, 292, 301, 307–9
    British colonies (1612–1947), *see* British India
    call centres in, 15
    caste in, 74, 159, 167, 171–6, 181–2, 183–4, 292
    Citizenship Amendment Bill (2019), 171
    French colonies (1664–1954), 104
    hijra community, 18, 133–7
    Hinduism in, 12–13, 74, 164–8, 171–6, 181–4, 251, 257, 292
    homosexuality in, 157
    Islam in, 165–8, 171–2, 257, 307–9
    Modi government (2014–), 13, 171, 279
    Parsis, 251, 304, 312
    Partition (1947), 12, 165
    Penal Code (1862), 157
    religious pluralism in, 257–8
    saris, 17
    Sikhism in, 168
    skin colour in, 65, 72–4
    third gender ruling (2014), 137
    Thuggees, 74
    Trinidad, migration to, 155–7
    Trudeau's visit (2018), 278–9
    UK, migration to, 1, 4–5
inferiority complex, 224–5, 228
Inglorious Empire (Tharoor), 257
integration, 220
Internal Racism (Davids), 224
internalised homophobia, 140, 143
internalised racism, 58–9, 96, 188, 224–5, 228, 231–2, 283
internalised whiteness, x, 233, 268
intersex people, 115, 118–20, 133
Intifada, Second (2000–5), 193, 195
inversion, 216, 217, 218
Iran, 185
Irish Republican Army (IRA), 132
Islam, 12–13, 46, 144
    Ahmadis and, 185
    al-Andalus (711–1492), 188–9
    Burton and, 241–9
    caste and, 167–8, 174
    conversion to, 167–8, 188

INDEX

cultural appropriation and, 241–9, 280–81
djinns in, 147, 149
Hajj, 241–9
Hinduism and, 165–8, 171
homosexuality and, 147, 149, 150, 159
in India, 165–8, 171–2, 257, 307–9
Islamophobia, 46, 171
Sufism, 136
Israel, 45, 109, 158, 159, 193–203
Izzard, Eddie, 15, 111

Jacir Palace, Bethlehem, 194
Jackson, Michael, 275, 282
Jackson, Samuel Leroy, 300
Jaffrey, Syed Ishtiaq Ahmed, 308
Jagdeep, 308
Jallianwala Bagh massacre (1919), 246, 278
James Bond, 297
Jamieson, George, 124
Japan, 110, 176–84, 295
jatra, 165
jazz music, 52–3, 63
Jefferson, Thomas, 44, 69, 204
Jenner, Caitlyn, 130
Jerkins, Morgan, 54, 55
Jerusalem, 128, 188, 191, 192, 193–203
Jewish people, 13, 16, 83, 93, 188, 314
  Ashkenazim, 195, 202
  conversion, 188, 189, 196
  crypto-Jews, 189–91, 196, 203, 204
  Egypt, captivity in, 27, 192, 205–6
  gentile-passing, 9, 188–93
  homosexuality and, 147, 149, 151–4
  Iberian, 188–93, 196, 203, 204
  Mizrahim, 195
  Nazi persecution (1933–45), 45, 171, 188, 312
  New Christians, 189, 196
  New Jews, 191
  Passover, 192, 203
  Pyramids, building of, 27, 192
  Second Temple (c. 516 BCE and 70 CE), 188
  Sephardim, 188–93, 196, 203, 204
  Shabbat, 316
  Yom Kippur, 319
  Zionism, 205–6
Jhabvala, Cyrus, 312
Jhabvala, Ruth Prawer, 227, 312–16
Jim Crow America (1865–1965), 41–63, 65, 70, 275
Joan, Pope, 100–103, 245, 292
job interviews, 45, 174
John, Elton, 157
Johnson, James Weldon, 47–8, 50, 87, 88
Johnson, Samuel, 91
Johnston, Harry, 244
Jolie, Angelina, 55, 295, 296
Jonas, Joyce, 233
Jones, Alice, 293
Jones, Suranne, 215
Jonker, Henk, 109

INDEX

Jordan, Neil, 131
Judaism, *see under* Jewish people
'Jump Jim Crow' (Rice), 275
Jungle Book, The (Kipling), 252, 255, 258, 259–61, 264

Kabuki theatre, 110
Kafka, Franz, 169, 232, 316
Kali, 74
Kaluuya, Daniel, 300
Kama Sutra, 136
Kardashian, Kim, 282–3
Kawash, Samira, 92
kayastho, 146
Kazi, Badruddin Jamaluddin, 308
Keats, John, 232
Keeping Up with the Kardashians, 130
Kerala, India, 5
Khan, Aamir, 308
Khan, Gauri, 172
Khan, Hamid Ali, 308
Khan, Irrfan, 308
Khan, Muhammad Yusuf, 308
Khan, Saif Ali, 308
Khan, Salman, 308
Khan, Sanjay, 308
Khan, Shah Abbas, 308
Khan, Shah Rukh, 172, 308
Khoesan people, 66
Kidman, Nicole, 303
Kim (Kipling), 1, 170, 252, 253–8, 260, 262, 264, 286
King, Martin Luther, 53, 55, 235, 302
Kingsley, Ben, 295
Kingston upon Thames, Surrey, 91

Kipling, Rudyard, 1, 3, 16, 170, 251–65, 271
  Jungle Book, The, 252, 255, 258, 259–61, 264
  Kim, 1, 170, 252, 253–8, 260, 262, 264, 286
  'Miss Youghal's Sais' (Kipling), 259, 261–2
  Something of Myself, 251, 253, 254
  'White Man's Burden, The', 252, 255, 256, 264
Kolkata, British India, 1
Kpelle people, 206
Krishna, 74, 164–5, 257
Krishnalila, 257
Kristallnacht (1938), 171
Kru people, 206
Krug, Jessica, 16
Kshatriyas, 173, 181
Ku Klux Klan, 57
Kumar, Dilip, 308
Kumari, Meena, 308
Kumasi, Ashanti Empire, 28

Lacan, Jacques, 232
Lady Chatterley's Lover (Lawrence), 218
Lahiri, Jhumpa, 273
Lahore, British India, 1
Lakshmi, 319
Lakshmi, Padma, 282
Lamming, George, 234
Larsen, Nella, 49–52, 59, 62, 70, 117, 143, 179, 235, 262, 294, 315
Laux, Charles, 115
Lawrence, Thomas Edward, 241, 271

INDEX

League of Nations, 283
Lebanon, 110
Ledger, Heath, 303
Lee, Spike, 222
Lennon, Anthony Ekundayo, 17, 86–91, 94, 96, 221, 285, 300, 314
Lennon, Vincent, 87, 96
Leo IV, Pope, 101
lesbianism, 4, 6, 212–18
   in Bangladesh, 144–51, 163, 214
   masculinity and, 216–18
   performing arts and, 303–5
   in United Kingdom, 124, 212–15
Liberia, 25, 203–7
Lincoln, Abraham, 38
Lincoln, Nebraska, 113, 117
Lipschutz, Alejandro, 75
Lister, Anne, 212–15
literacy, 31, 37, 175
Little House on the Prairie, 298
Liu Yifei, 301
Liverpool, England, 120, 122–4, 126, 127, 143, 304
Livingstone, David, 244
London, England, 228
   BBC in, 157, 231
   black community, 80, 87, 234, 269
   blackface in, 276
   Brixton, 1–7, 10, 11, 13–14, 16, 228, 289
   Jewish community, 83, 147
   multi-culturalism in, 269
   Notting Hill Carnival, 269
   Notting Hill riots (1958), 80

London Illustrated News, 34
Lone Ranger, The (2013 film), 296
Lonely Londoners, The (Selvon), 13, 234
Long Walk to Freedom (Mandela), 68
Lotter, John, 114
Louisiana, United States, 56, 62, 63, 305
Love, Loni, 286
'Love Jihad', 172

Macaulay, Thomas Babington, 1st Baron, 157
'Macaulay's Children', 156
Macon, Georgia, 30
Madhubala, 308
Mahabharata, 136, 164
Mahishashur, 318
Maimonides, Moses, 188, 190
makeup, 54, 70, 78, 199
Major, John, 14
'Make America Great Again', 46
'Making America White Again' (Morrison), 45
Malcolm X, 45
Malek, Rami, 303, 304
Mamdani, Mahmood, 66
Mandela, Nelson, 68
Mannan, Xulhaz, 144–5
March on Washington (1963), 53, 55, 235
Margaret, Countess of Snowdon, 306
Marie, Queen consort of Denmark, 213
Markle, Meghan, 93–6
marriage
   arranged, 145–6, 150

357

INDEX

in Bangladesh, 145–6, 150, 151
cassare, 27
caste and, 174
homosexual, 145–6, 148, 150, 215
in Jim Crow America (1865–1965), 44, 49, 293
in India, 73–4, 174
mixed-race, 44, 49, 155–6
mixed-religion, 146, 148, 163, 172
Singh maid murder case (2013), 172
skin tone and, 73–4
Stowe on, 37
straight-passing and, 140, 145–8, 150, 151, 158–60
marranos, 189
Martin, Christopher, 280–81
Martin, Trayvon, 26
Martinique, 39, 223
masculinity
  homosexuality and, 141, 142, 145, 155, 212, 213, 216–19
  male-passing and, 105, 114, 119, 209
mass passing, 185–208
Matisse, Henri, 217
McBratney, John, 258, 259, 261
McKellen, Ian, 306
McTeer, Janet, 107
meat consumption, 11
Mecca, 241–2, 245–6, 247, 248, 249
Medina, 241–2, 245, 248, 249
melanin, 56, 58, 71, 286
Memoirs of My People (Schwarz), 190–91

men
  female-passing, 2, 99, 100, 108–11, 116, 117, 120–37, 143–4
  gait, 119, 146
  gentlemen's clubs, 103–4
  passing as, 2, 99–108, 113–17, 125, 212
Merchant of Venice, The (Shakespeare), 100
Mercury, Freddie, 303, 304
Metamorphoses (Ovid), 99
Metamorphosis (Kafka), 169, 316
Mexico, 130, 274
Mezzrow, Mezz, xv, 53, 324
Middle Passage, 40, 191, 235, 331, 343
Middlesex (Eugenides), 118–20, 128, 129, 135, 146
Mighty Heart, A (2007 film), 295
Milk, Harvey, 303
Milk (2008 film), 303
minstrel shows, 53, 275–6, 277
Miranda, Lin-Manuel, 300
Mirren, Helen, 306
miscegenation, 46, 65, 204, 293–4
Misérables, Les, 306
'Miss Youghal's Sais' (Kipling), 259, 261–2
Mississippi, United States, 56
mixed-race people, 83–96
  apartheid and, 66–7
  black-passing, 4–5, 77–8, 85–91, 92
  in Brazil, 75–8
  Jim Crow and, 58

INDEX

One Drop rule and, 44–7, 65, 69, 70, 188
   slavery and, 29–40, 70
   in South Africa, 66–7, 70–71
   in United Kingdom, 83–4, 86–92
   in United States, 29–40, 44–7, 58, 65, 69, 70, 84–6
   white-passing, 2, 3, 29–39, 41–52, 60–63, 70, 84
Mizrahim, 195
Modi, Narendra, 13, 279
mofussil, 4, 6, 214, 228
Mohammed, Prophet of Islam, 165
Monster (2003 film), 303
Montefiore, Jan, 252
Montgomery, Alabama, 59
Moore, George, 107
Morris, Jan, 130
morris dancing, 276–7
Morrison, Toni, 45, 225
Moses, 205–6, 296
Mowgli (2018 film), 260
Mrs Doubtfire (1993 film), 111
Msamati, Lucian, 300
Mughal Empire (1526–1857), 136, 166, 167, 309
Mulan (2020 film), 301
'mulattoes' 30, 35, 36, 44, 70
Muller, Salomé, 33
Mulligan, Carey, 306
multi-culturalism, 220, 269
Multicultural London English, 17
Munich Olympics (1972), 110
Murray, Douglas, 270
'Muse of History, The' (Walcott), 227

Muska, Susan, 115
My Nine Lives (Jhabvala), 312–16
'Mythic Mannish Lesbian, The' (Newton), 216

NAACP, 46, 284
Nabataeans, 192
Naipaul, Vidiadhar Surajprasad, 191, 228, 231–2
National Health Service (NHS), 130
Native Americans, 17, 35–6, 296
'natives', 224
Nazi Germany (1933–45), 55, 171, 188, 289, 312
Nazrul Islam, Kazi, 165–6, 167, 169
Nebraska, United States, 113, 117, 148
Netherlands, 16, 25, 66, 104, 109, 277
New Christians, 189, 196
New Orleans, Louisiana, 56, 63, 305
New York City, New York, 49–52, 61
New York Times, 60, 61, 295
New Yorker, The, 61, 94
New Zealand, 6, 246
Newton, Esther, 216
Neymar, 76
Nigeria, 273
nisei, 180–83
Nissen, Marvin 'Tom', 114
Northern Ireland, 14, 131–3
Northup, Solomon, 33
Notting Hill, London Carnival, 269

riots (1958), 80
nternalised whiteness, 233, 268
Nyame, 23

Obama, Barack, 45, 93, 94, 95, 221–2
'octoroons', 44, 85
Ogidi, Ann, 80
okapi, 244
Ólafsdottir, Gréta, 115
Olaudah Equiano, 91
Old Testament, 190, 205, 206, 296
Oliver, Jamie, 271
Oliver!, 306
Oliver Twist (Dickens), 156
Olivier, Laurence, 278, 295
Olusoga, David, 91
Olympic Games
  1972 Munich, 110
  2016 Rio, 76
One Drop (Broyard), 85
One Drop rule, 44–7, 65, 70, 188
Orange is the New Black, 304
Orientalism, 241, 242, 252, 253, 258–9, 263, 279
Orlando (1992 film), 125–6
Orlando (Woolf), 108, 124–7, 216, 218–19, 315
Orwell, George, 252
Oscars, 94, 114, 276, 278, 295, 297, 303
#OscarsSoWhite movement, 300
Othello (Shakespeare), 91, 278, 295, 297
Ottoman Empire (1299–1922), 7, 185, 186, 188, 283

Oudh Kingdom (1732–1859), 257
Ovid, 99
Oxford University, 155, 157, 231, 232

Pakistan, 12, 136–7, 171, 185, 221, 308
Palestine, 159, 160, 193–203
Palgrave, William Gifford, 241–2
pansexuality, 124, 154, 305
Papacy, 100–103, 245, 292
Parasite (2019 film), 210–11, 292
Paris, France, 53–5
Parsis, 251, 304, 312
Passage to India, A (Forster), 227
passing, 1–19
  amnesia and, 39, 48, 57, 62, 72, 230
  apartheid and, 11, 47, 65–72
  caste/class, 9, 30, 31, 74, 95, 107, 117, 156, 174–83
  gender, 99–112, 113–37
  Jim Crow and, 41–63, 65, 293–4
  mass, 185–208
  performing arts and, 291–6
  religion, 163–4, 171–2, 185–203, 307–8
  reverse, *see* reverse passing
  sexuality, 139–60
  slavery and, 3, 8–9, 26, 29–39
  socio-cultural, 209–36
  Windrush generation and, 79–82
Passing (Larsen), 49–52, 59, 62, 70, 117, 143, 179, 235, 262, 294

INDEX

Passing of the Great Race, The (Grant), 44
Passover, 192, 203
Patterson, Eric, 142
Paxman, Jeremy, 247
Pearl, Mariane, 295
Peele, Jordan, 300
Peirce, Kimberly, 114
Pelé, 76, 182
Pennsylvania, United States, 34, 38
performing arts, 291–310
    black people and, 297–301
    blackface, 53–4, 275–9, 295
    class and, 291, 292, 301, 302, 306–7
    queer people and, 301–5
    religion and, 307–9
    whitewashing, 292–6
    women and, 110
Perry, Grayson, 112
Persia, 166, 168, 175, 316
Philadelphia, Pennsylvania, 34
Picasso, Pablo, 55, 217
Picton, Cesar, 91
Pink Floyd, 194
Piper, Adrian, 46
Pirojpur, Bangladesh, 144, 148
'play-whites', 68, 69, 70, 210
Playing in the Light (Wicomb), 47, 69, 70, 71–2, 84, 93
Poitier, Sidney, 88, 295
poll tax, 14
Pondicherry, India, 104
Pope Joan (Cross), 102
Population Registration Act (1950), 66, 68, 69
Portugal, 27

Potter, Sally, 125
Prada, 55
Premchand, Munshi, 173–4, 258
Production Code Administration, 293
Protestantism, 18, 100, 207, 248
Proulx, Annie, 140–43, 155, 160
psychoexistential complex, 225
Pudd'nhead Wilson (Twain), 44
Puerto Rico, 61, 300
punthi, 168
Purusha, 173
Pushkar, Rajasthan, 317
Pyramids, Egypt, 27, 192

'quadroons', 44, 70
Queen, 303, 304
queer people, 2, 3, 9, 139–60
    bisexuality, 6, 139, 154, 303
    'coming out', 3, 4, 5, 6, 144, 150, 152–3
    disowning of, 150
    drag, 110
    female-passing, 116, 117, 120–37, 143–4
    'fixing' of, 149, 304
    homosexuality, 4, 5, 6, 9, 16, 117, 121, 124, 139–54, 212–18
    'illness', labeling as, 129, 147, 152, 304
    male-passing, 106–8, 113–18, 125, 212
    'possession', labeling as, 147, 149, 152
    religion and, 16, 147, 149–50, 152–3
    straight-passing, 139–60

INDEX

trans people, 9, 18, 112, 113–17, 120–33, 140, 212, 302–3
transmasculinity, 212–18
Quran, 150

race science, 26, 28, 180, 283
race trials, 67–70
racialist hierarchy, 283–4
Radha, 165
Ragland, Doria, 93, 94, 95
Rai, Aishwarya, 199
Raj Quartet, The (Scott), 227
Ramallah, Palestine, 198, 201
Ramaswamy, Chitra, 299
Ramesses II, Pharaoh of Egypt, 296
Rana, Bindiya, 136
rap music, 89
rape, 44, 58, 100
Ratelband, Emile, xv, 16
Redmayne, Edward, 302–3, 306
Reed, Lewis 'Lou', 120
refugees, 4, 8, 279
religion, 18
    queer people and, 16, 147, 149–50, 152–3
    passing, 163–4, 171–2, 185–203
    white people and, 16
reverse passing, 1, 3, 9, 16, 239–49, 251–65, 267–89, 292–6
    affirmative action and, 77–8
    Araújo, 77–8
    Broyard, 85–6
    Burton, 241–9
    colonialism and, 241–9

cultural appropriation, 14, 17, 220, 239–40, 243, 261, 267–89
female-passing as, 108–11
Kipling, 1, 3, 16, 251–65
Griffin, 56–60
performing arts and, 292–6
trans people and, 131
Rhimes, Shonda, 303
Rhinelander, Leonard, 293
Rice, Thomas Dartmouth, 275
Rig Veda, 318
Rio Olympics (2016), 76
River With No Bridge, The (Sumii), 178
Robben Island, South Africa, 71
Rohy, Valerie, 111
Rome, Ancient (753 BCE–476 CE), 28, 99, 188
Romeo and Juliet (Shakespeare), 304
Room With A View, A (1985 film), 312
Rooney, Mickey, 295
Roth, Philip, 62, 296
Rousseau, Nicole, 3–4
Rowling, J.K., 298–9
Royal Geographical Society, 243, 245
Running a Thousand Miles for Freedom (Craft), 30–34, 38–9

Sackville-West, Vita, 125, 218
Said, Edward, 252, 258–9, 264
Saint Nicholas Parade, 277
Salieri, Antonio, 300
Salonica, 191
Salvador, Brazil, 77

INDEX

Sampa the Great, xiv, 286
Samurai, 177, 181–2
san benito, 189
Sancho, Ignatius, 91
São Paulo, Brazil, 180
Sapphire (1959 film), 80–81, 117, 230, 294
Saraswathi, 319
Schama, Simon, 204
Schwarz, Leo, 190–91
scientific racism, 26, 28, 85, 91, 122, 180, 283
Scott, Paul, 227
Scott, Ridley, 296
Sean Penn, 303
Second Intifada (2000–5), 193, 195
Secret Nation (Hadjian), 186
Self-Made Man (Vincent), 104
Selvon, Sam, 13, 234
Sephardim, 188–93
Sex and Character (Weininger), 216
sex reassignment surgery, 116, 122, 124, 128, 130, 134, 302
'Sexual Aberrations, The' (Freud), 216, 217
sexuality, 3
  bisexuality, 6, 139, 154, 303
  fluidity, 4, 6, 106, 123, 126, 139, 154
  gender and, 117, 121, 216, 217, 218
  homosexuality, 4, 5, 6, 9, 16, 117, 121, 124, 139–60, 212–18
  pansexuality, 124, 154
  performing arts and, 291, 302

Shaffer, Peter, 300
Shakespeare, William
  As You Like It, 100
  gender and, 100, 105–6, 111
  Hamlet, 297, 299
  Merchant of Venice, The, 100
  Othello, 91, 278, 295, 297
  Romeo and Juliet, 304
  sexuality and, 100, 105–6
  Tempest, The, 8, 105, 227, 228, 229, 236
  Twelfth Night, 100, 105–6
Sheeran, Edward, 271
Shia Islam, 185, 257
Shibden Hall, Yorkshire, x, xv, 213, 215
Shikoku, Japan, 179–80
Shinto, 177
Shirley, Don, 303
Shiva, 74, 148, 318
Shriver, Lionel, 272–3, 274, 275
Shudras, 173
Sierra Leone, 205
Sikhism, 168, 278
Silvermint, Daniel, 153, 154
Simpsons, The, 301
Singer, Isaac Bashevis, 151–4, 212
Singh, Dhananjay, 172
skin tone, 86, 283–4
  in Brazil, 75
  in France, 53–4
  in India, 72–4, 166, 168
  in Palestine, 199
  in South Africa, 67, 70, 71
  in United Kingdom, 92, 93–6
  in United States, 9, 29–39, 41–52, 61, 93
Slave Compensation Commission, 155

INDEX

slavery, slaves, 3, 8–9, 11, 24–40, 95, 122, 155, 203–7, 276
   abolition, 38, 41, 45, 77, 79, 95, 155, 180
   Anansi and, 9, 24–6, 29
   as 'civilising mission', 27
   guilt and, 58
   literacy, 31, 37
   Middle Passage, 40, 191
   One Drop rule, 44–7, 65, 69, 70, 188
   race and, 26, 28, 29–40
   rape of, 44, 58
   relocation to Africa, 203–7
   passing and, 3, 8–9, 26, 29–40, 70
Slaves to Racism (Dennis), 25
Smithsonian Institution, 275
Snell, Hannah, 104–5
social media, 10, 15, 187, 239, 273, 280–81, 282
socio-cultural passing, 7, 156, 209–36, 248–9, 263–4
Soho Theatre, London, 305
Somaliland, 241
Something of Myself (Kipling), 251, 253, 254
soul music, 53
South Africa, 47, 65–72, 76, 210
South Carolina, United States, 56
Southall Black Sisters, 14
Spain, 188–93, 196, 203, 204
Spartacus, 28
Spokane, Washington, 284
St Félix, Doreen, 94, 287
St Lucia, 39, 226, 227
Stallworth, Ron, 222–3
Stearns, Stephen, 76

'steenths', 44
Stein, Gertrude, 217–18, 219
Stern, Julia, 36, 207
Stone, Emma, 296, 303
Stonehenge, Wiltshire, 1, 229
Stowe, Harriet Beecher, 34–8, 205, 207, 255
straight-passing, 139–60
Strange Death of Europe, The (Murray), 270
strip clubs, 104
'subject races', 66
Sufism, 136, 248
Suits, 94
Sumii, Sue, 178
Sunak, Rishi, 221
Sunday Times, 88
Sunni Islam, 185
Swank, Hilary, 114, 302
Sweeney Todd (2007 film), 306
Syria, 9, 242

Table Mountain, South Africa, 71
Taboo, Bethlehem, 198
Tagore, Rabindranath, 74
Talawa, 88, 89, 90, 92
Talbot, Mary Anne, 104, 105
Talmud, 149, 153
tea, 249
Teena, Brandon, 107, 113–18, 128, 135, 148, 209, 302, 315
Tel Aviv, Israel, 198, 200
Tempest, The (Shakespeare), 8, 105, 227, 228, 236
Tender Buttons (Stein), 218
Texas, United States, 274
Tharoor, Shashi, 257–8
theatre, *see under* performing arts

INDEX

Theravada Buddhism, 166
Theron, Charlize, 303
third gender, 133–7
Thriller (Jackson), 282
Thuggees, 74
Time Out, 80
Times, The, 272
Tisdel, Lana, 113–14, 116
Toklas, Alice, 217
Tokugawa Shogunate (1603–1868), 176–7
Top Girls (Churchill), 102, 103
Torah, 190
trans people, 9, 112, 113–17, 120–33, 140, 212, 302
    cis-passing, 113–18, 128, 135, 140, 151–4
    homosexuality and, 117, 121
    'illness', labeling as, 129
    performing arts and, 302–3
    sex reassignment surgery, 116, 122, 124, 128, 130, 134, 302
Transformer (Reed), 120
transmasculinity, 217–18
transracialism, 286
transvestism, 110, 111–12
Trinidad, 13, 155–7, 231
Trudeau, Justin, 277–9
Trump, Donald, 270
Truth and Reconciliation Commission, 71
Turkey, 185–8, 203, 210
Turner (Dabydeen), 235
Turner, Joseph Mallord William, 235
Twain, Mark, 44, 45, 188
Twelfth Night (Shakespeare), 100, 105–6
Twelve Years A Slave (Northup), 33
Twitter, 26

Uganda, 66, 244
Ullmann, Liv, 102
Umm al-Fahm, Israel, 200
Uncle Tom's Cabin (Stowe), 34–8, 205, 207, 255
unconscious racial bias, 287
United Kingdom
    American War of Independence (1775–83), 205
    blackface in, 276
    Bloody Sunday (1972), 14
    Brexit (2016–20), 270
    class in, 301, 305–6
    Eastern Europeans in, 17, 221
    French Revolutionary Wars (1792–1802), 104
    general election (1992), 14
    homophobia in, 157, 158, 216
    homosexuality in, 157, 158, 212–16, 218–18
    immigration in, 17, 221, 269–70
    mixed-race people in, 83–4, 86–92
    morris dancing, 276–7
    Multicultural London English, 17
    multi-culturalism in, 220, 269
    Northern Ireland, 14, 131–2
    Notting Hill Carnival, 269
    Notting Hill riots (1958), 80
    performing arts in, 276, 298–9, 301, 305–6
    poll tax (1989–90), 14

INDEX

royal family, 93–6
segregation in, 80
Slave Compensation Act (1837), 155
slave trade, 28, 79, 95, 122, 155, 205, 235, 276
Slavery Abolition Act (1833), 79, 235
socio-cultural passing in, 221–2, 224–36
trans people in, 120–33
Windrush generation, 13, 79–82, 230, 232, 233–6
United Nations, 155, 157, 158–60
United States
  Black Lives Matter (2013–), 26, 284, 301
  Black Migration (1916–70), 43–4
  black nationalism in, 45–6
  Brown v. Board of Education (1954), 56
  Civil Rights movement (1954–68), 44, 45, 46, 53, 55, 220, 295
  Civil War (1861–5), 38, 204, 205
  Declaration of Independence (1776), 47
  Floyd murder (2020), 26, 301
  Fugitive Slave Act (1850), 30
  Hollywood, 9, 275, 292–8, 300–301, 302–5
  Homeland Security, 196, 197
  Immigration Act (1924), 180
  Jim Crow period (1865–1965), 41–63, 65, 275, 293–4
  Ku Klux Klan, 57
  March on Washington (1963), 53, 55, 235
  Martin murder (2012), 26
  minstrel shows, 53, 275, 277
  multi-culturalism in, 269
  Native Americans, 17, 35–6, 296
  Obama administration (2009–17), 45, 93, 94, 221–2
  performing arts in, 53, 275, 277, 292–306
  racial identity and, 45
  slavery in, 3, 8, 25, 26, 29–40, 41–2, 44, 45, 204–5
  Trump administration (2017–20), 46, 270
  War of Independence (1775–83), 205
  white nationalism in, 46, 285
Universal Studios, 293
UpStairs Lounge arson attack (1973), 305
Urdu, 174, 253

Vaishyas, 173
Vanity Fair, 285
variable identity, 4
Vatican, 100–103
Vedas, 173, 318
Venice, 191
Vested Interests (Garber), 130
Victoria Falls, 244
Victorian period (1837–1901), 18
View UpStairs, The, 305
Vijayadashami, 317–20
Vikings, 28

INDEX

Vincent, Norah, 104
Virginia, United States, 25, 29
Vishnu, 318
Vogue, 54, 55

Wajid Ali Shah, Nawab of Awadh, 257
Walcott, Derek, 7, 25, 39, 43, 164, 226, 227, 229–31, 312
'Walk on the Wild Side' (Reed), 120
Walker, Ann, 215
Walker, Johnny, 308
Wallis, Yae Nakayama, 181–3
Walters, Julie, 306
Wanted (2008 film), 296
Washington, Fredi, 293
Washington Post, The, 279
Waters, Roger, 194
Wegener, Einar, 116, 302
Weininger, Otto, 216
Weisz, Rachel, 303
Well of Loneliness, The (Hall), 216
Welles, Orson, 295
Wen Jiabao, 175, 176
West Indies
   socio-cultural passing and, 231–2
   slavery in, 24–5, 39
   Trinidad, 13, 155–7, 231
   Windrush generation, 13, 79–82, 230, 232, 233–6
Western culture, 269–70
   chauvinism, 192, 225, 270
   gender morals, 122, 123, 136, 145
   immigration and, 220–21, 269–70

socio-cultural passing, 156, 209–36, 248–9, 263–4
'White Man's Burden, The' (Kipling), 255, 256, 264
white nationalism, 46, 271, 285
white people, 2, 3
   apartheid and, 11, 47, 65–72
   black-passing, 16, 52–4, 56–60, 77–8
   Jim Crow and, 41–63, 65, 275, 293–4
   One Drop rule and, 44–7, 65, 69, 70, 188
   passing as, 2, 3, 29–52, 60–72, 79–82, 293–4
   slavery and, 3, 8–9, 11, 24–40
   socio-cultural passing as, 7, 156, 209–36, 248–9, 263–4, 281
White Tiger, The (Adiga), 175–6, 210, 211
White, Walter Francis, 46–7
Whittaker, Jodie, 297
'Who's Passing for Who?' (Hughes), 267
Why I'm No Longer Talking to White People About Race (Eddo-Lodge), 297
Wicomb, Zoë, 47, 69, 70, 71–2, 84, 93
Wiley, Samira, 304
Windrush generation, 13, 79–82, 230, 232, 233
women
   acting prohibition, 110
   male-passing, 2, 99–108, 113–17, 125, 212
   passing as, 2, 99, 100, 108–11, 116, 117, 120–37, 143–4

367

INDEX

Woolf, Virginia, 108, 124–7, 216, 218–19, 303, 315
Woolfian, 31
Wordsworth, William, 1
World Cup, 76
World Human Rights Day, 135
World Museum, Liverpool, 122
World War I (1914–18), 283
World War II, (1939–45), 55, 60, 79, 109
Wuornos, Aileen, 303

Xhosa people, 66

yakuza, 178
yamato, 177–80, 183, 184
Yates, Sarah, 66
Yazidis, 9
Yom Kippur, 319
Yoruba people, 90, 273, 274
Yoshino, Kenji, 186, 187
d'Ys, Julien, 271

Zimmerman, George, 26
Zionism, 205–6
Zoological Society of London, 244
Zwarte Pieten, 277